THE BULGARIAN ECONOMY: LESSONS FROM REFORM DURING EARLY TRANSITION

The Bulgarian Economy: Lessons from Reform during Early Transition

Edited by
DEREK C. JONES
JEFFREY MILLER

LONDON AND NEW YORK

First published 1997 by Ashgate Publishing

Reissued 2018 by Routledge
2 Park Square, Milton Park, Abingdon, Oxon, OX14 4RN
711 Third Avenue, New York, NY I 0017, USA

Routledge is an imprint of the Taylor & Francis Group, an informa business

Publisher's Note
The publisher has gone to great lengths to ensure the quality of this reprint but points out that some imperfections in the original copies may be apparent.

Disclaimer
The publisher has made every effort to trace copyright holders and welcomes correspondence from those they have been unable to contact.

A Library of Congress record exists under LC control number: 97070344

ISBN 13: 978-1-138-34958-2 (hbk)
ISBN 13: 978-0-429-43628-4 (ebk)

Contents

Figures and tables

Contributors

Will Bartlett is a member of SAUS at the University of Bristol. His research interests include small firms, with particular interest in Southern Europe and transition economies. With funding from various sources (including EEC Phare and the British Know How fund), he has collected new survey data on small firms in several countries, including Bulgaria. He has visited Bulgaria on several occasions.

Zeljko Bogetic is an economist at the World Bank who has worked extensively on Bulgaria. He led several World Bank missions and has had chief responsibility for preparing World Bank reports on public finance issues and private sector development. He has published a number of papers on economics of transition in professional economics journals. He co-edited a World Bank book, *Financing Government in the Transition: Bulgaria* (1995).

John A. Bristow is Professor of Economics at Trinity College, Dublin. His areas of research include international trade and public finance, with particular interest in transition economies. He has visited Bulgaria on many occasions as an advisor for the World Bank and the EEC. He is the author of *The Bulgarian Economy in Transition*, Edward Elgar.

Lubomir Christov holds a PhD from the University for National and World Economy (Sofia). He lectured at the same university for ten years. From 1991-94 he was Chief Economist and Member of the Managing Board of Bulgarian National Bank (Bulgaria's central bank). He is currently an advisor to the Executive Director of the World Bank in Washington, DC.

Tihomir Enev, a native of Bulgaria, is a doctoral student in sociology at the University of Delaware. He received a master's degree in economics from the University of

Delaware, and previously taught as an assistant professor at the Technical University, Varna, Bulgaria.

Heywood Fleisig is Director of Research at the Center for the Economic Analysis of Law in Washington, DC. He received his PhD in economics from Yale. In recent years he has written mainly on the economic analysis and economic impact of the reform of secured transactions and systems of registration. He recently retired from the World Bank where he held a variety of positions of Operations and Research, most recently as Economic Advisor in the Private Sector Development Department. Before joining the Bank, Mr. Fleisig served on the economic staffs of the Congressional Budget Office and the Federal Reserve Board. Prior to that, he taught at Cornell.

Derek C. Jones is the James Ferguson Professor of Economics at Hamilton College, New York, and Visiting Professor of Economics at the London Business School. His research interests lie in two broad areas: a) transition economies, especially questions concerning changes in labor markets and corporate governance in Russia, Bulgaria, and the Baltics; and b) employee ownership and employee participation.

Mark Klinedinst is Associate Professor of Economics at the University of Southern Mississippi. His research interests include: labor and management decision-making, transition policies in Eastern Europe – especially Bulgaria, cooperatives, credit unions, employee ownership, union strategies, and econometrics. He has visited Bulgaria on several occasions.

Kenneth Koford is Professor of Economics and Political Science at the University of Delaware. He has taught economics regularly in Bulgaria, and published a number of papers on incomes policies in western countries and Eastern Europe.

Christina Lenkova is completing her doctoral studies at CERGE in Prague and is currently an ACE scholar at the Institute for Advanced Studies in Vienna. Her research interests are labor economics and economies in transition.

Mieke Meurs is Associate Professor of Economics at the American University in Washington, DC. She was a Fulbright scholar to Bulgaria in 1991-92. Her research interests pertain to new institutionalist economics and transitional economies. She has various on-going projects in Bulgaria. These include a project on agricultural reform in Bulgaria funded by the McArthur Foundation. She has worked on similar issues in other former socialist countries including Romania. She has published several articles on Bulgaria including articles in *Soviet Studies* and *Comparative Economic Studies*.

xiii

Jeffrey B. Miller is Professor of Economics at the University of Delaware. He has taught regularly in the University of Delaware's program in Bulgaria. He has also published a number of papers in Bulgaria.

Garabed Minassian is a member and former director of the Institute of Economics, Bulgarian Academy of Sciences. He has done extensive research and published a number of papers on macroeconomic problems in Bulgaria.

Stoyko Nikolov is a graduate student in operations research at the University of North Carolina. He undertook extensive research on the Bulgarian economy for his senior thesis at Hamilton College, New York.

Hristo Pamouktchiev holds a PhD in economics. He is now Chairman of the Board of Directors of Bulgarian Consulting Group and a part-time lecturer at Plovdiv University. He is a former Chairman of the Supervisory Board of the Agency for Privatization in Bulgaria. He was also a senior research fellow at the Institute of Economics at the Bulgarian Academy of Sciences. His main fields of research are privatization, macroeconomics, and industrial relations.

Svilen Parvulov is Senior Consultant, Head of Department Portfolio Investments at Bulgarian Consulting Group. He is a former member of the Supervisory Board of the Agency for Privatization and a former member of the Foreign Investments Commission in Bulgaria. He was also a research fellow at the Institute of Economics at Bulgarian Academy of Sciences. His main research areas are investment projects and portfolio management.

Stefan Petranov holds a PhD in economics. He is a member of the Board of Directors of Bulgarian Consulting Group and a part-time lecturer at Sofia University and at University of Delaware-Bulgaria Coalition. Formerly he was deputy director of the PHARE program at the Ministry of Agriculture and a research fellow at the Institute of Economics at Bulgarian Academy of Sciences. His main research areas are in macroeconomics and investment analysis.

Rossitsa Rangelova is Senior Research Associate at the Institute of Economics, Bulgarian Academy of Sciences. Her main research is directed towards an analysis of the development of small business in an emerging market economy. She has taken part in several international research projects and was a visiting scholar at the University of Bristol. She is presently a member of the Consultative Committee at the Ministry of Economic Development.

Charles Rock is Professor of Economics at Rollins College. With partial support from IREX, he studied in Bulgaria during 1991-92. He was also a Fulbright scholar in Bulgaria for 1992-93. His work has also been supported by the NSF and ILO. His research interests include transition policies in Eastern Europe, especially Bulgaria, cooperatives, and labor unions. His publications on Bulgaria include an essay in *Privatization in Central and Eastern Europe*.

Darren Spreeuw is a graduate student at the American University in Washington, DC. His dissertation studies focus on production cooperatives and collective action problems.

Vassil Tzanov is a researcher at the Institute of Economics of the Bulgarian Academy of Sciences. He is a member of the Central and East European team of the ILO in Budapest. He wrote numerous articles on the transition process in Bulgaria, especially on labor markets, social policy and wages. He was co-author of the book *Bulgaria and the European Community; The Transformation of the Labour Market and Social policy: A View towards Europe*, Ivan D. Danov, 1993.

Daniel Vaughan-Whitehead is senior adviser on Wages and Incomes policies in the ILO Team for Central and Eastern Europe (ILO-CEET) based in Budapest. He published various books and articles on workers' financial participation, industrial relations and wages. He recently coordinated comparative studies on wage policies in Central and Eastern Europe, such as: *Minimum Wages in Central and Eastern Europe: From Protection to Destitution*, Central European University Press, 1995; and *Reforming Wage Policy in Central and Eastern Europe*, ILO-European Commission, 1995.

Michael L. Wyzan is Associate Professor at the Stockholm School of Economics, and research scholar at the International Institute for Applied Systems Analysis in Laxenburg, Austria. Recently he was a Senior Research Analyst at the Open Media Research Institute in Prague. During March 1994-September 1995, he was a US Treasury Department advisor to the Bulgarian Finance Ministry. He was a Fulbright awardee at the Higher Institute of Economics in Sofia during January-May 1985.

Acknowledgements

This project was undertaken because we felt that it was useful at this stage of the economic transition in Bulgaria to bring together in one place the work of both Bulgarian and non-Bulgarian scholars who were studying various aspects of the Bulgarian economy. The papers which comprise this volume were completed in the spring of 1996. Soon after a financial crisis occurred. In addition changes were made affecting the independence of the central bank and a mass privatization program went forward. For these reasons the period under investigation could be regarded as the first phase of the transition. Because the papers analyze a broad range of topics, they provide an overview of the situation as it existed when the economy entered the second phase of the transition.

We would like to thank all of the authors, who worked diligently to meet deadlines established to help publish this volume in a timely manner. We would like to thank Dawn Woodward who performed many coordination functions that enabled us to bring the volume to fruition. Debra Hagstrom deserves our special thanks for doing yeoman service in carefully preparing the manuscript for publication.

In support of some of the papers contained in this volume, we acknowledge support from NSF 9010591 and from the National Council for Soviet and East European Research. We would also like to acknowledge the logistical support from the University of Delaware-Bulgarian Coalition. Ross Abadjiev has been particularly helpful.

Derek C. Jones
Hamilton College

Jeffrey B. Miller
University of Delaware

Part One
INTRODUCTION

1   Early transition in Bulgaria: review and evaluation

Derek C. Jones and Jeffrey B. Miller

Introduction

The decade's immense political and economic changes in Central and Eastern Europe have generated tremendous interest amongst economists. Many seek a better understanding of the nature, scope, and effects of the key organizational and institutional changes as centrally-planned systems move towards economies based on markets. Others are more concerned with the implications of changes for heated theoretical debates – for example on the merits of neoclassical versus evolutionary theories of change (Murrell, 1992). On all such matters, unsurprisingly, most attention has been devoted to the larger economies (in particular Russia) and those economies which began the transition soonest (notably the Visegrad countries). However, there is now a growing interest in the economic analysis of the experiences of other transforming economies. In large part this stems from an awareness that the data on economic outcomes during early transition indicate much more diversity than many had initially predicted (e.g., Blanchard *et al.*, 1991, Fischer, *et al.*, 1996, Brada, 1996).

One of the countries in which attention has grown is Bulgaria. To some degree this enhanced interest reflects growing recognition that the Bulgarian experience has been comparatively neglected and that it is of interest in and of itself. It is also argued that deeper understanding of the Bulgarian case is needed because the volatile Balkan region has assumed much more strategic significance since the collapse of the Soviet Empire. But for many, the Bulgarian experience deserves closer attention because, according to many macroeconomic indicators, the Bulgarian performance lies somewhere in the middle range for transforming economies – poorer than the Visegrad group and the Baltic Republics but better than many other former communist countries, including Ukraine and Belarus and arguably Russia. Most noticeably, in Bulgaria declines in output and average real income are much greater

3

and unemployment and inflation much higher than in the former group, though often better than in the latter (e.g., Blanchard, 1996, Murrell, 1996).

In their review of the economic performance of countries that are undergoing transition Fischer *et al.* (1996) find a distinct difference between the output and inflation performance of the Eastern European countries and the countries of the former Soviet Union. In terms of cumulative output decline the Bulgarian performance (27.4 per cent) was worse than all the other Eastern European countries with the exception of Albania and Macedonia (which endured an embargo from Greece) but was better than the performance of all other countries except Mongolia and Uzbekistan. A similar picture emerges on the inflation front where they compare 'maximum annual inflation' across countries. The Bulgarian inflation (338 per cent) was worse than any other Eastern European experience and better than the experience in any other country with the exception of Mongolia (where it was very similar) (Fischer, *et al.*, 1996, Table 2, p. 52).

Where Bulgaria has been exceptional is its growth pattern. Most transition economies did not begin to grow until inflation was under 50 per cent. Fischer *et al.* report that only Bulgaria and Romania began to grow before inflation dropped below 50 per cent. (Of course, some countries in the former Soviet Union have not yet brought inflation down and have not begun to grow again.)

The chapters in this volume have been selected to shed light on this middling performance. Why have the costs of transition in Bulgaria been much greater than in other Eastern European countries? The puzzle arises in part because, in terms of many socio-economic indicators (e.g., per capita income, levels of education, and labor force participation rates), Bulgaria apparently started the process from a position similar to that of other Visegrad countries. However, on closer examination, it turns out that this starting position was not the same in Bulgaria as in other Visegrad countries. For example, there is evidence that there were important differences between Bulgaria and the Visegrad countries in areas including factors influencing wage determination (Jones and Ilayperuma, 1994) and the nature of industrial relations (Thirkell and Tseneva, 1992). Moreover, in many important respects Bulgaria resembled the Republics in the former USSR. Like many Commonwealth of Independent State (CIS) countries, Bulgaria was very centralized and heavily dependent on CMEA markets. There is abundant evidence in trade and capital flows and labor movements that Bulgaria was more Eastward than Westward looking. If one adopts a conceptual framework that provides an influential role for path dependence, such similarities in pre-conditions suggest that comparisons with the CIS countries might be more relevant than comparisons with the experiences of other countries in Eastern and Central Europe (such as Poland or the Czech Republic) which often had very different pre-conditions.

If we look beyond these differences in initial conditions to understand the reasons for the middling performance of the Bulgarian economy, we must also acknowledge the crucial importance of institutional and organizational change in determining economic outcomes (North, 1990, Ben-Ner *et al.*,1994). Contributors to this volume explore various aspects of the institutional reforms that have taken place in Bulgaria. Several papers analyze the changes from a microeconomic perspective; others evaluate their macroeconomic implications.

Given this starting point, how are we to characterize the Bulgarian transition strategy since 1990? This is not straightforward because, in some ways the Bulgarian approach has been quite radical – including rapid price liberalization, a new competition policy and extensive and swift small-scale privatization – and thus is reminiscent of 'big bang' experiences elsewhere. At the same time, the pace of change in other areas has been excruciatingly slow, most noticeably in the approach to privatization of large state-owned firms and in dealing with the problem of bad debts. Moreover, while formal policy changes have been heterodox, both the implementation of policy measures and the receptiveness of economic agents to changes seem to have been quite uneven. Consequently the *de facto* pace of institutional change often turns out to be far less than a casual observer might expect based on *de jure* changes. Hence it is not clear that our own assessment of the extent of change during early transition in Bulgaria would concur with that contained in studies such as those done by the European Bank for Reconstruction and Development (1994) and de Melo *et al.* (1996). Our sense is that the pace of change, in fact, has been far less dramatic than the indicators in these studies suggest.

Focus of this volume

When we began to assemble materials for this volume, there were no book-length studies of Bulgaria in the post-command economy era. However, since then good accounts of the main changes in the process of reform in Bulgaria have begun to appear (e.g., Bristow, 1996) and even some specialized studies of particular aspects (e.g., Bogetic and Hillman, 1995, on fiscal reform). At the same time there is presently no book-length study of the Bulgarian economy that assembles original research which analyzes and evaluates key aspects of these processes and draws more general lessons. For this volume, most contributors were encouraged to view their tasks as more analytical than expositional. In that process contributors build on the work of others who have emphasized description (e.g., Zloch-Christy, 1996).

We also encouraged contributors to draw more general lessons from their analysis of the Bulgarian experience. This has typically been done by consideration of new findings for Bulgaria in the context of the broader theoretical and empirical literature. In particular we were interested in whether the Bulgarian experience could shed light on questions regarding the value of specific strategies of economic reform. In that process authors draw on a diverse literature, including writings on the process of organizational change and the wider literature on transition including

5

debates such as: the appropriate sequencing of reforms; gradualism versus big-bang; privatization (and the relationship between creation of firms *de novo* and the restructuring of state-owned firms); and appropriate forms of ownership, property rights, and corporate governance.

Contributors focus on developments in key selected areas. These areas are chosen to illustrate the enormous variety and complexity of the process of reform in a transitional economy. Thus chapters include discussion of *macro* dimensions of reform including the determinants of inflation. During early transition there has been an extraordinary rate of inflation in Bulgaria (see *Appendix: statistical tables*). The causes and effects and the possible role of incomes polices are still not well understood. Several papers (e.g., Enev and Koford, Minassian, Tzanov and Vaughan-Whitehead) address these issues. With the current rekindling of inflation, these issues, as well as matters such as the institutional design of the new banking system, notably the central bank (see Christov) have assumed new importance.

At the *micro* level, we are interested in understanding whether changes in the macro context have been associated with changes in the behavior of firms and households and, if so, how pronounced have these changes been? The findings of some contributors (e.g., Meurs and Spreeuw) do *not* lend support to those who argue that standard stabilization programs can easily and effectively be introduced into environments where microfoundations are quite different from the context within which these theories were developed. Their findings point to the importance of specific institutional features in influencing economic outcomes and to evolutionary aspects of the nature of organizational and thus economic change, even during times of political revolution. As such these studies share conclusions with other work that has begun to appear for Bulgaria during the post-communist period.

For example, Koford and Miller (1995) found that the slow development of institutional infrastructure has retarded development of the economy. In a detailed survey of thirty-five managers (private, newly privatized, state, and cooperative) which focused on the development of market institutions, they found that a wide variety of market arrangements have evolved, with arrangements reflecting the special circumstances faced by traders in these markets. Many of these arrangements, however, are still influenced by the lack of trust among trading partners in these newly developing markets. Also Guevov (1994) finds that the transformation process of industrial enterprises has been quite slow. Another example is Jones (1995) in which it is shown that early transition has been characterized by much inertia in patterns of corporate governance, even when there have been legal changes in enterprise ownership. In a study which examines the determinants of executive compensation for Bulgarian managers, Jones and Kato (1995) find that, as in western firms, pay is positively related to size but unlike findings from western firms they find no link with profitability. Also, during early transition, pay differentials between Bulgarian managers and other workers were found to be quite narrow.

Several essays in this volume also point to the importance of specific institutional features in influencing change. For example, the contribution by Bartlett and Rangelova examines the crucial issue of the growth of small firms. While they find this sector is very dynamic, which is not the case in many other transforming countries (Brezinski and Fritsch, 1996), they also argue that a key impediment to its further expansion is the particular form that the evolving state bureaucracy has assumed in Bulgaria. Another example is the evidence presented by Jones and Nikolov. This shows that there are important differences and similarities in the character of the adjustment of Bulgarian firms compared to patterns of adjustment that have been observed in other transition economies. Their findings imply that supply elasticities in Bulgaria appear to be lower than in other transforming economies including Poland, Hungary and the Czech Republic (Estrin *et al.*, 1995, Svejnar, 1996).

Institutions can also influence the outcomes of policy initiatives. Given the substantial overlap in policy measures adopted in Bulgaria and in Poland, how are we to explain the major differences in macro outcomes between Poland and Bulgaria? To what extent are differences in outcomes attributable to differences in initial conditions and differences in other policies, rather than the greater rigidities in fundamental institutional and organizational processes in Bulgaria? In addressing some of these questions, Tzanov and Vaughan-Whitehead attribute great importance to the failed wage policy in Bulgaria. They argue that a key policy error was to impose too great a shock. This created great disorganization and enormous opposition to further change. In addition, in accounting for this bleak record it seems that a polarized political environment with alternating policy reversals and policy stagnation has played a part. The political instability has fed upon itself. In hindsight it would have been better had there been a more consistent and more gradual path.

Links between essays in the volume and the economic crisis of 1996

This book is being published at a somewhat awkward moment. Shortly after these papers were assembled in the spring of 1996, Bulgaria found itself in the midst of a foreign exchange crisis. Because the papers were completed before the crisis began, the authors did not have an opportunity to address the issues raised by the crisis. At the time this introduction was prepared, the economic implications of this event had not yet unfolded. The sharp depreciation of the lev will almost certainly mean higher inflation in the rest of 1996, but it is unclear whether this event will cause output to decline again after a short period of modest growth.

The crisis was precipitated by the conjunction of two events. Improved accounting systems now being utilized by the banks have clarified the enormous problem of non-performing loans. Secondly, as the Wyzan and Bristow papers make clear, the debt agreement signed with the London Club in 1994 did not solve these foreign debt problems. Before the 1996 crisis began, Bulgaria did not have an agreement

7

with the International Monetary Fund (IMF). Yet without IMF and World Bank assistance Bulgaria could not pay foreign debt and service obligations of approximately $1.25 billion in both 1996 and 1997.

To prevent a run on the banking system, actions were taken to close several large banks and create a deposit insurance system. To preserve its holdings of foreign currency reserves, the Bulgarian National Bank (BNB) chose to fight the sharp depreciation of the lev by sharply raising the base rate of interest rather than intervene extensively in the foreign exchange market. Even these actions were inadequate without an agreement with the IMF and World Bank.

How did such a crisis come about? The contributors to this volume analyze important aspects of the Bulgarian economy which shed light on these recent developments. As Bristow's paper points out, Bulgaria inherited large foreign debt problems from the communist period. Trade patterns also had to be significantly altered when CMEA trade collapsed. Despite these problems the present crisis was aggravated by a failure to reach agreement with the IMF earlier. As is described in more detail in Wyzan, there was a dramatic improvement in Bulgaria's foreign reserve position after the Bulgarian Socialist Party (BSP) came to power in January 1995. As Table 1.1 illustrates, this inflow in reserves slowed in the autumn, and it became increasing apparent that Bulgaria could not make its foreign debt payments without the assistance of the IMF.

Table 1.1
Gross foreign exchange reserves
(million US$)

Year	6/94	9/94	12/94	3/95	6/95	9/95	12/95	1/96	2/96	3/96
$	1124.4	742.3	1001.8	1127.4	1499.5	1433.7	1236.4	955.6	860	643.5

Source: BNB Monthly Bulletin (1996), April.

Many other problems that surfaced during the recent crisis have domestic origins. Restructuring has been slow, particularly of the large state enterprises. Fear of accelerating unemployment paralyzed the political process. However, the failure to restructure the large state enterprises has undermined the banking system and contributed significantly to the present crisis.

Pamouktchiev, Parvulov, and Petranov describe the various privatization programs and some of the political problems of moving the process along more quickly. While privatization is not a requirement for restructuring, the special interest groups they identify have also managed to retard attempts to restructure. Rather than look for ways to improve state enterprise efficiency by improving governance structures,

8

managerial positions have become part of the political spoils system. When the BSP came to power, many managerial positions were given to party loyalists. To the extent that managers are able to enhance their incomes through the 'shadow firms' described by Miller, these are indeed plum positions. Problems in the financial sector go beyond the state enterprises and the state banks, however. Many new private banks also have very weak balance sheets. Indeed one of the two banks closed during the crisis was the largest private bank. Poor bank supervision and problems in developing basic institutional arrangements to support credit markets have slowed the advancement of sound financial institutions. Bogetic and Fleissig analyze an important aspect of the credit market: collaterized lending. Inadequate bankruptcy laws are another contributing factor to the poor performance of the banking system.

Macroeconomic stabilization is also important. Several studies (e.g., Posen, 1993) have examined whether or not central bank independence can contribute to greater stability. Given the political pressures to keep state enterprises afloat by extending credit, central bank independence can be particularly important in the Bulgarian context. Christov evaluates the independence of the BNB. He finds that legally the BNB has substantial independence, but in practice its independence is much more limited. Adopting the conventional wisdom that money matters much in the inflationary process (but see on for discussion of several econometric studies that do *not* find that this has in fact been the case in Bulgaria), this may explain in part why inflation has been so high.

Price movements in Bulgaria have been difficult to explain. None of the usual culprits – nominal wages, money supply, exchange rates – have been growing as fast as the consumer price index (CPI). Enev and Koford and Tzanov and Whitehead look at inflation from the perspective of wage policies. After many attempts Minassian has found equations which explain both CPI movements and the producer price index (PPI) movements. Interestingly, he finds that money has no direct role and that the two price series depend on different variables.

Minassian's finding that different variables explain the movement of producer and consumer prices is not surprising when you look at the movement of these two series. Miller describes the gap between the two indices. The CPI rose much faster than the PPI during the first two years of the transition period. More recently the rates are closer together but the CPI continues to grow more rapidly than the PPI. Vulov (1996) has shown that the outlier appears to be the CPI. The PPI, the exchange rate and unit labor costs all grew at approximately the same rate from the beginning of 1992 until late 1995. (The sharp depreciation in the lev during the spring 1996 crisis may alter this relationship.) The CPI measures prices at the retail level. The retail sector is almost entirely private now. The PPI measures prices at the factory gate; the factories are still almost all state-owned. The unit labor cost series also measures activity in the state sector. The reasons for the discrepancies, therefore, may be that the indices are measuring activities in separate sectors of the economy, and these two sectors are operating quite differently (and the state sector appears to

9

be operating in ways more consistent with prevailing expectations about the macro-economic performance of a market economy!). As yet no one has fully analyzed what implications this might have for the performance of the overall economy.

Problems of measurement

One frustration in attempting to analyze the Bulgarian economy is the poor quality of the data. As Fischer *et al.* (1996) note, Bulgaria is not alone among the transforming economies in having this problem. In the movement to a market economy there is also a transition in data collection. Statistical collection agencies have been receiving assistance from western agencies to improve their methodology. Many contributions make clear the dependence of reliable applied work on the underlying data. Analysis can only proceed if relevant statistical information is available and credible. In this respect, the Bulgarian situation has improved significantly over what it was three or four years ago. For example, prompted by external lenders and other international organizations, now there is a labor force survey. This means that the data on such key matters as unemployment are much more reliable than was the case until quite recently.

At the same time the situation is far from ideal. This is reflected in the lack of confidence many have in even key financial statistics. (Bulgaria still does not have a page in *IMF Statistics* and that there is only limited inclusion in the International Labor Organization (ILO) *Bulletin of Labor Statistics*.) There are also crucial problems and puzzles concerning many key statistical series. In particular see the discussion by Miller on the pitfalls involved in measuring different price indices and implications this might have for the measure of GDP.

To this end we have assembled a *Statistical Appendix* with many monthly key series that researchers most commonly consult. (See also Wyzan's Table 2.1 for annual series.) While most of these are in the public domain, many are not easily obtained. We hope that this resource will assist interested students but we forewarn the reader that not all series are as frequently available as one might wish.

While in many papers the crucial role of data problems will be made clear, it will also be apparent that in the context of weak data provision by the central authorities (who are caught in a major fiscal crisis), one response is for researchers to try to collect their own data. During early transition in Bulgaria, many researchers have attempted to do this and several new and rich data sets have been generated. (For example, before the start of labor force surveys, a pilot sample of the registered unemployed was assembled. For details and analysis see Jones and Kato, 1993.) In this volume several papers make use of new survey data including Meurs and Spreeuw, and Klinedinst and Rock. Importantly, several of these efforts attempt the difficult task of drawing samples that are representative of the underlying populations – for example, the study of small firms by Bartlett and Rangelova.

Abstracts of contributions

Wyzan (Economic transformation and regional inequality: in search of a meaningful unit of analysis)

Wyzan sets the stage for his analysis of the regional divisions in Bulgaria by providing an overview of recent macroeconomic events since the reform began. This is followed by an investigation of the regional diversity within the country and its possible effects on the reform process. Unlike the former Czechoslovakia, the former Yugoslavia, and the former Soviet Union, Bulgaria has less geographic ethnic division. Still there are large populations of Turks, Bulgarian Muslims, and Roma. These factors along with differing regional conditions make it important to understand how the reforms are affecting various groups within the country. Using a general entropy model, Wyzan argues that, in many instances, the diversity of conditions within the nine existing *oblasti* is almost as great as it is between them. To understand the regional impact of the reforms it is important to break the analysis into small subdivisions.

Minassian (Inflation in a transition economy)

Minassian's paper analyzes the causes of inflation in Bulgaria. This has been an extremely difficult task. In an earlier paper Minassian (1994) was unable to obtain a satisfactory set of results to explain inflation in Bulgaria. With the longer (and more satisfactory) data series which is now available, the present paper takes a careful look at both the movements of the CPI and PPI. He now finds that the CPI can be explained by government borrowing, adaptive expectations of inflation, exchange rate movements and interest rates. In a less satisfactory equation describing the PPI, the most important variables are the exchange rate, interest rates, domestic credit and wages. Two interesting aspects of these results are: (1) the money supply does not enter directly into either equation, and (2) the two price indices have very different explanatory variables.

11

Miller (The price index gap)

Miller's paper can help explain why Minassian found that the two price indices seem so unrelated. They have been growing at different rates. The CPI has been growing much faster than the PPI. Miller explores the implications of this increasing divergence. First an attempt is made to explain why the divergence has occurred. In the second part of the paper he argues that the spreading gap has implications for the redistribution of income in the economy and the size of the private sector. The gap also raises the possibility that the present calculation of GDP is severely understated.

Enev and Koford (Incomes policies)

Enev and Koford analyze the effectiveness of incomes policies that were implemented to control the anticipated pressures on wages when the transition began. Before the transition began, many economists were correctly concerned that when prices were freed from the constraints imposed under central planning inflation would result. In Poland, Bulgaria and elsewhere, tax-based incomes polices were imposed to prevent wages from rising too rapidly. These programs taxed enterprises when wages rose too quickly. Enev and Koford describe the evolution of the program. They then evaluate the program by testing whether the program had any effect on inflation. Thus they present an alternative explanation of consumer price inflation which can be contrasted with the paper by Minassian. In their equation lagged price level and exchange rate movements are the most important explanatory variables. The dummy variable they use to test the effectiveness of incomes policy shows a small negative effect which suggests the program was mildly effective. Their money supply variable and wage variable enter with negative signs. (The wage variable is insignificant.) These results are largely consistent with Minassian who found that money supply variables were uncorrelated with consumer price inflation. Wages did not enter his equation although he found wages to be important in his producer price equation.

Tzanov and Vaughan-Whitehead (Macroeconomic effects of restrictive wage policy)

In their ambitious paper Tzanov and Vaughan-Whitehead present extensive econometric evidence on the effects of wage policy in Bulgaria on inflation, consumption, and employment. Since inflation was expected to be stimulated by 'excessive' wage demands, highly restrictive wage policies have existed in Bulgaria during early transition. (These include excess wages taxes on firms and other centralized incomes policies; see ILO, 1993). The authors present evidence that this is an erroneous view – that wages have not been the main cause of inflation. Moreover, they argue that the

12

restrictive wage policy has led to diverse unfavorable outcomes. Where rational re-structuring would be expected to lead to strong links between enterprise perfor-mance and average wages, their modeling of short-run wage determination indi-cates only a weak link between wages and productivity. In addition, they show how the erosion of real incomes has led to major changes in consumption patterns. They conclude by urging the adoption of an alternative wage policy.

Bogetic and Fleissig (Collateral, access to credit and investment)

Bogetic and Fleissig look carefully at the use of collateral in lending in Bulgaria. In an environment where economic uncertainty is so great, the use of collateral as the basis for business loans has been suggested by a number of economists (e.g., Tirole, 1994). Miller (1995) is even more pessimistic about the difficulties banks face in performing their roles as financial intermediaries in a transition economy. Bogetic and Fleissig find that real estate serves as collateral in Bulgaria but movable prop-erty does not. This limits the ability of businesses to borrow against inventory, for example. This impedes the development of new businesses as they try to expand since they are almost entirely dependent on owners' capital. While it is difficult to calculate the effect of these restrictions, cross country comparisons suggest that it may cost five to ten percent of GDP annually.

Christov (A role for an independent central bank in transition)

Christov explores the issue of central bank independence. This is an important ques-tion for transition economies because central banking is new for them and most transition economies have experienced initial instability. Bulgaria has also had four different governments (and an interim government) since the 'big bang' in February 1991. Christov finds that while the laws establishing the Bulgarian National Bank (BNB) were based on western practice and created a set of legal conditions condu-cive to central bank independence, the actual experience is very different. In practice the BNB has had much less independence. This is not unusual in countries where there is no legal tradition. Recently, the government has passed new laws which make it easier to dismiss the governor and the vice-governors of the BNB. This can be expected to further constrain the actions of the BNB.

Bristow (The international economy)

In his paper Bristow documents the central importance of external economic rela-tions to the transition in Bulgaria. Transition began under very unfavorable condi-tions, with external debts and dependence on CMEA markets, each at levels that were unusually high compared to many other transition economies. Moreover, this

13

adverse context was soon aggravated as UN embargoes were introduced in Yugoslavia. In these circumstances there is an acute need to reorient trade, a need which has not always been clearly and forcefully recognized by policy makers. The evidence on early successes and failures in this area are examined as are obstacles to further changes.

Pamouktchiev, Parvulov, and Petranov (The process of privatization)

Pamouktchiev, Parvulov, and Petranov analyze the uneven experience with privatization in Bulgaria. The initial privatization efforts were directed at housing and agricultural land. Large enterprise privatization has proceeded slowly. At the time their paper was prepared a mass privatization effort was underway. Undertaken by the socialist government, BSP, voucher privatization was perceived to be more equitable than cash privatization. There is popular support for the program, but there are important interest groups in the economy which oppose it and have slowed its implementation. Modeled on the Czech experience, an important part of the mass privatization effort is the establishment of privatization funds where citizens can buy shares in the funds instead of buying enterprises directly. Even after the mass privatization is complete, based on asset valuation, the state will retain a sizable ownership stake in more than half the enterprises to be privatized.

Bartlett and Rangelova (Nature and role of small firms)

One of the distinguishing features of industrial organization in many command economies in the past was the dominance of large firms. However, even within this framework, the Bulgarian economy was different from many Visegrad countries – unlike for example the Polish or the Hungarian economy, there was almost no experience with a small private sector. During early transformation, as Bartlett and Rangelova discuss, this legacy of the socialist 'red-hole' has begun to change. In their paper, after reviewing different conceptual frameworks on the role of small firms, Bartlett and Rangelova review findings from previous surveys of Bulgarian small firms. In addition they report findings based on both their own representative survey of 394 small firms in all Bulgarian sectors except agriculture in 1993 and on three case studies. The key problems that confront small firms are identified as weak demand, high cost of borrowing, high taxes, and bureaucracy. They conclude by relating their findings to the debate on privatization from below (and privatization from above).

Jones and Nikolov (Enterprise adjustment during early transition)

One area of heated debate in the literature is the nature and causes of enterprise adjustment during early transition (e.g., Estrin et al.,1995). By examining the adjustment patterns for 360 Bulgarian manufacturing firms (a sample that is much larger than that used in most studies on this topic) during 1989-92, the authors find evidence of change in some areas that is closely comparable to patterns observed for enterprises in other transition countries. However, compared to other countries, they find that there are important differences in the character of adjustment in Bulgarian firms. While in some areas, e.g., employment and investment, the pace of change has been dramatic, in other areas, including strategic behavior, it has been much less responsive. In accounting for these differences in adjustment patterns the authors' analysis suggests that several factors including initial conditions (especially size, sector and regional location), property rights, governance structures, and institutional and organizational infrastructure, all play important roles and that the links between enterprise adjustment and policy initiatives are quite complex.

Meurs and Spreeuw (The evolution of agrarian institutions: markets, cooperatives, and private farming, 1991-94)

In their informative paper Meurs and Spreeuw examine the development of transitional patterns of agricultural production following the collapse of central planning and state-managed agriculture. Whereas the conventional wisdom argues that decontrol and deregulation of the agrarian sector would lead to production dominated by private farmers, they discuss alternative conceptual frameworks which provide a rationale for choosing alternative organizational arrangements when markets are incomplete. Their new survey data indicate that, in fact, many agents have chosen alternative forms of production arrangements, notably the producer cooperative. In a concluding section they first develop a model of household choice and then estimate logit regressions to test hypotheses developed from that model. They find support for the view that weak market development results in the persistence of a strong cooperative presence.

Lenkova (Unemployment: the effects of policy)

Compared to many transition economies the Bulgarian experience is unusual insofar as unemployment soared very quickly to levels higher than those attained in many other transition economies, and subsequently has remained at comparatively high levels (see *Appendix: statistical tables*). In understanding whether, despite the comparatively high levels of unemployment, the factors influencing movements from unemployment in Bulgaria differ from the evidence for other countries (for a review, see Svejnar, 1996), Lenkova uses a proportional hazard function to estimate unemployment duration. In some respects Lenkova's findings are similar to those for other countries – for example, higher education enhances the probability of securing employment and the receipt of unemployment compensation lowers the likelihood

15

of an individual exiting from unemployment. However, her finding that the determinants of exits from unemployment differ for men and women is not strongly evident elsewhere. However, an earlier study by Jones and Kato (1993), using a multinomial logit framework to estimate the probability that individuals with particular characteristics will move within a given period from unemployment to employment, does find a similar pattern.

Klinedinst and Rock (Fringe benefits)

In previous studies of the Bulgarian labor market, evidence has been presented of the considerable erosion in base pay as well as of changes in the method of pay and form of contract during early transition (e.g., ILO, 1993). Also there is evidence that there is an increasing role for market forces both concerning pay determination in general (e.g., Jones and Ilayperuma, 1994) as well as for particular markets, such as the managerial labor market (Jones and Kato, 1996). However, these marketizing tendencies appear to be weaker than in other transforming economies. The paper by Klinedinst and Rock examines an aspect of this process that has been comparatively neglected, that of the nature and role of fringe benefits. Much of that research is based on a nationally representative panel survey of 500 firms and 4,600 employees in those firms. By using this extremely rich and unusual data source, they find that more and more workers at all levels are receiving smaller bundles of benefits than in the past. They also uncover evidence of increasing variation across regions and industries in the provision of such benefits than existed in the past.

Conclusions

These papers were written at an important juncture in the transition. Just over five years have passed since the 'big bang' in February 1991. In 1996 people more fully appreciate the immensity of task that confronts the country as it moves towards a market system. In many spheres more sophisticated markets are beginning to play a bigger role in directing the economy. Growth had just started to return and inflation had finally come down to more reasonable levels when the financial crisis occurred in the spring of 1996. With this crisis the IMF and World Bank are insisting on more structural reforms, including the closure of unprofitable firms, and new austerity measures. The mass privatization program should also bring about more structural changes. Substantial reforms which support this restructuring and improve the way investment resources are allocated are needed before the economy can grow significantly.

While some of these developments suggest cautious optimism, equally one cannot ignore the continuing central relevance of many of the initial conditions which placed

16

Bulgaria at an enormous disadvantage when transition began. Many of these inherited factors continue to plague and hinder efforts at reform – for example, the large foreign debt is still a major burden. Whether this debt will significantly hinder future economic development by sapping investment resources remains to be seen.

Many of the papers also point out key policy errors that have been made during early transition in Bulgaria. These include an ill-considered wage policy; a failure to have a consistent and well-thought out policy on privatization; a policy on price liberalization that initially was too rapid; and macroeconomic policies (especially a failure to get a tighter grip on fiscal balance) that have sustained macroeconomic trauma. Often the unfortunate effects of these policies have been compounded by various institutional failures and rigidities and the climate of uncertainty produced by a complex and often polarized political arena.

The urgent need to design effective policies that will produce sustainable reforms in Bulgaria is clear from the rising costs of the transition for the bulk of the population. Since the economic crisis began in spring 1996, the average wage is reported to have been halved – from $122 a month in March 1996 to about $60 in July (*Omri Daily Digest*, 15 July 1996). (In part this reflects a dramatic depreciation of the leva – with the Leva/US$ exchange rate approaching 200 in early August 1996). In addition, it is anticipated that the monthly rate of inflation will increase to 20 per cent in July, a level not seen since the 'big bang' of 1991. In the search for the new policy initiatives, it is apparent that the political context in Bulgaria continues to be far less than ideal. In particular, there do not seem to be many constituencies that have a genuine commitment to reform. However, it is conceivable that the accelerating economic crisis and mounting costs that have been imposed on the bulk of the population by the transition may produce the political will for more real and sustainable change.

References

Ben-Ner, Avner, Montias, J. Michael, and Neuberger, Egon (1993), 'Basic Issues in Organizations: A Comparative Perspective', *Journal of Comparative Economics*, Vol. 17, No. 2, June, pp. 207-42.

Blanchard, Olivier (1996), 'Theoretical Aspects of Transition' *American Economic Review*, Vol. 86, No. 2, May, pp. 117-22.

Blanchard, O., Dornbusch, R., Krugman, P., Layard, R., and Summers, L. (1991), *Reform in Eastern Europe*, MIT: Cambridge, Mass.

Bogetic, Z. and Hillman, A. (eds) (1995), *Financing Government in the Transition-Bulgaria: The Political Economy of Tax Policies, Tax Bases and Tax Evasion*, World Bank Regional and Sectional Study: Washington, D.C.

Brada, Josef C. (1996), 'Privatization is Transition - Or is it?', *Journal of Economic Perspectives*, Vol. 10, No. 2, Spring, pp. 67-86.

Brezinski, Horst and Fritsch, Michael (eds) (1996), *The Economic impact of New Firms in Post Socialist Countries: Bottom up Transformation in Eastern Europe*, Elgar: Cheltenham, UK.

Bristow, John A. (1996), *The Bulgarian Economy in Transition*, Edward Elgar: Cheltenham, UK.

de Melo, Martha, Deninzer, Cevdet, and Gelb, Alan (1996), 'From Plan to Market: Patterns of Transition', The World Bank, Policy Research Working Paper, No. 1564.

European Bank for Reconstruction and Development (1994), *Transition Report for 1994*, EBRD: London.

—— (1995), *Transition Report for 1995*, EBRD: London.

Estrin, Saul, Gelb, Alan, and Singh, Inderjit (1995), 'Shocks and Adjustment by Firms in Transition: A Comparative Study', *Journal of Comparative Economics*, Vol. 21, No. 2, pp. 131-53.

Fischer, Stanley, Sahay, Ratna, and Vegh, Carlos A. (1996), 'Stabilization and Growth in Transition Economies: The Early Experience', *Journal of Economic Perspectives*, Vol. 10, No. 2, Spring, pp.45-66.

Guenov, Kamen (1994), 'Real Sector Adjustment to Macroeconomic Policy Measure' in Avramov, R. and Antonov, V. (eds), *Economic Transition in Bulgaria*, AECD: Sofia.

International Labor Organization (1993), *The Bulgarian Challenge: Reform of the Labour Market and Social Policy*, ILO: Geneva.

Jones, Derek C. (1995), 'Employee Participation in Transitional Economies: Evidence from Bulgaria, 1989-1992', *Economic and Industrial Democracy*, Vol. 16, No. 1, pp. 111-35.

—— and Kosali Ilayperuma (1994), 'Wage determination under Plan and Early Transition: Evidence from Bulgaria', mimeo, Hamilton College: Clinton, N.Y.

—— and Takao Kato (1993), 'The Nature and Determinants of Labor Market Transitions in Former Socialist Economies', mimeo, Hamilton College: Clinton, N.Y.

—— and Takao Kato (1996), 'The Determinants of Chief Executive Compensation in Transitional Economies: Evidence from Bulgaria', forthcoming in *Labour Economics*.

—— and Svilen Parvulov (1995), 'Industrial Organization in a Restructuring Socialist Economy: Evidence from Bulgaria', *Empirica*, Vol. 22, pp. 23-46.

Koford, K. and Miller, J. (1995), 'Contracts in Bulgaria: How Agents Cope When Property Rights are Incomplete', Working Paper, Dept. of Economics, University of Delaware.

MacIntyre, R. J. (1988), *Bulgaria: Politics, Economics and Society*, Pinter: London.

Miller, J. B. (1995), 'The Price Index Gap: A Window to Understanding the Bulgarian Economy', *Bulgarian National Bank Review*, Vol. 3, pp. 12-22.

—— (1995), 'Industrial Policy and the Transition to a Market Economy', *Economics of Transition*, Vol. 3 , No. 3, September, pp. 289-99.

Minassian, G. (1994), 'Sources of Inflation in Postcommunist Bulgaria', paper presented at the Workshop on Central and Eastern European Countries in Transition, Institute of Economics, Hungarian Academy of Sciences, September.

Murrell, Peter (1992), 'Evolution in Economics and in the Economic Reform of the Centrally Planned Economies', in Clague, C. and Rausser, G. (eds), *The Emergence of Market Economies in Eastern Europe*, Blackwell: Cambridge, Mass., pp. 35-53.

—— (1996), 'How Far has the Transition Progressed?', *Journal of Economic Perspectives*, Vol. 10, No. 2, Spring, pp.25-44.

North, Douglas, C. (1990), *Institutions, Institutional Change and Economic Performance*, Cambridge University Press: Cambridge, England.

Nuti, Mario (1995), 'Employeeism, Corporate Governance and Employee Ownership in Transitional Economies', mimeo, London Business School.

Posen, Adam (1993), 'Why Central Bank Independence Does not Cause Low Inflation', *Finance and International Economy*, No. 7, Oxford University Press: Oxford, England.

Svejnar, Jan (1996), 'Enterprises and Workers in the Transition: Econometric Evidence', *American Economic Review*, Vol. 86, No. 2, May, pp. 123-27.

Thirkell, J. E. M. and Tseneva, E. A. (1992), 'Bulgarian Industrial Relations in Transition', *International Labor Review*, Vol. 131, No. 3, pp. 355-66.

Tirole, Jean (1994), 'Western Prudential Regulation: Assessment, and Reflections on Its Application to Central and Eastern Europe', *The Economics of Transition*, Vol. 2, pp. 129-150.

Vulov, V. (1996), 'Purchasing-Power-Parity Exchange Rates: The Bulgarian Experience', May, Masters Thesis, University of Delaware.

Zloch-Christy, Iliana (1996) (ed), *Bulgaria in a Time of Change: Economic and Political Dimensions*, Avebury: Aldershot, England.

2 Economic transformation and regional inequality in Bulgaria: in search of a meaningful unit of analysis

Michael L. Wyzan

Introduction

An important aspect of the economic transition process taking place in Central and Eastern Europe (CEE) is the effect of that process on the various regions of a nation. Those states constituted as federations of republics, each based around a 'titular' ethnic group – Czechoslovakia, the Soviet Union, and Yugoslavia – have already broken up; most of these republics have received their independence along the lines of their former 'internal' borders with other republics. There is already a substantial literature on the economics of secession (e.g., see Bookman, 1993) and on economic developments in the new states that have emerged (e.g., see the studies contained and cited in Wyzan, 1996a).

The regional economics of the transition process in other, nonfederal, CEE states, including Albania, Bulgaria, Hungary, Poland, and Romania, has received less attention.[1] Such a lapse can be problematic from a political/economic perspective, since much of the opposition to the rapid movement toward a market economy is regionally based, and legislatures are constituted around the territorial structures of countries. Central governments ignore the regional aspects of economic restructuring at their peril, especially where 'regional' and 'ethnic' are closely correlated.[2]

The subject of this paper is the effect of the postcommunist economic transformation taking place in Bulgaria on that country's regional economic development. This is a subject that has received little attention to date in the Western literature, although there are such exceptions as Koulov (1992), Levinson (1993), Tsekov (1992), and Vodenska (1992).[3]

Study of Bulgarian regional disparities is hampered by the fact that the country has since 1987 been divided up into nine *oblasti* (provinces), which seem too large and internally diverse to be useful for studying regional disparities (see below). The 28 *okræzi* (districts) that existed prior to the 1987 territorial reform appear intuitively to be more appropriate for this purpose.

Thus, for example, the oblast based in Haskovo contains three former okræzi – Haskovo, Kærdzhali, and Stara Zagora – which are extremely diverse in their characteristics. The Kærdzhali okræg is the most ethnically Turkish (65.7 per cent) and the most rural (67.6 per cent live in villages) in the country; the okræg is characterized by enormous emigration to Turkey since the mid-1980s, the population having fallen by almost 29 per cent between 1985 and 1992 (NSI/Demografska, 1993, pp. 126, 137). The Stara Zagora okræg, on the other hand, contains the major industrial center that is the country's sixth largest city (NSI/Naselenie, 1993, p. 199). Only four per cent of the population of Stara Zagora okræg are Turkish, 32.1 per cent live in villages, and the population fell by only 3.6 per cent between 1985 and 1992 (NSI/Demografska, 1993, pp. 126, 137).[4] The characteristics of Haskovo okræg lie between those of Kærdzhali and Stara Zagora, although they are far closer to the latter's.

In order to investigate more formally the extent to which the earlier territorial breakdown of the country gives a more accurate picture of Bulgarian regional disparities than the current one, data from below the level of the okræg are desirable. One would ideally like to know whether the various *obshtini* (municipalities) – of which there are 278 at the moment – were divided up among okræzi in such a way that the latter formed more homogeneous units than do the present oblasti. Unfortunately, very little information has been published recently on the obshtini. Nonetheless, the Bulgarian National Statistical Institute (NSI) is in the process of publishing separate books containing data broken down by obshtina on various aspects of the reform process; one on unemployment is discussed at length below (NSI/Bezrabotni, 1993). In addition, some demographic data are available for 235 *gradove* (cities)[5] (NSI/Naselenie, 1993).

So as to examine the applicability of Bulgaria's present and previous territorial subdivisions to the study of effects of economic reform, this paper presents generalized entropy (GE) indexes of inequality for various variables of interest. These indexes, introduced by Theil (1967), and subsequently generalized by Shorrocks (1980) (see also Shorrocks and Foster, 1987), are additively decomposable. A measure having this property is such that the overall regional inequality in a nation with respect to a certain phenomenon can be expressed as the sum of within-group – say, oblast or okræg – and between-group inequalities. This methodology has recently been put to good use by Tsui (1993), who examines interprovincial, interprovincial, intrarural, intraurban, and rural-urban inequality in per capita output, infant mortality, and illiteracy/semi-illiteracy in China in 1982.

22

This paper is organized as follows. The next section describes the reform environment in Bulgaria – focusing on macroeconomic stabilization and structural reform – so as to set the stage for the regional analysis that follows. The third section contains a short description of Bulgaria's various territorial subdivisions since the country's reemergence from the Ottoman Empire in 1878. The fourth presents data on, and various GE indexes of, regional inequality in an attempt simultaneously to obtain an overview of the regional dispersion of the economic transformation process and to evaluate the country's territorial subdivision. The fifth section concludes.

Bulgarian economy under reform

Economic reform in post-communist Bulgaria, which began in January 1991, has been relatively slow and uneven.[6] The key distinguishing features of the country's economic transformation have been heavy foreign indebtedness inherited from late communist days (see Zloch-Christy, 1996), off-again, on-again relations with the International Monetary Fund (IMF) and World Bank, and reluctance to make tough decisions on structural reform.

Upon admission to these bodies in September 1990, Bulgaria started Article IV consultations with the IMF, resulting in the filing of a Letter of Intent in February 1991. The stabilization program contained the following: price liberalization; establishing a market-determined, floating, and unified exchange rate and deregulating most current account transactions; checking the growth of nominal labor remuneration in the state sector; setting strict nominal targets for the budget deficit, while restructuring revenue and expenditure; and establishing a tight monetary/credit policy through both significant increases in nominal interest rates and bank-specific ceilings on the extension of credit.

The measures succeeded in eliminating the monetary overhang, liberalizing prices and trade, avoiding hyperinflation, keeping wages under control, and maintaining external balance (OECD/Bulgaria, 1992, p. 74). Still, 1991-94 was characterized by weak economic performance, occasional backtracking on reforms, and one severe crisis (in 1994) in terms of inflation and the exchange rate.

As can be seen from Table 2.1, real GDP declined by almost 29 per cent during 1989-93, and industrial production by over 52 per cent over this period. CPI inflation has averaged 4.5 per cent per month since April 1991 (ignoring the first two months under the program, when the big round of price liberalization occurred).

Table 2.1
Bulgarian macroeconomic indicators
(% change over previous year unless otherwise indicated)

	1989	1990	1991	1992	1993	1994	1995
GDP (billion leva)	35.60	45.40	131.00	201.00	299.00	543.00	852.00
GDP (billion USD)*	17.60	6.90	7.50	8.60	10.80	10.00	12.70
GDP per capita (USD)	1,957.00	769.00	836.00	1,010.00	1,280.00	1,190.00	1,499.00
Share of private sector in GDP (%)	n.a.	9.10	11.80	18.30	23.50	27.20	33.30
Unemployment (thousands, end-period)	0.00	65.00	419.00	577.00	626.00	488.00	424.00
Unemploy. rate (%)	0.00	1.60	10.80	15.20	16.40	12.80	11.10
Ave. monthly wage**							
–leva	274.00	378.00	1,591.00	2,305.00	3,930.00	6,248.00	8,952.00
–USD	136.00	58.00	73.00	94.00	120.00	95.00	127.00
Real GDP	-1.90	-9.10	-11.70	-7.30	-2.40	1.40	2.50
Gross industrial production	-1.10	-16.80	-22.20	-15.90	-10.90	4.50	7.00
Consumer price inflation***	10.00	72.50	338.90	79.50	63.90	121.90	32.90
Producer price inflation***	n.a.	n.a.	284.00	24.90	15.30	91.50	33.50
Budget balance (% GDP)****	-0.64	-4.90	-3.80	-5.30	-11.40	-6.80	-6.70
Broad money***	n.a.	n.a.	284.00	51.00	47.00	71.80	39.60
Exports (billion USD)*****	3.10	2.60	3.70	4.00	4.00	4.20	5.30
Imports (billion USD)*****	4.30	3.40	3.80	4.20	4.30	4.00	4.90
Trade balance (billion USD)*****	-1.20	-0.80	-0.03	-0.20	-0.30	0.20	0.40
Current account balance (billion USD)*****	-1.30	-0.90	-0.08	-0.40	-0.50	0.20	0.09 ******
Exchange rate							
–end-period	n.a.	n.a.	22.00	25.00	33.00	66.00	70.10
–average period	2.00	6.60	17.40	23.30	27.70	54.30	67.20

Table 2.1 (continued)
Bulgarian macroeconomic indicators
(% change over previous year unless otherwise indicated)

	1989	1990	1991	1992	1993	1994	1995
Gross foreign debt (end-period, billion USD)	9.20	10.00	11.40	12.10	12.50	10.40	11.40
BNB reserves (end-period, billion USD)	n.a.	0.10	0.30	0.90	0.70	1.00	1.30

*   Converted at average annual official exchange rate.
**   State sector only, not including women on maternity leave for 1989 and 1990, annual average; for 1991-95 figures apply to December of the relevant year.
***   On end-of-period basis.
****   Republican budget, cash basis.
*****   Data derived from customs statistics.
****** January-September 1995.
Source: Bulgarian National Bank; National Statistical Institute; International Monetary Fund; World Bank; *Business Central Europe* (1995, p. 17); Bulgarian Telegraphic Agency report of 21 December 1995.

Unemployment was 16 per cent at the end of 1993, before falling to about 11 per cent recently. As noted by Borensztein, Demekas, and Ostry (1993, p. 9), 'the state enterprise sector ... shed excess labor faster than in perhaps any other reforming country'. The rapid rise in the numbers of unemployed from 103,184 in February 1991 to 576,893 in December 1992 occurred despite the absence of bankruptcy legislation and of any breakthrough in large-scale privatization. Those numbers peaked at 631,987 in January 1994, before falling to 488,442 in December 1994 and 398,528 in October 1995, then rising to 423,773 in December 1995.

The monthly wage has remained low, bottoming out at $76 in April 1994 before rebounding to $127 in December 1995, still among the lowest in CEE. In real, domestic currency terms, the average monthly wage in 1991 was 298 leva (at the January 1991 consumer price level), rose to 332 in 1992, and then remained more or less constant (at 331) in 1993. More recently, the average monthly wage so measured fell to 263 leva in 1994, declining further to 246 in 1995. Accordingly, it appears heuristically as though relatively high real wages in 1991 and 1992 contributed to growing unemployment, while the real wage declines over the last two years have had the opposite effect.

For the domestic economy, 1995 was the first that can be characterized remotely favorably: moderate growth of the consumer price index (CPI; 32.9 per cent), rising GDP (2.5 per cent) and gross industrial output (seven per cent), and falling unemployment. However, during 1995 the foreign sector was the locus of wildly divergent trends. The trade surplus, preliminarily estimated at $426 million (Kænchev, 1996, Kyuchukov, 1996), was the largest in CEE that year; a small current account surplus was likely also earned.

These auspicious indicators were recorded despite the real appreciation of the lev, which moved only moved from 66.1 on 2 January to 68.0 on 9 October, in the face of about 25 per cent CPI inflation over that period. Bulgaria's traditional exports, still oriented around chemicals, metallurgy, and textiles, have been finding markets in the West. Moreover, modest direct foreign investment – officially put at $850 million over 1991-95, $284 million of that in 1995 (Mancheva, 1996) – and anemic recovery have not led to import booms, as in most Visegrád countries. The positive foreign sector balances coincided with growing foreign exchange reserves over most of the year, as they reached $1.5 billion on 30 June, up from $1.0 billion on 31 December 1994 (BNB, 1995, p. 23).

On the other hand, toward the end of 1995 foreign sector turbulence set in, as the lev weakened to close the year at 70.7 per dollar (it subsequently moved to 78.9 by 1 April 1996). Unlike the foreign exchange crises of January and March 1994, when the BNB seemed to stand by helplessly, the depreciation in late 1995 probably began as conscious policy. Letting the lev weaken is a way to help out banks and the state budget, as well as to head off another round of real appreciation like that preceding the events of early 1994.

Subsequently, the BNB began to intervene in the foreign exchange market, and the foreign reserves fell to $1.36 billion at year's end. The reserve decline picked up steam in early 1996, as they had fallen to $930 million by 29 February (*Trud*, 1996). With the country facing $1.25 billion in foreign debt and debt service payments in 1996 – and a similar amount in 1997 – and having as of late March 1996 no agreements on new lending with the IMF or World Bank, developments have turned ominous.

Despite the generally favorable macroeconomic developments presided over by the socialists, who took power in January 1995, five years into its reforms Bulgaria suffers from a vulnerability which the Visegrád lands do not. The low foreign reserves and large foreign debt and debt service payments have always carried the threat of sending the lev into a tailspin, setting off high inflation as in 1994. Troubled relations with the IMF and World Bank have meant that Bulgaria could never justifiably expect a given level of macroeconomic stability to be indefinitely sustainable.

Monetary, fiscal, and wage policy do not satisfactorily account for the deterioration in 1994, the improvement in much of 1995, or the turbulence late in 1995. The cash budget deficit in 1994 was only about half that of the year before as a share of GDP; more or less the same-sized deficit by that standard occurred in 1995. The country's large foreign and domestic debt burdens mean that large primary budget surpluses have been necessary in order to attain medium-sized cash budget deficits. This burden has been lessened somewhat by the June 1994 debt and debt service reduction (DDSR) agreement with the London Club.

While broad money growth accelerated in 1994, that was largely due to the revaluation of foreign currency deposits at the much depreciated exchange rate. In fact, growth of the lev component of broad money fell from 59 per cent in 1993 to 51 per cent in 1994. Thus, through 1994 the timing of the changes in broad money did not coincide with those in inflation or other performance indicators. However, the decline in broad money growth to under 40 per cent in 1995 is consistent with the lower inflation that year. In any case, the overall rapid growth of the lev-denominated money supply reflects the large-scale refinancing of state and private commercial banks, evincing the failure to deal with large bank and enterprise losses. At the end of 1995, bank losses stood at $410.2 million (*Pari*, 1996), while the World Bank estimates enterprise red ink over 1993-95 at $2 billion annually (Dimitrova, 1996).

It is these losses, along with inaction on other important structural matters, such as large-scale privatization, that are at the root of Bulgaria's macroeconomic instability. This is true not only with respect to the direct macroeconomic consequences of the chosen policies, but even more so due to the IMF's and World Bank's standoffishness in response to these policies. Bulgaria received $394 million from the IMF under the March 1991 standby agreement and another $131 million under that body's Compensatory and Contingency Financing Facility. A second standby agreement in April 1992 was to provide Bulgaria with $212 million, but the fifth tranche of this credit was never provided. After going without IMF credits in 1993, accord was reached in April 1994, which included a $97 million standby and a $324 million structural transformation facility (STF). The Fund also provided $102 million to support the London Club agreement of June that year.

The IMF never released the second $162 tranche of the STF, nor did it agree to a new standby, citing the country's failure to agree with the World Bank on a $150 financial and enterprise sector adjustment loan (FESAL). The Bank had agreed to a $250 million structural adjustment loan (SAL) in August 1991 and contributed $125 in support of the London Club deal. Recently, however, it has been displeased with Bulgaria's foot-dragging in dealing with enterprise and bank losses and in launching a mass privatization program.

There has been movement lately on several of these policy fronts. After four years of reliance on market privatization under an April 1992 law, which has resulted in the selling off of a small number of objects (NSI/Tekushta, 1996, p. 23, Dimitrov, 1996), a scheme of the mass variety began in January 1996. Between 8 January and 8 April 1996, the 6.7 million Bulgarian citizens aged 18 or over were eligible to acquire vouchers worth 25,000 leva ($348 at that day's exchange rate) for a token fee at local post offices. The vouchers can be used in auctions, to be held starting in June 1996, for shares in 1,063 enterprises with an aggregate book value of 80.47

billion leva ($1.1 billion), or can be entrusted to investment funds.

Interest in obtaining the vouchers has grown slowly, so that by 19 February only 350,000 (5.5 per cent of those eligible) had bought vouchers. Observers point to organizational flaws, including uncertainty over the value of the enterprises included and the fact that the list of those companies had been changed several times. Another problem is that the investment funds, which are expected to play a large role in the process, are not allowed to advertise or to call themselves 'privatization funds' during the three-month period for acquiring the vouchers (Damyanova, 1996). As the end of that period approached, one million citizens had obtained vouchers. Realistically speaking, this is an impressive figure, although those vouchers would allow them to purchase only 25 billion leva worth of the available over 80 billion leva in enterprise shares (Markov, 1996).[7]

As for banking reform, selected banks are to be recapitalized using government paper issued in a December 1993 attempt to replace unrecoverable enterprise debt with such paper (Wyzan, 1996b, pp. 93-95, Georgieva and Denkovska, 1996). The BNB has revoked the licenses of two insolvent private banks (Tsolov, 1996). Some 45 enterprises have been liquidated, with another 30-40 such bankruptcies expected shortly (Kirilova, 1996). The major question at this writing is whether the IMF and World Bank judge that there has been sufficient progress on structural reform to warrant new lending; some observers predict a positive outcome by the summer.

From a regional perspective, two aspects of the Bulgarian approach to privatization are noteworthy. First, since the restitution of small-scale property has been an important and successful component of the overall reform strategy, the geographical aspects of such restitution deserve particular attention. The most recent figures at the author's disposal show that as of 15 November 1994, 60.5 per cent of objects subject to restitution – including 82.1 per cent of stores, 82.7 per cent of restaurants, and 67.2 per cent of hotels and inns – had been returned to their precommunist owners (NSI/Spravochnik, 1995, p. 211). Second, since there has been relatively little large-scale privatization, any study of the regional effects of economic transformation in Bulgaria must inevitably focus on the territorial implications of the degenerative aspects of the process.

Brief history of Bulgaria's territorial administration

Bulgaria's system of territorial administration has gone through a series of major changes since the country's independence in 1878. Under both capitalism and communism periods with roughly 28 upper-level units have alternated with ones with fewer than ten such units. There has thus been a tension – especially in the communist era – between a centralizing tendency inherent in the economic development process and a desire to spread economic and social development evenly throughout the country's surface. As elsewhere in CEE, a movement to give more authority and revenue-raising capability to the lowest levels of government is afoot.

The 1880 Tærnovo constitution created 27 okræzi, 21 on the territory belonging at the time to Bulgaria and another six in Eastern Rumelia, the area that continued to belong to Turkey until 1885. Interestingly in view of subsequent experience, territorial reforms in 1887 and 1901 reduced the number of okræzi to 12, based in Burgas, Kyustendil, Pleven, Plovdiv, Ruse, Shumen, Sofia, Stara Zagora, Varna, Veliko Tærnovo, Vidin, and Vratsa. After the military coup in 1934, the number of territorial units was further reduced to only seven (Kyustendil, Ruse, Varna, Veliko Tærnovo, and Vidin were eliminated), although a further territorial reform in 1944 brought back the Ruse okræg and created one based in Blagoevgrad (Koulov, 1992).

What accounts for the ever increasing centralization during the precommunist period? Koulov (1992) credits the growing economic and administrative importance of Sofia relative to many of the okræg centers and the temporary loss of the Southern Dobrudzha to Romania in 1915. The seven such centers that survived the 1934 reform became the leading population and socioeconomic centers of the country, at the expense of demographic increase and economic development in the remainder of the land.

The socialist period can be divided into two subperiods. During the first subperiod, there was an emphasis on equalizing the level of development throughout the country, which ran counter to the centralizing tendencies inherent in Soviet-style central planning. Building on the prewar work of Anastas Beshkov on so-called 'economic regionalization' theory, the overriding principal was – in theory at least – for economic and administrative boundaries to coincide to the extent possible. By 1959, there were once again 28 okræzi (if one includes Sofia), which were sometimes referred to as 'economic regions', despite their lack of connection to the research attempting to delineate such regions by Bulgarian geographers during the 1950s (Carter, 1987, p. 72). That same year the 105 okoli ('counties') were abolished and 1,392 smaller obshtini created. The proliferation in the number of okræzi is said to have resulted in a 'considerable territorial deconcentration of capital investment, fixed assets, production and services, as well as a significant equalization of incomes and quality of life' (Koulov, 1992, p. 395, see also Hristov, 1989).

There was subsequently concern over the build-up of unnecessary bureaucracies in the okræg centers. The decentralization of decision making was in many respects purely formal and subnational governments largely lacked the ability to collect revenue independently. In 1977 another administrative layer, the selishtna sistema ('settlement system') was created; these 291 units were designed so as supposedly to reflect commuting and sociocultural links among communities. They had as their function to provide basic necessities and social infrastructure to their inhabitants (Hristov, 1989, Koulov, 1992). This reform, like so much else promulgated during the 35-year rule of communist leader Todor Zhivkov, proved to have only a formal character, and was thus unable to counteract the centralizing forces inherent in the command economy.

The final administrative reform of the communist era came in 1987, when the okræzi were abolished and the country was divided into the present nine oblasti. The motivation for doing so is said to have been that the okræzi were too small to reflect the size of the current heavy industrial complexes. This seeming recentralization was combined with continued talk of the need to decentralize and democratize decision making.[8] Thus, the obshtini – whose numbers were reduced by 52 – were supposedly given new authority in such spheres as encouraging local production, fostering self-sufficiency in agricultural products, and environmental protection, as well as new authority to levy taxes and fees (Grigorov, 1989, Koulov, 1992, pp. 397-99).[9]

Bulgarian economic geographers have argued in favor of a territorial subdivision of the country something like that which prevailed when communism fell in 1989 (e.g., Hristov, 1989, Koulov, 1992). On the other hand, there seems to be considerable sentiment in the country in favor of a return to a system like the one that prevailed between 1959 and 1987, with about 28 okræzi (or *regioni*, as they now sometimes called). There are undoubtedly good reasons to avoid an excessive bureaucratization of administration, and there may be well be criteria according to which a small number of large regions is optimal (as implied by Koulov, 1992, p. 398).

Nonetheless, the special considerations of the current era of postcommunist economic transformation suggest that having regions that are relatively internally homogeneous with respect to the socioeconomic consequences of that transformation may be desirable. As suggested in the introduction, many of the oblasti appear so heterogeneous internally that there may be as much variation within them as between them in important 'transition' variables. As part of its analysis of the regional effects of the transformation process, the next section examines this issue empirically using additively decomposable GE indexes of inequality.

Regional disparities: description and decomposition

In this section we examine Bulgarian regional disparities with respect to important variables characterizing the transformation of the economy from a centrally planned to a market basis. In carrying out such an analysis, two choices must be made. First, there is the issue of the variables to be examined. Unfortunately, while we have data at the level of the obshtina on unemployment broken by age, sex, education, and reason for separation, there is no national data set on employment by obshtina. This, of course, makes it impossible to calculate unemployment rates by obshtina, and we are forced to examine the regional dispersion of the ratio of unemployment to total population ('unemployment incidence'). Fortunately, we have unemployment rates by oblast, which can help in evaluating whether unemployment incidence is a good proxy for the state of a given labor market.

30

The second, and in many ways more difficult choice, at least in the Bulgarian context, is the territorial unit to examine. One might follow Zaniewski (1992) in his study of regional disparities in social well-being through Eastern Europe and take the oblasti as the units of analysis. However, the oblasti are considerably larger than the subunits in Hungary, Poland, and Romania, but not Czechoslovakia. Indeed, Zaniewski (1992, p. 345) admits that in the Bulgarian case 'the high degree of territorial aggregation...was probably responsible for the low value of coefficients of variation', that is, for the fact that Bulgaria appears to have a low degree of regional inequality.

In this section, we decompose the total national dispersion in certain variables into interoblast and intraoblast inequality and interokræg and intraokræg inequality. This enables us to evaluate whether the okræzi were more appropriate as upper-level territorial units than the oblasti for the purpose of observing whether changes associated with economic transformation have regionally variable effects.

It can be shown that only the class of so-called generalized entropy indexes of inequality across a given population satisfies the property of additive decomposability, in addition to the following other desirable features:

- it is continuous and symmetric in the variable under examination;
- it is such that its value is equal to zero when all observations are equal, that is, there is no inequality across the data set;
- it has continuous first-order partial derivatives; and it satisfies the Dalton-Pigou principle of transfers, namely that if a transfer is made from a unit of observation with a higher value of the variable in question to one with a lower value, the measured level of inequality falls.

An additively decomposable index is such that total inequality "can be expressed as the sum of a 'within-group' inequality term and a 'between-group' term, where the within-group contribution is itself a weighted sum of the sub-group inequality values" (Shorrocks, 1980, p. 614).

We follow Tsui (1993) and employ the variant of the GE index where the parameter $c = 0$. This not only simplifies matters computationally but also endows the indicator with the property of 'transfer sensitivity' and makes the within-group and between-group components independent of each other (Tsui, 1993, pp. 605-9). If transfer sensitivity holds, a transfer at the lower end of the distribution carries more weight in the index than would the same transfer higher in the distribution (see Shorrocks and Foster, 1987).

Accordingly, our measure of inequality is as follows:

$$I(y) = (1/n) \sum_{i=1}^{n} \log (m/y_i) \tag{1}$$

31

where I is the index of inequality, y is an nx1 vector containing the observations on the variable of interest, and m is equal to $(1/n) \Sigma y_i$ or the mean of the y_i.[10] The important characteristic of I that it is decomposable as follows,

$$I(y) = \Sigma w_g I(y_g) + I(m_1 e_1, m_2 e_2, ..., m_G e_G) \qquad (2)$$

where $w_g = n_g/n$ and y_g is a subvector of y including the observations belonging to group g, $g = 1, 2, ..., G$; $I(y_g)$ is the inequality index of the gth group; w_g, $g = 1, 2, ...,$ G, is the weight attached to inequality in group g in total inequality; n_g, $g = 1, 2, ...,$ G, is the number of observations in group g; and e_g, $g = 1, 2, ..., G$, is an n_gx1 vector of ones. The first term on the right-hand side of equation (2) is the measure of within-group inequality and the second term measures between-group inequality.

In order to apply these indexes to regional Bulgarian data, we choose the following variables: the progress of the restitution of small-scale urban property, the educational attainment of the population, rates of in- and outmigration, and unemployment incidence. Table 2.2 contains data broken down by oblast and okræg on restitution as of the end of October 1992, as contained in a special publication of the subject put out by NSI in March 1993 (NSI/Restitutsiyata, 1993). Nationally at the time 45.8 per cent of the objects subject to restitution had been returned, with a pecuniary value equal to 49.6 per cent of the total value of restitutable objects.

A glance at Table 2.2 indicates that there has been considerable inequality across the country in the progress of restitution. Using these data on the oblasti and okræzi, we are also able to note great variation across the latter within a given oblast: for example, Pernik (low) and Kyustendil (high) are both contained in Sofia oblast, and Tærgovishte (low) and Razgrad (high) cohabit the Ruse oblast. One's intuition that the oblasti are extremely internally heterogeneous with respect to this variable is borne out by the indexes of within- and between-group inequality presented at the bottom of Table 2.2. Fully 82 per cent of the total variation in the percentage of objects restituted, and 77 per cent of that in the total value restored, is accounted for within the oblasti.[11]

The next variable of interest is educational attainment. On the basis of the census of population and housing that began on 4 December 1992, NSI put out a special publication, based on a two per cent representative sample (i.e., about 170,000 people out of a national total of about 8.5 million), in May 1993 (NSI/Demografska, 1993). The publication contains data on the sex, age, educational attainment, family structure, ethnic affiliation, mother tongue, religion, internal migration, and invalidity (if any) of the respondents. Unfortunately for the present purposes, detailed data on the structure of the population are available by oblast and okræg (now called 'region'), with only a single table containing information on the obshtini; that table breaks the numbers down only into urban and rural.

Table 2.2
Progress of property restitution in Bulgaria
(as of 31 October 1992)

Oblast/Okraeg	Percent of objects restituted	Percent of total value of objects restituted
Sofia-grad	35	22.2
Burgas	45.2	51.7
Burgas-okraeg	53	49.2
Sliven	37.5	63.9
Yambol	43.3	41.5
Haskovo	45.3	45.4
Haskovo-okraeg	49.8	53.2
Kaerdzhali	45.3	34.6
Stara Zagora	41.7	46
Lovech	53.6	64.8
Gabrovo	56.5	68.7
Lovech-okraeg	41.8	34.3
Pleven	64.2	67.7
Veliko Taernovo	51.1	74.3
Montana	47.5	58.5
Montana-okraeg	53.4	63.5
Vidin	39.8	59.6
Vratsa	48.5	53.1
Plovdiv	49.9	71.2
Pazardzhik	47.7	50.3
Plovdiv-okraeg	51.2	81.9
Smolyan	50.2	33.5
Ruse	50.4	50
Razgrad	62.7	72.7
Ruse-okraeg	59.8	49.8
Silistra	40.6	42.9
Taergovishte	37.3	42.9
Sofia-oblast	37.6	37.4
Blagoevgrad	38.6	32.6
Kyustendil	61.4	61.8
Pernik	23.1	19.4
Sofia-okraeg	35.4	46.3

Source: NSI/Restitutsiyata (1993).

33

Table 2.2 (continued)
Progress of property restitution in Bulgaria
(as of 31 October 1992)

Oblast/Okraeg	Percent of objects restituted	Percent of total value of objects restituted
Varna	49.7	41.6
Dobrich	37.4	38
Shumen	45.7	55.5
Varna-okraeg	55	40
Total	45.8	49.6
Intraoblast inequality	0.0182 (81.8%)	0.0358 (77.3%)
Interoblast inequality	0.0040 (18.1%)	0.0105 (22.7%)
Total inequality	0.0222	0.0463

Source: NSI/Restitutsiyata (1993).

Following our practice for the restitution variable, we provide data in Table 2.3 on educational attainment by oblast and okræg. Although educational attainment is not a variable closely tied to the reform process *per se*, this variable is presumably positively correlated with other measures of regional socioeconomic status. Accordingly, regional inequality in education is worth watching as the reform process unfolds.

The first column in Table 2.3 shows the percentage of the population over seven years of age with higher and 'semi-higher' (i.e., post-secondary, non-university) education; the second column contains information on the percentage of such people who have failed to complete primary school. Note once again that there is considerable variation within at least certain oblasti. For example, Ruse oblast contains the Ruse okræg with a particularly high level of educational attainment, and Razgrad and Tærgovishte, with among the lowest such attainment. The presence of Varna (high) and Dobrich (low) within the same oblast is also striking.

Indeed, as demonstrated by the inequality indexes at the bottom of the table, for the high-education variable, 76 per cent of the overall inequality is within the oblasti. The finding is less striking for the low-education indicator – 57 per cent of the variation is intraoblast – but it is still the case that more of the variation is intraoblast than interoblast. Two observations are in order on the educational data before moving on. First, note that Sofia-city is extremely different from the rest of the country in terms of educational attainment; much of the regional variation in this variable is between Sofia and the rest of the country.

Table 2.3
Educational attainment in Bulgaria
(as of 4 December 1992)

Oblast/okraeg	Per cent of +7 population w/ higher education	Per cent of +7 population w/o complete primary education
Sofia-grad	25.3	13.1
Burgas	9.1	28.9
Burgas-okraeg	10.3	27.6
Sliven	7.6	30.7
Yambol	8.1	29.7
Haskovo	8.5	29.3
Haskovo-okraeg	8.7	30.3
Kaerdzhali	5.5	37.1
Stara Zagora	9.7	24.5
Lovech	10.4	21
Gabrovo	11.2	16.1
Lovech-okraeg	9.9	23.8
Pleven	10.3	22.5
Veliko Taernovo	10.4	20.3
Montana	8.8	24.6
Montana-okraeg	7.5	24.8
Vidin	8.8	27.7
Vratsa	9.9	22.6
Plovdiv	10.2	26
Pazardzhik	8.3	29
Plovdiv-okraeg	11.5	23.4
Smolyan	7.8	31.5
Ruse	8.8	27.7
Razgrad	6.8	33
Ruse-okraeg	11.1	20.5
Silistra	7.5	33.2
Taergovishte	7.4	30
Sofia-oblast	8	26.4
Blagoevgrad	7.9	30.4
Kyustendil	8.9	25.1
Pernik	8.3	22.1
Sofia-okraeg	7.5	24.8

Source: NSI/Demografska (1993, pp. 112-13, 132-33).

Table 2.3 (continued)
Educational attainment in Bulgaria
(as of 4 December 1992)

Oblast/okraeg	Per cent of +7 population w/ higher education	Per cent of +7 population w/o complete primary education
Varna	10.9	26.2
Dobrich	7.1	30.4
Shumen	8.4	31.1
Varna-okraeg	13.9	21.8
Total	11.6	24.3
Intraoblast inequality	0.0145 (76.1%)	0.0096 (56.9%)
Interoblast inequality	0.0045 (23.9%)	0.0073 (43.1%)
Total inequality	0.019	0.0169
Intraurban inequality	0.0148 (5.1%)	0.0302 (36.7%)
Interurban inequality	0.0356 (12.5%)	0.0116 (14.1%)
Rural-urban inequality	0.2352 (82.4%)	0.0405 (49.2%)
Total inequality	0.2856	0.0823

Source: NSI/Demografska (1993, pp. 112-13, 132-33).

Second, urban-rural inequality in educational achievement is more striking than the variation across and within oblasti. Following Tsui (1993, pp. 614-18), we have calculated intrarural, intraurban, and rural-urban inequality for our education variable. These calculations appear at the bottom of Table 2.3. Particularly noteworthy is the fact that fully 82 per cent of the inequality in the incidence across oblasti of high educational attainment consists of rural-urban inequality; only five per cent is accounted for by inequality across urban areas and 12.5 per cent by inequality across rural areas. The findings are less striking for low educational attainment, but even here rural-urban inequality is the largest component (49 per cent) of the total dispersion in the variable under examination.

We now move on to the decomposition of the inequality in variables for which we have data from below the level of the okræg. For in- and outmigration, we have figures from an April 1993 publication – unrelated to the 1992 census – that contains data on demographic processes in the country during 1991 (NSI/Naselenie, 1993). The migration data are provided for a total of 236 gradove (cities).[12] Inmigration and outmigration rates, whereby the raw migration numbers are divided by the relevant population totals, are summarized in Table 2.4.

Table 2.4
In- and out-migration in Bulgaria, 1991

Oblast/grad	Rate of inmigration	Rate of outmigration
Sofia-grad	0.0145	0.0138
Burgas	0.0217	0.0197
Burgas-grad	0.0246	0.0239
Sliven	0.0359	0.02
Yambol	0.0357	0.0388
Haskovo	0.0147	0.0167
Haskovo-grad	0.017	0.0244
Kaerdzhali	0.0497	0.0229
Stara Zagora	0.0173	0.0333
Lovech	0.0247	0.0218
Gabrovo	0.027	0.0333
Lovech-grad	0.0292	0.0285
Pleven	0.0205	0.0312
Veliko Taernovo	0.0628	0.0447
Montana	0.0176	0.0179
Montana-grad	0.0241	0.0227
Vidin	0.029	0.0314
Vratsa	0.0277	0.0342
Plovdiv	0.0186	0.017
Pazardzhik	0.0272	0.0278
Plovdiv-grad	0.0228	0.0248
Smolyan	0.0458	0.0496
Ruse	0.0073	0.0127
Razgrad	0.0338	0.0228
Ruse-grad	0.0097	0.0213
Silistra	0.0123	0.0246
Taergovishte	0.0015	0.0179
Sofia-oblast	0.0108	0.0128
Blagoevgrad	0.025	0.0208
Kyustendil	0.011	0.0213
Pernik	0.0279	0.0255

Source: NSI/Naselenie (1993, pp. 180, 189-99, 260-63).

Table 2.4 (continued)
In- and out-migration in Bulgaria, 1991

Oblast/grad	Rate of inmigration	Rate of outmigration
Varna	0.0018	0.0015
Dobrich	0.0114	0.0125
Shumen	0.0371	0.0272
Varna-grad	0.022	0.0199
Intraoblast inequality	0.5827 (84.0%)	0.1447 (62.6%)
Interoblast inequality	0.1114 (16.0%)	0.0867 (37.4%)
Total inequality	0.6941	0.2314
Intraokraeg inequality	0.4861 (67.0%)	0.1278 (51.3%)
Interokraeg inequality	0.2391 (33.0%)	0.1213 (48.7%)
Total inequality	0.7252	0.2491

Source: NSI/Naselenie (1993, pp. 180, 189-99, 260-63).

Although it appears virtually identical in structure to Tables 2.2 and 2.3, Table 2.4 is set up rather differently. The gradove listed under each oblast do not represent inclusive subdivisions of the territory of that oblast but are merely examples of the some of the gradove in each oblast; they are chosen only because they are the largest ones. Smaller gradove often have more extreme values for in- and out-migration and it is the distribution of these smaller places across the oblasti (and okræzi) that determines the overall level of regional inequality in the data. For every listed grad there is a corresponding okræg and a list of (unlisted) gradove that go with it.

As reported at the bottom of Table 2.4, in line with our findings for the other variables, the share of overall inequality accounted for by intraoblast inequality is always higher than that determined by interoblast inequality. This result is stronger for inmigration (84 per cent) than for outmigration (63 per cent), but is present for both variables. Since we have data from below the level of the okræg, we are also – for the first time – in a position to say something about whether the okræzi are more internally homogeneous. This is indeed the case, with intraokræg inequality accounting for 67 per cent of the total variation in inmigration and only 51 per cent of that in outmigration. The result for outmigration is the first instance in which the percentage of inequality of a between-group nature is close to that of a within-group nature. The okræzi look promising as units of analysis.

A high rate of outmigration may be associated with a declining locality and a high rate of inmigration with an expanding one. In practice, however, as shown in Table 2.4 and by the data on the smaller gradove not contained therein, in- and outmigration rates are often both high or both low for a given grad. Migration rates are thus rather

38

difficult to interpret as proxies for a locality's fate in the economic transformation process.

Perhaps the ideal measure of how a given region is faring is the state of its labor market. We are fortunate to have a very complete data set published in March 1993 on unemployment on 4 December 1992 (the census date) – broken down by reason for separation, education, age, and sex – in all of Bulgaria's 278 obshtini (NSI/Bezrabotni, 1993). Table 2.5 contains summary data on unemployment incidence (the number of unemployed relative to the total population) by oblast and okræg. Table 2.5 is again in the style of Tables 2.2 and 2.3, where the subdivision of the oblasti are okræzi that together encompass the oblast's entire territory. Like Table 2.4, however, a great deal of information, in this case on the obshtini, is not explicitly presented in the table. For the oblasti (only), we also have data on unemployment rates, where the denominator refers to the working-age, rather than the entire, population. These are presented in a separate column in the table.

The definition of unemployed applied in putting together the census data summarized in Table 2.5 was an especially inclusive one. Thus, the national total came to 680,228, at a time when the Ministry of Labor was showing a figure of only 565,138 (at the end of November 1992). The NSI counted those who left work voluntarily and those who completed school or military service without specializations, whom the Ministry's labor bureaus do not enumerate (NSI/Bezrabotni, 1993, p. 14). On the other hand, the director of the Ministry's National Employment Service expressed skepticism in January 1993 about the NSI's method, claiming that anyone who was not paid was considered unemployed (Dimitrova, 1993). Be that as it may, we can only note in passing that the data that we employ employs an extremely inclusive definition of the notion 'unemployed'.

Another question concerns the appropriateness of unemployment incidence as an indicator of the state of the labor market. It is possible, of course, that a given obshtina has a relatively young population, so that a low unemployment incidence is associated with a high unemployment rate. Unfortunately, we have at our disposal little data with which to evaluate the seriousness of this problem. However, if we compare the rank order of the oblasti by unemployment incidence and that by unemployment rate (see Table 2.5), we find them to be virtually identical; the only exception is the reversal of Lovech and Varna. Lovech oblast has a relatively large working-age population, so that its relatively low unemployment incidence rate is misleading.

With these caveats in mind, we turn our attention to the inequality in unemployment incidence. Note again the heterogeneity of the oblasti, with Haskovo, Plovdiv, and Sofia-oblast standing out in this respect. If we include Sofia-grad in the calculation – despite its obvious outlier status – we find that as much as 80 per cent of the variation in unemployment incidence is intraoblast. If we remove Sofia-grad from the calculation, we find that almost 89 per cent of the inequality is intraoblast. The oblasti are clearly dysfunctional as units of observation for labor market phenomena.

Table 2.5
Unemployment incidence in Bulgaria
(as of 4 December 1992)

Oblast/okraeg	Unemployment/ population	Unemployment/ working-age population
Sofia-grad	0.0582	0.1
Burgas	0.0847	0.152
Burgas-okraeg	0.0841	
Sliven	0.0927	
Yambol	0.0754	
Haskovo	0.0776	0.139
Haskovo-okraeg	0.0781	
Kaerdzhali	0.0976	
Stara Zagora	0.0723	
Lovech	0.0784	0.145
Gabrovo	0.0648	
Lovech-okraeg	0.0818	
Pleven	0.086	
Veliko Taernovo	0.0749	
Montana	0.0872	0.17
Montana-okraeg	0.0866	
Vidin	0.0867	
Vratsa	0.088	
Plovdiv	0.0869	0.152
Pazardzhik	0.1054	
Plovdiv-okraeg	0.0734	
Smolyan	0.1112	
Ruse	0.1	0.178
Razgrad	0.0999	
Ruse-okraeg	0.0887	
Silistra	0.1153	
Taergovishte	0.1059	
Sofia-oblast	0.0783	0.14
Blagoevgrad	0.0901	
Kyustendil	0.0705	
Pernik	0.0697	

Source: NSI/Bezrabotni (1993, pp. 7, 26-8, 38-96).

Table 2.5 (continued)
**Unemployment incidence in Bulgaria
(as of 4 December 1992)**

Oblast/okraeg	Unemployment/ population	Unemployment/ working-age population
Varna	0.0815	0.141
Dobrich	0.0926	
Shumen	0.0801	
Varna-okraeg	0.0766	
	Including Sofia-grad	Excluding Sofia-grad
Intraoblast inequality	0.0455 (79.8%)	0.0482 (88.5%)
Interoblast inequality	0.0115 (20.2%)	0.0063 (11.5%)
Total inequality	0.057	0.0545
Intraokraeg inequality	0.0551 (14.8%)	0.0538 (14.0%)
Interokraeg inequality	0.3172 (85.2%)	0.3299 (86.0%)
Total inequality	0.3723	0.3837

Source: NSI/Bezrabotni (1993, pp. 7, 26-8, 38-96).

When we reexamine the data by okræg, something dramatic happens: now 85 per cent of inequality – which has itself increased radically when the data are grouped in this manner – is accounted for by interokræg variation. In other words, the okræzi are ideally suited for understanding the spatial dimension of unemployment incidence in Bulgaria. In this instance, removing Sofia-grad from the data set affects the calculation only marginally – now 86 per cent of the inequality is interokræg.

The authors of NSI/Bezrabotni (1993, pp. 12-14) have divided the obshtini up into three groups based on the nature of unemployment in those localities. Such factors as age structure and the reason for being unemployed are taken into account. Table 2.6 provides data on some representative high-unemployment obshtini in each of the three groups.

In Group I – which contains around 50 per cent of the total number of obshtini – are found localities where about half of the unemployed were let go, where a relatively high percentage are secondary school leavers who have never worked or left their jobs voluntarily, and where more than half are generally under 30 years of age. In Group II, which largely consists of obshtini from the Blagoevgrad and Smolyan okræzi, a very high percentage of the unemployed were let go (from 65 to 80 per cent), voluntary quits are low, and the unemployed are older on the average than in Group I. In Group III, which contains only 26 obshtini in total, an unusually high

Table 2.6
Structure of unemployment in selected Bulgarian obshtini
(in %, as of 4 December 1992)

Obshtina (okraeg)	Let go	Quit	Never worked		
			After sec. school	After hi. ed.	After military
Group I					
Ardino (Kaerdzhali)	54.3	14	19.6	1.5	10.6
Aytos (Burgas)	53	13.5	22.8	1.5	9.2
Belovo (Pazardzhik)	55.1	13.9	21.1	1.5	8.3
Blagoevgrad	56	14.8	16.3	0.7	4.4
Gaelaebovo (Stara Zagora)	52.1	16.2	25.1	1.7	4.9
Karnobat (Burgas)	51.6	15.5	23.9	2	7
Preslav (Shumen)	51.6	15.6	23.1	1.9	7.8
Septemvri (Pazardzhik)	55.4	14.7	18.2	2.1	9.5
Simitli (Blagoevgrad)	51	14.2	24.6	2.3	7.8
Simeonovgrad (Haskovo)	50.3	15.8	25.1	0.6	8.2
Group II					
Borino (Smolyan)	82.4	3.6	7.8	0.3	5.9
Bregovo (Vidin)	71.3	11.4	7.9	1.5	7.8
Devin (Smolyan)	72.8	8.3	12.2	0.8	5.9
Dospat (Smolyan)	76.3	5	10.7	0.5	7.4
Gotse Delchev (Blagoevgrad)	65.2	8.1	15.2	1.7	9.8
Gaermen (Blagoevgrad)	68.9	4.6	14.4	0.7	11.3
Hadzhidimovo (Blagoevgrad)	66.7	5.9	16	2.2	9.2
Kirkovo (Kaerdzhali)	60.6	8.1	14.8	1.3	15.1
Kresna (Blagoevgrad)	66.4	8.9	15.5	0.8	8.3
Nedelino (Smolyan)	61.5	9.7	16	1.3	11.5
Razlog (Blagoevgrad)	66.1	6	17.7	1.8	8.4
Sandanski (Blagoevgrad)	67.9	7.9	14	2.3	7.9
Satovcha (Blagoevgrad)	71.6	4.9	12.9	3.4	7.2
Strumyani (Blagoevgrad)	70.5	5.3	13.6	0.9	9.6
Yakoruda (Blagoevgrad)	75.1	6.3	11.9	0.5	6.3
Group III					
Bankya (Sofia-grad)	38.2	17.3	38.2	1.2	5.1
Kaerdzhali	40.5	28.1	20.4	2	9
Momchilgrad (Kaerdzhali)	36.6	25.5	24.6	0.8	12.6
Stambolovo (Haskovo)	40.1	18.1	25.5	0	16.3

Source: NSI/Bezrabotni (1993, pp. 38-41, 46-7, 52-3, 60-1, 76-7, 80-1).

Table 2.6 (continued)
Structure of unemployment in selected Bulgarian obshtini
(in %, as of 4 December 1992)

Obshtina (okraeg)	Age			Sex	
	Under 30	30 to 50	Over 50	M	F
Group I					
Ardino (Kaerdzhali)	47.2	44.2	8.6	55.4	44.6
Aytos (Burgas)	56.4	38.4	5.2	46.8	53.2
Belovo (Pazardzhik)	52.1	42.7	5.2	57	43
Blagoevgrad	45.9	50.4	3.8	37.2	62.8
Gaelaebovo (Stara Zagora)	55.8	38.7	5.5	46.9	53.1
Karnobat (Burgas)	56.1	35.8	8.2	51.1	48.9
Preslav (Shumen)	57.1	38.2	4.7	49.7	50.3
Septemvri (Pazardzhik)	53.3	40.2	6.5	56.7	43.3
Simitli (Blagoevgrad)	61.8	34.5	3.6	47.5	52.5
Simeonovgrad (Haskovo)	57.7	37.3	5	44.8	55.2
Group II					
Borino (Smolyan)	38	56.1	5.9	43.3	56.7
Bregovo (Vidin)	35.7	54.3	9.9	53.7	46.3
Devin (Smolyan)	42.3	51	6.7	48.9	51.1
Dospat (Smolyan)	47.4	47.4	5.2	53.1	46.9
Gotse Delchev (Blagoevgrad)	56.7	37.2	6.1	65	35
Gaermen (Blagoevgrad)	52.2	43	4.8	63.6	36.4
Hadzhidimovo (Blagoevgrad)	49.6	44.3	6.2	68.1	31.9
Kirkovo (Kaerdzhali)	51.3	43.3	5.4	69.8	30.1
Kresna (Blagoevgrad)	50.1	43.6	6.3	46.2	53.8
Nedelino (Smolyan)	51.9	43	5.1	60.1	39.9
Razlog (Blagoevgrad)	52.6	41.8	5.7	53.3	46.7
Sandanski (Blagoevgrad)	47.5	46.4	6.1	55.3	44.7
Satovcha (Blagoevgrad)	52.6	43.2	4.2	62.8	37.2
Strumyani (Blagoevgrad)	47.8	42.6	9.6	56.3	43.7
Yakoruda (Blagoevgrad)	39.7	54.3	5.9	39.5	60.5
Group III					
Bankya (Sofia-grad)	47.2	47.9	4.8	59.9	40.1
Kaerdzhali	54.2	40.6	5.2	56.4	43.6
Momchilgrad (Kaerdzhali)	59.9	33.5	6.6	59.7	40.3
Stambolovo (Haskovo)	63.1	31.9	5	65.6	34.4

Source: NSI/Bezrabotni (1993, pp. 38-41, 46-7, 52-3, 60-1, 76-7, 80-1).

fraction of the unemployed left voluntarily or have never worked after leaving secondary school; not surprisingly, the percentage of the unemployed who are under 30 is particularly high for these obshtini. Note finally the great variation in the gender breakdown of the unemployed that exists within each group.

Conclusion

In this paper, we have examined the regional dimension of certain socioeconomic variables in Bulgaria. We have selected phenomena which we have argued are relevant for measuring the progress of the transition to a market economy in that country. The variables chosen are less than ideal and in each case we have only a snapshot taken at a given moment in time. Moreover, the applicability of the current, much-criticized Bulgarian territorial subdivision is unclear. We have accordingly devoted considerable attention to defining appropriate geographic subunits on which to base our analysis, rather than presenting a full-fledged analysis of important regionally-variable phenomena.

The most important finding of the paper is that the 28 former okræzi – abolished in one of Todor Zhivkov's many ill-conceived 'reforms' in 1987 – are far better units of analysis than the current nine oblasti. This is most strikingly so for our measure of the state of the labor market, the ratio of the number of unemployed to the total population. It remains to be seen whether this evaluation will also apply to other reform-relevant variables should data on such become available. In any case, we would argue that the results of this paper argue strongly in favor of returning to something like the earlier territorial subdivision, at least for the purpose of observing the progress of reform.

As for the success of the reform effort in Bulgaria, it is clear that the process is unfolding in a slower and more troubled fashion than in Central Europe and at least the two northern Baltic states. As the process proceeds, its regional variability should also increase, as some regions start to perform considerably better than others; in our data set one could already see that Sofia/Pernik/Kyustendil, Plovdiv, the Lovech oblast, and the coastal cities had certain advantages, at least with respect to labor market variables. Another interesting matter worth watching is the fate of border obshtini and of obshtini where ethnic minorities predominate.

It is possible to speculate that the obshtini of the Blagoevgrad okræg, which borders both Greece and Macedonia, may wind up with relatively favorable indicators. Trade relations have developed briskly in this region. For obshtini bordering Macedonia this was especially true during the 20 months beginning in February 1994 when Greece closed its border with that country. Although the fall of 1992 also saw a partial Greek blockade of Macedonia (Wyzan, 1993, p. 352), any benefits to the relevant Bulgarian obshtini cannot be found in Table 2.6. Nonetheless, the quality of the unemployment data is such that one wonders whether the labor market effects of an increase in small-scale trade activity would be observable. On the other hand, that obshtini where ethnic Turks, Bulgarian Muslims, and Roma predominate are often afflicted with particularly high unemployment is not difficult to surmise even from the data at hand.

In any case, as more and better data appear on the Bulgarian obshtini, a great variety of investigations of the regionally-variable aspects of the reform process there will become possible. This certainly seems a promising research agenda.

Acknowledgements

The author is especially grateful for the logistical and moral support of Yuri Aroyo and Anna Stoyanova in putting together a regional data set on Bulgaria, some of which is employed in this paper. He also wishes to thank Will Bartlett, Robert Begg, Pencho Dankov, Tsveta Kamenova, Gergana Kis'ova, Alfred Levinson, Nasko Nanev, Rositsa Rangelova, Örjan Sjöberg, Antonina Stoyanovska, Tanya Tocheva, and Stefan Tsatsarov for various forms of assistance. None of these individuals is responsible for the methods or conclusions of this paper.

Notes

1   This is not to say, of course, that there have been no studies of the regional effects of the reform process in Eastern Europe. Important examples of such work include Batchler (1992), Bulantsev and Wörgötter (1993), Ciechoci*f*ska (1993), OECD/Poland (1992), Papp and Tóth (1992), and Raagmaa (1993). Mention should also be made of the 1992, No. 5 issue of *Tijdschrift voor Economische en Social Geografie* (devoted to Central and Eastern Europe but not including the former USSR) and the 1993, No. 3 issue of *International Regional Science Review* (devoted to the former USSR).

2   In Bulgaria, one of the issues that led to the fall of the country's first postwar noncommunist government – that of Filip Dimitrov, in office from 8 November 1991, until losing a parliamentary confidence vote on 28 October 1992 – was an alleged lack of concern for the plight of the country's ethnic Turks. According to the population census of 4 December 1992, this ethnic minority makes up 9.7 per cent of the total population (NSI/Demografska, 1993, p. 95). Turks have been adversely affected disproportionately by the collapse of the tobacco industry and by the fact that they stand to gain relatively little – at least in certain regions of the country – from restitution of agricultural land and small-scale urban property.

45

3   Robert Begg of Indiana University of Pennsylvania and a group of other American geographers have recently been working on such issues in Bulgaria.

4   Due largely to a massive emigration of ethnic Turks during 1989 and a smaller movement of ethnic Bulgarians toward Western Europe beginning that year, and a very low rate of natural increase, the Bulgarian population fell by 5.3 per cent between the censuses of 1985 and 1992. See NSI/Demografska (1993, pp. 25 ff.).

5   Throughout this paper transliterated versions of the Bulgarian-language names for the various territorial units are employed. The English-language literature on this topic contains a great variety of translations for one and the same term. The reader who insists on such might find the term 'provinces' an appropriate term for the oblasti (following, e.g., Zaniewski, 1992) and 'districts' acceptable for the okræzi (following, e.g., Koulov, 1992, who unfortunately also calls the oblasti 'districts').

6   The treatment of macroeconomic stabilization in this paper is kept brief in the interest of space. More detailed treatments of events through the autumn of 1994 may be found in Wyzan (1996b) and in earlier papers cited there.

7   Many of the reports filtering in of the numbers who have acquired their privatization vouchers refer to particular localities. A novel object of study would be the regional variation in participation in mass privatization.

8   The carving up of the country into nine oblasti and the selection of such smaller cities as oblast centers seem to have been highly arbitrary, the arguments of Grigorov (1989) and Koulov (1992) in favor of such a regional breakdown notwithstanding. This author was told in mid-September 1993, for example, by Tsveta Kamenova, an expert on regional economics at the Ministry of Regional Development, Housing Policy, and Construction, that the number of oblasti corresponded to the number of Politburo members at the time.

9   A similar tendency to give the lowest territorial subunits more decision-making and revenue-raising authority has been taking place in other CEE countries, although it has generally been a postcommunist development; see, for example, OECD/Poland (1992, pp. 20-21) for a discussion of this issue in Poland.

10   The reader is cautioned that Tsiu (1993, p. 606) contains an important typographical error in which the 'log' term is left out of what we report as our equation (1). The correct formulation may be found in Shorrocks (1980, p. 622), equation 31.

11   It is not particularly easy to explain why various okræzi appear where they do on the list. It is easier to speculate about where cities stand with respect to the number of restituted sites per 10,000 people, a topic addressed in *168 Hours* (1993). It is possible that small cities that became major industrial centers only under communism, such as Pernik, have relatively little property to re-

store, as compared with long-standing centers of industry and crafts, such as Gabrovo. Another possibility is that in some areas with a high percentage of ethnic minorities, such as Sliven (Roma) or Razgrad (Turks), the current population stands to benefit relatively little from restitution, since much of the relevant property belonged to ethnic Bulgarians before communism. But this is apparently not the case in all areas, as it is said that in Kærdzhali ethnic Turks are eligible to have a considerable amount of property restituted.

12   The total number of cities is actually 238, but for two of them, Pirdop and Zlatitsa, no population total in NSI/Naselenie (1993) could be found, so that in- and outmigration rates could not be calculated.

References

168 Hours (1993), 'Close to 31,000 Sites Restituted by June 30th, 1993', *168 Hours BBN*, Vol. 3, No. 43, p.12, October 25-31.

Batchler, John (1992), 'Regional Problems and Policies in Central and Eastern Europe', *Regional Studies*, Vol. 26, No. 7, pp. 665-71.

Bookman, Milica Zarkovic (1993), *The Economics of Secession*, MacMillan: Basingstoke, Hampshire.

Borensztein, Eduardo, Demekas, Dimitri G., and Ostry, Jonathan D. (1993), 'An Empirical Analysis of the Output Declines in Three East European Countries', *IMF Staff Papers*, Vol. 40, No. 1, March, pp. 1-31.

Bulantsev, Vsevolod Yu. and Wörgötter, Andreas (1993), 'Many-Faced Russia: The Impact of Transition on the Russian Regions', Institute for Advanced Studies: Vienna.

Carter, Frank (1987), 'Bulgaria', in Dawson, Andrew H. (ed), *Planning in Eastern Europe*, pp. 67-101, St. Martin's: New York.

Ciechoci∫ska, Maria (1993), 'Gender Aspects of Dismantling the Command Economy in Eastern Europe: The Polish Case', *Geoforum*, Vol. 24, No. 1, pp. 31-44.

Damyanova, Diana (1996), 'Zashto Masite Ne Se Yurvat da Privatizirat', *24 Chasa*, 12 March.

Dimitrov, Mitko (1996), 'Privatization: Its Goals, Progress to Date and Prospects', in Zloch-Christy, Iliana (ed), *Bulgaria in a Time of Change: Economic and Political Dimensions*, pp. 107-18, Avebury: Aldershot, England.

Dimitrova, Svetlomira (1993), 'Spored Noviya Shef na Sluzhbata po Zaetost Bezrabotitsata Ne Veshtae Apokalipsis', *Demokratsiya*, 8 January.

Dimitrova, Yuliana (1996), 'Sporazumenie s MVF Nyama da Ima', *Demokratsiya*, 15 March.

Georgieva, Tanya and Denkovska, Krasi (1996), 'OBB Poluchava Zunkove za 100 Mln. Dolara', *Pari*, 12 March.

Grigorov, Nikolay (1989), 'Régions et Pouvoirs Régionaux en République Populaire de Bulgarie', in Radvanyi, Jean and Rey, Violette (eds), *Régions et Pouvoirs Régionaux en Europe de l'Est et en URSS*, pp. 83-121, Masson: Paris.

Hristov, Todor (1989), 'Les Structures Régionales Face aux Découpage Spatiaux', in Radvanyi, Jean and Rey, Violette (eds), *Régions et Pouvoirs Régionaux en Europe de l'Est et en URSS*, pp. 31-6, Masson: Paris.

Kænchev, Nikolay (1996), '35 Miliarda Leva Zagubiha Dærzhavnite Firmi za 1995 G', *Pari*, 22 March.

Kirilova, Galya (1996), 'Falit na Gubeshtite Dærzhavni Firmi I Bank Iska MVF', *Duma*, 15 March.

Koulov, Boian (1992), 'Tendencies in the Administrative Territorial Development of Bulgaria 1978-1990', *Tijdschrift voor Economische en Sociale Geografie*, Vol. 83, No. 5, pp.390-401.

Kyuchukov, Stefan (1996), 'Promishlenite Firmi Gubyat 35 Mlrd. Lv. za Minalata Godina', *Standart*, 22 March.

Levinson, Alfred (1993), 'The Impact of Privatization on Settlement Patterns in Southwestern Bulgaria', paper presented at the European Summer Institute in Regional Science, June, Joensuu, Finland.

Mancheva, Milena (1995), '$400 Mln. Chuzhdi Investitsii Se Ochakvat U Nas Prez 1996 G', *Standart*, 8 March.

Markov, Toni (1996), 'Masovata Privatizatsiya Zasega e Masova, No po Neuchastie', *Pari*, 1 April.

National Statistical Institute (1993), *Bezrabotni v Republika Bælgariya kæm 4.12.1993 Godina (Predvaritelni Danni)*, Natsionalen Statisticheski Institut: Sofia.

—— (1993), *Demografska Harakteristika na Bælgariya (Rezultati ot 2% Izvadka)*, Natsionalen Statisticheski Institut: Sofia.

—— (1993), *Naselenie*, Natsionalen Statisticheski Institut: Sofia.

—— (1993), *Restitutsiyata v Republika Bælgariya*, Natsionalen Statisticheski Institut: Sofia.

—— (1995), *Statisticheski Spravochnik 1995*, Natsionalen Statisticheski Institut: Sofia.

—— (1996), *Tekushta Stopanska Konyunktura*, January, Natsionalen Statisticheski Institut: Sofia.

Organisation for Economic Co-operation and Development (1992), *Bulgaria: An Economic Assessment*, National Statistical Institute: Paris.

—— (1992), *Regional Development Problems and Policies in Poland*, National Statistical Institute: Paris.

Papp, József and Tóth, József (1992), 'Industrial Crisis Zones in Hungary', *Eastern European Economics*, Vol. 30, No. 4, Summer, pp. 68-91 (translation of article originally appearing in *Közgazdasági szemle*).

Pari (1996), 'Zagubite na Bankite v Kray na 1995 G. sa 29 Mlrd. Lv.', *Pari*, 12 March.

Raagmaa, Garri (1993), 'New Enterprises and Regional Development in Estonia', paper presented at the European Summer Institute in Regional Science, June, Joensuu, Finland.

Shorrocks, Andrew F. (1980), 'The Class of Additively Decomposable Inequality Measures', *Econometrica*, Vol. 48, No. 3, April, pp. 613-25.

―― and Foster, James E. (1987), 'Transfer Sensitive Measures of Inequality', *Review of Economic Studies*, LIV, Vol. 3, July, pp. 485-97.

Theil, Henri (1967), *Economics and Information Theory*, North-Holland: Amsterdam.

Trud (1996), 'Navlizame Væv Vihæra na Nova Valutna Burya', *Trud*, 4 March.

Tsekov, Nikolay (1992), 'Regional Policy in Rural Settlements in Bulgaria', *Tijdschrift voor Economische en Sociale Geografie*, Vol. 83, No. 5, pp. 402-8.

Tsolov, Chavdar (1996), 'Kristalbank i ChIB Ostanaha bez Litsenz', *Pari*, 9 March.

Tsui, Kai-Yeun (1993), 'Decomposition of China's Regional Inequalities', *Journal of Comparative Economics*, Vol. 17, No. 3, September, pp. 600-27.

Vodenska, Maria (1992), 'International Tourism in Bulgaria: Problems and Perspectives', *Tijdschrift voor Economische en Sociale Geografie*, Vol. 83, No. 5, pp. 409-17.

Wyzan, Michael L. (1993), 'Monetary Independence and Macroeconomic Stabilisation in Macedonia: An Initial Assessment', *Communist Economies and Economic Transformation*, Vol. 5, No. 3, pp. 351-68.

―― (1996a) (ed), *First Steps Toward Economic Independence: New States of the Postcommunist World*, Praeger: Westport, Conn.

―― (1996b), 'Stabilization and Anti-Inflation Policy', in Zloch-Christy, Iliana (ed), *Bulgaria in a Time of Change: Economic and Political Dimensions*, pp. 77-105, Avebury: Aldershot, England.

Zaniewski, Kazimierz (1992), 'Regional Inequalities in Social Wellbeing in Central and Eastern Europe', *Tijdschrift voor Economische en Sociale Geografie*, Vol. 83, No. 5, pp. 342-52.

Zloch-Christy, Iliana (1996), 'External Balance and External Debt: An Overview', in Zloch-Christy, Iliana (ed), *Bulgaria in a Time of Change: Economic and Political Dimensions*, pp. 133-43, Avebury: Aldershot, England.

Part Two
MACROECONOMICS

3   Inflation in a transition economy: the case of Bulgaria

Garabed Minassian

Inflation is a phenomenon that is usually hard to explain in quantitative terms. Economic theory has not yet managed to find an unambiguous explanation of the relationship between inflation and other major economic indicators. For Keynesians the root cause of inflation is budget deficits and their financing. The well-known Phillips curve argues for functional dependence between inflation and unemployment. For monetarists, the growth of money supply accounts for inflation, whereas for the disciples of the school of rational expectations, people's expectations are to be blamed for the price rise.

This issue is further complicated today in the countries experiencing a transition to market economy. Their unique economic development only vaguely fits these visions of the causes of price adjustment. There have been many attempts to explain the sources of inflation in transitioning economies. Early in the transition the World Bank held a special conference in Laxenburg (Austria, March 1990), devoted to regulating inflation in the (then) socialist countries. As might be expected, contributors to this conference focused more on the past, evaluating the sources of inflation in qualitative terms and analyzing its various manifestations in centrally planned economies (Commander, 1992). Less forecasting of inflationary trends were undertaken. At this conference, Dornbusch (1992) carried out a comparative study of countries considered to be in a similar situation due to their high inflation rates. Even at that time, however, regulating inflation by means of the traditional macroeconomic policy tools was called into question (Calvo, 1992). The possible non-traditional consequences from stabilization programs introduced in the latter countries were not clear either (Calvo and Coricelli, 1992).

Many economists anticipated that the classical notions about the interaction of macroeconomic variables in a market economy would not apply to transition economies (Vanous, 1991, Heesterman, 1991). Typically, investigations of these processes showed little consistency in the results. Attempts at modeling inflation varied greatly, even though the same variables were almost always used as explanatory variables. (Barrionuevo, 1992, Bier, 1992, Kokoszczynsky, 1992, Welfe, 1992). Alternative approaches were used due to a lack of sufficiently reliable data.

The objective of the present study is to explain the inflationary experience in Bulgaria over the last four years (1992-95). The economic transformation in Bulgaria started in February 1991 with the liberalization of centrally fixed prices of goods and services. In February alone consumer goods prices more than doubled. All of 1991 could be described as an unusual year. For this reason we begin our study at the beginning of 1992.

The econometric results obtained should be viewed with caution. The poor quality of official statistics can be blamed for much of the noise in these series. Even though Bulgaria became an IMF member in 1990, it still has not gotten its page in International Financial Statistics, the most widely circulated IMF monthly edition. An example of the statistical problems is the debate over the CPI. In 1995 there was a lively debate on the methodology used for measuring the CPI. In spite of dramatic changes which had taken place in the composition of the market basket over the last three years, the National Statistical Institute (NSI) had been using the households' budget composition of 1992 as weights in the measurement of the CPI. In 1995 the NSI altered the manner of reporting price fluctuations in seasonal commodities (food primarily). Under the special conditions in Bulgaria, this substantially altered the calculation of households' monetary expenditure.

Another example where statistical validity is a problem is the measurement of unemployment. In the past unemployment data was based on the number of registered unemployed. Due to special features of the social security system in Bulgaria, these data systematically reported levels about 80 per cent of the level obtained by samples carried out by the NSI.

Banking statistics are not much better. In the middle of 1995 the Bulgarian National Bank (BNB) introduced a new accounting system which led to major adjustments in their time series. For example, receivables from the private sector rose from BGL 94.6 billion in May 1995 to BGL 154.9 billion in June. For the same time period domestic credit fell from BGL 588.8 billion to BGL 583.1 billion. In October 1995 BNB made public significant changes in the country's quarterly balance-of-payments figures for 1994 and 1995, declaring the 1994 figures as preliminary. Significant changes have been observed in a number of monetary aggregates, too. The relatively smooth series describing Net Domestic Credit first jumped 37.6 per cent in the spring of 1994 when the exchange rate nearly doubled from 37.4 BGL/USD at the end of February 1994 to 64.9 BGL/USD a month later.[1] A second jump in November 1994 was negative (-23.9 per cent) and attributed to the reduction of the country's foreign debt and liabilities.

Our econometric tests attempt to explain the behavior of two price series: the consumer price index and the production price index. The independent variables used to explain the price series are unemployment, the average monthly salary of employees in the public sector, the monetary aggregate M1, net domestic credit, the exchange rate, and BNB's base interest rate. All variables in the regressions were logarithmic transformations of the corresponding monthly indices. For the base interest rate, the monthly rate was used.

The Ministry of Finance borrows directly from the BNB to finance part of its fiscal deficits. The real value of these loans (deflated by the CPI) was used as a proxy for the impact of fiscal deficits. The value of this indicator was zero when no such loan was observed.

Special attention was paid to inflationary expectations. There is no doubt that inflationary expectations are important in determining price level changes, but their impact is difficult to account for in quantitative terms. Expectations are formed both through inflationary developments in the recent past and purely qualitative estimates made by economic agents. We follow Berndt (1990) and employ a geometric distribution, i.e.

$$P[t,q] = (1-q)\sum_i \{q^i P(t-1-i)\} \qquad (1)$$

where $P[t,q]$ represents inflation expectations at a moment, t, and q is a parameter of the geometric distribution ($0<q<1$). $P(t-1-i)$ is inflation at t-1-i. The impact of hypothetical inflationary expectations were assessed by assigning nine values between 0.1 and 0.9 to the parameter, q. To eliminate seasonal variation, we took first differences on the monthly data. This shortened the time period by one month, but the non-stationary effect due to seasonal fluctuations was eliminated.

The best equation for the CPI (out of many equations tested) was:

$$SP = .00037*SB + .45*SP9 - 1.01*SIP + .021*S\$(-5) +$$
$$(3.01) \qquad (3.54) \qquad (-79.3) \qquad (2.92)$$

$$.97*AR(1) + .33*MA(1) \qquad (2)$$
$$(16.9) \qquad (1.58)$$

$R^2 = .997$; Adjusted $R^2 = .996$; S.E. error of regression = .0031; LL = 129.4; D-W statistic = 2.02; Mean of dependent variable = -.008; S.D. of dependent variable = .054; Sum of squared residuals = .00022; F-statistic = 1649; Prob (F-statistic) = .00. The figures given in brackets represent the corresponding t-statistics.

The first letter S denotes, everywhere, the monthly divergence of logarithms from the respective indicators. P is the consumer price index; B, the monthly credits to the budget granted by the BNB; P9, the expectations' estimate of the monthly consumer price index, calculated according to (1) for q = .9; IP, the real yield from savings (monthly base rate adjusted by the CPI). AR(1) and MA(1) are the autoregressive and moving average components, respectively.

The equation describing the producer price index is:

$$SPP = -.573*SIPP(-1) + .229*S\$ + .463*SS(-3) + .131*SD(-1) \qquad (3)$$
$$(-4.86) \qquad\qquad (3.01) \quad (3.04) \qquad (2.13)$$

$R^2 = .683$; Adjusted $R^2 = .649$; S.E. error of regression = .031; LL = 68.1; D-W statistic = 2.06; Mean of dependent variable = -.0012; S.D. of dependent variable = .052; Sum of squared residuals = .027; F-statistic = 20.1; Prob (F-statistic) = .00.

PP is the producer price index; IPP, the monthly base interest rate adjusted by the production price index. S is average monthly salaries in the public sector; D, Net domestic credit; and \$ is the dollar exchange rate.

In the CPI equation the correlation coefficient is very high, and the Durbin-Watson statistic is satisfactory as well. These quantities are marginal ones and do not enable a direct estimation of the contribution of each of the factors discussed on the observed consumer price index level.

The importance of inflationary expectations on the CPI is confirmed. The coefficient is nearly one-half. This suggests a powerful expectations effect. We found that the larger the value of the parameter, q, the greater the impact. This suggests that people tend to base their assessment of future inflation on a reasonably long period rather than the latest observation. People find it hard to believe in immediate changes. Some time must elapse before they are fully incorporated into expectations.

The direct influence of the base interest rate on consumer price growth has also been confirmed. In 1994 the nominal base rate reached a record high level of 93.9 per cent. Still, real interest rates remained negative. In 1995 positive real interest rates prevailed, which evidently contributed to the drop in inflation.

Central Bank financing of the budget deficit has also influenced the general price level. The budget deficit's contribution to price change seems to be much higher owing to the special features of the country's budget deficit financing. The Ministry of Finance and the BNB are very active in issuing government securities which are largely bought by the commercial banks. The BNB offers to refinance the commercial banks at relatively acceptable terms with securities as collateral. This conceals its direct financing of the budget deficit. There have already been some instances where direct debt to the banking system was transformed into debt against the issue of long-term objective-oriented securities and bought up directly by the BNB.[2] Thus the data we use for deficit financing reflects only part of the actual financing.

The exchange variable is also significant in the CPI equation. The exchange rate at the organized currency market in Bulgaria is fixed by the market. BNB's foreign exchange policy has been decisive in a number of instances, however. In the spring of 1994, for example, there was a booming demand for hard currency and the exchange rate doubled. The limited currency resources of the national bank and uncertainty surrounding the negotiations to reduce the foreign debt stalled BNB's active interference in the foreign exchange market. The Bulgarian lev depreciated too much and this became highly visible in 1995. Throughout the first three quarters of 1995 the national bank continuously intervened in the foreign exchange market buying hard currency to prevent a fall in the dollar exchange rate on the local market. This enabled the BNB to accumulate considerable reserves (up to $1.5 billion) even though payments on the country's external obligations resumed and the signing of the next pending standby agreement with the IMF was postponed. Things changed in late 1995 and early 1996 when the dollar resumed its upward movement. This period, however, has not been included in the estimation of this correlation and does not have an impact on the statistical indicators. The latter implies a likely increased impact of the exchange rate.

Things are slightly different with producer prices. Here again there is a negative correlation with the real interest rate, but the impact is smaller. This can be partially attributed to the fact that the growth in production prices has not been as dramatic as the rise in consumer prices. A positive and statistically significant link has also been established with the growth of salaries in the public sector. Salaries have a direct impact on production costs and producer prices follow by a three-month lag with an elasticity of 0.46. Since the salaries are so low, market pressures have not led to significant increases in labor productivity.[3]

There is some evidence that producer prices are influenced by monetary aggregates. In this particular case these pressures are represented by the net domestic credit variable. It is worth mentioning that all attempts to obtain other statistically meaningful results for monetary aggregates for either producer or consumer prices failed.

These estimates show that producer and consumer indices are affected by somewhat different factors. There is evidence that producer prices have been influenced more by shortages of material and financial resources. Consumer prices have been changing more in response to inflationary expectations and money incomes. The indices have followed different paths. The disparity was particularly striking during the period between December 1991 and December 1993 when the PPI went up by 44 per cent and the CPI nearly tripled. During the next two years both indices followed a more similar growth path where the CPI increased three fold and the PPI rose by 156 per cent.

The producer price equation is less satisfactory than the equation for consumer prices. The PPI equation explains only about two-thirds of the variation. There are several factors which are difficult to quantify which have an impact on producer prices. Three important factors are:

(1) A large share of GDP is still generated in the public sector. This is particularly true in industry. 85-90 per cent of industrial output comes from state-owned enterprises. Managers in manufacturing do not have a secure future. Planning

time horizons are very short with little serious thought given to the future of the enterprise. Embezzlement is a widespread and frequent practice. Large-scale privatization has proved difficult to start and progress is slow. Mass privatization has begun after a significant delay. According to the official lists, the mass privatization will involve 1063 enterprises and is expected to begin (after the time specified for the setting up of privatization funds and initial sale of privatization coupon books) in April 1996.

(2)   The economy tries to work its way through to structural equilibrium. This is confirmed by relative price instability. There are significant differences between the CPI and PPI although the gap has been less dramatic since the middle of 1994.[4] The international embargo on Iraq (which owes Bulgaria significant sums) and the embargo on countries of the former Yugoslavia have had both open and hidden implications. In such a situation incidental factors might have an unpredictable impact on inflationary processes.

(3) Bulgaria is situated in a region of high inflation.

Bulgaria's foreign trade relations have undergone significant changes over the last four years. Until the end of the 80s, the country's foreign trade structure was dominated by the former COMECOM countries which accounted for about, and often more than, 80 per cent of the trade. By the mid-90s a system of four polar foreign trade groups took shape. The country's foreign trade was divided almost equally among four groups of countries: (1) those from the former Soviet Union; (2) Balkan and Central European countries; (3) European Community countries (without Greece); and (4) all other countries.[5]

All Balkan countries have had a sustained high growth of consumer prices. Greece was the notable exception, but while the Greek inflation was more moderate, it still was in the two-digit range. The countries of the former Soviet Union, almost all of whom have had hyperinflation, have maintained a substantial share of Bulgaria's foreign trade. A similar situation has existed in the countries of the former Yugoslavia. Tourist and trade regime liberalization encouraged active exchange of goods, frequently through illegal and unregulated channels. High inflation rates have been present in all countries in the region.

New institutional and legal foundations have been created at an unsatisfactorily slow pace. A very critical situation exists in taxation and customs control. Official statistical records have suffered from late submissions and unreliable information. This has hampered efforts to trace economic development and work out constructive economic policy proposals. According to some tentative figures, the underground economy may constitute a third of the country's GDP.[6] The macroeconomic policy pursued has often been dominated more by emotion than reason (Minassian, 1994). A major redistribution of national wealth has been occurring and the major players, primarily at the parliamentary level, have not been particularly concerned with nor interested in making their viewpoints and the processes clear. The state's economic functions in the transition economy remain unclear and unspecified. Initially there was enthusiasm and desire for the state to draw back from economic development. There was striving for a complete imitation of attitudes in some developed countries. What still lies ahead is the preparation of an alternative strategy to what D. Nuti and R. Portes (1993, p.15) named 'State Desertion'.[7] The structural transformation was substantially delayed, state-owned enterprises continue to operate under a situation of insecurity while waiting for decisions concerning their fate. After some movement in 1994, cash privatization slowed again and direct foreign investment fell.[8] This has created a situation where it has been difficult to identify sources of inflation since the main factors are closely tied to the low efficiency and wasteful spending of the public sector.

Forecasting economic dynamics in this situation has as much to do with art as science. Solid methodical foundations are hard to find in the large number of forecasts originating both in the country and outside it.[9] Many projections have been worked out in connection with the requirements of ministries such as the Ministry of Finance, the Ministry of Labor and Social Care, the Energy Committee, and the Ministry of Environment. As a rule these are mid-term forecasts and reflect their authors' views based more on intuition than quantitative methods. It will not be far-fetched to say that the main efforts are now being directed towards ensuring a satisfactory degree of coordination of the individual macroeconomic and branch indicators' development.

Notes

1   The annual average indicators are somewhat different: 36.8 BGL/USD and 47.2 BGL/USD, respectively.

2   The official domestic debt in Bulgaria consist of three components: (1) direct debt to financial institutions (including the BNB); (2) debt on government securities issued to finance the budget deficit; and (3) debt on government securities issued on non-performing credits of state-owned companies to commercial banks. Based on an agreement between the BNB and the Ministry of Finance there was an issue of treasury bonds which transformed government debt to the BNB into treasury securities.

3   At the end of 1995 they were in the range of $110 to $120 per month.

4   Detailed analysis of the CPI and PPI growth in Bulgaria is done by Miller (1994).

5   In 1994, foreign trade turnover of Bulgaria was distributed as follows: (1) former Soviet Union countries, 25.5 per cent; (2) Balkan peninsula and Central European countries, 21.2 per cent; (3) European Community countries (without Greece), 25.1 per cent; and (4) other countries, 28.2 per cent. In 1993 their respective shares were: 27.8 per cent, 21.0 per cent, 24.3 per cent, and 26.9 per cent ('Export and Imports', *NSI*, No. 4, 1993, pp. 5-6).

6   An OECD study quotes the share of Greek underground economy as 30 per cent of GDP (*Standard Newspaper*, 17 April 1994). Another estimation, published in the *Financial Times* (14 November 1995, p. 2) reports that about 40 per cent of the economy in Greece is a shadow economy. The direct comparative analysis suggests that in Bulgaria it has to be something similar.

7   "...the authorities should immediately take steps to reverse the 'state desertion' that has left state-owned enterprises floundering: commercialize them, pay attention to their management and the environment in which it operates, redirect managerial incentives, improve corporate governance in so far as is possible without privatization and rehabilitate industrial policy" (p. 15).

8   The report of the Minister of Economic Development, R. Gechev, states that somewhat more than half of the expected privatization contracts have been signed in 1995 (*Pari Newspaper*, 12 March 1996). Foreign investment fell from $105.4 million in 1994 to $90.4 million in 1995 (*BNB Annual Report*, 1995). Delays in structural transformation has brought about a dramatic foreign exchange crisis in the spring of 1996. The government has been forced to undertake urgent measures to close 67 state-owned enterprises without making prior attempts to offer them for privatization.

9   See the publications of OECD, PlanEcon, WEFA, WIIW, as well as reports of the local research team led by I. Angelov (1994), quoted in the references. Mention should also be made of participation in the LINK project of a team from Bulgaria.

References

Angelov, I., Doulov, S., Hubenova-Delissivkova, T., Yotzov, V., and Konsoulov, V. (1993), *Economic Outlook of Bulgaria 1994-1996*, Institute of Economics: Sofia.

Barrionuevo, J. (1992), 'Inflation and Fiscal Deficits: The Irrelevance of Debt and Money Financing', *IMF*, Working Paper No. 102, December.

Bier, W. (1992), 'Macroeconomic Models for PC', IMF, Working Paper No. 110, December.

Berndt, E. (1991), *The Practice of Econometrics: Classic and Contemporary*, Addison-Wesley Publishing Company: New York.

Calvo, G. (1992), 'Are High Interest Rates Effective for Stopping High Inflation? Some Skeptical Notes', *World Bank Economic Review*, Vol. 6, No. 1, pp. 247-60.

—— and Coricelli, F. (1992), 'Stagflationary Effects of Stabilization Programs in Reforming Socialist Countries: Enterprise-Side and Household-Side Factors', *World Bank Economic Review*, Vol. 6, No. 1.

Chadha, B., Masson, P., and Meridith, G. (1992), 'Models of Inflation and the Cost of Disinflation', *IMF Staff Papers*, Vol. 32, No. 2, pp. 395-431.

Charemza, W. and Deadman, D. (1992), *New Directions in Economic Practice*, Edward Elgar: Aldershot, U.K.

Commander, S. (1992), 'Inflation and the Transition to a Market Economy: An Overview', *World Bank Economic Review*, Vol. 6, No. 1, pp. 3-12.

—— and Coricelli, F. (1992), 'Price-Wage Dynamics and Inflation in Socialist Economies: Empirical Models for Hungary and Poland', *World Bank Economic Review*, Vol. 6, No. 1, pp. 33-55.

Dittus, P. (1993), 'Razrivat v izmenenieto na potrebitelskite I proizvodstvenite tzeni' ('Consumer prices outpacing producer prices: a problem?'), *Bankov Pregled*, No. 4, pp. 45-56.

Dobrinsky, R. (1994), 'Exchange Rate Policy and Macroeconomic Stabilization: Lessons From The Bulgarian Exchange Rate Crisis of 1993', presented at the conference 'Transition from the Command to the Market System: What Went Wrong and What to Do Now?', 22 February, Sofia.

Dornbusch, R. (1992), 'Lessons from Experience with High Inflation', *World Bank Economic Review*, Vol. 6, No. 1.

Economist Intelligence Unit (1993), 'Romania, Bulgaria, Albania: Country Report', The Economist Intelligence Unit, third quarter.

Heesterman, A. (1992), 'Inflation and the Transition to a Mixed Economy: Can it Work?', *Economics of Planning*, Vol. 24, No. 2.

Hunya, G. et. al. (1994), 'Central and Eastern Europe: Uneven Recovery', *WIIW Research Reports*, No. 204, February.

Kokoszczynsky, R. (1992), 'Recent Inflationary Processes in Poland: An Application of Western Modeling Approaches', presented at Research Seminar of the MEET Network, University of Leicester, May.

Koparanova, M. and Minassian, G. (1994), 'The Bulgarian Lev: An Uncertain Road to Stabilization', Discussion Paper No. 13, University of Leicester, July.

Miller, J. (1994), 'The Price Index Gap: Implications for Economic Restructuring and the Government Budget', *Ikonomicheska mis'l*, No. 7.

Minassian, G. (1994), 'The Bulgarian Economy in Transition: Is There Anything Wrong With Macroeconomic Policy?', *Europe-Asia Studies*, Vol. 46, No. 2.

—— (1995), 'Bulgarian Economy in the Mid '90s', *Eurobalkans*, No. 18, Spring, pp. 16-25.

Nuti, D. and Portes, R. (1993), 'Central Europe: The Way Foreword', in Portes, R. (ed), *Economic Transformation in Central Europe: A Progress Report*, CEPR.

Organization for Economic Cooperation and Development (1992), *Bulgaria: An Economic Assessment*, OECD: Paris.

PlanEcon (1993), *Review and Outlook: Analysis and Forecasts to 1998 of Economic Developments in Eastern Europe*, PlanEcon, December.

Solimano, A. and Yuravlivker, D. (1993), 'Price Formation, Nominal Anchors and Stabilization Policies in Hungary (An Empirical Analysis)', World Bank, WPS1234, December.

Vanous, J. (1991), 'Prospects for Economic Reform in Eastern Europe', *Proceedings of the World Bank Annual Conference on Development Economics*, World Bank: Washington, D.C.

Wharton Econometric Forcasting Associates (1994), 'Eurasia: Outlook for Foreign Trade and Finance', The WEFA Group, January.

Wendal, H. and Manchev, T. (1994), 'Mejdunarodnata stojnost na leva I otragenieto j vurhu vutreshnite tzeni', *Bankov Pregled*, No. 1, pp. 17-22.

4   Price index gap in Bulgaria

Jeffrey B. Miller

When the transition to market economies began in Eastern Europe two macroeconomic features initially emerged in many countries in the region: high inflation and declining industrial output. More recently inflation has subsided and these countries have begun to grow again.[1] Several countries also have another characteristic: the producer price index is rising much more slowly than the consumer price index. The gap between the growth rate in producer prices and retail/consumer prices has been particularly sharp in Bulgaria, but has also been observed in Poland and Hungary. A much smaller gap has appeared in the Czech Republic. In Romania the reverse has occurred; the producer price index has moved up more rapidly than the consumer price index (see Tables 4.1 and 4.2).

We begin by describing this price index gap in Bulgaria and suggest some reasons why the gap has appeared. Then, we explore some implications of the increasing difference between retail and producer prices. Focusing on movements in retail/consumer prices alone can lead to a misinterpretation of important economic trends. In particular, real exchange rate movements, real interest rates and real wage changes are very different when viewed from the perspective of the producer price index. When price changes are seen in this light, it is clear how state enterprises are now experiencing a profit squeeze caused by high real interest rates and rapidly increasing real wages.

Different growth rates of consumer and producer prices also mean changing relative prices between the retail and producer sectors of the economy. This shifting 'terms-of-trade' between the two sectors has created differential growth rates in the two sectors. Significant income is now being generated in the retail sector. Much of this income is being generated in the new private sector which the National Statistical Institute still has difficulty measuring.[2] Since almost all private sector activity (outside of agriculture) is in the retail/distribution sector, by measuring the growing

63

size of the gap between retail and producer prices we can obtain some clues as to the size of the private sector.

Table 4.1
Retail and producer price indices:
Poland, Hungary, Czech Republic, and Romania
(Base Month 100)

Country (beg. date = 100)	Poland (Jan. 1990)		Hungary (Jan. 1990)		Czech. Republic (June 1990)		Romania (Oct. 1990)		Bulgaria (Jan. 1991)	
	RPI	PPI	RPI	PPI	RPI	PPI	RPI	PPI	RPI	PPI
6 months	155	118	115	109	115	115	228	287	398	335
12 months	219	152	136	138	171	178	353	480	530	402
18 months	270	176	160	149	174	181	688	1054	731	484
24 months	335	197	175	154	181	191	1035	1406	969	513
30 months	387	227	190	165	197	197	1927	2599	1233	556
36 months	469	260	221	183	220	216	4291	5771	1543	595
42 months	528	302	231	186	232	220	6708	9735	2387	905
48 months	631	347	259	200	241	227	8104	11520	3429	1134
54 months	707	385	278	211	256	232	9019	12660	3863	1277
Ratio of RPI/PPI	1.83		1.32		1.1		0.71		3.03	

Source: PlanEcon Reports (various), National Statistical Institute (Bulgaria), and the Agency for Economic Coordination and Development (Bulgaria).

Table 4.2
Retail and producer inflation over previous 12 months:
Poland, Hungary, Czech Republic, Romania, and Bulgaria

Country (beg. date = 100)	Poland (Jan. 1990)		Hungary (Jan. 1990)		Czech. Republic (June 1990)		Romania (Oct. 1990)		Bulgaria (Jan. 1991)	
	RPI	PPI	RPI	PPI	RPI	PPI	RPI	PPI	RPI	PPI
12 months	119	52	36	38	71	78	252	382	425	300
18 months	74	49	39	36	52	57	301	367	81	42
24 months	53	28	29	12	5	7	294	293	84	26
30 months	43	27	19	9	13	9	280	147	65	15
36 months	40	32	26	19	22	13	315	311	59	16
42 months	36	33	22	13	18	12	248	274	94	63
48 months	35	34	17	9	10	5	89	100	122	91
54 months	34	27	20	13	10	5	34	30	62	41
Ratio of RPI/PPI as if 30 months = 100	1.07		1.14		1.1		0.96		1.36	

Source: Calculated from Table 4.1 on the basis of the movement in the index over the previous 12 months.

Retail/Consumer and producer price movements

Historical trends

Before 1991, prices in Bulgaria were largely determined by the central planners who directed the flow of resources in the economy. The winter of 1990-91 was characterized by severe shortages in anticipation of the decontrol of prices. As in other centrally planned economies, there was also concern about the 'monetary overhang' due to pent up savings of individuals. In February 1991 prices were released in all but a few crucial sectors of the economy. Retail prices almost immediately doubled, and by

June retail prices were more than three times the level in January. During the second half of 1991, the pace of inflation slowed, but prices still increased another 40 per cent (annual rate of 96 per cent) by January 1992. In 1992 the inflation slowed somewhat, but still retail prices rose by 80 per cent.

In 1993 the National Statistical Institute changed the method of calculating the index, moving from a calculation of a retail price index to a consumer price index with an identifiable market basket of goods. During 1993 reported CPI inflation slowed to 64 per cent. In 1994 two events in the spring pushed prices up sharply: a large adjustment in the nominal exchange rate and the imposition of a value-added tax. As a result consumer price inflation in 1994 was 122 per cent. 1995 was a year of relative calm with the exchange moving up slowly and the rate of consumer price inflation coming down dramatically to only 30 per cent.

Clearly, inflation has been and continues to be a serious problem for the economy.[3] Furthermore, traditional methods of controlling inflation have not been working. While the government deficits have been serious, the money supply on any measure has not been growing at the same pace as inflation. For example, by June 1995 broad money was approximately ten times the level it was in January 1991; by contrast, consumer prices were more than 38 times their January 1991 level.

On the other hand, the producer price index, which measures the changes in prices that state enterprises charge their customers at the producer level has not been rising nearly as fast as the retail/consumer index.[4] Initially the PPI rose more rapidly than the R/CPI. The PPI rose 118 per cent in February 1991 versus 112 per cent for the R/CPI. But by August 1991 the R/CPI was at 398 versus 335 for the PPI. From this point onwards the R/CPI continued to rise much more rapidly than the PPI. For example, in 1992 the PPI rose 25 per cent rather than 80 per cent for the R/CPI. As indicated at the bottom of Table 4.1, by the end of four and a half years the ratio of the consumer price to the producer price index (February 1991, base 100) was just over three to one. As illustrated in Table 4.2 the divergence between the consumer price and producer price indices continued during the last two years in the table (i.e., August 1993-August 1995) but was less dramatic.[5]

Normally we would expect the two indices to show approximately the same movement over time, although movements in the R/CPI tend to lag the PPI as producer price increases are passed on.[6] In Bulgaria, by contrast, the margin between producer prices and retail prices continues to spread. One way of envisioning what is happening is to imagine a particular good, e.g., kitchen pots. Suppose kitchen pots in January 1991 sold for 22 leva at retail. Of this 22 leva the producer might have received 20 leva and the retail establishment a ten per cent markup of two leva. If the prices of kitchen pots closely followed the movements in the general indices, by July 1995 the producer would be receiving 255 leva, but the pot would be selling at retail for 849 leva. The gap between producer and retail price would have gone from two leva to 594 leva. Instead of the ten per cent markup in January 1991, the markup in July 1995 would be 233 per cent.

As we will argue below, these numbers probably exaggerate the gap which is developing between producer and retail prices. Still they reveal important changes which are occurring during the transition in Bulgaria. These shifts in relative prices are also causing shifts in income sources. In our example, 91 per cent of the revenue from the retail sale of a kitchen pot went to the manufacturer in January 1991. By July 1995 only 30 per cent went to the producer and the other 70 per cent went to the wholesale and retail distributors.

Why the price gap is developing

There are at least three reasons why a gap is developing between the two measures of price change in Bulgaria.[7] First, for technical reasons the R/CPI, which is a Laspeyres index, will overstate the price change and the PPI, which is a Paasche index, will understate the change. The measurement of the R/CPI is based on a fixed market basket. When relative prices change and people shift away from higher-priced items, the effects of a changing market basket are not accounted for in the index. The PPI is calculated by dividing the revenue of state enterprises by the physical output units produced by the state enterprises so it has a changing basket.[8]

A second reason for the widening gap is quality change. The retail price index is based on a survey of goods. The person doing the survey is told to find an item, i.e., kitchen pots, and told to find and report the prices of six pots. No attempt is made to report quality changes.

If the quality changes were all in domestic goods both indices would be biased, and quality change itself would not produce a gap between the two indices. A major source of the quality change, especially during the first two years of the transition, was the influx of foreign goods. So when the survey was done, the price of German kitchen pots was averaged with Bulgarian pots to determine the new price level. These quality changes inflated the value of the R/CPI, but not the PPI. These effects were probably greatest during the first two years of the transition when many new Western products were suddenly available on the Bulgarian market. At first Bulgarians showed great interest in these new products. As time has passed imports have slowed. Bulgarians have found that many of their own, especially food, products are well-priced. It is not clear that the CPI measures that are presently being used are sophisticated enough to capture these changes in buying habits. If not, they are overstating the price effects that consumers are experiencing, especially when large exchange rate shifts occur as in 1994.

A third possible reason for the difference in the rate of change in the two price indices is due to market relationships. From a purely market concentration viewpoint, one might expect the opposite to occur, i.e., the markup between producer and distributor/retailer to narrow rather than rise. The manufacturing sector tends to be made up of large state enterprises. The retail sector has many small private firms.

With its market power, the manufacturing sector could attempt to squeeze the profits of a competitive retail sector. Clearly, this is not happening.

Viewed from a wider perspective which includes international as well as domestic competition, there may be less overall competition at the retail level. Services and non-tradable commodities do not have foreign competition and may have more freedom to raise prices. The CPI may rise more rapidly as a result.

Alternatively the answer may lie with the incentives for managers of state enterprises. There is considerable debate about what objectives state enterprise managers do seek. State enterprise managers do not share directly in the profits of the enterprise; therefore, they do not have the same motivation to increase profits as managers in private firms. Furthermore, the new environment presents many challenges for these managers. For many firms, demand for their products has fallen sharply as exports to the former Soviet republics have declined. Financially they are in serious difficulty and are dependent on loans from the banks for their survival.

The managers also face an uncertain future. The Law for Privatization which was passed in 1992 and amended in 1994 (to establish procedures for mass privatization) sets out a procedure for privatization of large enterprises, but actual privatization has been very limited. Managers, therefore, face a diverse set of possibilities: continuing to manage a state enterprise for some time to come, managing a privatized firm, an ownership role in the private enterprise, or having no further role in their present enterprise.

Evidence as to what managers are actually doing is scarce and anecdotal. Given such large future uncertainties, however, it would not be surprising if managers were short-sighted and attempted to exploit their present position at the expense of the future well-being of the enterprise. For example, decapitalization of the firm may create present profits, but lower its future value.[9]

Another concern is that managers may be establishing 'shadow firms'. Hillman, Mitev, and Peters (1995), in one of the few studies of firm behavior in Bulgaria, describe such a firm. These shadow firms are private firms where the management of the state enterprise has a stake. These shadow firms might be operated by friends or relatives of the management. The state enterprise sells its output to the shadow firm, and the shadow firm then sells the product to others, effectively privatizing the profits of the state enterprises. Distinguishing between these firms and legitimate elements of the growing private distribution/ retail system can be difficult.

The possible existence of shadow firms complicates the analysis of the price data. If a state enterprise sells to a shadow firm, the value of this sale is recorded by the PPI even though the actual price for most customers is actually higher. Shadow firms would also provide an incentive to keep producer prices from rising quickly. By keeping the state enterprise price low, the markup between the shadow firm's purchase and sale price can be increased. This widening markup would show up as a spread between the growth rates of the PPI and R/CPI.[10] Thus the desire to privatize profits may give enterprises with market power the incentive to keep prices down rather than raise them.[11]

Soft budget constraints make it easier to sustain shadow firms. To the extent that bank loans continue to support state enterprises which are losing money, there is only a loose connection between costs and revenues. Without financial discipline it is easier for the manager to maintain lower prices even in the face of sharply rising costs.[12] Indeed, by enabling state enterprise managers to hold down their sale prices, bank loans are effectively subsidizing shadow firms.

These subsidies could have long-run budget implications for the government. Bank loans are not officially part of the budget, but loans where money is siphoned off in this way are not likely to be repaid. As with the loans made during the Communist period, the government could easily find itself in a position where it expends additional resources to prevent the banks from failing.[13]

In such an uncertain environment it would be surprising if managerial behavior did not vary significantly across firms as managers pursued alternative survival strategies. Movements in aggregate price indices cover up large differences in managerial behavior across firms.

Since enterprise governance structures and the prospects for and the methods of privatization vary considerably across countries, managerial behavior should differ as well. The wide gap between the PPI and R/CPI in Bulgaria may reflect the relative importance of shadow firms. The fact that the spread is less dramatic or non-existent in other Eastern European countries may be an indication that managers in other countries are predominantly employing alternative survival strategies.[14]

Relative price movements interpreted through the PPI

In an economy with high inflation, nominal price movements need to be understood in relation to the rate of inflation. Because the growth rate of the PPI is so different from the R/CPI, a very different picture emerges when the analysis is carried out using the PPI. In this section we look at three important prices from this dual perspective: foreign exchange rate, interest rates, and wage movements.

Foreign exchange rates

Under central planning the foreign exchange rate was rigidly controlled. When the transition began in early 1991, Bulgaria had insufficient foreign exchange reserves to intervene extensively in foreign exchange markets. During the first year after exchange controls were relaxed, the lev was allowed to float and the exchange rate between the dollar and the lev fluctuated dramatically. From 2.83 lev/dollar in January 1991, the lev depreciated sharply to 15.9 lev/dollar in March 1991 and 23.9 lev/dollar in January 1992. Then the nominal rate stabilized, depreciating slowly to 24.5

lev/dollar in January 1993 and approximately 27 lev/dollar in July 1993. Then towards the end of 1993 the lev rose sharply to 32 lev/dollar. This was followed by a crisis in the spring of 1994. The lev depreciated to 55 lev/dollar. Since the first part of 1994 the lev has experienced nominal depreciation until it reached 70 lev/dollar in November 1995.[15]

The collapse of trade with the former Soviet republics has resulted in dramatic adjustments in Bulgarian trade patterns and trade flows are now far below historical levels. Still, the rapid initial depreciation of the lev made Bulgarian goods inexpensive on foreign markets and trade with Western Europe increased substantially. However, from early 1992 to July 1995 the R/CPI rose by 629 per cent while the nominal exchange rate rose only 179 per cent. A major concern has been whether the sharp increase in the real value of the lev will lead to trade deficits.

A different story emerges if the movements of the exchange rate are viewed from the perspective of the PPI. The lev still appreciates in real terms, but the increase is much smaller. To see the contrast, maintaining the real exchange rate at January 1992 levels would require a nominal exchange of only 75 lev/dollar in July 1995 on a PPI-adjusted basis (the actual rate was 66) versus 172 lev/dollar on a R/CPI-adjusted basis.[16]

The appropriate choice of index depends on the question posed. If the issue is import competition between domestic and foreign retail products, the R/CPI is better since it measures changes in relative prices between competing products. On the other hand, investigations of export competition should utilize the PPI-adjusted exchange rate. If the real-PPI-adjusted exchange rate is rising slowly, exports should continue to be strong.

A different story emerges if shadow firms are important, and these firms impose large markups on producer prices before exporting them. The state foreign trade monopoly has now been replaced by private traders. If their markup is high, then the PPI could understate the rise in export prices. Patterns, thus far, are difficult to discern because the composition of trade has changed dramatically since the transition began. The overall level of exports was higher in 1994 after a slight decline in 1993. Exports to the European Community have grown from $1.16 billion in 1992 to $1.4 billion in 1994. Exports to Turkey have declined, however. The most important shift has been exports to Macedonia which has become the largest importer from Bulgaria. Exports have risen from $158 million in 1992 to $368 million in 1994 (*PlanEcon Report*, 16 June 1995). (There may be re-exports in this data.)

Interest rates

When price controls were relaxed in February 1991, interest rates on loans and deposits were raised to reflect the higher inflation rates that were expected. Both inflation rates and nominal interest were volatile during 1991. In 1992 as inflation rates settled into the range of 80 per cent on the R/CPI and 25 per cent on the PPI, the base rate charged commercial banks on loans from the Bulgarian National Bank moved into the 60-65 per cent range. Loans to state enterprises and private business carried higher rates and interest rates on deposits lower rates.[17]

With the divergence in the two price indices, the choice of index again depends on what is being analyzed. From the point of view of depositors, who are trying to protect the real purchasing power of their savings, deposit interest rates of 55 per cent and R/CPI inflation rates of 80 per cent means that the real value of their savings is declining quickly. For a retail distributer holding stocks of goods whose value is rising at 80 per cent per year, paying nominal interest rates of 80 per cent per year should not be onerous.

On the other hand, for a state enterprise, whose prices are rising at 25 per cent a year, borrowing at 80 per cent means effective real interest rates are 55 per cent. Under more normal circumstances such a divergence in nominal interest rates and price increases would be a signal that this is a declining sector of the economy, and market adjustments would bring about the needed changes. The state enterprise sector is declining, but what makes this situation unusual is that it affects such a large core sector of the economy. Furthermore, if new private businesses attempt to compete with state enterprises in this sector of the economy, they will also be faced with very high real rates of interest.

Wages

At the beginning of the transition period real wages fell sharply. At the end of 1991 real wages (R/CPI basis) were approximately 63 per cent of their level in December 1990. From December 1991 to June 1995 average nominal wages rose from 1,685 lev to 7,812 lev, an increase of 364 per cent. During the same period retail prices rose 629 per cent. Workers, therefore, have seen a dramatic decline in their purchasing power. At the same time the identical increase in nominal wages has created problems for state enterprises. Since the PPI rose only 217 per cent, firms experienced close to a 46 per cent increase in real wages paid. While increases in labor productivity would normally offset some of these higher costs, firms have been trying to retain workers in spite of large output declines. Real industrial productivity is almost unchanged over this period.[18]

Given these high labor costs along with the burden of high real interest rates, it is not surprising that state enterprises are suffering. Only large subsidies in the form of loans from the banking system are keeping these enterprises alive. Few private firms facing these conditions could survive for very long. Indeed, if these conditions continue to prevail, most state enterprises could not be expected to survive as private firms. Privatization would lead shortly to private bankruptcy.

To survive as private firms these enterprises will have to make major adjustments.

71

First, they will have to improve labor productivity. Unless production expands rapidly this would require additional reductions in employment.[19] Secondly, they will have to raise prices to bring them more in line with rising wage bills. This may be possible if the existence of shadow firms is the reason for the relatively low rates of PPI inflation. Newly privatized firms, with greater incentives to capture profits for themselves, could squeeze these shadow firms and raise prices.[20] So enterprises which appear to be unsalvageable could turn out to be successful private firms.

Shifts in relative incomes

The gap between inflation rates recorded by the C/RPI and the PPI also describes a shift in relative prices. These shifts in relative prices also have an effect on relative incomes. Since the private sector of the economy has benefitted from many of these shifts, the analysis of these changes presents an indirect way of measuring the size of the private sector. During the early stages of the transition the National Statistical Institute had great difficulty measuring the size of the private sector. This was during a period when large declines in output were being recorded. Calculations using price gap statistics suggest that the private retail/wholesale sector was quite significant during this period. This suggests that the national income statistics might have significantly unreported output levels during this period.

The rise in retail prices relative to producer prices has created a shift in the terms-of-trade between the producer sector and the retail/distribution sector. More income is being generated in the retail sector. The shift is dramatic. In our earlier example of the kitchen pots, an original markup of ten per cent becomes a markup of 233 per cent by June 1995. More than half the income being generated in the consumer goods sector of the economy is flowing to distributors and retailers.

To understand the implications of these income figures, they need to be modified in terms of size of the consumer goods sector. The 1992 figures from the National Statistical Institute put the consumption share of GDP in Bulgaria at 67 per cent. The other 33 per cent of GDP was investment activity or government services and products not sold on the market. In the first section we calculated that 70 per cent of the income in the consumption sector was being captured at distribution and retail.[21] Thus approximately 47 per cent (.70 x .67) of income is now being generated in the distribution/retail sector of the economy. If we use the same methodology to calculate the size of the private sector in 1993 it would be 39 per cent, much larger than the projection of the National Statistical Institute figure of less than 20 per cent. Almost all of this activity is private sector activity. While it would not be appropriate to argue on this basis that the private sector is 47 per cent of the economy, this figure at least provides a starting point for judging its overall importance.[22]

There are several important qualifications before one could claim all this activity is private. First, there is the bias caused by differences between the Laspeyres and the Paasche indices. Then there is the import-good-quality bias. The impact of the quality change on the price index can be seen if we continue with our kitchen pot example. Suppose in January 1991 there were only Bulgarian pots selling for 22 leva and in the June 1995 survey one-half the pots are Bulgarian pots selling for 281 leva and one-half the pots are German pots selling for 1,417 leva. The R/CPI, therefore, stands at 849 (the same as the actual reported figure). Large quality differences are occurring but are being reported as price changes. Suppose further that Bulgaria is exporting pots to Germany at 255 leva each (which reflects the PPI movements) and importing German pots at 1,289 leva each.[23] Note that in this example in spite of the apparent gap between the C/RPI and PPI, the markup is ten per cent in January 1991 and is still ten per cent for both goods in June 1995.

Since the markup is still ten per cent, there is no large income increase due to the widening gap between the two indices. Imagine the same trader involved in both sides of the transaction: 5.04 Bulgarian pots are sold for one German pot. The trader has the same income as before. So to the extent the C/RPI picks up these changes, there is no relative income shift towards the retail sector, *but* there is no rise in the actual cost of living either. The C/RPI is overstating the increase. The option of Bulgarian pots still exists.

Quality changes are also occurring in the domestic economy. In this case both the PPI and C/RPI overstate the change in prices, but these quality changes do not bias our relative income calculation.[24] Our concern, therefore, is with the bias created by quality changes in imported goods.

It is difficult to calculate how large a combination of import-quality-change bias and Laspeyres/Paasche index bias might be. Since approximately half of Bulgarian production is traded, the import quality bias should be significant.[25] The divergence between Laspeyres and Paasche indices will also be greater when the basket of goods being purchased is changing rapidly, as it is in Bulgaria. Still the biases created by use of a Laspeyres index and the quality changes are not additive. The Laspeyres index is biased because the original market basket is no longer representative after relative prices change. People shift to cheaper goods. If there are quality changes and people recognize the quality differences, they will not change their market basket as dramatically as they would if there were no quality changes. So the Laspeyres index will be less distorted than it would be in the absence of the quality changes.

We might ask how sensitive our results are to adjustments in the inflation rates calculated for the C/RPI. Table 4.3 presents relative income results under different scenarios for both 1993 and 1995. Two alternatives are compared with the actual data. In the first alternative the R/CPI is assumed to have risen to only four-fifths of its actual level; in the second, to only three-fifths. During the January 1992–July 1993 period the inflation rate was actually 80 per cent. The first scenario would be equivalent to an inflation rate of 65 per cent, the second to an inflation rate of only 48 per cent.

73

Table 4.3
Relative income calculations for retail sector with adjusted inflation scenarios

	Actual data (%)	Change in C/RPI = 4/5 of actual value (%)	Change in C/RPI = 3/5 of actual value (%)
1993	39	33	23
1995	47	41.5	33

While these results show much smaller levels of income generated in the retail/distribution sector, they are still large. To the extent that they represent unmeasured private sector activity, these activities are an important unreported element of economic activity in the Bulgarian economy.

Income distribution and future price trends

The growing importance of the private retail sector also supports casual observation and anecdotal evidence from the economy. Sofia and other cities give an air of affluence which belies the statistics which show ever declining GDP. At the same time income inequalities are also growing with both fancy cars on the streets and more people carefully rummaging through the trash.

People who are dependent on state income have seen a decline in their purchasing power. Because of the government's financial problems neither state pensions nor state wages can make up the losses in real income that were suffered during the early months of the transition.[26] On the other hand, there is a strong perception that wages in the private sector are much higher than wages in the state sector. This differential is drawing workers out of the state sector in spite of a hesitancy to relinquish the security of a state sector job.[27]

Under central planning the service sector was small relative to similar sectors in market economies. So this shift in resources to the retail sector can be viewed as valuable restructuring. If the growth of the retail sector is being reflected in the disparity between the inflation rates recorded by the PPI and the C/RPI, then we would expect that, once the retail sector has established itself, the difference between the two growth rates would merge.

If the other major factor causing the discrepancy in the two inflation rates is the importation of high quality foreign goods, this process should also slow. Now that markets are open, the big influx of new foreign goods should soon pass and this distortion in the measured change in the C/RPI should have a much smaller effect. For these reasons we would expect that the rate of change of the two indices would begin to move closer together. This has already happened to some extent, but the fact that the gap has not narrowed more in recent years is somewhat surprising.

Not only might we expect that inflation rates would converge, we might expect the rates to converge to a rate which more closely reflect monetary growth. During the period from January 1992-June 1995 broad money grew about 270 per cent. This is far below the C/RPI increase of 629 per cent. In a transitioning economy rapidly changing institutions should cause velocity to change and in a high inflation economy people will try to conserve on their monetary balances. Another possible reason for the difference in these growth rates, however, is that the C/RPI overstates the price change of the average transaction. Given the large gap between the C/RPI and the PPI, the price change of the average transaction is somewhere between the C/RPI and PPI. Indeed the growth rate of broad money is closer to the growth rate of the PPI (217 per cent) Once financial institutions become more stable and the C/RPI and the PPI merge, the inflation rate should be determined more by these monetary factors.

Conclusions

Analysis of the gap between movements of the C/RPI and the PPI reveals that some positive changes have been occurring in the Bulgarian economy but also suggests that there are some disturbing trends that could create serious problems in the future. If our calculations are correct, the private sector in Bulgaria has been growing rapidly, providing additional retail services that were not present before. This is an important beneficial restructuring of the economy. The growth in this sector has offset substantial declines that have occurred in the state sector. At the same time it creates a challenge for the government which must find ways to tax this new sector without impeding its growth. The value-add tax passed in the spring of 1994 is a movement in that direction.

We have also argued that the underlying inflation problem is not as bad as the rates measured by the C/RPI. The PPI is increasing much more slowly. Furthermore, the C/RPI overstates the rate of inflation because it has not been adjusted for significant quality changes in the market basket of goods now available to consumers.

The picture which emerges from analysis of the PPI and C/RPI is a Bulgarian economy which has a sizable private sector, a more moderate decline in output than official figures describe and less inflation.

However, there are some serious dangers on the horizon. Since the C/RPI seriously overstates the rate of inflation, policy decisions based on the C/RPI could create difficulties for the economy. When the government uses the existing C/RPI as a guide for determining nominal expenditure levels, government deficits will be large. Furthermore, if interest rate and wage change policies are geared to exaggerated measures of inflation, they can have negative consequences for the future viability of Bulgaria's industrial base. Even well-managed firms cannot survive in this environment. The result may be costly and unnecessary restructuring. Some of these problems can be avoided if movements of the PPI as well as the C/RPI are considered when policy choices are analyzed.

The analysis also suggests some movements that are not so positive. A recurrent theme throughout this paper has been the possible establishment of shadow firms in the distribution system. The wide gap between the PPI and C/RPI provides some possible evidence of their presence. Shadow firms are a reflection of poor management in the state enterprise sector.[28] Because of these management problems, restructuring the state enterprise sector is going to be all that much more difficult whether it is done before or after privatization. Since the privatization process is moving slowly, the logical way to counter these trends is to alter the governance structures of state enterprises so that managers have a larger stake in the future of their enterprises.

Notes

1   See Fisher, Sahay, and Vegh (1996) for a more detailed description of these trends both in Eastern Europe and the former republics of the Soviet Union.

2   Tax evasion is a major problem. As in other counties where there is a large 'underground' economy, there is a serious undermeasurement of total output.

3   Inflation will certainly rise again when the effects of the rapid nominal depreciation of the lev in the spring of 1996 filter through the economy.

4   The National Statistical Institute does not calculate a separate primary good and intermediate good index so this index also reflects the prices that state enterprises charge when they sell inputs used by other state enterprises.

5   By contrast, the last row in Table 4.2 also shows that in the other four countries after 30 months the prices indices no longer seriously diverge.

6   Dittus (1993) provides some historical examples where gaps between the R/CPI and PPI have previously appeared. However, none of these show rapid divergences as great as those now being experienced in Bulgaria and Poland.

7   A fourth possible reason which is not explored here is differential productivity improvement across sectors. This is an important explanation for price gaps which have appeared in other countries. For example, between the late 1950s and the early 1990s, the PPI doubled in Japan while the CPI rose more than five times. During this period industrial productivity improved enormously while productivity improvements in the service sector were more modest (Dittus, 1993). Since industrial productivity has seen little change in Bulgaria, there must be other explanations.

8   The collection of information on revenue and output both come from the same state enterprise. In some instances it may be beneficial for the enterprise to overstate their output to justify its existence. Price change may be understated in this instance.

9   Similar arguments have been made about state enterprise managers in other countries. Pinto, Belka, and Krajewski (1993) have surveyed managers in Poland and have reached different conclusions. They argue that managers are trying to make their enterprises profitable while waiting for privatization. Some are more successful than others. Poland is interesting because its price indices are also diverging, although not as dramatically as in Bulgaria.

10   Even if competitive pressures in the retail markets tended to push retail prices downward, retailers would all be experiencing the higher cost of buying from shadow firms. The R/CPI would still rise rapidly.

11   The existence of shadow firms is widely acknowledged in Bulgaria. For example, in a survey of business firms the author conducted with Kenneth Koford (see Koford and Miller, 1995) during the summer of 1994, some managers described situations where they were unable to buy directly from the state enterprise.
     There is much less written about 'shadow firm' type activity in other countries. This may be one of the distinguishing features of the Bulgarian economy and may explain why the price index gap is greater in Bulgaria.

12   This is discussed at greater length below.

13   As Hillman, Mitev, and Peters (1995) point out, the money being accumulated in these shadow firms is supporting eventual privatization of the economy – a form of privatization which may or may not be desirable. So if the government is able to stop this flow of money, the privatization process may be even slower.

14   In Russia the relationship between movements of the CPI and PPI is opposite of those described here; the PPI is rising much more rapidly than the CPI. Commander and Yemtsov's (1994) explanation is that large enterprises are using their market power to raise prices because managers are able to extract the profits for their own use. If this is true, the price effects are opposite, but both Russian managers and Bulgarian managers are trying to siphon off funds from the state enterprise. These are simply different strategies to achieve the same result.

15   In the spring and summer of 1996, there was been another financial crisis. The nominal level of the lev fell from 78 to over 180 lev/dollar. At the time of this writing it is not clear where the new rate will settle.

16   There are many forces acting on the exchange rate. While the lev floated during the early stages of the transition, more recently the Bulgarian National Bank has been an active trader. The foreign trade picture has been further clouded by the large discrepancy between the balance described by customs-

based trade figures and the financial flows data.

17   The base rate and interest rates on deposits and loans described below are based on weighted average interest rates reported for the first four months of 1993 (Bulgarian National Bank, *News Bulletin*, No. 10, p. 35).

18   Estrin, Schaffer, and Singh (1993) have identified similar problems in Czechoslovakia, Hungary, and Poland.

19   While this may make sense from a business point of view, politically it is a very sensitive issue. The Agency for Privatization is trying to prevent this from happening by placing conditions on new owners of privatized firms that would prevent them from reducing their employment levels.

20   If state enterprise managers are benefitting from the profits generated by shadow firms, they could be opponents of privatization unless they expected to share in the profits of the newly privatized state enterprise.

21   We have assumed here that the original markup was ten per cent. The larger the original markup, the larger is the markup in June 1993. If there were no markup in January 1991, the income share in retail in June 1993 would be 55 per cent; if 20 per cent in January 1991, it would be 62 per cent. Since we are dealing with approximations here, they are all in the same range.

22   If we use the data in Table 4.1 to do a similar calculation for Poland, the country with the second largest price index gap, the figure would be 31 per cent. At the other extreme, in Romania the PPI index has risen more than the C/RPI suggesting a shift in the other direction.

23   While the numbers here are illustrative, actual prices for Bulgarian pans during the summer of 1993 were between 40 and 60 lev. Imported 'Tefal' pans were selling at prices between 220 and 500 lev.

24   Quality improvements at retail such as better service would bias the C/RPI index and not the PPI index, but it would not distort the income calculation. More income is being created at retail because more services are being provided in the retail sector.

25   The composition of imports can also provide a clue to the degree of distortion. Approximately a third of Bulgarian imports are fuels. About 15 per cent are consumer good products including clothing and footwear, automobiles, photographic supplies, tobacco products, pharmaceutical, paper products, and beverages (*PlanEcon Report*, 29 June 1993).

From January 1992–April 1995 categories where consumer prices had risen more rapidly than the R/CPI were foodstuffs, clothing and footwear, hygiene, and public health. The largest increase was in hygiene and public health (*PlanEcon Report*, June 1995). The related electricity and heating, coal mining, oil extraction sector experienced the highest price increases in the PPI in 1992 (AECD, 1992).

26   Real wages and pensions are, however, higher than presently thought. The upward bias in the consumer price index distorts this calculation.

27   The labor market in the private sector is unusual in several respects. People
      who have businesses are very cautious about the people they hire. Connec-
      tions are important because finding trustworthy employees is considered dif-
      ficult. The other way to get full-time private sector employment is to start a
      business with all the uncertainty that this entails.
28   Minassian (1993) is also concerned that Bulgarian state enterprise managers
      are not acting in the public interest.

References

Agency for Economic Coordination and Development (1992), *1992 Annual Report
    on the State of the Bulgarian Economy*, Agency for Economic Co-ordination
    and Development: Sofia, December.
Bulgarian National Bank (1993), *News Bulletin*, No. 10, 16-31 May.
—— (1993), *News Bulletin*, No. 11, 1-15 June.
Commander, Simon and Yemtsov, Ruslan (1994), 'Privatization in Russia: Does it
    Matter? Some Early Evidence on the Behavior of Privatized and Private Firms',
    World Bank (mimeo), January.
Dittus, Peter (1993), 'Consumer Prices Outpacing Producer Prices: A Problem?',
    Bank Review: Quarterly Journal of the Bulgarian National Bank, No. 4, pp.
    45-56.
Estrin, Saul, Schaffer, Mark, and Singh, Inderjit (1993), 'Enterprise Adjustment
    in Transition Economies: Czechoslovakia, Hungary and Poland', in Blejer,
    Mario, Calvo, Guillermo, Coricelli, Fabrizio, and Gelb, Alan (eds), *Eastern
    Europe in Transition: From Recession to Growth?*, World Bank: Washington,
    D.C., pp. 111-36.
Fischer, Stanley, Sahay, Ratna, and Vegh, Carlos A. (1996), 'Stabilization and
    Growth in Transition Economies: The Early Experience', *Journal of Economic
    Perspectives*, No. 2, pp. 45-66.
Hillman, Ayre L., Mitev, Lubomir, and Peters, R. Kyle (1995), 'The Private
    Sector, State Enterprises, and Informal Economic Activity', in Bogetic, Z. and
    Hillman, A. (eds), *Financing Government in the Transition – Bulgaria: The
    Political Economy of Tax Policies, Tax Bases and Tax Evasion*, World Bank
    Regional and Sectional Study: Washington, D.C., pp. 47-70.
Koford, Kenneth and Miller, Jeffrey (1995), 'Contracts in Bulgaria: How Agents
    Cope When Property Rights are Incomplete', working paper, Center for
    Institutional Reform in the Informal Sector, University of Maryland.
Minassian, Garabed (1993), *Bulgarian Economy in Transition: Is There Anything
    Wrong with Its Macroeconomic Policy?*, Institute of Economics, Bulgarian
    Academy of Science: Sofia, Bulgaria.

Pinto, Brian, Belko, Mark, and Krajewski, Stefan (1993), 'Transforming State Enterprises in Poland: Evidence on Adjustment by Manufacturing Firms', *Brookings Papers on Economic Activity,* No.1, pp. 213-70.
PlanEcon, PlanEcon Reports (various).

Acknowledgements

The author would like to thank Tanya Hubenova, Anastassia Mlteva, Kenneth Koford, and Evangelos Falaris for helpful comments. Special thanks are due Kamen Atanassov, Valentin Chavdarov, and Valentin Vulov who assisted on the project and provided useful insights. Remaining mistakes are the author's responsibility.

5   Incomes policies in Bulgaria

Tihomir Enev and Kenneth Koford

Introduction

In advanced industrial countries with national unions and a monetary policy that accommodates wage and price increases, an incomes policy may be a means to improve the tradeoff between inflation and unemployment. This follows from the argument that wage increases carry a negative externality in the form of inflation. In the former centrally planned economies there are additional factors favoring incomes policy. First, most of the firms are either fully state-owned or under state control, and second, the state often fails to act as an effective owner both in terms of making decisions based on a long-term horizon and enforcing hard-budget constraints. In most of the economies in transition high inflation has become a chronic problem. Therefore, wage control is a necessary part of the stabilization program as a means 'of breaking the momentum of inflation and dampening inflationary expectations in order to mitigate the output consequences often associated with fiscal and monetary stringency...' (Commander, 1993, p. 127). While there are substantial problems with these policies, they appear to be ones of design and enforcement, not the shortages implied by neoclassical models.[1]

The goal of this paper is to examine the role of wage control in wage dynamics, and its impact on inflation in Bulgaria for the period from 1990-93.[2] We first describe the introduction and development of the incomes policy in Bulgaria and then find its effect on the CPI.

In order to assess the influence of the various factors on inflation in Bulgaria over 1990-93, we run a regression similar to that used by Fabrizio Coricelli and Rezende Rocha (1991) in a paper describing the stabilization programs in Poland and Yugoslavia. Coricelli and Rocha use the regression to determine the factors determining inflation in Poland during the 1980s, a period in which the economy was largely state-owned, but in which decision-making authority in firms had been largely decentralized. They consider two types of factors: cost push factors and monetary factors. The first includes lagged inflation, the exchange rate, and wages. The second consists of the ratio between broad money and retail sales as a measure of monetary disequilibrium. To consider incomes policies, we add more regressors to the equation to act as 'control' variables, plus a dummy variable representing the wage-bill regulation (zero when it is not present, one when it is). This tests the hypothesis that wage-bill controls can reduce inflation, other factors held constant.

We begin with some theoretical observations on incomes policies, then review the Bulgarian inflation policy and wage bill controls over 1990-93. Next we provide our best econometric estimate of the effects of the wage bill controls. A conclusion follows.

Incomes policies and a wage-bill policy

All of the major transition countries have adopted some form of incomes policy – largely by controlling wages or the wage bill. The objective has clearly been to reduce inflation, which has become substantial in almost every country (the major exception being the Czech Republic). Bulgaria's monthly inflation rate is shown in Figure 5.1. Clearly, monthly inflation in the range of four to ten per cent is a serious problem, particularly after many years of price stability under communism. In addition, the inflation was accompanied by sharp declines in output, suggesting a movement like that shown in Figure 5.2. The overall framework is that of aggregate demand (AD) along with the full-employment level of output (Y_f). Point A shows a shortage economy, while point B shows the new equilibrium.

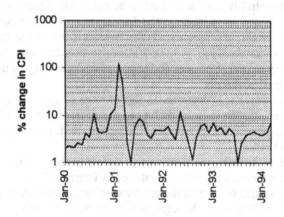

Figure 5.1   Per cent change in CPI, January 1990-March 1994

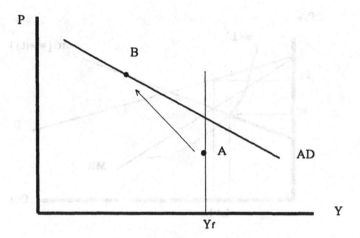

Figure 5.2

However, transition countries avoided the 'standard' policy of controlling prices or value added.[3] Most probably, after many years of price controls, these governments wanted to avoid any appearance of continuing to control prices in general. A more political explanation could be that the new democratic governments tended to be allied with business interests and opposed to labor.

In any case, the universal approach has been to control wages or the wage bill. The latter is particularly easy for a state enterprise to calculate (and it had been done under the communist regime). However, the effects of a wage-bill policy are likely to be perverse. Figure 5.3 shows a firm with some market power, in which the major cost is the wage, w. Assume that in the short run, output is proportional to labor, so $Q = aL$.[4] A particular wage bill, $w*L*$, constrains output and wages to a rectangular hyperbola through $w*L*$. Also, wages must be at or above the labor supply function, $w(L)$. If $w*L*$ is to the right of the profit-maximizing quantity and price, then the constraint is not binding. On the other hand, if $w*L*$ is to the left of the profit-maximizing quantity, L_1, and price, the firm is constrained to choose a higher price and lower quantity than it would otherwise do (as argued in Koford and Miller, 1986, for a constraint on a firm's total revenue, where a similar principle applies).

A quite similar story uses the competitive model of firm behavior. If the demand curve in Figure 5.3 is horizontal, the conclusions remain the same: either the wage bill constraint is not binding, or it causes a perverse effect.

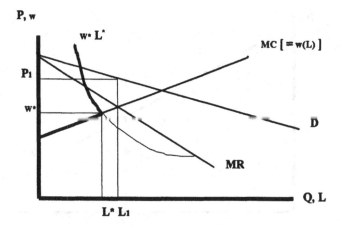

Figure 5.3

To rationalize the policies chosen by the countries that favored a wage-bill, two additional assumptions seem required. First, the actual wage paid by firms must be above the competitive supply of labor, so that there is a margin to force down wages. Second, the firm must be unable to reduce the number of employees; for example, this could be a matter of negotiation with a labor union.[5] In that case, the marginal

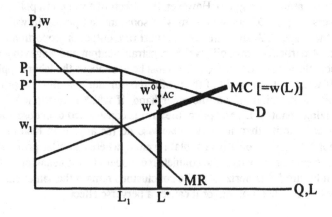

Figure 5.4

84

cost of labor is zero up to the fixed level of labor, L*. This creates a large jump in the marginal cost function at L*, so that for many demands and marginal revenues L* will be the optimal point. Finally, the firm must – in the absence of the wage-bill controls – desire to raise price and reduce output, as in Figure 5.3. In Figure 5.4, the firm would choose L_1P_1 if not constrained, paying wage rate w_1. But if required to maintain the labor supply at L*, the firm will set price at P*. However, in this frame-work, the wage-bill constraint does not play a role. So, in addition, consider the firm's average cost function, based on the wage rate. Then if the constraint pushes the wage from w^0 to w^*, the firm will make a profit at P*Q*.

This story *does* rationalize the wage-bill as a way to reduce wages and so prices. But one must consider that it is very complex and ad-hoc. Keep in mind that at least the Bulgarians *thought* that a wage-bill constraint should reduce inflation. So they may have had some story along these lines in mind.

Bulgarian macroeconomic and incomes policies, 1989-93

Economic environment at the start of transition

Bulgaria started to implement its liberalization and stabilization program under ex-tremely unfavorable conditions. Having had one of the most centralized economies in the Soviet bloc, with the private sector producing around five per cent of the GDP in 1989 and foreign trade extremely concentrated within the CMEA (GDP declined 16 per cent due to the collapse of the CMEA), Bulgaria has had to solve many hard problems during the transition. GDP declined 12 per cent in 1990 and 23 per cent in 1991. The inflation rate reached a 950 per cent annualized monthly rate by the end of 1991 and the unemployment rate soared to 10.7 per cent, both starting from al-most zero at the end of 1989. This rapidly deteriorating economic situation resulted from a combination of domestic and external conditions.

Against this background, the government embarked on a radical reform program in February 1991 which was in scope and speed much like Poland's. The main pillars of the Bulgarian stabilization program were restrictive monetary and fiscal policies, and an incomes policy that controlled the nominal wage bill for state enter-prises and institutions. The floating exchange rate system adopted at the beginning of the program led to almost complete depletion of its international reserves and put enormous pressure on incomes and financial policies. The incomes policy was the result of a tripartite agreement among the government, the employers, and the larg-est national trade union federation. The conditions for a consensus and a successful incomes policy were relatively favorable in Bulgaria because of the uncertainty and high social homogeneity.

Controlling wages before the transition

From 1982, according to a government decree, wages were to be computed as a residual between income earned and all other input costs. This aimed to align wages and enterprise performance. However, wage funds continued to be provided centrally and enterprises faced a soft budget constraint. In fact, wages were paid first, equal to the amount each enterprise was able to obtain from the Central Planning Office. Government subsidies and bank loans were used to cover the difference (if any) between revenues from sales and expenditure for inputs. Thus, the system of centrally determined prices couldn't provide a linkage between wages and productivity (Jones and Meurs, 1991).

During 1985-87, the General Assembly of each firm, consisting of all employees (for firms with less than 500 employees) and of workers' representatives in bigger ones, was allowed to vote on guidelines for determining individual wages. On 1 January 1988 the important Decree #56 was passed by the Government regulating the whole economy. Under this decree the total sum of wage funds for groups of firms (called associations) was made dependent on a certain percentage of sales, value added, or specified as an absolute amount, according to the industry to which they belonged. The associations then determined the exact sum for each firm's wage fund. The whole process was regulated by the Ministry of Economy and Planning. In 1988 a tax on excess wage and salary increases was introduced, with highly progressive tax rates.[6]

1990

1990 was not a year of dramatic changes for the Bulgarian economy, but a period of political euphoria after the democratic changes in November 1989 and psychological preparation for radical economic reforms. The socialist government of Mr. Loukanov tried to solve tactical problems rather than to undertake strategic changes. Between November 1989 and February 1991 the budget deficit was allowed to run out of control and the money supply grew rapidly. Prices, still controlled in the prevailing government sector, and existing stocks of goods, prevented high inflation for a time. The control over wage increases was not strict, mainly because of political interests.

It is interesting that the average nominal wage grew by 173 per cent till the end of the year, while inflation was 165.1 per cent. This shows a 4.6 per cent increase in the real wage, which in a economy in transition with shrinking output and vague monetary and fiscal policies was a strong precondition for cost-push inflation.

1991

Negotiating wages in Bulgaria started in 1991, although the first steps were made in 1990 with the creation of the tripartite system of workers, government, and trade unions. At the beginning the priorities were to determine the minimum wage and the mechanisms of indexation. Only during 1991 did the process of negotiating wages really get started.

In February 1991 prices of 90 per cent of the goods were liberalized. There were 14 monitored prices of essential commodities, four goods were priced by the state, and a special policy was introduced to control energy prices (Pishev, 1992). In this situation the role of incomes policy was to restrict cost-push inflation as much as possible. An important question at that time was what to control: the average wage or the wage bill? The decision was based on a judgment as to which macroeconomic indicator could be considered more predictable: labor productivity or output. Wage controls aim to stabilize (or keep down) unit labor costs (ULC) which can be expressed either as the ratio of the average wage to productivity, or the ratio of the wage bill to output:

$$ULC = AW/P = (WB/L)/Q/L = WB/Q$$

In Bulgaria, labor productivity was viewed as a more uncertain indicator than output, since productivity depends on more unpredictable decisions like whether to hoard or to shed labor where labor has zero marginal productivity in a hugely over-staffed state sector. Control over the wage bill was considered to provide a better nominal anchor.[7]

This is what we know the authorities said. As we noted in the previous section, putting this in a straightforward microeconomic framework is difficult. As Koford and Miller (1986) have argued, when, under certainty, profit maximizing firms have market power, controlling the wage bill is likely to lead to a perverse effect of increased wages and reduced labor input. A non-microeconomic approach that is implied by the authorities' claim is that firms were expected to act in an entirely passive fashion, keeping planned L and Q fixed, and setting P as a markup over average cost. However, it is hard to think of any rationale for such beliefs. In the context of the Bulgarian incomes policy, there could have been some quite indirect effects on inflation, due to the policy's reduction in consumer incomes and of output.

During the first half of 1991 the incomes policy limited wages by imposing a ceiling on the nominal wage bill of individual enterprises and requiring that an absolute amount of wage compensation be granted to each worker to offset the initial price adjustment. The government planned to enforce compliance with the wage-bill ceiling by a tax on excess wage bill increases. In the first phase of the reform the

87

wage bills were calculated by the formula:

$$WB(91:s) = WB(90:s) * [W(90:4)/W(90:s)]$$

where WB(90:s) is the wage bill of the firm in 1990 quarter s, and W(90:s) is the average monthly wage in 1990 quarter s.

The tax on the excess wage bill was determined by the scheme in Table 5.1.

Table 5.1
Tax on excess wage fund increase, February–June 1991

Quarterly increase above fund	Marginal tax rate on increment
<1%	100%
1-2%	200%
2-3%	400%
>3%	800%

Average real wages fell 45 per cent in the first half of 1991. This was more than anticipated. The decline was due mainly to higher than expected inflation of 134 per cent. 120 per cent had been expected. This should be interpreted in connection with the large increase of the real wage in the last quarter of 1990, almost 20 per cent. This earlier increase in real wages meant that there was little opportunity for firms to provide a wage bill high enough to reach the allowed limit (Bogetic and Fox, 1993).

In July 1991 wage bargaining was decentralized to bilateral bargaining between enterprise managements and trade unions. The government retained two constraints imposed on wage negotiation: a minimum wage level and a wage fund ceiling for individual enterprises. At this stage several adjustments of the formula were made to incorporate explicit 100 per cent indexation to retail prices and to allow wages to reflect productivity growth. The formula became:

$$WB(t:s) = WB(t-1:s)*[W(t:s-1)/W(t-1:s)]*[P(t:s)/P(t:s-1)]*[R(t:s)/R(t:s-1)]$$

where P(t:s) is the retail price index in year t quarter s, and R(t:s) is output per employee (productivity) in the firm in year t quarter s.

The tax on the excess wage bill was reduced to reflect more adequately the condition of companies' wage funds. In practice, firms set wages based on inflation forecasts, but the excess wage tax was levied *ex post* on the excess of the wage bill over the ceiling calculated on the basis of actual inflation during the quarter.

Against this background, enterprises showed considerable wage-bill restraint. Nominal wage bills remained about 15 per cent below the controlled levels at which taxes would be imposed. This was mainly due to the compression of intra-enterprise wage differentials (Stoikov, 1992), the early retirement policy, hiring freezes, and the increased number of workers on unpaid furlough rather than layoffs. Thus, both wages and number of workers were constrained.

During the third quarter of 1991 the tension between the government and the unions grew and the tripartite agreement was dissolved. The incomes policy during the second half of 1991 was in fact based on a decentralized system of enterprise level bargaining. Average real wages rose by eight per cent as inflation slowed and unemployment increased. In the last quarter real wages rose by 47 per cent as a result of the seasonal recovery of output, payment of year-end bonuses and the efforts of the trade unions. The minimum wage was raised, but the real wage was still 34 per cent below its value at the end of 1990. With the considerable decline in output, unemployment soared from 1.6 per cent at the end of 1990, to 3.2 per cent in March 1991, and to ten per cent by the end of the year. This forced the government to raise the contribution rate on the wage bill to the unemployment fund from 3.7 to 5 per cent (Bogetic and Fox, 1993).

The following conclusions could be reached from the results of wage contracting and regulation in 1991. First, the increase in wages was a result of efforts to compensate for the fall in real income after the first price shock. Second, in general, the incomes policy caused a decline in the real wage bill. It may have reduced real wages, if the assumption that reductions in output and labor inputs were exogenous was correct. That is, the reductions in output were largely caused by such shocks as the collapse of trade with the CMEA, and the reductions in labor were constrained by union agreements. Thus, it may be that the incomes policy was useful in avoiding an escalating price-wage spiral. Still, at the beginning the norm was set too high and wages were far below it. If the rule had been more fully binding, the wage bill would have fallen more, but this could have caused the perverse result of a further fall in output described by Koford and Miller (1986). Third, the path of unemployment was determined by the closing of state-owned firms and the contraction of production, while the inflation rate was dominated not so much by the increased wages as by such factors as declining production, the deteriorating terms of trade, the floating exchange rate, high mark-ups partially reflecting inflationary expectations, and the budget deficit.

The incomes policy in 1992 was created as a result of the high inflation during the first quarter of the year (approximately five per cent a month), and continued reliance on the floating exchange rate regime. Its role did not change over that period and it was considered one of the most important elements in controlling inflation. The key elements of the 1992 incomes policy included: a wage-bill ceiling for every enterprise to keep real wage bills at their last quarter of 1991 level which allowed some real wage increase from declines in employment; and a quarterly adjustment of wage bills based on the changes in the average wage rate for the last three quarters, anticipated quarterly changes in inflation and a partial allowance for any divergence between anticipated and actual quarterly inflation (Bankov, 1994). A universal minimum wage was set for all full-time workers at 750 Lv. per month (about $30 at that time) during the first half of 1992. In July 1992, changes were made for the remainder of the year, since wage fund limits had been calculated on the basis of the first quarter of the year, and had taken into account the forecast rate of inflation rather than allowing it to adjust ex post to actual inflation. The progressive tax was reduced again, the top rate remaining 400 per cent but being applicable only if the wage fund grew by more than six per cent (Table 5.2). The excess wage tax now had to be paid regardless of the enterprise's profitability. (Previously, the tax was supposed to be paid, but enterprises were able to avoid paying.) The wage fund limits had to take into consideration layoffs, and the fund was reduced if employment was substantially reduced. Unemployment continued to increase, reaching 15 per cent by October 1992.

The degree to which penalties should be enforced can be problematic. When many state firms are in deep financial trouble, it is not always clear what sort of sanction an additional tax liability can be. Bulgaria is an extreme case where in 1992 only ten per cent of the total excess wage tax revenues was actually collected from 27 per cent of the firms owing taxes. To the extent that firms are insolvent, enforcing the tax may only force the firms to close. When unemployment is high and there is political opposition to further job losses, the short run trade off may keep the government from enforcing the tax. This occurred in 1992 and in 1993.

1993

In 1993 the private sector accounted for 37 per cent of GDP, though, according to official estimates, that did not include the 'gray economy', this figure was 18 per cent.[8] During 1990-91 personal consumption declined by almost 25 per cent in real terms before rising slightly in 1993 by 0.3 per cent. Average real wages continued to

Table 5.2
Incomes policy mechanisms in Bulgaria

Basic design	Ceilings on the wage bill enforced with excess wages tax.
Norm developments	
Feb 91-Jun 91	The WB ceilings were set at the 90 Q:4 WB. The number of workers was recalculated to account for layoffs.
Jul 91-Jun 92	WB ceilings fixed at former quarter WB, indexed by inflation rate. WB ceilings were also related to productivity.
Jul 92-Dec 92	WB ceilings set at the first quarter of 1992 WB, indexed by inflation.
Jan 93-Dec 93	Partial indexation for the past inflation. Reduced adjustment for changes in productivity.
Indexation	In Q:1 90 there were flat rate compensations for unexpected increases in prices.
	From May 1991 on, there was full wage indexation.
	From Jan. 1993, there was partial indexation based on the previous 12 months' price increases.
Penalties	Taxes were applied to the difference between ceilings and actual WB.
Feb 91- Jun 91	tax rate for excessive WB up to 1%: 100%
	1-2%: 200%
	3-4%: 400%
	>4%: 800%
Jul 91-Jun 92	up to 1%: no tax
	1-2%: 50%
	2-3%: 100%
	3-4%: 200%
	>4%: 400%
Jul 92-Dec 92	up to 3%: no tax
	3-4%: 50%
	4-5%: 100%
	5-6%: 200%
	>6%: 400%
Jan 93-Dec 93	up to 2%: no tax
	2-3%: 50%
	3-4%: 200%
	4-5%: 600%
	>5%: 800%

drop. PlanEcon estimates show a decline of ten per cent. But it is important to notice that in Bulgaria, as in other East European countries, the relative importance of non-wage income is rising significantly, and it indicates an increase of 48.6 per cent (PlanEcon, 1994, p. 4). For 1993 real income was 97 per cent of the 1992 level.

Incomes policy continued to be an important instrument in the fight to control inflation and a factor for balancing real incomes, unemployment and inflation in the dominant public sector of the Bulgarian economy. The mechanism regulating the wage fund formation and its growth was modified in two respects. First, the adjustment coefficient was changed to partial rather than full compensation for actual or forecast inflation. The partial compensation was calculated using the previous twelve months' price increase as a base amount, with full adjustment for the first nine months plus 85 per cent of the increase for the last three months. Second, the adjustment for productivity was reduced from 100 to 30 per cent of the changes in output per capita (Commander and Coricelli, 1995). The tax rates on the excess wage bill were also increased for the first time. Experience showed that this mechanism was milder than the one applied during the previous year. Some enterprises and organizations managed to attain higher 'ceilings' while under the same restrictions.

The results at the end of 1993 showed that, as a whole, the wage funds in industrial enterprises were below the ceilings, as firms' depleted financial reserves. During that period some weak features of the mechanism were revealed, too. In a difficult market situation with uncertain product realization, some firms continued to pay high wages to their employees in order to keep their wage fund base high for the next year. The methods of indexation of wages in different industries based on present and past quarter inflation led to some disproportional movements in nominal gross wage among industries. The factor 'volume of retail sales per capita' included in the norm to stimulate market activity by firms was not very reliable. Many firms faced the problem of collecting payments from their clients, which made it difficult to effectively apply this indicator. Only 33 per cent of the firms that violated the norm paid their punitive taxes, which shows that the policy was not applied firmly (Jackman and Pages, 1993).

Evidence from regression analysis

In order to assess the role of wage controls over the wage dynamic and its influence over the inflation in Bulgaria we estimated several time-series regressions. The following regression closely follows the Coricelli and Rocha (1991) approach and appeared to fit the data best:

$$DLCPI = .083 + .561 \, DLCPI(-1) + .358 \, DLEXR - .211 \, DLRA - .111 \, DLWG -$$
$$(7.00) \quad\quad (12.98) \quad\quad (-2.36) \quad\quad (-1.53)$$

$$.287 \, DLUN - .056 \, DUMMY$$
$$(-2.29) \quad\quad (-2.39)$$

where $R^2 = .88$; $N = 45$; D-W = 1.87. t-statistics are given in parentheses. DLCPI is the change in the logarithm of the consumer price index; DLEXR is the change in the logarithm of the exchange rate; DLRA is the change in the logarithm of the ratio of broad money to retail sales; DLWG is the change in the logarithm of wages; DLUN is the change in the logarithm of unemployment; DUMMY shows the wage bill norm and equals zero before the reform (April 1990-February 1991) and one after its implementation.

The data is monthly from April 1990 to December 1993. There are 47 observations, of which two are lost due to the need to calculate lags, and no significant outliers distort the results.

All coefficients are statistically significant, though some signs need additional explanation.[9] The coefficients for DLCPI(-1) and DLEXR are highly significant and their relative weight is rather high, too. Taking these terms as elasticities, we see that inflation is somewhat damped, since the coefficient on DLCPI(-1) is less than one. This confirms our hypothesis that important factors in the Bulgarian inflation are past inflation and the floating exchange rate. The first factor has a role in the adjustment of the wage norm and influences the overall economic behavior of people and firms. The second is reflected in the deteriorating terms-of-trade and increasing prices of imports. Wendel and Manchev (1994), in another econometric study of Bulgarian inflation, find a coefficient in a linear regression of the foreign exchange rate on the CPI of .78 (with a standard error of .59). This is about half the effect found in our estimates, when one takes antilogs of the coefficient on DLEXR.

Two control variables have puzzling signs that are inconsistent with economic theory, and with our prior expectations. The negative sign of the coefficient on the change in the wage rate could be explained by the fact that wage adjustment in the public sector is based on forecasted inflation, which in most cases was underestimated. The norm is corrected afterward if the difference is too big. This error-correction mechanism makes the changes in wages lag behind these of the CPI and causes them to have opposite signs. The fact that the sign on wages is negative at least supports the hypothesis that wages are not the dominant factor for the inflation dynamic in Bulgaria. The coefficient is also not statistically significant at conventional levels.

The negative coefficient for the Broad Money/Retail Sales ratio is also puzzling and inconsistent with monetary theory. It could be explained by the monetary policy of the central bank and the government trying to correct the money stock for the inflation dynamics. These two variables were kept in the regression, despite their puzzling coefficients, since they are really control variables to assure a proper measure of the effect of the dummy.

The wage control dummy variable is negative and statistically significant, showing that wage controls played a role in restricting wage growth and inflation, and the coefficient is fairly impressive. Taking the 'preferred' value of -.056 and taking antilogs, the change in the average CPI due to the controls is -7.6 per cent per month, from around 13.3 per cent before the controls to 5.4 per cent afterward.[10] However, the relative 'beta' weight of the coefficient is relatively small, since other factors, particularly the past inflation rate and the exchange rate were more important in explaining monthly changes. The negative sign indicates that the Bulgarian authorities were probably correct in thinking that output and employment were determined externally and that firms were not able to reduce employment freely. Otherwise, their constraints could easily have increased the inflation rate. Almost surely, there was some indirect effect from the reduction in total labor income, which in turn reduced demand.

The relation between inflation growth and unemployment growth is negative, which just confirms the evidences from the Philips curve model. There is a significant tradeoff between these two macro variables. A more complete analysis would examine the effect of the controls on output, but the limited data and the many other factors that have influenced output make that a difficult undertaking.

The regression was tested for robustness by varying the number of regressors. The most important variables are the exchange rate and lagged inflation; the first one contributing most to the high R^2. We also ran the regression with the same variables but quarterly data. Again, the most important variable with a statistically significant coefficient is the exchange rate.

The regression with monthly data is tested for autocorrelation using Durbin's h-test due to the lagged CPI variable. The figures from the test show that there is no autocorrelation (h = .55; the critical value is 1.6).

Conclusions

In a country with a highly centralized economy like Bulgaria, enforcing an incomes policy with social consensus and a compliance mechanism was achieved with modest success for several years.

Starting from the second quarter of 1991 direct controls on wages were applied using a tax on excessive wage increases. The regulation was based on actual and forecasted inflation, average wages, and labor productivity.

94

The adjustment was done quarterly, and the tax system was extremely progressive. In the second half of 1992 some corrections were made reducing the rates and the way gross wages were calculated. Rates were adjusted again for 1993.

Experience shows that the restrictive incomes policy had variable success over 1991-93, but the main goal of decreasing real wages and thus of consumer demand (though, to an undesired extent) was achieved.

A specific weakness of the wage control system was that companies could redistribute their wage funds during the fiscal year so that they could indicate lower wage increases than the norm. The wage control system can also influence the unemployment rate. Theory implies that controlling the wage bill increases individual wages and reduces employment (consistent with Koford and Miller, 1986), while wage control maintains jobs and reduces wages. This could explain the correlation between real wage increases and rising unemployment in Bulgaria.

It is also well known that taxes on excessive wage increases is not effective in a soft budget regime. The fact that some unprofitable companies were able to get credits and subsidies from the government worked against hardening the financial constraint. Firms that realized gains from their monopolistic market position increased wages above the norm and paid the penalties.

In general, after the price liberalization, inflation dynamics were high. This means that anti-inflation policy was not very effective and could not prevent inflation's high drift. This was similar to other former planned economies, in which inflation seemed to 'take off' and was difficult to stop despite increased unemployment. In our regression, the exchange rate fall is the major source of the inflation, but that seems to miss other factors. The factors that most experts consider dominated inflation in Bulgaria at this time were the high budget deficit, the floating exchange rate, inflationary expectations, high mark-ups, and the unstable political environment and legal system. A fact that supports the argument for rising markups is the enormous gap between the CPI and PPI and their dynamics for the last three years (Miller, 1995). The changes of the PPI are lagged and much smaller than those of CPI, which provides some evidence against the hypothesis that the cost-push inflation is due to high wages.

In the private sector of the economy there are no wage regulations or controls. Wages are established by agreement between the employer and the employees. The statistical data for private companies is very scarce but, as a rule, wages are higher than in the state-owned companies. This is a positive tendency because it moves workers to the private sector, but it also puts pressure on wages in the public sector.

Finally, similar estimates were made of the effect of both wage and wage bill controls in Poland over 1990-94. The results did not indicate a statistically significant effect of the policy, although the controls there changed often, and did not always bind.

References

Bankov, G. (1994), 'The Incomes Policy for 1994 and the Mechanisms of its Implementation', *Economic Thought*, No. 3, pp. 3-25 (in Bulgarian).

Bogetic, Zeljko and Fox, Louise (1993), 'Incomes Policy During Stabilization: A Review and Lessons from Bulgaria and Rumania', *Comparative Economic Studies*, Vol. 35, No. 1, pp. 39-57.

Commander, Simon (1995), 'Russia' in Commander, Simon and Coricelli, Fabrizio (eds), *Unemployment, Restructuring, and Labor Market in Eastern Europe and Russia*, The World Bank: Washington, D.C.

—— and Coricelli, Fabrizio (eds) (1995), *Unemployment, Restructuring, and Labor Market in Eastern Europe and Russia*, The World Bank: Washington, D.C.

Coricelli, Fabrizio and Lane, Timothy (1993), 'Wage Control During the Transition from Central Planing to a Market Economy', *The World Bank Research Observer*, Vol. 8, No. 2, July, pp. 195-210.

Coricelli, Fabrizio and Rocha, R. (1991), 'Stabilization Programs in Eastern Europe: A Comparative Analysis of the Polish and Yugoslav Programs of 1990', paper presented at the World Bank Symposium: *Reforming Central and Eastern Europe*, September, Washington, D.C.

Dudov, T. (1993), 'Distribution of Profit and Motivation', *Wage, Income, and Standard of Living*, No. 6, pp. 3-16 (in Bulgarian).

Enev, Tihomir and Koford, Kenneth (1996), 'Incomes Policies in Bulgaria and Poland', Working Paper, University of Delaware: Newark, DE.

International Labor Organization (1994), 'The Bulgarian Challenge: Reforming Labor Market and Social Policy. A Review of the Commission of the European Communities', PHARE PROGRAMME, ILO, Budapest.

Jackman, Richard and Pages, C. (1993), 'Wage Policy and Inflation in Eastern Europe', paper prepared for a World Bank Conference, 7-8 October.

Jones, Derek C. and Meurs, Mieke (1991), 'Worker Participation and Worker Self-Management in Bulgaria', *Comparative Economic Studies*, No. 4, Winter, pp. 47-81.

Koford, Kenneth and Miller, Jeffrey B. (1986), 'Incentive Anti-Inflation Policies in a Model of Market Disequilibrium', in Colander, David C. (ed), *Incentive-Based Incomes Policies*, Ballinger: Cambridge, MA.

—— and Colander, David C. (1993), 'Application of Market Anti-inflation Plans in the Transition to a Market Economy', *Eastern Economic Journal*, Vol. 19, No. 3, Summer, pp. 379-93.

—— and Schneider, Jerrold (1986), 'Plans for Fighting Inflation with Microeconomic Incentives', in Colander, David C. (ed), *Incentive-Based Incomes Policies*, Ballinger: Cambridge, MA.

Miller, Jeffrey B. (1995), 'The Price Index Gap: A Window to Understanding the Bulgarian Economy', *Bulgarian National Bank Quarterly Review*, No. 1.

Pinto, Brian, Belka, Marek, and Krajewski, Stefan (1993), 'Transforming State Enterprises in Poland: Evidence on Adjustment by Manufacturing Firms', *Brookings Papers on Economic Activity*, No. 1, pp. 213-70.

Pinto, Brian and van Wijnbergen, Sweder (1995), 'Ownership and Corporate Control in Poland: Why State Firms Defied the Odds', CEPR Discussion Paper No. 1273, December.

Pishev, Ognyan (1992), 'Bulgaria: Political Economy', Paper for the Hoover Institution Conference on Economy, Society, and Democracy, 7-9 May, Washington D.C.

PlanEcon (1994), *Bulgarian Economic Monitor*, Vol. 10, Nos. 20-22, 18 July.

Stoikov T. (1992), 'Differentiation of Income', *Wage, Income, and Standard of Living*, No. 2, pp. 3-14 (in Bulgarian).

Wendel, Helmut and Manchev, Tsvetan (1994), 'The International Value of the Lev and Its Effect on Domestic Prices', *Bulgarian National Bank Review*, No. 1, pp. 16-20.

World Bank (1990), *Bulgaria: Crisis and Transition to Market Economy*, Vol.1, October, Washington, D.C.

—— (1994), 'Structural Reforms in Bulgaria', Vol. 5, No. 4, April, Policy Research Division/Transforming Economies newsletter.

Notes

1   See Miller, Koford, and Schneider (1986) for a review of different incentive policies, and Koford, Miller, and Colander (1993) for an application to the transition economies.

2   A companion paper considers Poland as well, and examines the contrasts in the two countries' policies. These countries have applied different types of incomes policy in different socioeconomic environments and have different approaches for implementing their stabilization programs, giving some opportunity to learn from the comparison.

3   Wage controls have usually been chosen by western governments. Hungary also controlled wages in the 1970s. Value-added has been advocated by many economists, including Lerner and Colander, Vickrey, and Koford, Miller, and Colander (1993).

4   The same basic argument would still apply if the relationship between Q and L were nonlinear.

5   Some Polish economists actually favored a wage-bill policy because that would cause labor-shedding. Such a policy would not be consistent with the stylized

facts of Polish firms reported in Pinto, Belka, and Krajewski (1993) and Pinto and van Wijnbergen (1995).

6 The World Bank (1990) study gives a good background in English for this early period.

7 See International Labor Organization (1994). This PHARE report gives some background on the labor market and its inflexibility under shocks.

8 See World Bank (1994).

9 More details, including alternative regressions that were estimated, are contained in the working paper Enev and Koford (1996).

10 The average DLCPI was 0.073.

6 Macroeconomic effects of restrictive wage policy in Bulgaria: empirical evidence for 1991-95

Vassil Tzanov and Daniel Vaughan-Whitehead

Introduction

The Bulgarian economy entered its sixth year of reform suffering from abnormally large declines in output, employment, demand, and real wages. In the course of only a few years, unemployment has risen alarmingly and inflation has stabilized at a high level.

Although five years of reform is not a long period it is sufficient to enable us to draw some general conclusions about the efficiency of the macroeconomic policy which was applied and the relationships between macroeconomic indicators.

Since 1991, the Bulgarian authorities have pursued the radical economic strategy also applied in other countries of the region to varying degrees and known as 'shock therapy'. This has involved a particular sequencing of macroeconomic reforms, beginning with price liberalization, followed by a stabilization policy which involved an attempt to impose a tight monetary and fiscal policy in which a restrictive incomes policy always figured prominently.

This restrictive incomes policy as it applied to industrial and public employees was intended to contain cost-push inflation while permitting wages to adjust to increases in living costs. In the event, it led to a sharp fall in real wages over the whole period, and to a growing number of social tensions, in light of which the Government redesigned its incomes policy on a number of occasions. The principal claim of the present paper is that this policy resulted not only in negative social effects, but in extremely adverse economic effects.

We will analyze in detail why this restrictive policy has not been as effective as expected on the macroeconomic side and why it also served to harm production. Using empirical evidence from the period 1991-95 and econometric models for analyzing short-term dynamics, we will test the impact of Bulgarian wage policy and other elements of the restrictive incomes policy on wages, inflation, consumption and employment in a number of different equations.

Wage dynamics, 1991-95

Restrictive incomes policy and the fall in real wages

The changes which this involved were implemented only from 1991.[1] After price liberalization, a tax-based incomes policy was introduced to control cost-push inflation, while simultaneously attempts were made to try to limit the inevitable adverse social effects. This incomes policy was central place to the stabilization program and consisted in the levying of a progressive tax on wage fund increases with the aim of limiting wage growth and keeping inflation under control. After the Government had determined national norms for wage funds, enterprises had to fix wage increases accordingly; those whose wage funds were above the limit were subject to a progressive tax. A number of variants of this policy were applied one after another. At first wage fund norms were to be set annually, but from early 1991 it was decided that they should be adjusted at the end of each quarter. Since then the reference period for the calculation of wage fund growth for the current quarter has also changed several times, variants including the same quarter as the previous year, the first quarter of the current year and the previous quarter. The rate of the progressive tax was also changed several times. In 1991 there was no compensation for inflation and wage fund limits were held constant. With the introduction of collective wage bargaining in July 1991 a new wage regulation system was introduced which preserved the basic principle but allowed for inflation. From 1991, wage fund norms were also supposed to take account of changes in productivity. Following an upsurge in wages and inflation in late 1991, the productivity link was severed in 1992, only to be reintroduced in March the following year. The productivity coefficient was then regularly increased, first in 1994 (from 0.3 to 0.6) and again in 1995 (to 0.95). However, unexpected inflation growth in 1994 led to a considerable tightening of wage regulations in 1994 and 1995.[2]

Public employee wage controls were another important component of the Government's restrictive incomes policy. Public sector wages and salaries were tightly controlled by means of an inflexible grid of job classifications and pay scales. The system of calculating public sector wages on the basis of the statutory minimum wage was retained, the level of these wages remaining constant for more than a year from 1991-92, after which they were adjusted to inflation on an irregular basis. Over the whole period, another important means by which policy-makers controlled public expenditure was the maintenance of the minimum wage at constant or very low levels; this was particularly important because many other public payments were tied to the minimum wage, including public sector pay, unemployment benefit, school and university grants, retirement pensions and child allowances. The value of all these payments fell in real terms.

As a result of these restrictive policy measures, nominal wages lagged well behind consumer price inflation (Figure 6.1). After the implementation of price liberalization at the beginning of 1991, real wages fell by more than 42 per cent over the rest of the year.[3] The switch to a wage bargaining system caused nominal and real wages to increase slightly in 1992-93. However, although wages more than kept pace with prices during this time, the real wage increases of about 19 per cent and one per cent respectively were insufficient to compensate for the vertiginous fall suffered in 1991. Real wages in 1992 remained 28 per cent below their 1990 level. Moreover, a second sharp decrease intervened in 1994 and real wages dropped again by more than 20 per cent, falling again in 1995, although this time by only three per cent. Real wage falls were greatest in the public sector, particularly in education, health and culture which were all subject to severe budgetary restrictions. Sectoral differences continued to grow throughout the period, leading to social tensions and demands for wage increases in some sectors.

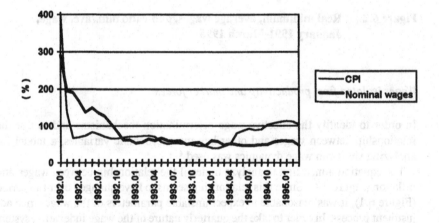

**Figure 6.1   Wage-price inflation (12-months rates),
January 1992-March 1995**

As a result of its delayed and irregular adjustment, the minimum wage broke loose of inflation. The fall in the minimum wage was even greater than the fall in real wages. The Government took advantage of the breakdown of the Tripartite Commission in 1991 to keep the minimum wage unchanged for one year (between July 1991 and July 1992) in order to control the whole wage structure. As a result, the real value of the minimum wage fell by 48 per cent; it also fell relative to the average wage, from 53 per cent in 1991 to 34 per cent in 1995 (Figure 6.2).

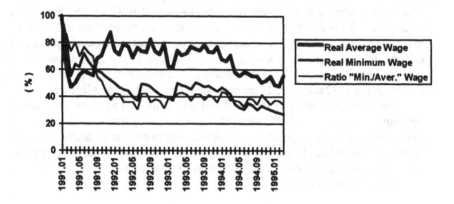

Figure 6.2   Real minimum, average wages, and ratio min./ave. wage, January 1991-March 1995

Wages isolated from productivity and market forces

In order to identify the effective wage determination mechanisms and to test the relationship between wages and other key macroeconomic variables, a model for analyzing short-run wage dynamics was used.[4]

The equation aimed first to analyze in detail the relationship between wages and inflation (Figure 6.1). Since this relationship seems to have changed over the period (Figure 6.1), it was reasonable to expect unstable parameters of the wage-price adjustment process. In order to take the quarterly nature of the wage indexation system into account, the wage variable was integrated in the appropriate 'lagged' form; the unemployment rate was also included in the equation with the necessary lags. This variable was expected to be negative, because an unemployment increase would be expected to reduce wage claims; and because the minimum wage plays an important role in the control of wage increases, a minimum wage variable was included in the equation. A variable measuring real wage progression was expected to appear with a negative coefficient and should be interpreted as the speed of adjustment of wages to

102

the deviation from their long-term path. All variables are in logarithms.[5]

The corresponding wage equation is as follows:

$$\Delta nw_t = \alpha_0 + \alpha_1 \Delta nw_{t\text{-}i} + \alpha_2 \Delta unem_{t\text{-}i} + \alpha_3 \Delta minw_{t\text{-}i} + \alpha_4 \Delta prod_{t\text{-}i} + \alpha_5 \Delta cpi_{t\text{-}i} + \alpha_6 \Delta rw_{t\text{-}1} + \epsilon_t \tag{1}$$

with:

  nw = nominal wage;
  $unem$ = unemployment rate;
  $minw$ = ratio of the minimum wage to the average wage;
  cpi = consumer prices;
  $prod$ = productivity;
  rw = real wages;
  Δ = first difference operator;
  α_i = parameters.

On the basis of these assumptions, we estimated many different wage equations for different periods and with different lagged variables, using 56 monthly observations carried out over the period as a whole (January 1991-September 1995) and over three sub-periods: 1991-92, 1991-93, and 1991-94. This division allowed us to investigate the differentiated impact of the different variants of the restrictive incomes policy. The results are presented in Table 6.1. The dependent variable is nominal wages in Model A and real wages in Model B.

The reported results for Model A show that parameter stability is extremely disturbed when 1994 is included; most parameters became statistically insignificant. This was due to the strong disconnection between wages, prices and productivity which occurred in 1994. The implementation of a very restrictive incomes policy that year succeeded in breaking the close relationship observed until then between wages and prices, and in interrupting the indexation adjustment process.

The results can be summarized as follows. First, the equation shows that the indexation mechanisms implemented between 1991 and 1993 played a crucial role in adjusting wages to price growth, as shown by the positive coefficient of the price index in Model A for 1991-93. It is interesting to note that price increases affected wage increases only at the end of the quarter when a partial adjustment to inflation was implemented (*cpi-4* positive and significant while *cpi* was not significant). It is important to note that the interruption of indexation mechanisms in 1994 is directly reflected in the equation, since the same equation including 1994 results in a non-significant coefficient on the *cpi-4* variable for the whole period (equation 3). At the same time, this result tends to show that wages have not been adequately indexed to

103

Table 6.1
Estimation of the wage equation

Variables	Model A (nominal wage)				Model B (real wage)
	(1) 1991-92	(2) 1991-93	(3) 1991-94	(4) 1991-95	(5) 1991-95
$\alpha 0$	(1.63) 4.1	(1.41) 4.5	(0.38) 2.3	(0.081) 1.1	-
Nw-1	(-0.11) -0.49	(-0.22) -1.4	(0.02) 0.13	(0.227) 1.6	
Nw-3	(0.24) 2.1	(0.117) 1.7	(0.04) 0.7	(-0.148) -1.9	-
Cpi	-	-	-	-	(-1.29) -11.5
Cpi-4	(1.034) 4.2	(0.89) 4.3	(0.113) 0.8	(-0.065) -1.7	-
Unem	(-0.92) -2.1	(-0.31) -1.0	(0.39) 1.9	(0.248) 2.4	(0.033) 2.8
Unem-1	(-0.162) -2.7	(-0.098) -2.2	(-0.04) -0.82	(0.00021) -0.3	(-0.0013) -1.1
Prod-3	(0.15) 2.3	(0.14) 2.8	(0.074) 1.3	(0.103) 2.1	(0.102) 6.0
Minw	(0.38) 2.5	(0.20) 1.7	(0.001) 1.6	(0.095) 2.1	-
Minw-3	-	-	-	-	(0.186) 2.3
Rw-1	(-0.28) -3.1	(-0.26) -3.8	(-0.061) -1.3	(-0.019) -0.8	-
R-squared	0.89	0.77	0.47	0.62	0.81
SE	0.02	0.013	0.025	0.024	0.011
DW	1.66	2.14	2.14	2.1	2.08
LM test for serial correl.(3), p-value	0.04	0.52	0.15	0.14	0.21
ARCH-test, p-value	0.93	0.91	0.17	0.96	0.83
Heterosked. test	0.67	0.42	0.01	0.6	0.62

inflation over the whole period, as both main trade unions, CITUB and Podkrepa, have often claimed. The positive coefficient on the minimum wage variable in the nominal wage equations tends to confirm that the minimum wage has an impact on the whole wage structure. The negative sign of the real wage variable (*rw*) is an indication of how nominal wages and real wages tended to go in different directions. Despite continuous growth in nominal wages, real wages fell significantly – by more than 54 per cent – over the whole period (Tzanov, 1995). The negative and impressively high coefficient (greater than one) on *cpi* in the real wage equation (Model B) confirms that the price increases led to a sharp fall in real wages over the period 1991-95. Equation B confirms the effect of the minimum wage on real wages over the whole period: the downward trend of the minimum wage contributed to the fall in real wages. The Government's pressure on the statutory minimum wage, which was kept at a constant or extremely low level, thus successively contributed to the fall in real wages. Tragically, for millions of workers and their families, in Bulgaria like in all other countries of Central and Eastern Europe, the minimum wage became a means by which impoverishment was intensified (Standing and Vaughan-Whitehead, 1995). However, it is interesting to observe that the coefficient of *minw* lost significance over the period, and was found to be particularly weak when 1994 was included in the equation. This would confirm that the restrictive wage policy implemented in 1994 helped progressively to lower the impact of the minimum wage on the whole wage structure by keeping the minimum wage at extremely low levels. The continuation of such a policy, apart from exacerbating already extreme and widespread poverty, would gradually reduce the Government's ability to control wage progression in the economy.

A positive relationship was found to exist between unemployment and real wages. Normally – for example, as observed in market economies – there is an inverse relationship between wages and unemployment: wages fall when unemployment rises and rise when unemployment falls. Such a relationship seems to have prevailed in the period 1991-93, as shown by the negative coefficient on *unem* and *unem-1* in the nominal wage equation (equations 1 and 2 for Model A). Nevertheless, this negative coefficient disappeared when 1994 was included in the analysis (eq. 3), and was found to be positively correlated to real wage growth for the period as a whole (eq. 5). This result is important because it seems to confirm that a very restrictive wage policy can modify the normal relationship between wages and employment. This result may reflect the following combination of phenomena, observed in the first years of reform in Bulgaria: first, a low wage policy may have induced enterprises to maintain existing labor force levels and to delay their restructuring and layoff programs; this policy appeared to be particularly advantageous in 1991 because the wage fund was calculated according to the number of employees at the enterprise; in 1992-93 real wages increased while unemployment continued to grow (Figure 6.6). A reverse trend appeared in 1994, when unemployment started to decline while real wages began to fall dramatically. Second, most enterprises in the public sector maintained very high levels of employment despite very low productivity and poor performance. At the same time, they also experienced their highest fall in real wages, public sector wages being determined on the basis of the minimum wage which was kept at a constantly low level. This restrictive policy also led in these sectors to serious delays in restructuring. Third, because of the wage fund tax, the most profitable sectors experiencing higher productivity and employment growth could not convert performance and employment growth into higher wages, so contributing to the reinforcement of the positive relationship between unemployment (or negative between employment growth) and wage levels.

Another important result found in the wage equation was the very weak connection (with a positive but very low coefficient) between productivity and wage increases, despite government attempts to accompany wage regulations with a formula aimed at linking wage fund norms to productivity growth. This coefficient was found to be insignificant when 1994 was included in the analysis (eq. 3), so indicating that severe wage restrictions helped to disconnect wages from productivity altogether. The same productivity variable appeared with a positive but small coefficient in the real wage equation, probably reflecting the developments induced by the tax-based incomes policy (ILO-CEET, 1994). Real wages have grown the most in enterprises where productivity was the lowest – for example, monopolistic enterprises – and have been severely limited in the most profitable and productive enterprises which were constrained by the tax-based incomes policy. The restrictive wage policy was found to hamper enterprises in their efforts to link wages to productivity and economic performance (Tzanov, 1995), a result also found in other countries of the region (ILO-CEET and EC, 1995). This lack of a strong correlation between wages and productivity is also shown in Figure 6.3 which presents real wage and productivity dynamics from 1992-95. This lack of connection clearly appears again in 1994, when real wages started to fall sharply again while productivity rates tended to grow in a very irregular manner.

This weak connection between wages and productivity combined with the evidence suggesting that the *cpi* is one of the most significant determinants of wage leads us to question the feasibility of linking part of wages to something other than price growth when prices are suddenly liberalized, especially in economies in which initial wage levels were already extremely low, as in the former communist countries. In such a context, wage negotiations, if any, tend to focus on inflation and leave no room for linking wages to productivity or enterprise performance. This also seems to show that 'shock therapy' with the aim of liberalizing prices in a very short period of time was not the way to solve the tremendous fall in production experienced by the economies in transition. In order to leave some room to link part of wages to productivity and so help to solve the production crisis, a more progressive policy would certainly have had better results. This also calls into question the efficiency of a centrally determined formula linking wages to productivity, which can only reflect an easily observable output measure: the ratio sales/number of employees which was adopted by the Government, for example, only provides an approximate measure of productivity. In a context of progressive decentralization of wage determination, and in a period in which productivity is the result of the microeconomic behavior of workers – and so more and more difficult to monitor – a scheme that would link part of wages to productivity determined at the enterprise or establishment level between employers and unions would be much more efficient.

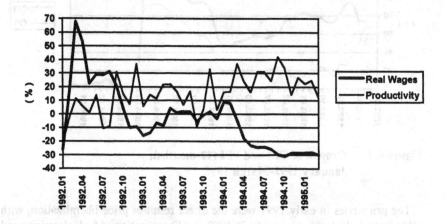

Figure 6.3   Real wages and productivity (12-months rates), January 1992-March 1995

Wrong anchor for inflation

Because of the presentation of wages as the leading inflationary factor throughout the reform process the Government decided to use wage controls as the main anchor of inflation. It was therefore important for us to test the precise impact of wages on inflation.

The price liberalization initiated early in 1991 immediately led to active inflationary processes and a high rate of inflation. After 1991, consumer price dynamics can be characterized by episodic price shocks and by short or long periods of acceleration and deceleration (Figure 6.4).

Besides seasonal fluctuations, Figure 6.4 shows that the general tendency towards a progressive deceleration of inflation was interrupted in 1994, only to be resumed later in the same year and in 1995. The most striking characteristics of inflation in Bulgaria from 1992 seem to be its changing nature and its numerous determinants which also tend to change over time.

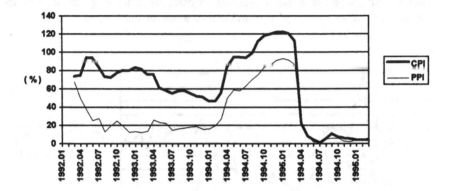

**Figure 6.4   Growth of CPI and PPI (12-months),
            January 1992-March 1995**

The price rises in early 1991 were the direct result of price liberalization, with other factors playing a minor role. In 1992, the liberalization of fuel, electricity and agricultural prices led to a further upsurge in inflation. Other inflationary sources such as the budget deficit, the falling exchange rate and inflationary expectations also seem to have played a part, mainly in the second half of 1991 and in 1992.

However, Figures 6.5, 6.6, and 6.7 which compare monthly inflation rates (presented on an annual basis) to the growth of money supply (M1), exchange rates, unemployment and nominal wages show that these variables did not closely follow changes in the rate of inflation; in some cases, they even seem to have moved in a totally different direction.

For instance in 1992, as shown in Figure 6.5, the depreciation of the Bulgarian leva did not correspond to the movements of inflation observed in the first six months. A similar picture can be drawn in respect of money supply growth (M1) which clearly lagged well behind price increases. From Figure 6.7, we can draw similar conclusions with regard to nominal wage increases which lagged well behind price increases in 1991-92. Unemployment and inflation in 1992 experienced a similar upward trend indicating the absence of any trade-off between them.

A constant fall in monthly inflation rates characterized 1993, annual inflation being limited to 59 per cent. The moderate depreciation of the currency and the growth of M1 did not affect inflation dynamics. At the same time, unemployment continued to grow but at a lower rate; in some months the number of unemployed even fell. It is also important to note that the growth of the budget deficit in 1993 (11 per cent of GDP) was accompanied by lower inflation.

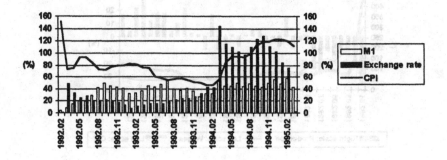

Figure 6.5   Inflation, money supply (M1), and exchange rate, February 1992-March 1995

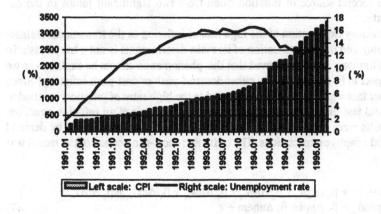

Figure 6.6   Inflation and unemployment, January 1991-March 1995

Contrary to expectations, inflation in 1994 exploded again with a magnitude comparable to 1991. Between January and December, accumulated inflation reached 122 per cent, double its 1993 rate. Although monetary policy was tightened up in the second half of the year inflation continued to rise. In addition, drastic restrictions on wage increases led to a further dramatic fall in real wages, with serious social and economic effects.

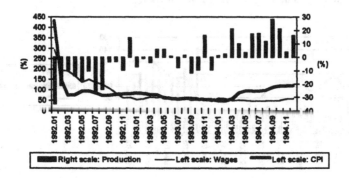

Figure 6.7   Inflation, wages, and production, 1992-94

Two elements in particular seem to have affected inflation in 1994: the first was
the introduction of VAT (April 1994), which stoked up existing inflationary expectations; the second source of inflation came from two significant jumps in the exchange rate.

A satisfactory explanation of the high rate of inflation in the transitional Bulgarian economy and the quantification of its main determinants is not a trivial task. In
fact, a preliminary analysis showed that this phenomenon cannot be explain – as we
might expect to be able to do – by either demand-push or cost-push inflation.[6] Since
many other factors seem to have contributed to the high rates of inflation, we tried to
identify and test those factors by the econometric analysis of an inflation equation.
Good results were obtained using the Phillips curve model augmented by demand
factors and adaptive expectations. The estimated short-run version of the model was
as follows:

$$\Delta cpi = \beta_0 + \beta_1 \, \Delta cpi_{-1} + \beta_2 \, \Delta nw_{-1} + \beta_3 \, \Delta nw_{-4} + \beta_4 \, \Delta exr_{-1} + \beta_5 \, \Delta M1_{-1} +$$
$$\beta_6 \, \Delta prod_{-4} + \beta_7 \, \Delta ppi + \beta_8 \, \Delta unem + \epsilon_t \tag{2}$$

with:

    cpi = consumer price index;
    nw = nominal wages;
    exr = exchange rate;
    M1 = money supply;
    prod = production;
    ppi = producer price index;

unem = unemployment rate;
Δ = operator of the first difference;
β_i = parameters.

The results show high and statistically significant coefficients of multiple correlation, a relatively low standard error of estimation and an appropriate misspecification test for serial correlation, parameter constancy and heteroskedasticity (Table 6.2).

Table 6.2
Estimation of the inflation equation

Variable	Estimation	t-statistics
β0	0.013	2.5
Cpi-1	0.311	2.8
Nw-1	-0.06	-0.5
Nw-4	0.09	1.3
Exr-1	0.128	2.5
M1-1	0.081	1.9
Prod-4	-0.095	-1.8
Ppi	0.336	4.2
Unem	0.124	2.3
R-squared	0.73	-
SE	0.013	-
DW	1.93	-
LM-test (3) p-value	0.87	-
ARCH-test (3), p-value	0.74	-
Heteroskedasticity test, p-value	0.69	-

The current level of inflation was found to be determined mainly by previous levels, emphasizing the important role of inflationary expectations in a self-sustaining process.[7]

Wage increases did not create any inflationary pressure, as shown by the insignificant coefficient on nominal wages despite the indexation mechanism used between 1991-93 and 1995. Although this result might be partly due to the restrictive wage policy, which may have contributed somehow to limit the spiral of wage and price increases, the fact that inflation continued to grow while wages were under strict control supports the view that wages have not been the main inflationary factor in

111

Bulgaria at any time during transition: in fact, given that wage costs represented only a minor proportion – 13 per cent in 1992 – of total production costs, the impact of wage growth on inflation could only have been small.

This result confirms the often contradictory trends characterizing prices and real wage increases (Figure 6.7): while in 1991 price liberalization and inflation growth led to a sharp fall in real wages, there was no jump in inflation when wages were more regularly adjusted to inflation in 1992 and 1993. In 1994, real wages started to fall again, while inflation increased rapidly, clearly the result of other inflationary sources.

These results indicate that wages were not the main inflationary factor and that the macroeconomic policy based on strict control of wages and incomes was ill-advised. Inflation has continued to grow at accelerating rates despite wage controls and appears to be determined by several other factors, as is also shown by other variables included in the equation.

In particular, the development of exchange rates, notably the depreciation of the leva, was found to be of crucial importance: *exr* has a positive coefficient in the inflation equation. Exchange rate coefficients were extremely unstable throughout the period. Recursive estimations resulted in higher coefficients during 1994 which means that the influence of exchange rates on domestic prices became stronger that year. The efforts of the National Bank of Bulgaria to support a non-inflationary exchange rate seem to have been unsuccessful, particularly in 1994; the adaptation of the exchange rate to the purchasing power of the leva was carried out by means of major adjustments which generated significant inflationary impulses and provoked further inflationary expectations and speculations.[8]

In the short-run equation M1 appears with a positive but low coefficient, and a more significant but still positive coefficient in the long run.[9] This low coefficient in the short-run equation means that money creation did not have much effect on inflation, at least in the short term. We saw in fact in Figure 6.5 that the growth of M1 lagged well behind inflation growth, a phenomenon which could be due to the application of restrictive monetary measures. Nevertheless, its still positive – and more significant in the long run – coefficient tends to underline the limited effectiveness of monetary instruments (such as control of M1) in the long run, given the influence on inflation of other factors outside the monetary sphere. In this context, the application of even more restrictive measures would not lead to better results in the fight against inflation.

The increase in producer prices, for example, played a major role in pushing up consumer prices, as shown by the positive and strong effect of *ppi*. The rising cost of raw materials, fuel and electricity constituted the major source of inflation: their share of total costs was 72 per cent in 1990 and 69 per cent in 1992 (ILO-CEET, 1994). The fall in industrial production also had a significant effect on inflation growth, although this was only to be expected in light of the marked falls in demand and output.

Unemployment appeared to be positively connected to inflation, both having experienced continuous growth over the period.

Interest rates that we had included in the equation were not significant, although the National Bank of Bulgaria used a gradual increase in the base interest rate to restrict the money supply and limit inflation (BNB, 1995).

The above empirical results entitle us to draw some general conclusions about the nature of inflation over the period under investigation and the effectiveness of the various policy instruments applied by the Bulgarian Government.

First, the estimations do not support demand-push inflation, suggesting rather an inflation process fed by production costs (mainly raw materials) and inflationary expectations. Strict control of monopolistic enterprises and the adoption of corresponding anti-monopoly laws should progressively help to limit this inflationary source.

Second, the model ruled out a causal relationship between wages and prices: an inverse causality was found from prices to wages (interrupted in 1994). Moreover, the low share of wages in production costs and falling real wages render highly questionable the attribution of part of inflation to wage rises for the purpose of justifying the tax-based incomes policy.[10] Third, the restrictive monetary policy – controlling both the money supply and interest rates – does seem to have had a limited impact on inflation. Its limited effectiveness in the long run seems to show that the application of more restrictive measures would not lead to better results, since many other inflationary sources seem to be outside the monetary sphere. Moreover, monetary policy did not manage to control exchange rates which also turned out to be a considerable source of inflation. The depreciation of the leva substantially reduced the National Bank's ability to control the money supply, so undermining its whole monetary policy (BNB, 1995). This underlines the need to back up macroeconomic programs with a careful exchange rate policy, particularly in light of the important role played by inflationary expectations and speculations identified in our equation.

Collapse of consumption

Surprisingly, the impact of the fall in real average and minimum wages on the national level and structure of consumption has not been stressed in debates on wage developments in Central and Eastern Europe. In all countries of the region, the early phases of reform have undoubtedly been accompanied by severe adverse effects on aggregate demand.[11] In Bulgaria, over a period of four years (1991-94), personal consumption fell by 40 per cent and continued to fall in 1995.

An analysis of the determinants of real consumption clearly identified two major factors which explain its decline: the fall in real incomes and the growth of interest rates on bank savings accounts. Figure 6.8 shows how closely consumption levels

113

followed real income changes between 1991 and 1995; Figure 6.9 shows how consumption progressively declined alongside interest rate increases.

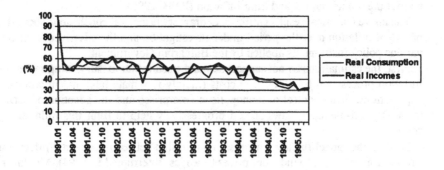

**Figure 6.8   Household real incomes and real consumption,
January 1991=100**

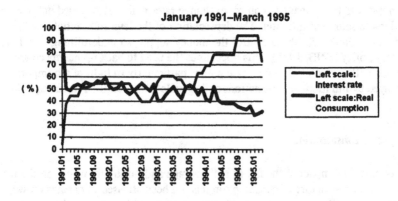

**Figure 6.9   Consumption and interest rates,
January 1991-March 1995**

Interest payments became an important source of income, increasing from 0.6 per cent of total income in 1990 to 12 per cent in 1991 and 14 per cent in 1992. According to Table 6.3 savings increased significantly in 1991 (especially early 1991) and 1992 due to interest rate growth. Savings accounted for more than 24 per cent of households incomes in 1991. Apart from the jump in interest rates, economic uncertainty and growing unemployment also encouraged people to save more as a precautionary measure in spite of accelerating inflation.

Table 6.3
Distribution of disposable income, Bulgaria, 1990-94 (%)

Year	Consumption	Taxes	Savings	Other
1990	74.9	7.4	2	15.7
1991	71.9	6.5	14.4	7.2
1992	62.8	8.1	24.3	4.8
1993	69.4	6.8	19.8	4
1994	73.8	6.9	16.9	2.4
1995	75.4	7.1	15.4	2.1

The recomposition of income and wage structures also contributed to modify consumption patterns. The restrictive incomes policy and consequent erosion of real wages led to two major phenomena: a fall in the wage share of total income – from 55 per cent in 1990 to less than 40 per cent in 1995 (Tzanov, 1995) – and the substitution of monetary incomes by non-monetary payments which rose above 20 per cent. Both these phenomena can be accounted for the high consumption by households – particularly rural households – of their own production. From 1990 to 1995, the share of non-monetary income in agriculture increased from 21 per cent to more than 35 per cent. It is interesting to note that non-monetary sources of income mainly grew under the restrictive incomes policy of 1991 (up to 20 per cent of total income). Relaxation of incomes policy in 1992-93 caused a reverse trend, with a reduction of non-monetary sources of income (to less than 14 per cent); the more restrictive wage regulations applied in 1994 resulted in another increase (to nearly 16 per cent) in the share of non-monetary sources of income (Tzanov, 1995).

The fall in the purchasing power of Bulgarian households and the continuous price increases led them to restructure their consumption patterns and in particular to increase the proportion of their budget spent on food items at the expense of other basic items of expenditure (Table 6.4). It is interesting to observe that the structure of consumption closely followed changes in the restrictive incomes policy and consequent falls in real wages. For instance, the percentage of expenditure on food items rapidly increased in parallel with the 42 per cent drop in real wages of 1991, fell slightly after the real wage increases of 1992-93, but increased again in 1994 when real wages started to fall again. Expenditure on food reached nearly 50 per cent of the average household budget in 1994. It is important to note that the share of food expenditure in Western countries is rarely more than 30 per cent of total household consumption. Other expenditure, though no less basic – for example, on clothes and transport – necessarily fell in periods of severe wage restraint (mainly 1991 and 1994). Other reports indicate that expenditure on education and health also fell dramatically (Tzanov, 1995).

Table 6.4
Structure of household consumer expenditure, Bulgaria, 1991-95

Year	Food	Cloth	Housing	Equipm't	Transport	Other
1990	36.3	11.9	7.3	4.3	8	32.2
1991	47.4	8.6	7.3	3	6.7	27
1992	46.9	8.3	7.3	3.9	7.7	25.9
1993	42.9	8	8	4	7.9	29.1
1994	45	7.4	7.5	3.7	7.7	28.7
1995	46.3	7.1	7.9	3.8	7.5	27.1

We tried to confirm these relationships by the econometric analysis of a consumption equation. The consumption equation was defined in accordance with traditional macroeconomic consumption functions, based on the assumption of permanent income. Since consumption appeared to be stable during the transition period, we decided to test, in both the short and long term, the possible explanatory factors of consumption changes.

We first tested the following long-run consumption model:

$$\text{rcons}_t = \beta_0 + \beta_1 \text{rinc}_t + \beta_2 \text{cpi}_t + \beta_3 \text{itr}_t + \epsilon_t \qquad (3)$$

with:

rcons = real consumption;
rinc = real income;
cpi = consumer price index;
itr = interest rate.

The explanatory variables were found to have a long-term relationship with consumption with a valid correction mechanism. The estimated propensity to consume in the long run was found to be reliable and economically rational.

The equation confirmed that the restrictive wages and incomes policy and the subsequent fall in real incomes (very strong positive coefficient on *rinc*) had as their direct effect a decrease in the level of global consumption, as already shown in Figure 6.8. The equation also confirmed the negative influence of price increases on consumption, the variable on *cpi* appearing with a significant, although surprisingly low coefficient. Its low coefficient could be due to the fact that the real income variable – which already incorporates inflation – captured part of the effects of inflation on consumption. It is also possible that consumption had reached its lowest level so rendering it more or less insensitive to further price increases.

Table 6.5
Estimation of the long-run consumption function, Bulgaria

Variable	Coefficient	T-statistics
β0	1.54	4.9
Rinc	0.703	12.5
Itr	-0.059	-1.6
Cpi	-0.064	-3.6
R-squared	0.97	-
DW	2.31	-

The short-run consumption model incorporated the same factors as the long-run version but with appropriate lagged variables:

$$\Delta rcons = \beta_0 + \beta_1 \Delta rcons_{-1} + \beta_2 \Delta rcons_{-2} + \beta_3 \Delta rinc + \beta_4 \Delta rinc_{-1} + \beta_5 \Delta\, itr + \beta_6 \Delta cpi + \beta_7 \Delta cpi_{-1} + \epsilon_t \qquad (4)$$

The estimated parameters confirmed that the relatively low short-run propensity to consume was mainly the result of low real incomes, high inflation and savings compensations (Table 6.6).

The short-run consumption equation clearly confirms the direct and strong negative effect of the fall in real incomes on consumption levels that was found in the long-run model. Although this positive relationship between the two variables (income and consumption) appeared very strongly in both (short- and long-run) equations, it has been systematically neglected in the economic policies followed by the successive governments. Government and in the macroeconomic models put forward by the IMF and the World Bank. We, on the other hand, would like to empha-

117

size the important negative macroeconomic effect that falls in real wages, not only in Bulgaria but also in other countries of the region, have had in terms of consumption and production. Further, the collapse of domestic aggregate demand and internal markets have had a detrimental effect on foreign investment, another phenomenon which has not attracted much attention from policy-makers and requires more in-depth analysis.

The *cpi* variables were found to have strong coefficients on consumption levels, this negative price elasticity contradicting the assumption of a 'money illusion effect' in favor of expected inflation.

Table 6.6
Estimation of the short-run consumption function, Bulgaria

Variable	Coefficient	t-statistics
β0	0.015	0.9
Rcons-1	-0.546	-3.7
Rcons-2	-0.221	-2.5
Rinc	0.528	3.3
Rinc-1	0.361	2.9
Itr	-0.243	-1.4
Cpi	-0.272	-2.3
Cpi-1	-0.243	-1.8
R-squared	0.77	-
SE of estim.	0.04	-
DW	2.2	-
Ser. cor. LM-test, p-value	0.28	-
ARCH-test, p-value	0.76	-
Heterosked.	0.56	-

Dubious effects on employment

Under the communist regime there was a firm commitment to the preservation of so-called 'full employment' within the framework of which unemployment was not recognized officially, wages were kept at very low levels and labor hoarding was practiced at all enterprises. Since the beginning of the reform process, there has been a massive change in the level and pattern of employment: the overall decline between 1990 and 1992 was proportionately greater than in any other Central and East European country. According to the National Statistical Institute, total employment between 1990 and the end of 1994 fell by nearly 45 per cent (Table 6.7). Industry, agriculture, construction and transport were most seriously affected. All industrial sectors contributed to the employment decline, with the exception of the small financial services and banking sector. A rapid rate of increase in private economic activity (by 24 per cent between 1990 and 1994) could not compensate the heavy job losses in the state and cooperative sectors.

This rapid growth in unemployment can be explained mainly by the collapse of both the CMEA and internal markets which led to a plummeting industrial output. Other factors, such as the restrictive stabilization program, the unsteady progress of property restitution, the dissolution of agricultural cooperatives and massive labor hoarding under the communist regime also played an important role.

Table 6.7 shows how the fall in employment closely followed the collapse of industrial output.

Table 6.7
Employment dynamics, Bulgaria, 1990-94 (rates of growth – %)

	1990	1991	1992	1993	1994	1995
Real wages	100	63.4	76.7	72.6	47.7	44.1
Employment	100	81.2	68.9	60.6	55.4	-
Output	100	77.8	65.4	58.3	60.9	63.0

A clear picture of both employment and industrial output trends is presented in Figure 6.10. After experiencing a simultaneous reduction until 1993, they started to follow different trends in 1994.

Real wages also experienced a general downward trend over the whole period. Between 1990 and 1994 employment fell sharply by 45 per cent, while real wages fell by more than 53 per cent (Figure 6.10). However, they also followed different trends in 1992 and 1993 when real wages started to increase while employment continued to fall. This relationship also varied by sector. Five different types of enterprise could be distinguished:[12]

• in budget-financed enterprises employment cuts were less drastic but real wages declined, mainly because of the budget situation. This was particularly the case in education, health, science and culture where the number of employees between 1990 and 1994 was reduced by only seven per cent but real wages fell by more than 50 per cent. As a result, the public sector share of employment increased;

119

- in monopolistic branches that received substantial subsidies and credit (such as energy, ferrous metallurgy and coal mining) and generally experienced a decline in production and productivity, there was no production restructuring or massive layoffs, but real wages remained well above the national average and continued to increase. Despite the wage fund tax, these enterprises were ready to pay penalty taxes from their subsidies in order to distribute higher wages;
- in other poorly performing industries (such as machine-building and textiles), both employment and relative wages fell;
- in some profitable sectors (such as printing), productivity increased after restructuring and layoff programs, but enterprises could not convert this better economic performance into higher wages because of restrictive regulations on wage fund growth. Real wages in these sectors fell by much more than the national average; in other profitable enterprises, employment and productivity simultaneously increased but real wage increases remained limited;
- in the highly successful financial services and banking sector, high profits led to an increase in employment and wages.

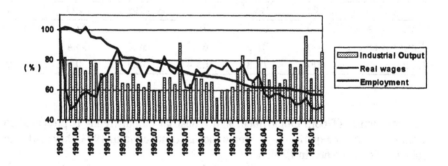

Figure 6.10   Employment, real wages, and industrial output, January 1991-March 1995 (January 1991=100)

In order to identify short-run employment dynamics, the following model was applied:

$$\Delta empl = \beta_1 \Delta empl_{-1} + \beta_2 \Delta empl_{-2} + \beta_3 \Delta rw_{-3} + \beta_4 \Delta prod_{-1} + \beta_5 \Delta prod_{-3} + \beta_6 \Delta itr + \beta_7 \Delta cpi + \epsilon_t \tag{5}$$

The estimated coefficients confirmed the assumption of a strong relationship between employment, production and wages (Table 6.8).[13]

Table 6.8
Estimation of the employment equation

Variable	Coefficient	t-statistics
Empl-1	-0.59	-5.2
Empl-2	-0.489	-6.3
Rw-3	0.06	-6.7
Prod-1	0.045	2.5
Prod-3	0.04	1.9
Itr	0.123	-1.8
Cpi	0.039	2
R-squared	0.84	-
DW	1.89	-
LM-test for ser. correlation	0.56	-
ARCH-test (3), p-value	0.37	-
Heteroskedasticity, p-value	0.78	-

Real wages were found to be inversely related to employment growth. Falls in real wages thus corresponded to employment growth. This result is in accordance with the traditional theoretical relationship expected between employment and wages, employment growing when wages are lower, and employment decreasing when the labor force becomes too expensive. This result, however, which matches the positive relationship found with unemployment in the wage equation also reflects the specific nature of the Bulgarian economy. We saw that although both real wages and employment declined over the whole period, they often followed different directions in the short term: after 1991 when they both decreased, employment continued to fall in 1992 and 1993 while real wages increased; in 1994, employment reductions decreased (the unemployment growth rate fell, as shown in Figure 6.6) while real wages dropped dramatically. It might also reflect the effects of the tax-based incomes policy which clearly encouraged enterprises – through a policy of low wages – to maintain their labor force levels and to delay their restructuring and layoff programs. This result also applies to the situation prevailing in enterprises in the public sector which maintained very high levels of employment despite very low productivity and poor performance, but also experienced the highest fall in real wages. Finally, this negative relationship might have occurred in profitable sectors which experienced higher productivity and employment growth but could not convert performance and employment growth into higher wages.

Production was also found to be positively related to employment levels, confirming that employment fell as a direct consequence of the production crisis.

The negative and significant coefficient on *itr* would confirm the role lowering interest rates might play in promoting productive investment in industry and employment creation, especially in the dynamically emerging private sector and among new small and medium-sized enterprises.

The strong coefficient of lagged employment variables also shows the considerable inertia in the process of employment reduction. Enterprises which have already carried out restructuring and implemented layoff programs will be less likely to continue to reduce employment.

Conclusion

The tax-based incomes policies pursued in many transitional economies were expected to control inflation and to help enterprises to restructure and improve efficiency. The situation in Bulgaria after five years of reform shows that this policy can lead not only to the increasing social inequality which is observable everywhere, it can also exacerbate economic inefficiency. Bulgaria is one of the few countries in Central and Eastern Europe persisting with a tax-based incomes policy despite its questionability as a macroeconomic tool.

Our econometric analysis confirmed that the fall in real wages led to a tremendous fall in consumption; further investigation showed that its structure was also profoundly affected.

Moreover, this policy was found to have limited the scope for linking wages to productivity and other indicators of economic performance. Wage regulations over the period in question allowed wages to be partially and irregularly adjusted only to price increases which appeared to be the most significant determinant in the wage equation. No doubt low wages also helped to reduce human capital and affected workers' motivation and productivity.

These two factors – low productivity and the fall in consumption – clearly aggravated the production crisis and certainly had indirect adverse effects on employment. Low wages probably also led several employers to maintain overemployment and so to reduce or delay the necessary restructuring.

Finally, the advantages of such an anti-inflationary policy were revealed to be dubious to say the least. Wages were found to have no significant inflationary effect: our results showed that inflation was led by many other factors, particularly exchange rates, money supply, production prices and inflationary expectations. The fact that wages represent a minor proportion of total production costs is an additional argument for considering wage controls as unnecessary in the present phase of the transformation process.

To summarize, quite apart from the constraints to which it subjected microeconomic behavior, this restrictive policy cannot be shown to have achieved anything on the macroeconomic side. This is an issue of strategic importance relative to the restrictive incomes policy pursued by the Bulgarian Government under pressure from the IMF and other international advisory bodies. Although introduced as an anti-inflationary device, it seems to have distorted the wage mechanism and prevented it from fulfilling its all-important incentive and productivity-enhancing role. By promoting a fall in aggregate demand and amplifying the productivity crisis, it tended to worsen the most serious production crisis that Bulgaria has yet faced.

In this context, it is important that the Bulgarian authorities reconsider their restrictive incomes policy and its central place at the heart of their economic reforms. The Government might consider the potential benefits that a progressive relaxation of wage controls – in tandem with an appropriate monetary policy – might have for the economy, boosting consumption and productivity and so progressively improving employment prospects. A process of national negotiations on wage increases, with some collective agreements at more decentralized levels, may also be a more appropriate mechanism for fixing wages in accordance with economic conditions. The removal of wage regulations in other countries of the region shows – at least provisionally – that it is possible, through consultation and negotiation with employers' and workers' representatives, to design an incomes policy able to provide the necessary microeconomic incentives without having detrimental effects on inflation.

Notes

1   For a more detailed description of the wage determination and wage policy followed during the period 1990-93, see ILO-CEET and EC (1994) and Bankov (1993).

2   The inflation rate during 1994 (January-December) was 122 per cent, while expected inflation was 45-55 per cent.

3   According to the World Bank (1993), this should be seen in the context of a substantial increase in real wages in 1990. This increase in real wages, however, was of only eight per cent, compared to the mentioned fall of 42 per cent in 1991.

4   The short-term wage dynamics model assumes that wages are set on imperfect competitive markets, with exchanges taking place outside equilibrium because of imperfect competition in respect of both goods and labor markets (Charemza, 1994). This means that wages are the result of both the bargain-

ing process and expected prices, the latter being set as a mark-up on expected costs (Layard and Nickell, 1991). Since the concept of imperfect competitive markets is not fully satisfactory for explaining wage dynamics in Bulgaria, however, we incorporated in the basic model other features specific to the Bulgarian wage determination system.

5   This equation is given in error correction mechanism (ECM) form where real wages are used as a direct ECM. In support of this, it is reasonable to assume that there is a long-term co-integration relation between wages and prices. This is supported by the evidence that real wages are integrated in the order of 1- I(1) and lrw = lnw-lcpi.

6   Preliminary estimations based upon pure inflation models – the results of which are not presented here – did not support either a demand- or a cost-push explanation of inflation in Bulgaria.

7   This inertia characterized the whole period under study – the recursive estimation of the coefficient is also extremely stable.

8   This result seems to confirm other analyses of inflation determinants, according to which the impact of the exchange rate was considered to be quite important – around 0.4 per cent – indicating that a one per cent change in the exchange rate would have entailed a 0.4 per cent change in inflation (Minasian, 1995). According to the same study, the budget deficit would have accounted for 25 per cent of inflation growth and monetary aggregates – represented by internal debt – nearly 30 per cent. The effects of production were found to be low and statistically insignificant. Wages did not appear to be a major determinant of inflation.

9   The results of the long-run regression are not presented here.

10   According to the World Bank, 'the increase in the wage bill was an important factor in the resurgence of inflation towards the end of 1991' (World Bank, 1993, op. cit., p. 25).

11   For evidence of the adverse effects of restrictive wage policies on aggregate demand and consumption in the region, see Vaughan-Whitehead, Daniel (1995).

12   This typology of enterprises in which the relationship between wages and employment is totally different shows the need to further investigate employment determinants of employment by a cross sectional analysis.

13   The high coefficient of adjusted R^2 and the relatively low standard error of the estimation supported the sound specification of the model. However, serial correlation and heteroskedasticity effects appeared in residuals, although the model was estimated by a procedure which incorporated first order autocorrelation and second order moving average terms.

References

Angelov, R. (ed) (1995), *Economic Outlook of Bulgaria*, Sofia.

Bankov, G. (1993), 'The Cabinet New Views on the Policy Concerning the Incomes of the Population', paper presented at the ILO Conference on 'Restructuring Labor Practices in Bulgarian Industry', 18-20 May, Sofia.

Bulgarian National Bank (1995), *The Bulgarian Banking System*, Sofia.

Charemza, W. (1994), The LAM Models for East European Economies: General Description, University of Leicester, mimeo.

ILO-CEET and European Commission (1994), *The Bulgarian Challenge: Reforming Labor Market and Social Policy*, Country Objective Review, Budapest.

ILO-CEET and European Commission (1995), *Reforming Wage Policy in Central and Eastern Europe*, Vaughan-Whitehead, Daniel (ed), prepared for the ILO-EC International Symposium on 'Wages, Efficiency and Social Cohesion: Towards a Negotiated Wage Policy in Central and Eastern Europe', 29 November-1 December, Budapest.

Layard, R. and Nickell, R.S. (1991), 'Unemployment in Britain', *Economica*, Vol. 53, pp. S121-69.

Minasian, G. (ed) (1995), *Bulgarian Economy: Today and Tomorrow*, Book 4, Sofia.

Standing, G. and Vaughan-Whitehead, D. (1995), *Minimum Wages in Central and Eastern Europe: From Protection to Destitution*, ILO-CEET and Central European University Press.

Tzanov, V. (1995), 'For a Negotiated Alternative to Tax-based Incomes Policy in Bulgaria', Chapter 4 in Vaughan-Whitehead, Daniel (ed), *Reforming Wage Policy in Central and Eastern Europe*, ILO-CEET and European Commision.

World Bank (1993), *Bulgaria: An Economic Update*, World Bank Report, May.

World Bank-EDI (1994), *Unemployment, Restructuring and the Labor Market in East Europe and Russia*, Commander, S. and Coricelli, F. (eds).

Part Three
MONEY AND CAPITAL MARKET

7   A role for an independent central bank in transition? The case of Bulgaria

Lubomir Christov

> *The tragedy of Bulgaria is that its Central bank is independent.*
>
> Stoyan Alexandrov,
> Minister of Finance (1993-94)

Introduction

The process of transition from centrally planned to market economies, evolving in Central and Eastern Europe (CEE), is perhaps the most challenging event of the 20th century. The pace and the depth of the political, social, economic and institutional reforms are unprecedented under peaceful (luckily, in most of the countries) conditions. Privatization and financial sector reforms are two pillars of the re-establishment of market-guided economic structures in the countries in CEE.

The financial sector reforms encompass a long list of profound structural and institutional changes. Banking reform lies at the heart of the financial sector restructuring. The creation of capital markets comes second in importance. The goal of reforming the banking sector is to put in place a functioning two-tier banking system. The commercial banking 'tier' would presumably be able to support private sector development by mobilizing the savings from non-financial sectors and channeling them to the most efficient investments. The monetary authority (central bank) 'tier' would be responsible for conducting the monetary policy and supervising and regulating the banking system. This paper examines the five-year old Bulgarian experience with central banking reform. It applies the methodology developed by Cukierman, Webb, and Neyapti (1992) to measure the degree of independence of the Bulgarian National Bank (BNB), both legally and in practice, for the period January

1991 to April 1996 when the Law on the Bulgarian National Bank was amended. Finally it argues that the unsuccessful experiment with central bank independence in Bulgaria should be seen rather as a missed opportunity to gradually achieve a reasonable degree of price stability, rather than a complicated institutional arrangement inapplicable to transition economies in general.

The Bulgarian National Bank was established in 1879. No central banking tradition evolved, however, due to episodes of inflationary financing during war periods and the period of central planning (1947-90) when the BNB was channeling credit into real sector activities according to the plan and printing money to cover government expenditures. The transformation of the BNB into a genuine central bank started in January 1991 when a governor and three deputy governors were elected by Parliament. Shortly after, a new Law on the Bulgarian National Bank was promulgated in June 1991, thus providing the legal basis for reform of the Bulgarian National Bank and its new role in the financial sector and policy making. The Law provided for a central bank responsible for monetary policy and banking and payments system supervision. It also provided for a central bank independent of the government and accountable to the Parliament.

Mr. Lyubomir Filipov was elected as governor of the BNB in January 1996. In April 1996 the Law on the BNB was amended to allow a parliamentary majority to dismiss the governor. The law does not constrain the Parliament by limiting the conditions under which the governor can be dismissed. The amendment effectively rejects the concept of legal independence of the BNB from political interference. Therefore, the five-year period 1991-96 forms a natural, relatively complete phase in the history of the BNB.

We argue that, although rejecting the concept of central bank independence (CBI) in Bulgaria was not unnatural, there was a missed opportunity to successfully implement this complex institutional arrangement in the context of transition to a market economy. The difficulties of the starting conditions of transition are marked by a lack of financial markets that form the infrastructure and the environment in which a central bank operates. The case of Bulgaria provides evidence that rapid progress is possible on this technical side. The main reason behind rejecting BNB independence was the slow and inconsistent progress of market reforms in Bulgaria. Bulgaria provides an example of the 'anti-Geraschenko' effect where revolving-door governments were reluctant to start genuine structural reforms and allowed both state-owned enterprises and emerging private businesses to continue operating under soft-budget constraints. Losses in the real sector continued to be covered by bank loans, thus destabilizing the banking sector, monetary policy and the central bank itself. The behavior of the BNB during that period was far from flawless, but the BNB's mistakes were of only secondary importance. Therefore the concept of CBI cannot be seen as incompatible with transition itself.

Only after a full-fledged financial crisis, accompanied by steep depreciation of the currency and a run on the banks erupted in April-May 1996, did the government design and endorse a bold program of liquidation and restructuring of loss-making enterprises. It will be difficult, time consuming, and expensive to restore confidence, even if the program is fully implemented. Bulgaria will need to reestablish an institutional framework for monetary stability. Given that CBI has already been compromised, we speculate in the conclusion that fixing the exchange rate or even introducing a currency board arrangement will be necessary. One can ask whether it would not have been useful to start the reform process in Bulgaria with a more binding monetary arrangement. We come back to this question in the conclusion.

The remainder of the paper is organized as follows. The next section describes briefly the starting conditions for reform of the BNB. The third and fourth sections deal with the rationale and the concept of CBI in the context of transition. In the fifth and sixth sections the legal and real independence of the BNB in 1991-96 are measured, applying the methodology of Cukierman, Webb, and Neyapti (1992). The seventh section characterizes the amendment of the Law on the BNB passed in April 1996. The final section summarizes the conclusions.

Challenges of transition

This section outlines the initial conditions when the BNB started transforming itself into a pure central bank in January 1991.

Macroeconomic conditions

A coalition government with a mandate to start market-oriented reforms took power in December 1990. The economic circumstances were characterized by falling output for two consecutive years, severe shortages in the consumer goods market, and complete isolation of the country from the international financial markets as a consequence of the default on the foreign debt announced earlier that year. The coalition government implemented a package of bold reforms. The prices of goods accounting for about 85 per cent of the turnover were freed. Both deposit and lending interest rates were deregulated and the authority to set the discount rate was transferred from the government to the BNB. The exchange rate was unified and floated. The deregulated exchange regime was coupled with substantial trade liberalization.

Inflation skyrocketed, reaching 123 per cent in the month of February 1991 and rising again by 50 per cent in March, but was restrained to the 3.5-5 per cent range for the rest of the year. The exchange rate depreciated sharply for a few days in February, reaching 28-29 leva per US dollar, but appreciated soon thereafter and remained in the range of 17-19 leva per US dollar for the rest of the year.

Monetary restraint was to play a central role in the stabilization effort for 1991 and onwards. Due to a lack of foreign exchange reserves and uncertainty about what a competitive and 'defensible' exchange rate might be, Bulgaria had no recourse but to use the exchange rate as a 'nominal anchor'. Given the chosen monetary regime and the crucial role monetary policy had to play to erase inflationary pressures in the years to come, the institutional arrangements and capability of the BNB to formulate and conduct monetary policy was of utmost importance. The independence of the BNB was the only institutional 'anchor' supporting stabilization efforts. Other transitional economies had additional choices and opted for rule-bound monetary policies like fixed exchange rates (or crawling peg) or even straight currency board arrangements (Estonia, Lithuania).

BNB: institutional conditions

The BNB was not prepared for its new role and responsibilities. It had to combine its day-to-day operations with a daunting agenda for both internal reform and reform of the banking sector.

The BNB had neither foreign exchange reserves, nor a structural unit with experienced staff to manage foreign exchange operations. The first foreign currency reserves were borrowed from the IMF.

The monetary policy instruments available to the BNB in the beginning of 1991 were: the discount (so-called 'basic') interest rate applied to BNB loans to commercial banks and the government, credit ceilings on commercial banks' lending to the real sector, and reserve requirements. There were no government securities and virtually no money market.

There was no expertise or legal basis for bank supervision activities. The banking system consisted of 79 mostly small, undercapitalized, and regionally concentrated commercial banks. The majority of these 'banks' were BNB branches until 1989. Their management was weak and inexperienced. Their portfolios were burdened with non-performing loans inherited from previous state-directed lending.

The accounting practices were complicated and out of touch with the GAAP. The payment system was functioning reasonably well, but under the prevailing regulations, the BNB was lending to commercial banks interest-free by automatically creating float to cover the obligations of banks with insufficient liquidity.

Transforming the BNB

Five years later the BNB is a full-fledged central bank with a complete structure and functions. The interbank foreign exchange market has been operating virtually without interruption since February 1991. It is regarded as the best functioning segment of the financial market in Bulgaria. The payment system was reformed profoundly by late 1992, and 99 per cent of the inter-bank payments are now completed within 24 hours. It is a gross-settlement based system and no settlement occurs unless the paying bank has a sufficient balance on its account with the BNB. Thus the payment system no longer interferes with monetary policy.

By mid-1993 the BNB had issued prudential regulations in a number of areas including regulations governing licensing of commercial banks, banks' liquidity, loan classification and provisioning, and capital adequacy. Unfortunately the BNB failed to strictly enforce these regulations and banking supervision is acknowledged both inside and outside the BNB as its major weakness.

By 1994 the BNB completed the gradual process of developing instruments for indirect monetary control and phasing out its direct instruments. Open market operations and Lombard loans gained in importance and are now the main levers used by the BNB to control liquidity in the banking system. Credit ceilings were abolished.

By 1993 new accounting standards for banks were adopted in conformity with the Bulgarian law on accounting. These were close to international standards. They were implemented in mid-1995.[1]

Over this period enormous, but publicly less visible, work was accomplished to transform the BNB into an institution that is well-positioned to formulate and conduct monetary policy.

Rationale for central bank independence

The issue of CBI has been extensively studied from both theoretical and empirical perspectives. Measurement of CBI across countries and the association of CBI with macroeconomic variables such as inflation, growth and unemployment has been subject to considerable research.[2] It is now widely accepted that CBI is closely correlated with lower and less variable inflation.

The Cukierman, Webb, and Neyapti (1992) study stands out in this body of literature as the most comprehensive. It proposes an index of CBI based on indicators from both a legal perspective and actual experience in the respective countries. The coverage of the study is substantial both in terms of number of countries studied (72) and the length of the period (1950-89). In the next two sections, their methodology is applied to measure the degree of independence of the BNB during the period 1991-96. This allows us to compare Bulgaria with the other 72 countries.

The Cukierman-Webb-Neyapti study does not find that there is a strong association between CBI and inflation across the entire sample of countries. Rather it establishes a positive correlation between legal independence of central banks and price stability in the subset of 21 industrial countries over the period 1950-89. Inflation for the 51 developing countries appears to be significantly correlated with the turnover of central bank governors, but not with the degree of legal CBI. This result hints that legally similar institutional arrangements may not be sufficient to produce similar outcomes in countries with different historical backgrounds. This in turn leads to the general question of what causal links exist between CBI and price stability and whether these links are the same in the context of transition.

The independence of a central bank is not an end in itself. It is an institutional arrangement to improve economic performance by producing price stability through credible commitments. To stress the desirability and importance of price stability on broader social and political grounds, central bankers often reverse the statement of Lenin who is quoted as saying 'to destroy a bourgeois society, you have to destroy its monetary system'. Hence, the development of a free market society entails the development of a sound monetary system (Schlesinger, 1993).

More specifically high and variable inflation hinders growth by discouraging investment and causing inefficient resource allocation. As monetizing the formerly planned economies lies at the heart of the transition, these relations apply equally to the countries of Eastern and Central Europe. Some evidence has already been accumulated to support this view: 'While the economies in transition from planned systems are partly *sui generis*, their experience fits a larger pattern. Output has began to recover in those economies in Eastern Europe that have stabilized inflation, while no recovery is in sight for those economies of the FSU where inflation remains high' (Bruno and Easterly, 1995).

It is now widely accepted that low inflation is essential for sustainable growth and not an alternative to it, a view popular in the past. The vertical Philips curve, to use the economics jargon, provides a theoretical foundation of this perception. In other words there is no trade-off between inflation and growth (unemployment) in the medium and long-term. Hence monetary policy should be steered with a view to stabilize prices in the longer-run. Politicians, on the other hand, and especially prior to elections, cannot credibly commit themselves to avoid the printing press. Monetary surprises can still temporarily affect growth and employment. (Politicians have an incentive to behave in a time-inconsistent manner.) The way out for politicians is to grant independence to the central bank which then can pursue price stability more single-mindedly and more credibly.[3]

This general line of thinking is even more valid for countries in the initial stage of their transition, given the prevailing political instability and lack of central banking tradition. In Bulgaria, for example, five cabinets changed in the period of 1991-95. One governor of the BNB worked with five different prime-ministers and three ministers of finance.

The politicians' way out of this credibility/time-inconsistency trap would be to tie their hands and delegate the objective of achieving price stability to a separate institution, a central bank independent (autonomous) of the government. Thus the requisite of a longer-term horizon, compatible with the long and variable lags between the major monetary policy decisions and their effect on the real economy, is ensured.[4]

Concept of central bank independence

What does independence of a central bank actually mean? Fischer (1995a) introduces a distinction between *goal independence* and *instrument independence*. 'A central bank that is given control over levers of monetary policy and allowed to use them has instrument independence; a central bank that sets its own policy goals has goal independence' (Fischer, 1995b, p. 202). He goes on to assert that 'the most important conclusion of both the theoretical and empirical literature is that a central bank should have instrument independence, but should not have goal independence' (p. 202). One can even strengthen this statement by recognizing that instrument independence of a central bank is indispensable to allow it to effectively pursue the goals that a legislature defines for it. Instrument independence is the means to achieve the goal: '...it should be inconsistent to give the central bank the task of maintaining the value of the currency while interfering with its freedom of action in pursuit of that goal' (O'Grady Walshe, 1990, p.102).

Instrument independence for a central bank boils down to the existence of efficient monetary policy instruments and the political and economic freedom to use them. The extent to which a central bank enjoys instrument independence and the freedom to use the instruments available to it can be judged by two indicators: the institutional and the personal independence of the central bank. Institutional independence refers to the freedom of the bank to act without regard to any instructions from the government or the Parliament. Personal independence refers to freedom of the members of the central bank's decision-making body to act regardless of any outside mandate or advice.

Cukierman, Webb, and Neyapti (1992) develop detailed measurement structures along these lines. We proceed to apply their methodology to characterize the legal and actual independence of the BNB in the 1991-96 period.

Measuring the legal independence of the BNB (1991-96)

The Parliament elected Mr. Todor Vulchev, a respected economist, governor of the BNB in January 1991. His three deputies were also elected by the Parliament at the same time. A new Law on the Bulgarian National Bank, providing legal basis for the bank to transform itself into the central bank of Bulgaria, became effective in June 1991. This law remained intact until April 1996 when it was amended, curtailing the personal independence of the governor and the deputy governors. In this section the legal independence of the BNB is measured according to the original law that was in effect until April 1996.

Cukierman, Webb, and Neyapti (1992, p. 360-61) construct an index of legal CBI for 21 industrialized and 51 developing countries. In a two-stage process 16 variables are aggregated first into eight groups and then into a single index. These eight groups characterize:

1. appointment and term of office of the governor of the central bank,
2. monetary policy formulation,
3. objectives the central bank is required to pursue, and
4. limitations on lending to the government (five variables).

The 'objectives' variable measures how precisely the law defines the goals for the central bank. The more narrowly and more clearly the goals of the central bank are defined, the greater is the index of independence. In other words, a lack of goal independence for the central bank is treated as an indicator of stronger instrument independence.

The indicators under 'monetary policy formulation' capture the institutional independence of the central bank. 'Appointment and term of office' stands for the governor's personal independence and 'limitations on lending to the government' measures the political and economic freedom of the central bank to use the monetary policy instruments at hand.

Table 7.1 reproduces the original 16 legal variables with the weights used for their aggregation. An additional column contains marks of the respective numerical coding of each variable that corresponds to the provisions of the Law on the BNB (1991-96).

The aggregate index for legal independence of the BNB is 0.545. This score is approximately the same as the score given to the Bank of Greece (0.55). This would make these two central banks the highest ranking central banks among a set of 52 developing countries.[5] When the group of industrialized countries is considered, the BNB is placed between the Austrian National Bank (0.61) and the Danish central bank (0.50). Curiously, indexes for the Federal Reserve System (0.49), the Dutch central bank (0.42), and Bank of England (0.27) are lower than the index of BNB independence (Table 2, p. 362).[6]

Two observations should be emphasized. The original Law on the BNB was in line with modern thinking as regards central banks independence. It was perhaps somewhat overly ambitious given the early stage of transition and virtual absence of financial markets at that time.

The following is a brief characterization of each of the 16 legal variables that underlie the index. We rearranged the order in which they appear starting with the group of 'Objectives' and proceeding through 'Policy formulation', 'Chief executive officer', and finally 'Limitations to lending to the government'.

136

Objectives – 'Price stability is one goal with other compatible objectives'

The law defines as primary the mandate of the BNB to preserve the internal and external stability of the currency and empowers it to formulate and implement monetary policy. The BNB is also assigned the task to supervise and regulate commercial banks and maintain an effective and efficient payment system. There is no provision whatsoever for the BNB to support the economic policies of the government.

Policy formulation

a) Who formulates monetary policy? – 'Bank alone' The law provides that the general direction of monetary policy be endorsed by the Plenary Council of the BNB. The members of the council are the nine member Managing Board of the BNB and six financial experts that are not employees of the bank. They are appointed by the governor of the BNB for a three-year term.

b) Who has the final word in conflict resolution? The Law on the BNB does not contain explicit provisions on resolution of conflict. The government, however, has no legal means to impose its opinion in case of conflict. Article 47 of the law explicitly prevents the BNB from seeking or taking advice from 'the Council of Ministers or other governmental agencies'. To the extent that the BNB reports to the Parliament, it is conceivable that in case of conflict, a meeting between the Minister of Finance and the BNB board could be intermediated by the budgetary or economic committee of the Parliament. The closest proxy of the Law on the BNB would then be 'a council of the central bank, executive branch, and legislative branch'.

On three occasions there were differences of opinion concerning monetary policy issues. These conflicts were addressed once by a meeting initiated by the budgetary parliamentary committee and twice by special meetings of the Plenary Council. The Minister of Finance and other government officials were invited to attend these meetings. No formal decisions, obligatory to the bank, however, were taken in either case. In one instance politicians felt that subsequent monetary policy did not take into account what was felt to be the prevailing opinion of Plenary Council members that are not members of the board and the invited government officials.

c) Role in government's budgetary process – 'Central bank has no influence' The law remains silent on a possible role for the BNB in the budgetary process. Moreover, the deadlines for the BNB annual report on monetary policy to the Parliament are not coordinated with the timetable for the budgetary procedure.

In practice this has proved to be a major weakness and is inconsistent with the main thrust of the law. Once the budget, and especially the deficit and its financing is set with no respect of its impact on the money supply growth, very little scope for independent monetary policy is left.

Limitations on lending to the government

Advances (non-securitized lending) Advances to the government are allowed by the Law, but they should: a) be limited in amount, for the balance of such advances cannot exceed at any moment five per cent of the projected budget revenues for the current year and must be repaid in full by the end of the fiscal year; b) be limited in maturity since the maturity of such advances cannot exceed three months; and c) bear a floating interest rate, decided by BNB with no scope for the government to influence it.

Securitized lending Direct securitized lending to the government is prohibited by the law. The BNB is not allowed to buy or sell government securities in the primary market. The BNB can engage in government securities transactions only on the secondary market for the purpose of conducting its monetary policy.

Potential borrowers from the BNB Only the central government can borrow from the BNB for bridging a temporary gap between revenues and expenditures. Individual ministries, local authorities or non-financial enterprises, public or private, do not have access to central bank lending.

Chief executive officer

Term of office The governor and three deputy governors of the BNB serve for a five-year term. This provision allows for substantial personal independence given the fact that general elections for Parliament are held every four years.

Appointment The governor and three deputy governors are elected by Parliament. Five other members of the bank board are appointed by the President of the Republic after being proposed by the governor.

Dismissal The tenure of a board member can only be interrupted if the person has been sentenced for a premeditated crime of public character or is prevented from performing his function for more than a year.

Other offices in government Members of the BNB managing board are explicitly forbidden to hold other positions within or outside the government or to engage in any other activity for remuneration.

An additional dimension of safeguarding the personal independence of members of the central bank's decision-making bodies is providing for their individual tenure on a staggered basis. This ensures that whoever is empowered to appoint them has no opportunity to replace at any given moment the entire decision-making body of the bank or a majority of its members. The Bulgarian law does not provide for staggered terms of office for individual members of the board. It stipulates that if and when a member of the board resigns for some reason, a successor is appointed to serve the rest of his term.

In summary, the Law on the BNB, adopted in 1991, provides a solid legal basis for an independent Bulgarian National Bank. It is consistent with virtually all important dimensions of central bank independence. It should not be surprising that the BNB scores higher on the index of legal independence than some industrial countries. One possible interpretation is that the Law on the BNB represents a major break with the institutional tradition of the 45 years under a centrally-planned economy. That is why it was possible and desirable to provide for such a degree of independence. It reflects modern thinking on central bank independence and at the same time underlines the breach with the past. Central banking laws in a number of industrialized countries, on the other hand, date back to the years around the Second World War or earlier. They bear the seal of the prevailing thinking on the role of central banks at that time. The continuity of their institutional evolution made it possible to gradually develop real independence and the economic performance associated with it. The Bank of Japan is one such example. While the index of its legal independence places it at the bottom of the group of central banks from twenty-one developed countries in 1980-89, the average inflation rate in Japan for the 80s was three per cent. This is comparable to the experience in Germany and Switzerland, countries with the most independent central banks, and superior to the inflation performance of the US, UK, France, and Italy.[7]

When we turn to measuring actual central bank independence in the next section, the relative position of the BNB on the scale of CBI changes.

Measuring the actual independence of the BNB

The statute of a central bank, though important, is not the only basis for central bank independence. Traditions, personalities of the governor and other members of the decision-making body of the bank, as well as day-to-day practice also matter. Laws cannot always provide detailed provisions to regulate all kinds of real life situations.

But even when the law is detailed and explicit, reality may be very different. To capture the independence in reality Cukierman, Webb, and Neyapti (1992) construct another index of independence, based on the responses of a non-random sample of specialists on monetary policy in the central banks of 23 countries. The seven variables used here partly overlap and partly supplement the indicators used to measure legal independence.

These variables, together with their numerical coding and the weights for aggregation into a single index, are listed in Table 7.2. As before, a separate column marks the numerical coding of the respective variables as it applies to the BNB in 1991-96.[8]

The aggregate index of actual independence for Bulgaria is estimated to be 0.55. This places the BNB just below the median for the sample of 23 countries (0.60), and between Ireland (0.57) and Barbados (0.54).[9] Central banks in virtually all industrialized countries including the Bank of England and the Bank of France, which appeared to have less legal independence than the BNB, enjoy higher actual independence. It appears that the BNB was actually more independent in 1991-96 than the central bank of Belgium was in 1980-89. Central banks of several developing countries also enjoyed greater real independence. Among them were the central banks of Costa Rica, the Bahamas, South Africa, Zaire, and Lebanon.

The large difference in ranking for the BNB under the two indices suggests a large disconnect between the provisions of the Law of the BNB and reality. This disconnect is analyzed in greater detail in the following section. Here are some comments on the individual variables from the questionnaire.

Actual priority given to price stability

The situation facing the BNB is best reflected in the following statement: 'Price and exchange rate stability are among the bank's objectives, but not first priority'. This is not to say that the Bank is required by law or pressed by the successive governments to explicitly keep growth or employment considerations in view when deciding on the stance of monetary policy. Concerns over liquidity problems of some large banks, however, have too often taken precedence in monetary policy decisions.

In 1994, for example, between 60 and 70 per cent of the incremental liquidity injected in the banking system was channeled through two large state-owned banks in distress. The first time the board was equally split in taking a decision was in February 1994 when increasing minimum reserve requirements was considered for the first time since their introduction in 1990. The lev had been under pressure since November 1993. Foreign exchange reserves were low. The cost of the forthcoming Debt and Debt Service Reduction Agreement on repayment of Bulgaria's foreign debt were clear. (The agreement was actually signed in June 1994.) The trade account was in deficit as exports and import show seasonal patterns with imports at their peak and exports at their lowest level in the first quarter. Several upward adjustments in interest rates starting from the beginning of the year were not sufficient to support the lev. The board had recourse to the reserve requirements instrument to drain liquidity and calm the foreign exchange market. In a long and heated debate the eight members of the board (at that time) split into two groups. Four members supported a proposal to increase reserve requirements by one percentage point effective immediately and to announce a further upward adjustment in a month's time. The other four members were concerned about the consequences of such a decision for the liquidity and profitability of the banks given the weakness of a few large state-owned banks in particular. The decision was postponed. Eventually the reserve requirements were increased, effective April 1994. Meanwhile, the lev depreciated by close to 100 per cent in the month of March.

Intermediate targets

Defining and announcing intermediate targets for monetary policy and a record of good adherence to the targets is a primary vehicle for a central bank to establish the credibility of its monetary policy. The BNB has not yet developed a practice of publicly announcing intermediate monetary policy targets. The issue of intermediate targets and indicators in economies in transition is particularly complex. Abrupt structural changes make it close to impossible to establish an association between financial variables and indicators measuring inflation, growth, and employment. This suggests that monetary policy in transition should be defined in a framework as simple as possible and guided by transparent and easy to understand rules. A fixed or pegged exchange rate is one such option. This option was, however, not open to Bulgaria at the outset of the transition due to the lack of foreign reserves and higher than usual uncertainty with respect to the exchange rate.

Monetary stock targets The floating exchange rate regime, adopted in Bulgaria, placed emphasis on restricting money supply growth as the most important nominal anchor for prices. Controlling the money supply requires that monetary policy be guided by intermediate targets. These targets should be simple and observable by the markets and the general public. Several choices for defining such a target are open in principle: growth of a chosen monetary aggregate, growth of nominal GDP, or price change directly.

It is extremely difficult, however, to develop a monetary framework in the early stages of transition. The difficulties stem mainly from two sources. First, there is no record (time series) of the relevant variables and their association with price level dynamics. (In fact there is no record of price level dynamics.) Second, there are rapid (revolutionary) changes taking place in the structure of the financial system.

The BNB has explicitly adopted intermediate targets only in the framework of standby agreements with the IMF. The target, defined as quarterly performance criteria, was in the form of a ceiling on the growth of net domestic assets of the banking system (with a subceiling on government borrowing from the banking system). Targeting net domestic assets of the banking system and net international reserves of the BNB at the same time was effectively a form of money supply target. This particular form of money supply target was in line with the direct monetary policy instruments of the BNB such as credit ceilings, to control credit expansion. One problem with targeting net domestic assets was that it was only applied in the years 1991, 1992, and 1994 when Bulgaria had standby agreements with the IMF. The second and more important problem is that these targets were never announced publicly. Thus the BNB was not able to build credibility through transparency.

The general public spontaneously offset the lack of an announced target by an implicit, easily monitored 'performance indicator': the nominal exchange rate. BNB performance came to be judged by its ability to keep the nominal exchange rate of the lev stable. Thus, most of the time, Bulgaria experienced the same advantages and costs as if a fixed exchange regime had formally been adopted. The monetary policy decisions were often driven by exchange rate considerations. Against the background of domestic inflation, sustained in the higher two-digit range, this led to excessive and unsustainable real appreciation of the lev, followed by episodes of drastic nominal depreciation. In March 1994, for example, the lev depreciated by 62 per cent in two weeks time. Other episodes of steep depreciation occurred in November 1993, September 1994, February and April-May 1996. In the first four and a half months of 1996 the lev depreciated by 51 per cent. These episodes eroded the hard won reputation that the BNB had acquired during 1991-93.

Interest rates targets Since 1991 the BNB has enjoyed autonomy in its interest rate policy not only legally, but also in practice. This was instrumental in avoiding hyperinflation in the early stages of transition. This is not to say that, in retrospect, the interest rate policy of the BNB was always flawless. The point is that the BNB was never effectively constrained from outside when it was deemed necessary to use such a powerful blunt instrument as interest rate adjustment.

One, so far unsuccessful, but repeatedly used vehicle to apply pressure on the BNB to adopt at least an informal interest rate target, were the annual budget discussions in Parliament. The governor of the BNB was usually invited to participate in these discussions and invariably was asked whether he would concur with the budgetary assumption of the average interest rate for the coming year. This assumption was often seen as a constraint on the interest rate policy of the BNB. The practice so far, however, does not support such views. 1996 provides the most recent example. While the budget for the current year assumes an average basic interest rate of 25 per cent, the BNB did not hesitate to hike this rate several times to relieve pressure on the lev. The base interest rate went from 34 per cent in January to 42 per cent in February, to 49 per cent in March, to 67 per cent in April, and to an historic high of 108 per cent in May. An interesting detail is that the first interest rate adjustment happened between the first and second reading of the Law on the Budget, thus putting the government into a delicate position. Finally the budget was promulgated in its original form. The situation is now domestically perceived as an implausible budget. The BNB has no obligation to offset the higher interest rate in the beginning of the year by substantially lowering interest rates later.

Limitations on lending in practice

Breaching the limits on lending to the government is the most serious and consistent practical deviation from the Law on the BNB. The annual Law on the Budget effectively overrides the provisions of Article 49 of the Law on the BNB on a regular basis. 'These actions call into question the BNB's independence at a practical if not a legal level' (Miller and Petranov, 1996). The Law on the Budget usually contains a requirement that the BNB print money to partially finance the approved budget deficit. The wording is that the BNB should provide direct unsecured credit to cover up to 50 per cent of the deficit for the current year.[10] Once this door to circumvent the Law on the BNB was open, it was used as an additional channel to finance the deficit. It became common practice for the government to roll-over the limited (both in terms of amounts and maturity) advances, which should normally be paid off before the end of the fiscal year. In order to formally comply with the law, any short-term debts outstanding at the end of the year are renegotiated with the BNB and converted into long-term loans within the ceiling established by the Law on the Budget.

There have been two basic reasons for this infringement of monetary independence, especially in the early years of transition. a) It was impossible to immediately balance the budget in the first years of transition. The transition process only increased the normal political controversies which typically accompany any fiscal adjustment in any economy. It added a cyclical dimension (i.e. the collapse of output and rise in unemployment) to the budget deficit. In addition tax revenue in former socialist economies was overwhelmingly dependent on taxing the profit of state-owned enterprises, while the share of income and indirect taxes was much lower than the average in market economies. But liberalization of prices and the collapse of external (CMEA) markets rendered many state-owned enterprises loss-makers. b) Government securities did not exist.

It seems that direct lending from the central bank was the only possible way to cover the budget deficit. However, as time passes, it is harder to make this argument. One possible way out of this situation is to allow for a temporary deviation from the ban on BNB lending to the government, while implementing supporting measures such as tax reform and development of a market for government securities. In retrospect this seems to have been possible. In 1992, 94 per cent of the budget deficit was monetized. In 1993 and 1994 direct BNB lending covered 29 per cent and 21 per cent of the central government borrowing requirement respectively (BNB, 1995a). In 1995, for the first time during the transition, the government did not engage in long-term borrowing from the BNB (BNB, 1996, p. 138).

The failure to commit to phasing out direct BNB lending to the state budget contributed to delays in tax reform with negative consequences for fiscal prudence and stabilization. For instance, the VAT law had been prepared in draft form by mid-1992 but was not promulgated and put into effect until March 1994. In April 1996 a new profit tax law was still under discussion in Parliament.

Resolution of conflict

A number of conflicts between various governments (Ministers of Finance) occurred during this period, mainly due to the lack of institutional tradition. There was one, particularly acute and publicly open case, which was definitely won by the BNB. Nevertheless, we do not assign the highest mark (1.0) to this indicator, but rather 0.5 which stands for 'all other cases'. The main reason is that this remained an isolated case and did not set a pattern or incentive for subsequent governments to avoid open clashes with the BNB.

The conflict evolved as follows. In mid-1992 the Ministry of Finance stopped paying interest on government debt to the BNB. There were no spill-over effects in the nascent financial markets from this default by the government because only the direct unsecured debt of the government on the books of the BNB was affected. The Minister of Finance took these extraordinary steps to avoid going back to Parliament before the end of the fiscal year to request authorization for a higher deficit. At the end of the year, however, he reversed himself and accused the BNB, publicly, of failing to make transfers to the budget out of its net income. He gave this as the reason for the Ministry to default on its debt to the BNB.

Because the first step was taken by the Minister of Finance in public, the BNB also presented its case publicly. It explained that the government's liability is legally binding since it follows from a formal contract. On the other hand, BNB's obligation to transfer its net income, after setting part aside part as reserve accumulation, applies only to the extent such net income is actually earned. Moreover, as government debt is an asset of the BNB, the amount of actual gross (and net) income of the BNB depends on timely servicing of government debt obligations to the BNB. To adopt the minister's point of view, namely that the projections of the transfers in the budget is mandatory for the BNB, would have infringed on the financial independence of the BNB. During an extensive period before the dispute was settled, the BNB announced and effectively stopped extending advances or transfers of funds to the Ministry of Finance.

The conflict was settled by a special parliamentary resolution that states that the domestic debt is increased by the overdue interest payments to the BNB. Only after that decision were the financial relationships between the government and the BNB normalized again. It is very unlikely that a similar episode will be repeated, given that most government debt is now in the form of securities widely held by banks and the non-bank public. This case is an example of how bumpy a road toward establishing the rule of law can be in the context of an economic transition where no (or forgotten) institutional traditions exist.

Tenure of central bank CEO overlap with political authorities

Todor Vulchev was elected governor of the BNB directly by the Parliament in January 1991, and in anticipation of the new Law of the BNB, he served a full five-year term and resigned in January 1996. During that period two general elections were held (1991 and 1994) and five cabinets changed. On the face of it, there was virtually no overlap between revolving-door governments and the BNB governor's tenure. Formally the BNB scores high on this indicator of actual independence.

However, the real situation is much more complicated than it appears. As noted earlier, in Bulgaria the law stipulates that not only the governor but also the three deputy governors are directly elected by Parliament. For the purposes of measurement of actual independence and international comparisons, the tenure of all four BNB leaders should be analyzed.

The shield of personal independence provided by the Law on the BNB proved too weak to protect them. In July 1993 the key deputy governor of the BNB, Mr. Emil Harsev, was removed by vote of Parliament, thus rendering the legal provision that specifies only a limited number of reasons for interrupting the tenure of a governor (or his deputy), a dead letter. The role of Mr. Harsev is described here as 'key' for two reasons. First, the operational departments such as foreign currency operations, national currency operations (lending to banks) and currency issue (banknote issue) reported to him. Second, he played a leading role in banking sector regulations such as designing prudential regulations, reforming the payment system and the accounting standards. For all practical purposes he was the CEO of the BNB in 1991-93.

A conflict between Governor Vulchev and the rest of the board arose in early 1993 over issues regarding the governance of the BNB. The board members were concerned that, what they felt were urgent decisions with respect to both bank reform and normal operations affecting the commercial banks, were constantly postponed. Moreover, there were indications that these delays were due to informal external influence. In this situation members of the BNB managing board offered Vulchev the opportunity to submit his resignation to Parliament to prevent further, and especially open, conflicts. Governor Vulchev initially appeared to agree and requested advise as to when would be the most appropriate time to resign. It was suggested that

145

submission of the annual report to Parliament a couple of months later would be a suitable occasion. Governor Vulchev took a leave. As later became apparent, he used this time to arrange political support so that he could remain in office.

Assessed retrospectively, the failure of the board members to keep the BNB scandal-free served as a direct invitation to politicians to interfere. The way the Parliament resolved the conflict created ambiguity as to when the tenure of Governor Vulchev and the remaining deputy governors had started. This ambiguity served as an excuse to amend the Law on the BNB in April 1996 and to effectively negate the personal independence of the BNB's board members.

The case described may sound amusing to many readers, accustomed to stability of institutions in their countries. However, this illustrates the enormous pressure that reform of the banking sector can place on people and institutions; pressure that they are not always able to withstand.

The rest of this section describes how politicians abused their powers to further increase the uncertainty surrounding the BNB and to open an opportunity to interfere in the future. In essence, the Parliament stepped in to resolve a conflict between Governor Vulchev and the rest of the board. Formally, however, the case was presented in Parliament as a need to resolve a legal issue. The issue was that the governor and deputy governors were elected several months before the Law on the BNB was enacted. Hence, it was argued, they were not elected according to the law. This needed to be corrected by a new formal vote by the Parliament which, it was claimed, would be according to the law. Parliament voted for the governor and three deputy governors in two votes. The first concerned the governor and two deputy governors together. In one vote they were 'elected'. In a separate vote deputy governor and executive director, Mr. Harsev, 'was not elected'. The voting procedure made it crystal clear that the goal was to remove Mr. Harsev from the bank. The use of the term 'elect', however, created legal confusion as to when the terms of the governor and the two deputy governors began, for they were elected twice by the Parliament: once in January 1991 and a second time in July 1993. If the reason for the second election was to be taken seriously, then the logical conclusion would have been that only the second election was made under Article 15 of the Law on the BNB. Therefore, the five-year term of the elected governor and deputy governors only started from July 1993 and expires in July 1998. This, however, was not unanimously accepted. At least not by Governor Vulchev himself who insisted that his term had started in January 1991. This uncertainty was explored in late 1995 and early 1996 and led to a formal amendment to the Law on the BNB in April 1996. This amendment effectively negated the concept of a secure tenure for the governor of the BNB and his deputies.

Financial independence

The financial independence of the BNB, as provided by law, was also maintained in practice during the period 1991-96 in terms of budgetary decisions, the salaries of high bank officials, and allocation of the BNB's profit.

The budget of the BNB is endorsed annually by the Plenary Council, in which the BNB board members hold a majority. It is not this formal majority, however, but the prudence in administrative spending by BNB management that never provoked criticism.

There was one case, however, in which a proposal was made for the BNB to invest in a new building. One member of the Plenary Council, a member of Parliament, objected. Finally this was dropped from the budget. This kind of objection was not repeated in subsequent years.

Ensuring financial independence of the BNB in terms of allowing it to set aside 25 per cent of its net income for reserve accumulation was strictly observed, thus making it improbable that the bank will have to request financial assistance from the state budget.

The law provides that all salaries of BNB staff be decided by the Managing Board, subject to a floor set by the average remuneration for staff with similar functions in commercial banks. This has been strictly adhered to. The salaries of board members were decided by the Plenary Council following the same guidelines. This practice allowed the BNB to offer competitive compensation and to attract and keep qualified professionals. At the same time the salaries in the BNB, although consistently higher than in government agencies, were never perceived as exorbitant.

Function as a development bank, granting credit at subsidy rates

The BNB is not allowed to lend directly to the non-financial sector and this provision was strictly observed. However, it has given in to pressures from Parliament and the government to provide additional funds to banks for lending to specific sectors, especially in the early years of transition. The BNB was also required from time to time to adjust upwards credit ceilings to individual banks to allow them to provide credits to particular sectors. In both cases the BNB did charge banks the prevailing interest rate.

The management of the BNB has consistently resisted (not always successfully) such pressures. With the elimination of credit ceilings in mid-1994, this source of pressure was also eliminated. When the BNB started to require government guarantees, the *ad hoc* requirements from Parliament and the government to lend to individual banks also appears to have ceased. Functioning as a kind of development bank, which can conflict with the objective of price stability, was a short transitory phenomenon in the case of Bulgaria. More generally, however, the pressure on the central bank to continue functioning as a development bank is very high in the context of transition. This is due to the previous practice of automatic lending to certain branches (most notably agriculture) on preferential terms. These branches need to adjust to market-based lending before they are cut from access to base money.

In sum, the experience of the first five years of transition shows numerous and substantial deviations from the legal basis for independent monetary policy. Part of these deviations, especially in the initial years of transition, were perhaps unavoidable. The underdeveloped financial markets provided further hurdles for implementing an anti-inflationary monetary policy. The independence of the BNB gradually eroded in 1994-95 and was effectively abolished by amending the Law on the BNB in April 1996.

One question is whether it was a good idea to start the banking sector reform by establishing an independent central bank? The two available alternatives were to have opted either for a more rule-based monetary framework (like fixed exchange rate regime or even currency board), or to have postponed the introduction of an independent central bank until financial markets had matured. Before turning to this issue, let us review the election of the second governor of the BNB and the amendment of the law in 1996.

1996: End of BNB independence

In April 1996 the Law on the BNB was amended. The amendment essentially negated the status of independence of the BNB by providing that Parliament can terminate the term of the governor and/or the deputy governors by a 60 per cent majority vote without specifying any particular reason for the termination. In these circumstances it will only be plausible to perceive future decisions of the BNB's Managing Board as being influenced by considerations of the possible reaction from influential groups of politicians. This is by no means compatible with pursuing price stability.

An additional provision states that the term of the present members of the BNB Board expires on 29 June 1996, i.e. five years after the law came put into effect. This also applies to Governor Filipov who was only elected on 26 January 1996. Thus Parliament has now interfered for a second time (after 1993) with the provision of the law regulating the term of office for the governor and deputy governors. It also formally removed the security of office for them. This amendment, together with the regular overriding of the limitations on lending to the government, openly subordinates the BNB to anonymous political 'guidance'. Under these institutional arrangements, it will be more difficult, if not impossible, for the BNB to gain credibility for its determination to fight inflation. The protracted conflict was finally resolved between the mandate the Parliament gave to the BNB to safeguard the currency and the reluctance by the same Parliament to give the BNB the means to pursue that objective. This resolution, however, lifts institutional barriers to price instability and cannot be expected to be durable. At some point price instability will become economically and socially intolerable, and medicine stronger than central bank independence will be needed. The current financial crisis in which Bulgaria finds itself suggests that this time will come soon.

This amendment is a softer form of a previous draft proposed and discussed informally in January 1996. This draft proposed that the Law on the BNB be changed to provide that the term of office of every member of the board be terminated once the term of the governor expires or is terminated for some other reason. The reasoning behind this proposal was that the governor should be given the opportunity to choose a 'team' with whom to work. Reportedly this draft gained substantial informal support from both the majority and the opposition. The draft was never presented for formal discussion (after strong objections from the BNB and the press). The Plenary Council of the BNB published its objections and submitted to Parliament minutes of its discussion together with information on how the term of office of the central bank chief executive officer is regulated by the law of European Union member countries.

The 1996 amendment has to be judged against the background of the policies pursued by the socialist government that came into power in early 1995. The main thrust of these policies has been anti-market. The government has attempted to revive administrative controls in the banking sector as well as in other sectors of the economy. The government changed the management and appointed prime minister advisors as chairmen of supervisory boards of state-owned banks with the view to ensure financial support of its industrial policies. Pouring new money into large loss-making enterprises was at the heart of the government's industrial policies in 1995. And indeed 2.5 per cent real growth was reported in 1995, but the costs were huge. The state-owned enterprises reported consolidated losses around eight per cent of GDP for 1995. Already impaired portfolios of commercial banks deteriorated rapidly. In April-May 1996 a full-fledged financial crisis broke out. International reserves were depleted; the lev started depreciating rapidly, and depositors started withdrawing savings from the banks in panic. The weakening of the BNB, although not the main reason, undoubtedly contributed to the crisis.

Conclusion

One way or another, the change of the Law on the BNB seems to have put an end to a protracted period of attacks against the independence of BNB. These attacks came mainly from members of Parliament who were supposed to have expressed their commitment to price stability (at least in the long run) by granting independence to the BNB.

What went wrong? The unsuccessful Bulgarian experiment with central bank in-

149

dependence seems to provide additional evidence to support the theory that central bank independence and low inflation are associated, not because they are causally linked, but because they have common underlying causes and interest to support both. What really matters are interests rather than institutions. Five years after launching the transition, strong interest groups opposing inflation did not emerge to support a commitment to price stability through central bank independence.

a) Introducing central bank independence early in transition proved halfhearted because it was not complemented with a medium-term framework for fiscal adjustment and gradual enforcement of a ban on government recourse to the printing press for covering deficits. Ironically, the monetary tightening in 1991 that prevented hyperinflation as well as the tightening in 1994 that restored the confidence in the lev gave relief to governments and allowed them to further postpone the necessary fiscal and structural reforms.

b) The state and state-owned enterprises which still dominate industry are net debtors. Many banks have negative net worth. They all stand to benefit from higher inflation.

c) Bulgaria has failed so far to attract foreign private investment which could have imposed a cost to politicians openly showing their negligence to price stability.

As mentioned above, the BNB successfully restored confidence in the national currency after it was seriously shaken by loose policies in 1993. This, however, came at the cost of high positive real interest rates that contributed to worsening portfolios and liquidity problems. Systemic instability has weakened general public support for an independent BNB.

The case of lost independence for the Bulgarian National Bank fits well with Posen's analysis as to why central bank independence does not cause low inflation.[11] Given that the concept of CBI is a delicate and technically complicated arrangement, it is not surprising that it could not be sustained during the transition in Bulgaria. What is surprising is that there was a chance for success. Huge progress was made in developing and deepening financial markets (e.g. the foreign exchange market, the government securities market including gradual development of a secondary market, and the interbank money market.) This created a financial infrastructure in which standard monetary policy can be implemented. The BNB introduced and mastered the full range of monetary policy instruments. Initially in 1991-93, the BNB gained credibility and respect by providing for a reasonable degree of stability by subduing inflation and stabilizing the exchange rate.

This temporary 'umbrella' of relative stability provided an opportunity to implement deep market-oriented structural adjustment and market oriented reforms. This opportunity was missed. Privatization has stalled and hard-budget constraints were

150

not imposed on state-owned enterprises (SOEs). The state partially assumed non-performing debts of SOEs in several steps, thus creating a huge moral hazard problem since enterprises will be repeatedly bailed-out. The delays in introducing and implementing legal procedures for bankruptcies and debt collection have also contributed to further worsening of banks' portfolios.

The tightening of monetary policy in 1994 to offset earlier fiscal loosening resulted in high real interest rates. The share of substandard loans in banks' portfolios reached 75 per cent of loans to the non-financial sector in 1995.

Thus delays in reforming the Bulgarian economy demonstrated clearly that the commitment of politicians to price stability, as expressed in the Law on the BNB in 1991, was not serious. Logically, the BNB was formally put under the vague control of politicians.

Bulgaria will still need a reasonable degree of price stability regardless of how the banking crisis develops in the near future. Next time, however, a genuine commitment to price stability will need to be supported by stronger evidence and more rigid arrangements like a fixed exchange rate or currency board. The associated real costs of disinflation will correspondingly have to be higher.

Given that CBI in Bulgaria did not succeed, one is tempted to explore a counterfactual. Should monetary policy in Bulgaria have been controlled by a currency board or clearly defined rule like a fixed exchange rate or a crawling peg? Without elaborating further, our answer to this question is negative. As a small open economy, such monetary arrangement may be suitable in principle. With virtually zero international reserves in February 1991, it was inconceivable to make such a strong commitment. A fixed exchange rate would have made the necessary structural adjustments unacceptably costly. In fact, as mentioned above, the BNB used monetary policy to stabilize the economy in 1991-93 and provided a unique window of opportunity for the government to act on structural adjustment. In 1991-93 the prevailing real interest rates on credits were negative, but the savings in banks were still growing because of even lower yields on foreign currency deposits in the context of a nominally stable exchange rate. This opportunity was missed, however. A currency board or a fixed exchange rate would only have been successful if there was the political will on the part of government to discipline its fiscal policy as well as to impose hard-budget constraints on the state sector. And it was exactly this political will that was missing in Bulgaria. A more stringent monetary regime cannot substitute for the lack of political commitment. The case of rump Yugoslavia, where the highly respected governor of the central bank has recently been removed after successfully halting the most severe hyperinflation in the 20th century, clearly illustrates this.

On the other hand, the danger that confidence in the BNB will totally collapse as a result of the current banking crisis in Bulgaria suggests that a currency board may remain one of the very few options to restore confidence in the country's monetary system in the near future.

Notes

1   For more details, see BNB (1995b).
2   See Grilli, Masciandro, and Tabellini (1991), Cukierman (1992, Chapter 20), Alesina and Summers (1993), Cukierman, Kalaitzidakis, Summers, and Web (1993), de Gregorio (1996), among others.
3   '... the point of the Bundesbank was never to prevent pain; it was to ensure that the guardians of Germany's money were free to ignore pain, in a way that elected politicians could not be trusted to do'. *The Economist*, 12 June 1993, p. 20.
4   'All other functions [of a Central Bank] could in principle be carried out quite well by a ministry or department of the government, but maintaining the value of the currency domestically and externally is of such importance to the well-being of the economy that it is felt to be appropriate to give the task to an institution that can pursue it single-mindedly, without the danger of being thrown off course by some short-term economic or political objective'. (O'Grady Walshe, 1990, p.102).
5   The index of legal CBI for developing countries ranges from 0.10 for Poland to 0.55 for Greece, with a median of 0.34 for India. (Cukierman, Webb, and Neyapti, 1992, p. 362, Table 2).
6   The index of legal CBI for developed countries ranges from 0.17 for Belgium to 0.69 for Germany, with a median of 0.33 for Luxembourg (Cukierman, Webb, and Neyapti, 1992, p. 362, Table 2).
7   Cukierman, Webb, and Neyapti (1992), p. 362, Table 2.
8   Assigning numerical values to the variables in Table 7.2 as they apply for BNB is my sole responsibility. My judgment is based on my service to the BNB as Member of the Board and Chief Economist from 1991 through August 1994 and on external observations afterwards.
9   Cukierman, Webb, and Neyapti (1992), p.368, Table 5.
10   This has been true since 1993. Earlier the ceiling was higher.
11   See also Mas (1995).

References

Alesina, A. and Summers, L.H. (1993), 'Central Bank Independence and Macro-economic Performance: Some Comparative Evidence', *Journal of Money Credit and Banking*, Vol. 25, May, pp. 157-62.

Bruno, M., and Easterly, W. (1995), 'Inflation Crises and Long-Run Growth', *Policy Research Working Paper*, The World Bank, July.

BNB (1995a), *Annual Report 1994*, Bulgarian National Bank, Sofia.

—— (1995b), *The Bulgarian Banking System*, Bulgarian National Bank, Sofia.

—— (1996), *Annual Report 1995*, Bulgarian National Bank, Sofia.

Cukierman, A. (1992), *Central Bank Strategy, Credibility, and Independence: Theory and Evidence*, MIT Press: Cambridge, MA.

——, Webb, S., and Neyapti, B. (1992), 'Measuring the Independence of Central Banks and Its Effect on Policy Outcome', *The World Bank Economic Review*, Vol. 6, September, pp. 353-98.

——, Kalaitzidakis, P., Summers, L.H., and Webb, S.B. (1993), 'Central Bank Independence, Growth, Investment, and Real Rates', *Carnegie-Rochester Conference Series on Public Policy*, Vol. 39, pp. 95-140.

de Gregorio, J. (1996), 'Inflation, Growth and Central Banks: Theory and Evidence', *Policy Research Working Paper 1575*, The World Bank, February.

Fischer, S. (1995a), 'Modern Central Banking', in Capie, F., Fischer, S., Goodhart, C., and Schnadt, N. (eds), *The Future of Central Banking*, pp. 262-308, Cambridge University Press: Cambridge, England.

—— (1995b), 'Central-Bank Independence Revisited', *American Economic Review*, Vol. 85, May, pp. 201-06.

Grilli, V., Masciandro, D., and Tabellini, G. (1991), 'Political and Monetary Institutions and Public Financial Policies in the Industrial Countries', *Economic Policy*, Vol. 13, pp. 341-92.

Mas, I. (1995), 'Central Bank Independence: A Critical View from a Developing Country Perspective', *World Development*, Vol. 23, October, pp. 1639-52.

Miller, J. B. and Petranov, S. (1996), *Banking in the Bulgarian Economy*, Bulgarian National Bank.

O'Grady Walshe, T. (1990), 'Managing a Central Bank: Goals, Strategies, and Techniques', in Downes and Vaez-Zadeh, Reza (eds), *The Evolving Role of Central Banks*, International Monetary Fund: Washington, D.C., pp. 93-117.

Posen, A. S. (1994), 'Why Central Bank Independence does not cause low inflation', *Finance and the International Economy*, No. 7, pp. 51-63.

Schlesinger, H. (1993), 'Prof. Schlesinger underlines the importance of central bank independence for German and European economic policy', *BIS Review*, Vol. 4, No. 1, January, pp. 1-4.

Table 7.1
Variables for legal central bank independence

Variable number	Description of variable	Weight	Numerical coding	BNB 1991-96
1	**Chief executive officer (CEO)**	0.20		
	a) Term of office			
	- more than 8 years		1.00	
	- 6 to 8 years		0.75	
	- 5 years		0.50	X
	- 4 years		0.25	
	- less than 4 years, or at discretion of appointer		0.00	
	b) Who appoints CEO?			
	- Board of central bank		1.00	
	- Council of central bank board, executive branch, and legislative branch		0.75	
	- Legislature		0.50	X
	- Executive collectively (e.g., council of ministers)		0.25	
	- One or two members of executive branch		0.00	
	c) Dismissal			
	- No provision for dismissal		1.00	
	- Only for reasons unrelated to policy		0.83	X
	- At discretion of central bank board		0.67	
	- At legislature's discretion		0.50	
	- Unconditional dismissal possible by legislature		0.33	
	- At executive's discretion		0.17	
	- Unconditional dismissal possible by executive		0.00	
	d) May CEO hold other offices in government?			
	- No		1.00	X
	- Only with permission of executive branch		0.50	
	- No rule against holding another office		0.00	

154

Variable number	Description of variable	Weight	Numerical coding	BNB 1991-96
2	**Policy formulation**	**0.15**		
	a) Who formulates monetary policy?			
	- Bank alone		1.00	X
	- Bank participates, with little influence		0.67	
	- Bank only advises government		0.33	
	- Bank has no say		0.00	
	b) Who has final word in conflict resolution?			
	- Bank, on issues clearly defined in law as its objective		1.00	
	- Government, on policy issues not clearly defined as bank's goals, or in case of conflict with bank		0.80	
	- Council of central bank, executive branch, and legislative branch		0.60	X
	- Legislature, on policy issues		0.40	
	- Executive branch, on policy issues, subject to due process and possible protest by bank		0.20	
	- Executive branch has unconstitutional priority		0.00	
	c) Role in government's budgetary process?			
	- Central bank active		1.00	
	- Central bank has no influence		0.00	X
3	**Objectives**	**0.15**		
	- Price stability is major or only objective in the charter, and central bank has final word in case of conflict with other government objectives		1.00	
	- Price stability is only objective		0.80	
	- Price stability is one goal, with other compatible objectives, such as stable banking system		0.60	X

Variable number	Description of variable	Weight	Numerical coding	BNB 1991-96
3 (cont.)	**Objectives**			
	- Price stability is one goal, with potentially conflicting objectives, such as full employment		0.40	
	- No objectives stated in bank charter		0.20	
	- Stated objectives do not include price stability		0.00	
4	**Limitations on lending to government?**			
	a) Advances (limitation on nonsecuritized lending)	0.15		
	- No advances permitted		1.00	
	- Advances permitted, but with strict limits (e.g., up to 15% of government revenue)		0.67	X
	- Advances permitted, with loose limits (e.g., over 15% of government revenue)		0.33	
	- No legal limits on lending		0.00	
	b) Securitized lending	0.10		
	- Not permitted		1.00	
	- Permitted, but with strict limits (e.g., up to 15% of government revenue)		0.67	
	- Permitted, with loose limits (e.g., over 15% of government revenue)		0.33	
	- No legal limits on lending		0.00	X
	c) Terms of lending (maturity, interest, amount)	0.10		
	- Controlled by bank		1.00	
	- Specified by bank charter		0.67	
	- Agreed between central bank and executive		0.33	
	- Decided only by executive branch		0.00	

Variable number	Description of variable	Weight	Numerical coding	BNB 1991-96
4 (cont.)	**Limitations on lending to government?**			
	d) Potential borrowers from bank	0.05		
	- Only central government		1.00	X
	- All levels of government (state as well as central)		0.67	
	- Those mentioned above and public enterprises		0.33	
	- Public and private sector		0.00	
	e) Limits on central bank lending defined in...	0.025		
	- Currency amounts		1.00	
	- Shares of central bank demand liabilities or capital		0.67	
	- Shares of government revenue		0.33	X
	- Shares of government expenditures		0.00	
	f) Maturity of loans	0.025		
	- Within 6 months		1.00	
	- Within 1 year		0.67	
	- More than 1 year		0.33	X
	- No mention of maturity in the law		0.00	
	g) Interest rates on loans must be...	0.025		
	- Above minimum rates		1.00	
	- At market rates		0.75	
	- Below maximum rates		0.50	
	- Interest rate not mentioned		0.25	X
	- No interest on government borrowing from central bank		0.00	
	h) Central bank prohibited from buying or selling securities in primary market?	0.025		
	- Yes		1.00	X
	- No		0.00	

157

Table 7.2
Questionnaire variables, weights, and numerical codes

Variable number	Description of variable	Weight	Numerical coding	BNB 1991-96
1	**Tenure of central bank CEO overlap with political authorities**	0.10		
	- Little overlap		1.00	X
	- Some overlap		0.50	
	- Substantial overlap		0.00	
2	**Limitations on lending in practice**	0.20		
	- Tight		1.00	
	- Moderately tight		0.66	
	- Moderately loose		0.33	X
	- Loose or nonexistent		0.00	
3	**Resolution of conflict**	0.10		
	- Some clear cases of resolution in favor of bank		1.00	
	- Resolution in favor of government in all cases		0.00	
	- All other cases		0.50	X
4	**Financial independence**	0.10		
	a) Determination of central bank's budget			
	- Mostly central bank		1.00	
	- Mixture of bank and executive or legislative branches		0.50	X
	- Mostly executive or legislative branches		0.00	
	b) Determination of salaries of high bank officials and allocation of bank profits			
	- Mostly central bank or fixed by law		1.00	X
	- Mixture of bank and executive or legislative branches		0.50	
	- Mostly executive or legislative branches		0.00	

Variable number	Description of variable	Weight	Numerical coding	BNB 1991-96
5	**Intermediate policy targets**	**0.15**		
	a) Quantitative monetary stock target			
	- Such targets exist, good adherence		1.00	
	- Such targets exist, mixed adherence		0.66	
	- Such targets exist, poor adherence		0.33	
	- No stock targets		0.00	X
	b) Formal or informal interest rate targets			
	- No		1.00	X
	- Yes		0.00	
6	**Actual priority given to price stability**	**0.15**		
	- First priority		1.00	
	- First priority assigned to a fixed exchange rate		0.66	
	- Price or exchange rate stability are among bank's objectives, but not first priority		0.33	X
	- No mention of price or exchange rate objectives		0.00	
7	**Function as a development bank, granting credit at subsidy rates?**	**0.20**		
	- No		1.00	
	- To some extent		0.66	X
	- Yes		0.33	
	- Central bank heavily involved in granting subsidized credits		0.00	

8   Collateral, access to credit, and investment in Bulgaria[1]

Zeljko Bogetic and Heywood Fleisig

Rarely do investors have sufficient savings to fund their investment projects; rarely do savers have enough investment projects to absorb their savings. When credit markets function well, they bridge that gap. They allocate savings to their most productive investment.

When government institutions attempt to fill that role, they must be scrupulous in their evaluation of investment projects. The more profitable an investment project, the more it will contribute to growth. When private institutions fill that role, they often depend more on the private borrower to evaluate the quality of the investment. But the private lender will typically require collateral as proof of the borrower's intention to repay and as recourse in the event that the borrower does not pay.

In Bulgaria, however, private Bulgarian banks typically accept only real estate as collateral for these loans, or the personal guaranty of someone who owns real estate. They usually will not accept movable property as collateral – property like inventory, accounts receivable, livestock or industrial equipment – unless that property remains in the physical possession of the bank or the borrower also offers a supplemental security based on the ownership of real estate. Private banks require this guaranty either directly, through a mortgage, or indirectly, by requiring proof that the borrower owns land that the bank could lien and sell in the event of non-payment or by requiring the personal guaranty of another property owner.

Besides banks, other potentially important private suppliers of credit operate in Bulgaria. These include non-bank financial intermediaries, such as finance companies and pawnshops, and non-bank non-financial intermediaries, such as equipment, automobile, and primary commodity dealers. These potential lenders followed lending practices similar to those of banks. Only material in the possession of the lender served as collateral for loans; otherwise, loans were given only to borrowers meeting the most stringent personal loan qualifications. Consequently, even loans commonly observed in industrial and other developing countries, like loans for auto-

161

mobiles and trucks, are unknown in Bulgaria. Other types of private financing, for heavy machinery, livestock, fertilizer, air conditioning and heating equipment, are unknown in Bulgaria.

Broadly, this gap in the granting of credit arises from Bulgaria's problems in devising a workable system of secured transactions – a system for securing loans with movable property.[2] The following sections discuss the economic cost to Bulgaria of its secured transactions problem – restrictions on the use of movable property as collateral. It shows how these secured transactions problems limit investment by raising the interest rate and the availability of funds, and how, in turn, these higher interest rates and lower volumes of lending limit economic growth and aggravate poverty. It then gives examples of how the secured transactions problem limits lending. Discussing the transactions of some important borrowers and lenders, it traces the effect of the problem through the channels through which credit flows. First, directly, by limiting the lenders' willingness to lend against movable property to finance their sales. Second, indirectly, by limiting the lenders' own ability to borrow against their movable property, making it difficult to finance their own operations and their own sales on credit. Finally, the chapter sets out a preliminary view of the legal and institutional roots of the secured transactions problem in Bulgaria and sets out some options for consideration by Bulgarian policy makers.

Secured transaction problem reduces output and growth

Business people and farmers get loans with three types of guaranties: real estate, movable property, and their reputation. Typically real estate is the best collateral, movable property is second best, and reputation is the worst. As we move from real estate to reputation, lenders will extend smaller loans and charge higher interest rates for them. This is true in Bulgaria, in Bolivia, and in the United States. It is true at Citicorp and at banks in developing countries.

The problem that arises in Bulgaria, however, emerges from crippling problems associated with using movable property as collateral. Bulgarian business and farm borrowers may get limited credit at the relatively low rates secured by real estate but once they run out of real estate to mortgage, they immediately face the high interest rates on loans secured by reputation alone. Unlike the industrial countries, a Bulgarian borrower's possession of movable property – equipment, inventories, accounts receivable – does not reduce the risk to the lender. Hence lenders who accepted movable property as collateral neither lent more nor charged lower interest rates.

This restriction of credit can be particularly severe when farmers or businessmen work from rented premises or do not own their own land. In these cases, restrictions on the usefulness of movable property as collateral will restrict their access to credit. They pay higher interest rates for loans than they would with better collateral loans.

Even then, often no loans are available. Smaller loans and higher interest rates lead investors to invest less; they do not undertake projects whose rate of return is less than the interest rate.

The secured transactions problem also affects the allocation of investment, not just its volume and price. Even for farmers and businessmen who do own real estate, a credit system linked rigidly to real estate will limit development. Different types of businesses and farms will require different combinations of fixed and working capital for their most efficient operation. For example, as a distribution business expands, it will increase sales. This higher volume of business may not require much more physical space, but it will require higher inventories. Credit to finance that inventory will be harder to obtain, however, if the inventory cannot itself serve as collateral. Similarly, expanding farm output often involves increasing yields per acre by using more machines or livestock on a given amount of land. Under such production conditions, optimal investment in both machines and livestock would rise relative to the investment in land. However, credit for those machines and livestock will be more restricted where they cannot serve as collateral.

In each of these examples, the most rapidly growing businesses will be forced to finance their expansion from the owner's capital and will have limited access to borrowed funds. A system that directs credit toward less rapidly growing business and away from more rapidly growing businesses is not most conducive to rapid economic growth.

Of course, farmers should not invest in projects whose rates of return are less than the interest rate. Such investments would earn less than their cost and would harm, not help, growth in Bulgaria. Nor can the government of Bulgaria address this problem by simply offering these loans through a subsidized or state-directed lending program – the private market charges more for these loans because they are, in fact, more risky. Spreading the risk over the whole population in a state supported subsidy program might make the losses less politically objectionable, but it would not reduce their size and would not reduce the drag they exert on Bulgarian growth. However, Bulgarian policy makers have a different option: the high interest rate charged in Bulgaria for loans against movable property contains a substantial risk premium to cover the higher cost of using movable property as collateral. Introducing a socially efficient way to reduce that risk would reduce interest rates, leading investment to increase and growth rates to rise.

Measuring the economic loss from the existing secured transactions system

Developing countries face many legal problems – many possible improvements in legal systems exist. Equally, developing countries display many types of economic inefficiency and many possible improvements in economic performance exist. Does

163

the secured transactions problem merit any special attention?

Preliminary calculations indicate that it does. When they can get a loan, Bulgarian borrowers pay 24 per cent to 36 per cent interest on US$ denominated loans ostensibly secured by movable property. Three major features explain those high interest rates: macroeconomics policy, high bank intermediation spreads, and the secured transaction problem. Obviously, the mortgage interest rate on houses in Bulgaria, typically a four or five year loan, is just as subject to macroeconomics risk as a four or five year equipment loan. Similarly, such mortgages would have intermediation spreads similar to the spreads on equipment loans. However, the mortgage interest rate in Bulgaria is only 16 per cent. The difference between the mortgage interest rate and the interest rate for loans for movable property can only be explained by differences in the quality of the collateral -- the secured transactions problem. That difference amounts to eight to 20 percentage points (see Table 8.1).

How much could that difference be reduced in a system that efficiently solved the secured transactions problem? In one such system, in the United States, rates of interest on loans for a wide array of equipment, cars, and other movable property typically run one-half to one per cent above the mortgage interest rate.

An efficient collateral system in Bulgaria, therefore, could reduce the cost of financing movable equipment by seven to 19 percentage points. The amount of movable property so financed would increase substantially – noting that under the existing system such credit is only offered to those with land. In the United States, approximately one-third of the capital stock is movable property. Moreover, since movable property depreciates somewhat faster than buildings or land, investment in movable property represents close to one-half of investment. This importance in the physical capital stock is mirrored in the credit structure: nearly 40 per cent of the country's credit is secured by movable goods alone. Unfortunately, similar statistics are not available for Bulgaria. There is a strong presumption, though, that the same broad conclusion would apply.[3]

What is the likely impact of such an expansion of credit on movable capital? This calculation remains to be done for Bulgaria. Previous work on Bolivia and Argentina, where the frameworks for secured transactions are similar to those of Bulgaria, indicated that problems with that system cost five to ten per cent of GDP annually.[4]

Secured transactions problem

The combination of high interest rates and limited access to credit in Bulgaria are caused by different elements: macroeconomics uncertainty, high bank spreads, insufficient saving, and the inability of borrowers to offer lenders satisfactory collateral. While a full discussion of these issues is beyond the scope of this paper, it is possible to decompose these elements.[5] Much of the access to credit problem in Bul-

164

garia arises from insufficient collateral; this problem will not go away if Bulgaria's other macroeconomics problems are addressed.

Table 8.1
Explaining high interest rates for loans in Bulgaria

	United States (in %)	Bulgaria (in %)	Difference (in %)
1. Effect of greater macroeconomics risk in Bulgaria			
(There is no risk that the US Government will be unable to pay its bonds in dollars, because it has the legal monopoly on printing dollars. the government of Bulgaria must get its dollars by raising taxes or cutting spending. These are politically difficult actions and lead to perceptions of macroeconomics risk. The difference between the US interest rate on dollar bonds and the Bulgarian interest rate on dollar bonds is entirely macroeconomics risk.)			
Government borrowing rate in dollars (3-month dollar-denominated notes)	5.5	11.4	5.9
2. Effect of higher bank intermediation spreads and greater difficulty in collecting against real estate collateral			
Mortgage interest rate	7.5	18.0	10.5
* Estimated size of impact	–	–	4.6
3. Estimated impact of the difference in the framework for secured transactions			
(Differences in macroeconomics risk and intermediation cost apply equally to loans secured by real estate and loans secured by movable property. In the United States, loans secured by movable property have interest rates close to the interest rates on mortgages; in Bulgaria, banks do not make loans secured only by movable property and non-bank credit charge runs about 60 per cent.)			
New car loan	9.7	21.0	11.3
Used car loan	14.1	26.0	11.9
Equipment	14.1	60.0	45.9
Personal unsecured loan	16.2	60.0	43.8
* Estimated size of impact	–	–	0.8 (new cars); 33.3 - 35.4 (other equipment and personal loans)

Source: U.S. data taken from *Federal Reserve Bulletin*, July 1993, tables 1.35, 1.53, 1.56. Bulgarian data are from wire services carrying Bulgarian data. Rates for loan secured by movable collateral based on evidence given during interviews.

What are the sources of the problems with secured transactions in Bulgaria? A number of explanations have been posited. This section examines those explanations and sets out the reasons for believing that the source of the problem lies in legal problems in the creation, perfection, and enforcement of security interests in movable property.

Legal roots?

Those who have worked in commercial banks, or for agencies that supervise and regulate banks, know that the first question any loan officer is taught to ask is 'How do I get my money back?'. The answer to that question involves: first, an evaluation of the business prospects of the borrower and the proposed loan; and second, a plan of action that the lender can pursue in the event that the borrower does not pay.

In most countries, that plan will rest on the prospects for seizing the collateral that secured the loan, selling the collateral, and applying the proceeds from the sale to the outstanding balance of the loan. It may also mean attaching and seizing other property of the debtor and selling that too, in the event that the proceeds of the sale of the collateral do not cover the loan. The clarity that the law permits in the loan agreement and the amount of time that repossession and sale of collateral takes, therefore, is an important element in determining whether the collateral can satisfactorily secure the loan. Three problems, therefore, underlie the secured transactions problem in Bulgaria: the creation of security interests, their perfection, and their enforcement.

Creation

A workable and efficient system for securing transactions has several desired traits: the interest should be inexpensive to create, legally unambiguous, and readily extended to most transactions of economic importance. At the other extreme, it should not contain gaps in coverage or arbitrary prohibitions on certain types of assets.

The present Bulgarian legal system makes it impossible for certain economic agents to use certain kinds of property as collateral. However, some of these parties and some of these transactions have great potential economic importance. These gaps in legal definitions or economic unsound prohibitions will not be remedied by speeding up repossession and sale; rather, they can only be addressed by fixing the underlying laws and procedures.

For example, the Law of Contracts (1952) makes no provision for the 'non-possessory pledge' – the main loan contract for movable property when property remains in the hands of the borrower. Given this absence, there is no practical way to write enforceable contracts for equipment financing, even though in principle this is consistent with the law. More recent laws do contemplate the 'non-possessory' pledge

166

but restrict these security interests to foreign investors[6] and banks.[7] The law on agricultural financing[8] would allow farmers to use crops, stock, and farm equipment as collateral for loans when this merchandise remains in the debtor's possession. However, such pledges are limited to those issued by state-owned banks and bearing a rate of interest below the market. These provisions will be of little comfort to non-bank lenders or to non-farm borrowers. The restrictions have no obvious public policy justification but bear a high economic cost.

Perfection

Perfection, the establishment of the rank of priority of the claim against the collateral, is crucial in determining the risk of the lender in a secured transaction. The key element in the determination is the registration of the security interest in the collateral. If that determination is not made in a public way, all lenders face heightened risk and will react by lending less.

Because of this, differences in perfection systems may seem small from the perspective of their legal structure, but confusion about priorities and the chance of a shift in priority can have disastrous effects on lending. The problem can be seen easily with a simple example. Suppose a lender has a first claim against an asset with an expected resale value of $100,000, whose resale value would range between $80,000 with probability 50 per cent and $120,000 with probability 50 per cent. A loan of $60,000 in the first position would appear to that lender to be quite secure – it would have zero per cent chance of loss because the lowest possible realized value of the collateral would be $80,000. But move the same loan to the second position, with, say, a $30,000 loan in the first position, and now the lender faces a loss of $10,000 with a 50 per cent probability (lender defaults, property realizes $80,000, and first position claimant takes $30,000, leaving $50,000 in equity to cover the $60,000 loan). Evaluated relative to the size of the loan, that is a 50 per cent chance of a loss of 16.7 per cent ($10,000/$60,000) – so a 'safe' loan becomes much riskier solely because of the change in the priority of the claim. A system that conceals information about priorities, therefore, makes it impossible for lenders to judge the risk of the loan and, therefore, to price the loan or set its size. Not surprisingly, lenders respond by demanding other collateral that can be registered or physically possessed. Two serious problems afflict the perfection: properties of the law that create uncertainty and the lack of unified public registries. The law itself contributes to uncertainty about priority by giving many claimants priority over the possessor of the security interest: the law assigns a higher priority to court costs of liquidation, legal fees, and, possibly, to taxes and worker severance payments.[9] As all of these costs are uncertain but potentially high, a lender will have a great deal of difficulty analyzing how much collateral will suffice to cover a loan.

No functioning registry for security interests in movable property exists in Bulgaria nor is the creation of it contemplated in the law. Rather, the pledge with dispossession – the security agreement used when the collateral is movable property and remains in the possession of the borrower – is filed in the scattered offices of notaries. Any notary in Bulgaria can register a pledge, or, more precisely, assign the 'certain date' that determines the priority of the pledge. Even if the lender knew which of Bulgaria's notaries had assigned the certain date, the index within each notaries office might stymie the search for the document. This is a critical defect in the Bulgarian pledge. Like other legal systems, the priority of the claim of the Bulgarian lender against the collateral is identified by the time of the filing; unlike other systems, however, it is impossible for a Bulgarian lender to determine a position in the order of priority.

No rational lender will consider that such collateral is safe; no rational lender will make such a loan. No credit line designed to disburse against equipment or working capital and administered by private banks will disburse unless the borrower can offer sufficient other guaranties based on real estate holdings or personal reputation. If the borrower can offer such guaranties, the borrower would have gotten the loan anyway and the credit line would have no additionality.

Moreover, this problem with the registry for the pledge where the collateral is held by the debtor contaminates the otherwise promising Bulgarian system for the 'ordinary' pledge, the pledge wherein the collateral remains in the hands of the lender. Registration is less important for this pledge, because the physical possession of the collateral by the lender is public proof of the lender's security interest in the collateral. However, suppose the borrower pledged the goods to another lender before delivering them to the custody of the lender offering the 'ordinary' pledge – then that earlier pledge with dispossession would still have priority. The first lender could demand delivery of the collateral from the second lender in the event of default but the second lender could not protect himself with a search of the registries. Consequently, only inventory with 'impeccable' credentials that reaches the country through importation and is immediately placed in bonded warehouses is really at low risk for Bulgarian lenders.

In this way, the lack of public registries stymies the warehouse lending system that is used all over industrial countries and in many developing countries to routinely finance agricultural and industrial stocks.

Enforcement

Slow Bulgarian court procedures make movable property poor collateral in Bulgaria. Those businesses interviewed indicated consistently that repossessing and selling movable property used as collateral can take six months to two years. Banks reported no collection and sale experience under six months. This is too long for movable property. Farm and industrial equipment will depreciate substantially over such a time; inventory will become shopworn; livestock can die; equipment bought used can become valueless; and accounts receivable will be gone. For all such collateral, the lender faces a constant threat that the collateral will disappear. Its movability and its physical possession by the debtor threaten the creditor in many ways. Dishonest debtors may sell the collateral or flee with it. Even honest debtors, however, may have the collateral taken from them by others when, as they are unable to service their debt, their business affairs fall into disarray.

Real estate is less subject to these risks than is movable property like farm and industrial equipment, inventory, or livestock. While its market value can fluctuate, real estate typically would not depreciate substantially during the two-year collection period. Moreover, by definition, real estate is always located in the same place; it cannot be moved. Even with a long court action, lenders know that the real estate will be where it was when the action began. When collection procedures are slow, as they are in Bulgaria, lenders will only take real estate as collateral. They will not take movable property.

Problems with secured transactions limit access to credit by both borrowers and lenders

This section discusses how problems with the creation, perfection, and enforcement of security interests combine in different ways to hinder different types of economically important activities in Bulgaria. It illustrates the problems with examples of farmers, equipment dealers, retail businesses, and private banks. It is not, in any sense, an exhaustive treatment. Many more problems with secured transactions will affect each of these agents; they will also affect many more agents than those discussed here.

Farmers

Farmers in Bulgaria cannot get credit secured alone by livestock, crops, or equipment. They cannot pledge the livestock, crops, or equipment that they already own to get, say, working capital. Nor, effectively, can they get working capital by offering a security interest in a 'future' crop under cultivation to get working capital; nor can they buy livestock or equipment on credit from dealers or banks. If they cannot mortgage land or show evidence of ownership of land without encumbrances, they can get no appreciable credit at all.

Even for land where title is clear, the existence of cooperatives presents a problem. Pledging the property of cooperatives requires a separate legal infrastructure to permit pledging shares in the cooperative. Without this infrastructure, cooperative members cannot get credit. As understanding of this fact seems to be quite limited, those holding property cooperatively are often subjected to politically-contentious plans to break up cooperatives so that the members may obtain credit. While these pressures may have merit on other grounds, they are not necessary to permit access to credit.

While this situation is taken for granted in Bulgaria, under different credit and collateral systems movable property does serve readily as collateral. The reasons for this arise from the problems of speed of collection and definition of security interests in collateral.

Consider first the definition of the underlying security interest. Lending against wine or grain stored in elevators or cattle in feedlots is quite common in the United States and many other countries, but rare in Bulgaria. Why? As mentioned above, the critical defects arise from the slow speed of repossession and the absence of a pledge registry. However, even if these problems were solved, Bulgarian law appears to contain no definition of a floating pledge that could be used to lend against goods that were subject to replacement while in storage. That gap makes the floating pledge a risky instrument for both cattle in feedlots or grain in elevators. There, the normal practice of trade requires revolving part of the inventory. And once the inventory revolves, under the law, the collateral legally 'disappears'.[10]

Consider the speed of repossession and sale. In Bulgaria, cattle owned by a farmer operating only on rented land are unacceptable to any private bank as collateral. Bulgarian banks regard such cattle as too risky because the six month to two-year collection period is too long. In Kansas, by contrast, cattle are the preferred collateral for bank loans. Machinery stands second and real estate a poor third. The bank examiners at the Federal Reserve concur in this judgment. Why? Because loan contracts written with cattle as security have no difficulty identifying the underlying collateral, because claims against those cattle can be clearly registered and demonstrated to other possible borrowers, and because cattle that secure a loan in default in Kansas can be repossessed and sold without judicial intervention in one to five days.

Providing farmers with working capital by lending to finance standing crops is also nonexistent in Bulgaria. The law appears to contain no 'pledge against after-acquired property' so a loan written against future crop is difficult to defend in court and, therefore, risky. This crucially blocks the flow of credit. When intermediaries like feed lot and grain silo operators cannot borrow, they cannot pass credit back down the production line to the farmers that sell to them. That limits competition in the lending market facing farmers. They must try to gain access to bank lenders, which will be difficult for them. Also, banks are not well-represented in rural areas and typically lack the customer knowledge to directly serve much of the rural population; dealers and merchants often do.

Equipment dealers

Equipment dealers face the same problem as banks in extending credit to finance equipment sales: if, as a practical matter, movable property cannot serve as collateral, equipment dealers cannot sell equipment on credit secured only by the equipment sold.

In other countries, such sales on credit are a highly lucrative business, and dealers actively compete with banks to arrange the financing of equipment sales. Dealers can be a major conduit providing access to credit – they can funnel credit to a group of borrowers that commercial banks cannot reach. The equipment dealer has frequent dealings with the customer through servicing the machines and, consequently, can often know better than a bank both the reputation of that customer and his likely performance as a borrower. Dealers have a natural advantage in repossessing and selling collateral, as they already deal in the market for that equipment. A tractor dealer, for example, can more easily repossess and sell a tractor than can a bank. Moreover, when the dealer finances a sale, the dealer makes the profit from the sale as well as the profit from handling the financing contract or selling it to a finance company. This additional profit from the sale can make smaller loans more attractive to a dealer than to a bank. These dealers can service equipment customers less expensively than can most banks.

But the secured transaction problem in Bulgaria penalizes equipment dealers in several ways that make it difficult for them to fill this role. The typical equipment dealer in Bulgaria has a credit line with a bank or manufacturer. For nearly all dealers, the size of this credit line is determined by the net asset position of the firm, with only its real estate having an important weight in its assets. While a few banks would accept inventories and accounts receivable as collateral, they deducted the ensuing loan from the overall credit line. Consequently, the dealer's own inventory of new and used equipment actually does not serve as collateral for *additional* loans; nor would the assignment of credit sales to the bank yield loans above the existing credit line. Unable to use inventories of equipment or accounts receivable to *expand* access to credit, equipment dealers are constrained in their ability to offer credit for equipment sales.

These collateral-related problems prevent strong links from developing between banks, the dominant financial institutions in Bulgaria, and potential non-bank sources of credit that are often better suited to lend to farmers and to small- and medium-scale enterprises, which are the foundation of a vibrant, competitive, private economy.

In many countries, dealers also have credit lines with their manufacturers. These manufacturers will typically offer a credit line to dealers based on their network and the volume of sales they generate. Dealers often take used equipment in trade when they sell new equipment. Taking in used equipment is crucial in selling new equipment. At the same time, selling used equipment provides an important input for smaller and less wealthy farmers and business people.

In many countries, dealers compete with banks to arrange the financing of equipment and livestock. Such dealers however, must themselves borrow to extend this credit or make arrangements with finance companies. Movable property can secure those loans in two different ways. First, the dealers' inventory of movable goods can serve as collateral for loans. Banks and financial institutions can extend credit to the enterprise to finance their holding of inventory. Second, dealers can rediscount or sell the loans they originate in the course of selling their equipment.

In Bulgaria, all equipment dealers interviewed reported that there was no practical *way* to sell or rediscount loans that they originated, whether or not the purchaser was offered recourse in the event of non-payment. All dealers interviewed reported that the total credit available to them was determined by the value of their real estate holdings and the unsecured line of credit that company income would support; total credit was unrelated to their holdings of inventory. Consequently, businesses must finance both their inventories and any dealer-financed sales out of their own capital.

Retail businesses

Retail businesses – such as office supply stores, hardware stores, plumbing supply houses, seed dealers or fertilizer suppliers – often provide working capital to farmers and small businesses by extending unsecured credit for short periods of time, 30 to 180 days. Such supply stores constitute an important part of the credit chain. They advance revolving credit to farmers and businesses, providing useful financing for the purchase of seeds, fertilizer, or light equipment.

The credit they grant is unsecured. The stores assign credit lines in line with the borrowers' net worth, income, and their repayment history. They rarely ask for written pledges on loans extended to their customers.

However, collateral-related problems create obstacles for retail businesses in raising credit to finance their own credit sales. In countries where secured transaction problems are less serious, retail enterprises can take their 'accounts receivable' and refinance them with other financial intermediaries – they can discount them with banks or finance companies or sell them to factors. This permits them to roll over their capital and extend more credit for new purchases by their customers. These retail stores can then specialize in extending limited credit to clients that they know well and intermediating between such small borrowers and larger financial intermediaries.

Banks and finance companies could not profitably make such small loans to the dealer's final customers. However, they might find the same small loans attractive if the store that extended the original credit 'bundled' these accounts into a larger block. The larger financial intermediaries would then use these accounts receivable to secure a loan to the store that extended the original credit. Unlike the smaller loans to individual customers, the loan to the store would be large enough to warrant the attention of the bank or the finance company.

Because of collateral-related problems, retail business in Bulgaria cannot discount their accounts receivable or pledges with the banks to finance their sales.[11] While

172

banks may appear to take such documents as collateral, they actually deduct the sums provided from the overall credit line whose size depends mainly on the real estate of the business. No additional credit is actually supplied; the documents have no standing in and of themselves as collateral for loans.

Private banks

No private bank interviewed in Bulgaria would lend for movable property unless the borrower delivered the movable property into its possession. The financing of car sales provides an instructive example of the large possible consequences of that policy. Financing car sales is an enormous business in industrial countries. For example, the total consumer credit secured by automobiles in the United States in mid-1994 amounted to $285 billion, of which $130 billion was held by commercial banks.[12] In comparison, commercial bank mortgage lending amounted to about $940 billion.[13] Consequently, in the United States, car financing is a business that equals 15 per cent of bank mortgage lending and for which banks contest in a market that amounts to about 30 per cent of mortgage lending. That is, car financing is a big and important business to commercial banks in the United States; the car-financing referred to here all arises from financing cars that are in the hands of the borrowers.[14]

Yet, in Bulgaria, only one private bank would finance a car sale when the car remained in the hands of the borrower and then only after approval of the loan by the board of directors of the bank. This a more severe problem than exists in other countries where the World Bank has undertaken similar work: even in Bolivia, Honduras, Argentina, and Uruguay, where the credit system for movable property is severely impaired, car loans function better.

The roots of the unusually severe Bulgarian difficulties lie in several areas. The lender has no effective ability to *perfect* the lender's security interest in the car – that is, to establish the existence and the rank of priority of a lender's security interest in the collateral. That problem arises because the Bulgarian automobile registration system does not keep track of security interests in the car. Therefore, no system exists to keep the owner of a pledged car from selling it to another person free of the security interest. Even if that buyer wanted to find out whether the car was pledged, it would be technically impossible to do so – the pledge is not in the automobile registry but rather in the hands of an undetermined notary.

Second, even if records were in order, most parties believe that seizure and sale of the car would require a six month to a two year court proceeding. A car depreciates substantially during that period; with such procedures, a loan secured by a car is not appreciably better than an unsecured loan.

In many countries with collateral and guaranty problems, the only movable property that can be financed is cars. That is because cars are licensed and registered, so it is relatively easy for the lender to establish the priority of the lender's claim.

173

Moreover, cars are only useful if they are driven on public roads, so it is relatively easy to locate and seize the car. Often the lenders can get the aid of the police and use the same channels used to locate stolen cars.

If cars are this unattractive as collateral in Bulgaria, then other movable equipment will be considerably less attractive. Loans on other equipment must be registered in the scattered notary offices; moreover, technically such equipment can be concealed and still retain its economic usefulness. Not surprising, no private Bulgarian lender would make such a loan unless the borrower qualified for the loan under the strictest personal lending criteria.

Options for solution

Taking into account the above discussion, Table 8.2 summarizes a preliminary list of identified problems and solution strategies in addressing the collateral-related problems of credit in Bulgaria.

Table 8.2
Addressing the legal and institutional roots of the limits to access credit

Problems	Solutions
Creation of security interests	Expand the range of movable property that can serve as collateral for a loan; permit different types of property rights in that property such as floating security interest in proceeds, after-acquired property clauses; consider the advantages of broad functional approaches to security interests, such as the EBRD model code, Canadian Personal Property Security Act, or the US UCC-9; weigh these advantages against more piecemeal but simpler reforms along the lines of the German or French model. Consider the advantages of extending the abilities to write non-possessory security interests beyond the banks and foreign parties.
Perfection	Public registration of security interests; consider the type of public registration; consider using public access as a way of providing private registration; consider possibilities of linking and making public the existing notarial registries; consider requiring the registration of security interests in automobiles in the automobile registry.
Enforcement	Consider options of improving the speed and lowering the cost of public enforcement agents; of expanding public enforcement beyond the judiciary; of changing laws to permit private repossession and sale of the collateral underlying debt contracts.

174

Notes

1   This chapter draws on the background paper prepared for the World Bank Report by Fleisig, Simpson, and Rover (1996). We are particularly obliged to Mark Beesley, Ronald Cuming, Ulrich Drobiig, Alejandro Gaffo, Lubomir Mitov, and John A. Spanogic for their guidance and helpful comments on this section of the report.

2   In broadly accepted legal usage, personal property is all property other than real property. Real property is also known as real estate. This paper treats movable property as roughly synonymous with personal property. Personal property includes all movable goods such as fertilizer, inventory, machinery or livestock. However, it is broader in that it includes 'intangible' property. This excludes 'fixtures', items such as equipment that would be physically fastened to a building or to land. Fixtures are items that were once personal property but that are now attached to real property in a way that removing them will damage the real property. This paper does not discuss the Bulgarian system of financing fixtures.

3   While wages in Bulgaria are considerably lower than those in the United States, this would tend to lead Bulgarian businesses to economize on capital and, in aggregate, for Bulgaria to have a lower capital labor ratio. However, them is no reason to believe that labor substitutes differently for fixed than for movable capital. Assuming this substitution is the same, and that Bulgaria and the United States have technological possibilities by virtue of their similar educational levels, we would expect a lower overall level of capital but about the same proportions of fixed and movable capital.

4   See Fleisig (1995).

5   For a fuller discussion, see Fleisig (1996).

6   Zakon za spopanskata deyunost na chuzhdestram-iite litsa i za zakrils na chuzhdetnlanite investitbii, Darzhaven Vestnik, No. 8 (1992), hereinafter 'Foreign Investment Law'.

7   Zakon za bankite i kreditnoto delo, 27 March 1992, hereinafter 'Banking Law'.

8   Law on Agricultural Financing, 1993-94.

9   Zakon za zadalzheniyata i dogovorite, Darzhaven Vestnik, No. 12 (1993), hereinafter 'LOC', Art. 136.

10   An important exception exists for the non-possessory pledge provided for in the new Banking Law. However, the non-possessory pledge may only be taken by banks and will not be used by other creditors.

11   Theoretically, the contract law of 1952 treats accounts receivable 'as transferable money claims that can be the object of a traditional pledge', like a stock certificate or a bond. However, the difficulty with accounts receivable in the

Bulgarian framework that requires physical transfer to the lender arises from the lack of any intrinsic value to their 'paper embodiment'. What would the store owner transfer – the account books, sales slips? The prospective lender against accounts receivable needs a system to establish the lender's interest in the payments from those receivable in a public and dependable way. Therefore, while the Bulgarian law may give the theoretical possibility of accounts receivable financing, it has not provided the necessary legal logical structure required by the underlying economic transaction.

12   *Federal Reserve Bulletin*, August 1994, table 1.55.

13   *Federal Reserve Bulletin*, August 1994, table 1.26.

14   Mindful of this, the World Bank mission asked all private banks if they lent for cars and all private banks said they would not. In one instance, however, the credit director stated that they 'would be happy to lend for cars so long as the import documents were in order and the cars were delivered directly to the bank's bonded warehouse'. Upon being asked if the bank would consider extending credit for a car in the possession of the borrower, the credit director flatly answered 'no'. On consideration, however, the director said that a couple of such loans had been granted but only to extremely well-known and affluent people and even then only when the loan application had been approved by the board of directors. Upon a follow-up question of whether the director meant to say 'the loan committee', the director said 'no' – approval by the board of directors. That is, a car loan in Bulgaria was a lending decision that required management attention on the order of a decision to float a bond or a stock issue.

References

Fleisig, Heywood W. (1995), 'Assessing the Economic Cost of Deficiencies in the Framework for Secured Transactions: Examinations of Argentina and Bolivia', World Bank Report.
—— (1996), 'The Economic Functions of Security in a Market Economy', in Norton, Joseph J. (ed.), *Emerging Economics: Devising Secured Transactions Laws for Security in Movables and Intangibles*, Kluwer Emotional Publishers: London.
——, Simpson, John, and Rover, Jan-Hendrick (1996), 'How Legal Restrictions on Collateral Limit Access to Credit in Bulgaria', World Bank Report.

Part Four
TRADE

9   The international economy[1]

John A. Bristow

External economic relations are at the center of Bulgaria's transition experience. The communist era ended with the country having huge debts in hard currencies; failure to service that debt from the spring of 1990 onwards made new non-official borrowing impossible, thus hardening the balance-of-payments constraint, inhibiting both exports and capital inflows; the overwhelming dominance of the Council for Mutual Economic Assistance (CMEA, otherwise known as Comecon) in Bulgaria's foreign trade meant that the collapse of that institution in 1990 not only caused an exogenous shock to aggregate demand much exceeding that experienced by other countries in the region but also made trade-reorientation especially significant as a transition objective; difficulties over exchange-rate policy have had adverse effects on macroeconomic conditions, international trade and investment; and Bulgaria has suffered considerably as a result of the United Nations embargoes on Iraq and the rump of Yugoslavia. In this paper we examine these issues.

The significance of the CMEA

The Council for Mutual Economic Assistance was established in 1949, its membership consisting of the USSR, all European communist countries other than Albania and Yugoslavia, and certain non-European communist states. Four features of this organisation are important to an understanding of the nature of intra-CMEA trade. First, that trade was conducted on the basis of bilateral agreements of an essentially barter nature. Second, the system was explicitly designed to promote national specialization based on the assumed existence of economies of scale but having little to do with comparative advantage. Third, the implicit exchange rates and relative prices for this barter trade were not equal to world prices and were not even equal to domestic relative prices. Fourth, for the purposes of clearing, planning and statistics

179

there was developed an artificial currency, the transferable ruble, which was no more than a unit of account and had none of the other features of money.

From the 1960s onwards the CMEA became the most important external influence on Bulgaria's economic development, because such a high proportion of the country's trade was with other members, and especially with the former Soviet Union (FSU). Official figures for the importance of inter-member trade are shown in Table 9.1.

The table indicates that the CMEA was much more important for Bulgaria than for any other country in the region. However, these official figures are seriously misleading because of the problems of aggregating CMEA and non-CMEA trade. The unit of account had no fixed, and no easily determinable, relationship with the dollar. The official aggregation from which the above percentages were derived was accomplished by measuring all trade in terms of a 'currency lev' (or an equivalent artificial currency in other member countries) whose exchange value was different from official exchange rates. Indeed, the relationship between the exchange value of the currency lev and official exchange rates was not constant across currencies. The overall effect was a serious overvaluation of trade denominated in transferable rubles (that is, CMEA trade) compared with that denominated in dollars. On top of this, the official exchange value of the lev against the dollar (which is used in the aggregation for non-CMEA trade) was itself administered and greatly exceeded the market-clearing value. This compounded the distortion by causing non-CMEA trade to be undervalued in the aggregation.

An estimate of these biases was attempted by the World Bank,[2] which indicated that, in 1989, the CMEA accounted for 62 per cent of Bulgaria's exports (as opposed to the 83 per cent shown by the official figures) and for 52 per cent of imports (as opposed to 73 per cent). This strongly suggests that, because the official figures of trade structure prior to transition overstate the dependence on the CMEA, later indicators of changes in trade structure also overstate the degree of trade-reorientation and, more generally, of the impact on Bulgaria of the changing trade regime.

Of course, notwithstanding these statistical problems, the dominance of CMEA trade for Bulgaria cannot be doubted[3] and so the country had more than any other member to lose when the system collapsed.

Quantitative estimates of the effect on Bulgaria of the end of the old trading system are difficult to derive because of the statistical problems already mentioned. However, one set of estimates, referring to the change between 1989 and 1991, suggests the following.[4] The first effect results from the collapse of export markets in the former Soviet Union (FSU), which is estimated to have generated a decline of around 40 per cent in total Bulgarian export volume over the period in question. Some of this could have been expected to have been compensated for by a reorientation of exports to other markets, but a figure of 33 per cent is suggested for the proportion by which import volumes would have had to diminish to preserve exter-

Table 9.1

Shares of CMEA in total trade of member countries (%), 1989ᵃ

	Exports	Imports
Bulgaria	83	73
	(66)	(54)
Czechoslovakia	54	55
	(31)	(30)
Hungary	39	39
	(24)	(22)
Poland	35	32
	(21)	(18)
Romania	40	55
	(23)	(32)
FSU	46	50
	(0)	(0)

a   Figures in parentheses are for trade with the FSU.
Source: Schrenk (1992), p. 221.

nal balance. Then, the move to world prices for intra-CMEA trade produced a serious deterioration in the terms of trade on both sides of the account. Dominating Bulgarian imports were fuels from the FSU and, over the two-year period, prices of these products more than doubled. On the other hand, the country's major CMEA exports were machinery and equipment, of which prices fell somewhat. The overall terms-of-trade effect (that is, the decline in import volumes required to preserve external balance with no change in export volumes) was estimated to be 27 per cent.[5] In other words, the two effects together required a 60 per cent reduction in the volume of imports if the balance of payments were to be unaffected. Such a reduction would have represented something between 12 and 25 per cent of 1989 GDP.[6]

These estimates should not be taken too literally (and even their authors warn that they involve a series of unverifiable assumptions necessitated by data deficiencies and so are only very approximate orders of magnitude), but no reasonable estimation procedure could refute the hypothesis that the fall in exports to the FSU and the deterioration in the terms of trade administered a catastrophic shock to the Bulgarian economy – a shock which is more than enough to explain why the output decline after 1989 was deeper than in any other country of the region. Figures for the same trade, but viewed from the Soviet side, also support this conclusion. In 1991, total Soviet imports were 44 per cent lower than in the previous year, imports from all CMEA partners were 56 per cent lower, but those from Bulgaria had declined by 63 per cent.[7]

In addition to these real effects, mention should be made of the adverse effects of the inadequacies of the financial regime under which Bulgarian-FSU trade has been conducted since the collapse of the CMEA. Under the old system, if a bilateral clearing account failed to balance in transferable rubles, no debt in the financial sense was established: the debit or credit was simply used as the starting-point in future physical barter agreements between the two countries. Unfortunately for Bulgaria, this system came to an end at a time when the country was in credit in its balance with the Soviet Union (by one estimate, to the value of $300 million).[8] Since the Bulgarian exporters had already been paid in leva by the Foreign Trade Bank, the Russians were in effect debtors of the Bulgarian government and the latter had to carry the financial costs. This is one reason why the state's financing requirement has exceeded its budget deficit. Since the credit was interest-free but its financing was not, the existence of this unredeemed debt added a burden to the Bulgarian budget.

Trade between the two countries has, from 1991, been conducted in so-called 'clearing dollars'. These are still really only units of account but balances are domestically transferable at a publicly quoted exchange rate – but a rate which bears no real relationship to the lev/US$ rate. Trade continues to be on a negotiated bilateral basis, but the newer system may be slightly less distorted than the old transferable ruble in that price-ratios for traded goods bear a closer relation to international price ratios than they did.[9]

The reorientation of trade

Origin and destination

The issues here are central to Bulgaria's transition process since the ability to reorientate trading relationships in response to the collapse of traditional markets in the former CMEA is a necessary condition for the country's future economic success.

Table 9.2 indicates the geographical structure of Bulgarian trade for the first four years of the transition process (at the time of writing, no reliable statistics for 1995 were available).

When comparing this table with Table 9.1, two points must be remembered: first, Table 9.1 uses unrefined figures which overstate the importance of CMEA trade; and second, that table includes the former GDR as CMEA (that country accounting for approximately six per cent of both exports from and imports to Bulgaria in 1989).

Table 9.2
Geographical structure of trade* (%), 1991-94

	1991	1992	1993	1994
Exports				
Former CMEA	55	29	26	36
OECD	26	42	43	47
Other	19	29	31	18
Imports				
Former CMEA	47	37	43	40
OECD	33	44	43	47
Other	20	19	14	13

a   The former German Democratic Republic is counted as OECD rather than as former CMEA.
Source: Bulgarian National Bank.

The table appears to indicate a very dramatic change in the geographical pattern of Bulgaria's trade, with the proportion of exports accounted for by the former CMEA (excluding GDR) declining by over 40 percentage points and the proportion accounted for by OECD increasing by more than 30 percentage points. Qualitatively similar though quantitatively less dramatic changes are shown for imports. The problem is to know how much of this is real reorientation and how much is statistical illusion.

The potential illusion has two, related sources. First, there is the general problem – already noted – of aggregating trade in transferable rubles with trade in convertible currency, a problem which causes the official figures to overstate the relative importance of trade conducted in non-convertible currency. Since, from 1991 onwards, trade with the former CMEA other than Russia has been conducted in convertible currency, this statistical bias correspondingly diminishes and so changes between the pre-transition and transition years are exaggerated. The other factor confusing the picture is the devaluation of 1991 when the lev/dollar rate was unified and became market-determined. Since the method of valuing trade with Russia did not adjust proportionately, the effect of the devaluation was to increase the significance of dollar-denominated trade relative to trade denominated in transferable rubles.

Thus, Table 9.2, when combined with Table 9.1, is certainly misleading as a statistical picture of the change in the geographical structure of Bulgarian foreign trade. However, there is no reason to believe that it is misleading qualitatively. No data exist for trade volumes (and, even if they did, some of the same issues would arise

183

since such data consist of value figures deflated by price indices, the latter being notoriously difficult to construct reliably) but there can be no doubt that there has been a reorientation away from the FSU, especially on the export side.

Commodity structure

As already noted, the patterns of intra-CMEA trade took little account of comparative advantage and, as a result, industrial structures were seriously distorted with excessive representation of those activities which would be expected to be uncompetitive in liberalized markets. These distortions were investigated in a major research project covering several transition economies, including Bulgaria.[10] Among other things, this project studied what would have happened in the late 1980s if the inputs and outputs of Bulgarian industry had been valued at world prices (which were taken to represent competitive prices). The results were dramatic. On average for manufacturing industry, measured value added would have been more than halved, but in some cases the distortion (more or less, artificial profitability) was much greater. For example, in transport equipment (which includes the famous fork-lift trucks in which Bulgaria had a CMEA monopoly), the distortions increased measured value added by almost nine-fold. In the case of basic chemicals, cement and fruit and vegetable products, value added at international prices was actually negative (which means that GDP measured at international prices would have been higher if that sub-sector had not existed). The situation became even worse after an effort to make adjustments for the alleged inferior quality of many Bulgarian products: this suggested that the industrial sector as a whole had negative value added.

The exact numbers generated by this research are of no concern, especially since they have to be accompanied by many qualifications. The important point is qualitative: that the planning and trade systems generated a structure of prices and quantities which led value added to be exaggerated. This is exactly what would be expected of systems which created an industrial structure which had no reference to comparative advantage, and would lead one to predict that price- and trade-liberalization themselves (that is, independently of any associated or coincidental effects on demand) would lead to a decline in the activities whose survival depended most on the distortion of markets.

Therefore, when trade and foreign-exchange markets were liberalized, one would expect to see a fairly rapid change in the commodity structure of GDP and, more important here, of international trade.

The change in trade patterns is, unfortunately, difficult to track – not only for the statistical reason already referred to, but because the method of classifying trade by commodity changed in 1991: continuous series are not available covering both the pre-transition and transition periods. Nonetheless, a broad picture can be sketched.

Table 9.3 reveals very clearly the nature of Bulgaria's international trade in the last full year under the old system. In relation to the CMEA, the country was predominantly one which imported equipment, fuels and minerals and used them to produce capital goods for export. In addition, it had net exports of food products and of manufactured consumer goods.

Table 9.3
Commodity structure of trade (%), 1989

	CMEA	Other	Total
Exports			
Machinery, equipment	65	24	50
Fuels, minerals	3	33	15
Chemicals, rubber	3	7	5
Non-food materials	3	9	5
Food, related products	13	18	15
Consumer goods	12	8	10
Other	-	2	1
Imports			
Machinery, equipment	29	25	37
Fuels, minerals	36	32	34
Chemicals, rubber	3	10	7
Non-food materials	3	14	8
Food, related products	3	13	8
Consumer goods	5	6	6
Other	1	1	1

Source: derived from World Bank (1991), Vol. 1, pp. 152-3.

As regards non-CMEA, the picture is different with, at the level of product differentiation shown in the table, quite a close match between the commodity structure of imports and exports (one exception being agricultural produce, which includes wine and tobacco). However, the table disguises important differences between trade patterns with, on the one hand, OECD members and, on the other, developing countries. For most of the 1980s, Bulgaria's exports to developing countries considerably exceeded those to the developed world, whereas the situation as regards imports was the reverse. In 1989, 64 per cent of imports from developing countries consisted of fuel and minerals – a reflection notably of growing oil imports from the Middle East and North Africa – and machinery accounted for 38 per cent of exports to developing countries. Bulgarian capital goods were, however, less successful in penetrating western markets (machinery representing only ten per cent of exports to developed countries) and exports to those countries consisted particularly of food and materials (27 per cent) and fuels and minerals (44 per cent). Imports from OECD members consisted especially of machinery (36 per cent) and food and materials (25 per cent).

Transition has brought very significant changes in the commodity structure of Bulgaria's trade, as is shown if Table 9.4 is compared with the final column of Table 9.3.

Table 9.4
Commodity structure of trade (%), 1991-94

	1991	1992	1993	1994
Exports				
Food, drink, tobacco	25	26	21	22
Minerals, fuel	5	8	10	9
Chemicals, plastic	27	15	17	17
Metals	7	15	19	20
Machinery	29	19	15	13
Other	7	18	18	19
Imports				
Food, drink, tobacco	10	8	9	11
Minerals, fuel	56	38	38	30
Chemicals, plastics	8	12	12	12
Metals	3	6	6	7
Machinery	16	24	22	24
Other	8	13	13	16

Source: Bulgarian National Bank.

Despite the difficulty created by the lack of continuity in commodity-classification, the broad pattern is clear, and it shows just how much the structure of trade had been distorted under the CMEA, especially on the export side. Machinery and equipment had accounted for almost half of total exports in 1989, and two-thirds of exports to the CMEA, whereas the contribution of those products to exports fell to 13 per cent by 1994. This is not surprising, given the collapse of major markets and the time needed to penetrate new markets. The longer-term prospects are, however, not encouraging since (apart from computers and related products) the structure of Bulgaria's engineering exports bears little resemblance to the structure of OECD imports of such goods.[11] On the other hand, food, drink and tobacco – where some comparative advantage exists – have increased their contribution noticeably. In general, total export structure in 1994 was quite similar to the structure of non-CMEA exports in 1989, as would be expected with the dramatic reduction in the effect of distorted CMEA trade patterns. The change on the import side is less marked, primarily because of the low price-elasticity of demand for energy from the FSU: the contraction in the volume of fuel imports has been small relative to the huge increase in prices. Nevertheless, again the total commodity structure is moving towards the earlier non-CMEA structure.

Relations with the European Union

In March 1993, Bulgaria became the fifth transition economy to conclude an association agreement with the European Community (now the European Union), the others being the former Czechoslovakia, Hungary, Poland and Romania. Trade aspects were dealt with under a so-called interim agreement which was intended to become operable in July, but was postponed for six months. The agreement provides for the establishment of a mutual free trade area over a period of ten years, the rate of elimination of tariffs and non-tariff barriers varying very significantly among products. In the generality, EU tariffs will be removed immediately and the overall complexion is asymmetrical in Bulgaria's favour – that is, trade barriers will be eliminated more quickly by the EU than is required of Bulgaria. However, this apparent favour is offset by the choice of goods for which free trade is to be delayed.

The goods in question are 'sensitive' products – notably iron and steel, chemicals, clothing and textiles and, above all, agriculture. As regards the industrial products in this list, EU trade barriers will be dismantled on a phased basis, the period in question varying among sectors. Of course, the EU's common agricultural policy is the very antithesis of free trade and this is reflected in the agreement, under which the mixture of quotas and tariffs will, for most products, continue to operate.

While the agreement is clearly welcome in providing opportunities for trade reorientation, its value to Bulgaria is restricted as a result of the special provisions for trade in sensitive goods.

In fact, imports of sensitive products from the five associate members have historically been of no significance to the EU, in the mid-1980s equalling much less than one per cent of EU output and only about four per cent of total EU imports of those products. However, such products are of much greater consequence to the associate members, and especially to Bulgaria. In 1989, sensitive products accounted for 50 per cent of Bulgaria's exports to the EU – higher than for any other transition economy except Hungary. Furthermore, exports of those products from Bulgaria to the EU increased by 45 per cent in the next two years – the highest figure for any of the five associate members.[12]

The restrictions on access therefore have the capacity to deny to Bulgaria considerable opportunities to expand trade, but that is not all. Trade restrictions reduce the incentives for EU firms to invest in transition economies and, more generally, inhibit the efficient restructuring of economic activity which the movement to a market economy is designed to achieve. While the EU has expressed some generosity through PHARE and other programs, when it comes to trade policy the imperatives of inter-member federal politics dominate the outcome.

The balance of payments

The issues addressed above as regards the structure of trade of course arise again in relation to aggregate trading performance. Movements in the balance of payments are difficult to track in all countries. Data come from two sources – customs declarations and the banking system – and there are often a marked divergence between these sources. The major problem arises from the fact that the figure of most interest (the balance of trade or the balance on current account) is the difference between two large numbers and so quite small mismeasurement of these large numbers can create very large proportional discrepancies in the number of interest. This has been very serious in Bulgaria where one data source can show a deficit when the other shows a surplus and revisions of a single data source can turn a surplus into a deficit or *vice-versa*. These problems are reflected in the volatility of the 'errors and omissions' item in the balance-of-payments statistics: in the annual figures for 1991-94, this item varies from a -2 per cent to a +58 per cent of the recorded current balance and, in the statistics for the first half of 1995, it is 130 per cent of the balance on current account.

In the light of these difficulties, one can have faith only in the very broad movements shown by the official statistics. Those statistics are shown in Table 9.5.

Given that, in the light of the statistical difficulties, only broad orders of magnitude are at all reliable, the most noteworthy feature of this table is the marked deterioration in both merchandise and invisible trade in 1993. Exports declined by six per cent (even in nominal terms), nominal imports increased by ten per cent, and net earnings from services declined by 30 per cent. This could hardly have been the result of any delayed impact of the collapse in trade among former CMEA members. It was almost certainly attributable to the cumulative effects of the combination of high inflation and relative stability in the nominal exchange rate. This is dealt with in more detail below: it is sufficient to note here that the two years up to late 1993 had seen an inexorable rise in the real exchange value of the lev – a process which had seriously undermined international competitiveness.

Table 9.5
Balance of payments on current account (US$ mn.), 1991-94

	1991	1992	1993	1994
Exports	3,737	3,956.4	3,726.5	4,159.2
Imports	3,769	4,168.8	4,611.9	4,007.6
Trade balance	-32	-212.4	-885.4	151.6
Services, net	-114	-191	-249.5	-170
Transfers, net	69.1	42.9	36.9	164.1
CURRENT BALANCE	-76.9	-360.5	-1,098	145.7
(as % of GDP)	(-1)	(-4.2)	(-10.2)	(1.5)

Source: Bulgarian National Bank.

By the same token, it is difficult to attribute the significant recovery in 1994 to other than the huge devaluation during the winter of 1993/1994. Exports rose and imports fell by more than ten per cent and the invisibles balance, while remaining negative, also improved considerably. The improvement appears to have persisted into 1995, with nominal exports being 14 per cent higher and imports slightly lower in the first six months than in the same period of 1994. However, the real appreciation of the lev re-established itself during 1994 and continued in 1995. While there is bound to be a lag in the response of trade volumes to movements in the real exchange rate – and so the outcome for the whole of 1995 may be satisfactory – one cannot be sanguine about longer-term prospects if competitiveness continues to be eroded by real currency appreciation.

Exchange-rate policy

There are three major reasons why the exchange rate is of concern to policy makers in an economy like Bulgaria: depreciation of the currency can be a potent source of inflationary pressure; changes in the real exchange rate have effects on the balance of payments and on the capacity to expand the volume of exports; and the exchange rate influences the domestic value of obligations to service external debt.

In countries whose transition started with a significant monetary overhang – such as Bulgaria, Poland and Russia – an immediate effect of price liberalization was an explosion in the general price level and the urgent objective of stabilization policy was to prevent this from degenerating into hyperinflation. The problem arises because of inertia in the system: inflation causes a variable to change and that in turn perpetuates the inflationary process. The quest was mounted for a nominal anchor –

189

that is, exercising control over a variable in such a way that it cannot add the next twist to the inflationary spiral. One candidate is the exchange rate. However, the use of the exchange rate as an anchor requires foreign exchange reserves to be available so that a central bank can intervene in a market where inflationary forces cause downward pressure on the external value of the currency. This in turn requires a past surplus on hard-currency trade or access to a stabilization fund financed, for instance, by the IMF. For this reason, only Poland attempted to use the exchange rate as an anchor (the dollar rate of the zloty was fixed for sixteen months beginning in January 1990). Such a strategy was not feasible for Bulgaria, whose convertible currency reserves at the end of 1990 (that is, one month before the big bang of price liberalization) provided just two weeks' cover for hard-currency imports.[13]

In these circumstances, a fixed exchange rate as an anchor could not be contemplated, even in the short run. The BNB described its approach in the following terms: 'A basic task of the exchange rate policy was to secure relative stability in the nominal exchange rate. With a floating rate and with heightened inflation, the Central Bank aimed at supporting the exchange rate of the lev on a level that would not exert inflationary pressure in the country, but would preserve the international competitiveness of Bulgarian producers in international markets'.[14] The best term for such a policy is probably 'managed float'.

Bulgaria introduced its liberalization package when the central, official exchange rate was BGL2.88 to the dollar and, in the initial stages, the now floating rate behaved more or less as would have been expected: the lev immediately devalued to BGL28 to the dollar but quickly began to recover, reaching under BGL21 by the end of February and remaining better than BGL20 per dollar until almost the end of the year. That is, the immediate devaluation represented serious overshooting, which the market soon rectified.

Table 9.6 presents a summary history of the exchange rate since transition began with the big bang of February 1991. For the first two years or so, the stability objective of exchange-rate policy was achieved, with almost no trend in the nominal rate between April and November 1991, a devaluation of around 30 per cent over the following three months, and then again almost no trend up to the late autumn of 1992.

This stability in the exchange rate was attributable to two factors: a creditable performance on the balance of payments in 1991 and 1992, and intervention in the market by the BNB, which was able to buy foreign currency as a result of assistance from the IMF and the European Union. Support from international institutions began to flow in early 1991, starting with an IMF standby facility, approved in March of that year and delivered in five tranches. This loan was explicitly designed to support the foreign exchange reserves. The first tranche of a World Bank structural adjustment loan was delivered in August and this could also be regarded as support for the reserves since it was all spent on inescapable imports of oil. The second tranche of this loan was withheld because of failure to meet the conditions relating to structural reform and was not delivered until April 1993. Other support from the European Bank for Reconstruction and Development and the EU was also received in 1991, 1992, and 1993. A further IMF standby, to be delivered in five equal tranches, was agreed in March 1992. The first four tranches were paid during the year, but breach of the conditions of the loan caused the fifth tranche to be cancelled and the following year was a difficult one for relations between Bulgaria and the IMF, with no new assistance approved.

Table 9.6
Exchange rate (BGL/$), end quarter, 1991-95

	1991	1992	1993	1994	1995
Q1	15.2	23.3	26.5	64.9	66.2
Q2	17.6	23	26.7	53.7	66.1
Q3	19	22.6	28	61.2	68
Q4	21.8	24.5	32.7	65.5	70.7

Source: Bulgarian National Bank.

Although nothing dramatic happened in the early part of 1993, there were already signs of nominal weakening: by August, the lev had already devalued by the 11 per cent by which it had depreciated over the whole of the previous year. More rapid decline then set in, the rate of depreciation over the last four months of 1993 being 16 per cent, making 25 per cent over the year as a whole.

A number of explanations can be suggested for the steady weakening of the lev in the last five months of 1993. In the first place, there was, as noted above, a definite deterioration in the balance of payments during the year. There may have been some pressure on the lev as a result of inflationary expectations (which would cause Bulgarian residents to switch into dollars) and there may have been some outflow of money temporarily lodged in Bulgaria by foreign residents but, since the dollar value of foreign-currency accounts changed very little over the year, these factors cannot be judged significant.

This situation tested both the nerve and the judgement of the BNB since it was the first occasion when its objective of exchange-rate stability could be achieved only by selling large amounts of foreign exchange. It was not helped by the fact that the IMF had suspended its current standby agreement and so that kind of support for the reserves was not available. Gross reserves, which had reached a peak of $990 million in May 1993, then went into steady and accelerating decline as the Bank struggled to sustain the lev. By February 1994 they had fallen to $593 million. The BNB very sensibly gave up the fight, the lev collapsed in March, and the reserves immediately

191

began to recover. It appears that the IMF, in negotiations for a new standby facility, had earlier advised the BNB to conserve reserves by withdrawing from the market and the heeding of this advice was rewarded by the granting in April of new credits from the Fund and the World Bank, thus boosting the reserves, which rose as high as $1,133 million in June. They then fell back to $581 million in July as those funds were used to buy securities to guarantee debt payments under the agreement with the London Club (see below). To replenish the reserves in response to these new liabilities, an additional loan of approximately $100 million was granted by the IMF in September.

It is hard not to criticize the BNB's behavior in persisting so long in its struggle against devaluation. A managed float is always a difficult policy to operate because one can never be sure when to resist market movements and when to allow them to take their course. The Bank has ample company around the world in throwing reserves at an unsupportable currency, and hindsight always facilitates analysis. Nonetheless, it could, and should, have been realized that the lev had become seriously overvalued since it had recovered the real exchange value it had immediately prior to liberalization in February 1991. Of course, if the Bank had given up buying leva in the autumn, there would have been a period of instability and almost certainly some overshooting in the devaluation, but this happened anyway, but six months later. In the meantime, enough foreign exchange to buy nearly a month's imports had been jettisoned to no avail. The lesson to be learned is that the market keeps its eye on the real and not the nominal exchange rate, and it behooves central banks to do the same (we return to the question of the real exchange rate shortly).

Although the budget deficit is almost certainly the main cause of the high underlying rate of inflation, the surge in the general price level in early 1994 is equally certainly attributable to the behavior of the exchange rate (with some help from the implementation of VAT in April). Further research would be needed to quantify with any precision the way lev import prices feed through to domestic prices, but a rough calculation can be made. It has been suggested that a ten per cent nominal devaluation will create 3.3 per cent inflation in the first month afterwards and a further 1.8 per cent after six months, following the adjustment in nominal wages.[15] If even remotely correct, such estimates would suggest that, of the 22 per cent inflation in April 1994, 15 percentage points resulted from the immediate impact of the March devaluation and the feed-through of the weakening of the lev in the previous autumn.

Regardless of the validity of such quantification, the qualitative conclusion is unavoidable. The dilemma for stabilization policy is then this: should all efforts be focused on the domestic sources of inflation (notably fiscal policy) and exchange-rate policy be concentrated on maintaining stability in the real rather than the nominal exchange rate? The danger when there are conflicting policy objectives is that none of them will be achieved. The underlying balance of payments situation will continue to be difficult until there is serious restructuring of domestic activity, productivity improvements and recovery in former CMEA markets. There will therefore continue to be downward pressure on the nominal value of the lev, a process which will be exacerbated as Bulgaria attempts to improve the servicing of foreign debt through its own earnings, as opposed to credit from the IMF. If domestic inflationary pressures are not contained, this in turn will lead to real appreciation, with further harmful repercussions for the balance of payments. Thus, the use of a managed float as an instrument of domestic stabilization policy is likely to be counterproductive if the real sources of inflation are not tackled.

As Table 9.6 shows, there was overshooting in the devaluation of March 1994 and the lev strengthened again until the middle of the year, but continued to weaken thereafter. The mid-year recovery may have been associated with improved performance on the trade front (we have already noted the considerable improvement in the balance of trade in 1994), but trade movements cannot explain the subsequent weakening of the currency. The answer may lie, at least to some extent, in an increase in non-trade, domestic demand for dollars. Over the whole year, that part of the nominal money supply denominated in convertible currencies increased significantly faster than the part denominated in leva.[16] Also, the changes in the currency composition of the money supply match very closely the movements in the exchange rate. This suggests the possibility that changes in the currency composition of the domestic demand for money, related to expectations concerning the rate of inflation and of the exchange value of the lev, provide a major part of the explanation of exchange-rate movements during 1994 after the crash in March.

The lev remained remarkably stable during most of 1995. This does not appear to have been attributable to intervention on the part of the BNB but, at the time of writing, insufficient data were available to permit a confident judgement, although the continued improvement in the balance of payments in the first half of the year has already been noted.

To summarize, the exchange rate has gone through a number of phases since the liberalization of early 1991. After adjusting to the initial overshooting, the rate of nominal depreciation was quite slow for the next two and a half years, accelerating in late 1993 and with a dramatic devaluation in early 1994. Thereafter, stability has been resumed, with renewed signs of weakness in late 1995 and early 1996. Clearly, if the only objective were to minimize the effects of devaluation on the inflation rate and on the domestic cost of external debt service, then over the period as a whole exchange-rate policy has to be judged more successful than it might have been. The qualification is, however, important.

Although, with the exception of 1993, trading performance has been creditable, it could be argued that it could have been even better since it was inhibited by a policy which achieved stability in the nominal exchange rate at the expense of, taking the transition period as a whole, a very significant *appreciation* in the *real* international value of the lev.

It has not been possible to construct an index of the true real exchange rate because a sufficiently detailed breakdown of the origin and destination of Bulgaria's trade is not available. Trade with former CMEA members still represents a considerable proportion of the country's total trade and some of these partners (those in the FSU) have had inflation rates markedly in excess of Bulgaria's, and so the real exchange rate with respect to those countries depreciated, whereas others had markedly lower inflation. A further complication is that OECD countries did not have currencies which were fixed *vis-à-vis* the US dollar. However, concentrating on trade with non-CMEA countries, and accepting that such trading partners had inflation rates which were trivial relative to Bulgaria's, one can construct a crude estimate of movements in the real exchange rate if one simply deflates the nominal dollar rate by the domestic inflation rate. This is done in Table 9.7. So that an increase in the index indicates a real appreciation, it is based on the inverse of Table 9.6 (that is, it shows $/BGL).[17]

Table 9.7
Index of real exchange rate ($/BGL, Dec 1990=100), end quarter, 1991-95

	1991	1992	1993	1994	1995
Q1	72	82	132	87	182
Q2	68	101	150	145	188
Q3	77	111	153	149	196
Q4	76	121	149	165	203

Source: author's estimates.

After the initial huge real devaluation in February 1991, there was a steady real appreciation until, by mid-1992, the real exchange value of the lev against the dollar had climbed back to its pre-liberalization level. For the reasons mentioned in the previous paragraph, this is certainly an overestimate of the degree of real appreciation, but the extent of that overestimate declines over time with the decline in the relative importance of trade with the high-inflation countries of the FSU. In the light of these estimates, the export performance, with the value of exports to OECD more than doubling and those to the EU almost tripling between 1991 and 1992, is remarkable. Whatever the explanation, exporters certainly received no help from the exchange rate. Of course, it could not last.

This real appreciation of the lev continued until the autumn of 1993 and, as already noted, trade performance deteriorated substantially in that year. This significant overvaluation of the lev could not be sustained and, again as seen above, the collapse came in late 1993 and, dramatically, in early 1994. This provided some relief but the old trend of an inexorable real appreciation was soon reestablished and has continued up to the present, with the real external value of the lev being twice what it was five years previously.

In the light of this, a judgement on the success or otherwise of exchange-rate policy becomes more complex. Nominal stability helps to contain inflationary pressures and the fiscal burden of external debt service: it also reduces uncertainty, with desirable effects on the real economy. On the other hand, real appreciation is inappropriate for an economy whose development prospects are so closely tied to improvements in international competitiveness. It is difficult to escape the conclusion that a managed, progressive, nominal devaluation would have been superior to a policy which permitted nominal stability with periodic, significant nominal devaluations. Experience elsewhere suggests that an over-valued currency is one of the greatest inhibitors of trade-based development and it is perhaps time for this lesson to be learned by Bulgaria.

Foreign debt

The legacy of hard-currency debt has, after the collapse of the CMEA, been the most severe constraint on Bulgaria's international economic relations. Although external debt had increased in the 1970s, primarily to finance the importation of capital goods and other industrial inputs from the west, the first half of the 1980s saw significant retrenchment as capital imports declined and the current balance of payments was helped by the re-export of Russian oil products. By 1985, 'Bulgaria was widely regarded as a good borrower'.[18] Serious deterioration then set in until, by the end of 1989, the country's net foreign debt in convertible currencies had reached $9.2 billion (over $1,000 per head of the population) – an increase of almost three-fold since 1985. About four-fifths of this was owed to western commercial banks with half of this debt being denominated in US dollars, 30 per cent in Deutschmarks, and the remainder being divided approximately equally among Japanese yen, Swiss francs, and Austrian schillings. The main creditor countries were West Germany, Japan, the United Kingdom, and Austria.[19]

The main reason for the accumulation of this debt was that, during the 1980s, there were increasing quantitative and qualitative difficulties over inputs from CMEA suppliers, which were replaced by supplies from the West. Since these western inputs were used to produce exports to the CMEA, the economic process did not generate hard currency to service this debt. Interest continued to be paid, but by 1989 the ratio of debt to annual hard-currency exports had reached three and the debt service ratio 74 per cent. With a hard-currency deficit on current account of $1.3 billion, this position was obviously unsustainable, but the crisis came in early 1990 because of immediate problems of liquidity. The overriding cause of the liquidity crisis was the bunching in 1990 of the debt service profile, with almost $3 billion due in that year, compared with $1.3 billion and $800 million in 1991 and 1992 respectively. Subsidiary, but nonetheless significant, problems were created by arrears in receipts from the $2.4 billion in export credits which Bulgaria had advanced to less developed countries, especially Iraq and Libya, the difficulties with the former being exacerbated by the developing crisis in the Gulf. These arrears amounted to over $700 million by early 1990.[20]

On 29 March 1990 the Bulgarian Foreign Trade Bank (the formal holder of all external liabilities) announced a moratorium on repayments of principal, which was extended to interest payments in June. The unilateral declaration of a moratorium obviously deprived Bulgaria of further access to commercial credit from the West, and the restoration of normal servicing of foreign debt became a central objective of monetary policy as transition proceeded. In the meantime, the unavailability of non-official finance from abroad placed a major constraint on macroeconomic policy. Access to official credit clearly became an urgent necessity and in February 1990 Bulgaria applied to join the International Monetary Fund and the World Bank, becoming a member in September.

This huge volume of unserviced debt has severely constrained various aspects of transition policy: inability to borrow abroad has inhibited exchange-rate policy, has forced the government to use the most inflationary method of financing budget deficits, has inhibited hard-currency exports because of lack of access to trade credit, and has severely limited restructuring strategies since direct investment has been the only means of access to foreign capital. It is no wonder that so much effort has had to be extended in efforts to reschedule the debt. Having been the subject of intermittent and frustrating negotiations for four years, an agreement with the commercial creditors of the London Club for debt forgiveness and rescheduling finally came into effect on 28 July 1994. Since most of the debt was short-term and had been incurred in the 1980s, it was all past maturity by the time of the agreement.

The basis of the agreement was the substitution of new instruments for existing debt and, for this purpose, the latter was divided into two parts – principal and accrued interest. The first action, performed instantaneously, was a buy-back at a 75 per cent discount of 12 per cent of the principal and a portion of the accrued interest. The remainder of the principal was dealt with by two instruments.[21] The first, covering 62 per cent of the principal, replaces debt with government bonds at a 50 per cent discount and with a 30 year maturity. These bonds pay interest at LIBOR (the London Inter-Bank Offer Rate) every six months and redemption will occur in a single tranche on maturity. The second, which covers the remaining 26 per cent of the principal, is a front-loaded interest-reduction bond. It pays an increasing rate of interest, beginning at two per cent for the first two years and rising in periodic steps to slightly above LIBOR after seven years. This bond has a full maturity of 18 years, with redemption taking place in tranches beginning in the eighth year.

These two bonds are fully collateralized by US Treasury Bonds and other foreign government securities. The acquisition of this collateral required more than half the country's foreign exchange reserves in July.

The remaining instrument, which covers most of the accrued interest, is a non-collateralized interest arrears bond. With a full maturity of 17 years, it is to be redeemed in stages beginning in the eighth year and pays slightly above LIBOR from the outset.

By any standards, this is a satisfactory deal for Bulgaria. Of the principal, 40 per cent has been written off, 31 per cent involves only interest payments for 30 years, 26 per cent requires only interest for seven years, and only the remaining three per cent had to be repaid immediately.

This agreement signalled the end of the moratorium which had been in operation since early 1990 and which, although very slightly relaxed with some debt-service in 1992 and 1993, had effectively isolated the country from any credit from non-official sources, be it import/export credits for Bulgarian hard-currency trade or foreign participation in the financing of the budget deficit. With the current state of their balance sheets, most commercial banks (certainly the state-owned ones and possibly the private ones too) would be a very poor credit risk, especially if the Bulgarian National Bank desists from its practice of generous support and is prepared to harden significantly the budget constraints under which the banks operate. Certainly, any foreign bank will for some time be very careful about the collateral on offer before lending to most commercial banks in Bulgaria, although a window may be provided by the expected expansion of local branches of foreign banks.

By late 1994, gross external debt amounted to approximately $10 billion, about half of which was owed to the London Club and was fully collateralized by Brady bonds, with a further 20 per cent owing to multilateral international organizations such as the IMF and another ten per cent being official debt to Paris Club members. Against this was about $2 billion owed to Bulgaria by developing countries and by Russia (the credit balance on old CMEA transactions). Even after the London Club agreement, and even if foreign debtors were servicing their debts to Bulgaria (which they are not), the net servicing requirement is still very significant. If the average interest rate on this debt were six per cent, interest liabilities alone would amount to over $400 million per year, or more than ten per cent of merchandise exports in 1994. Although in principle these apparent net liabilities are balanced by assets (at least some of which are fixed assets owned by state enterprises), these assets are probably predominantly non-performing – they are loans to enterprises – and more certainly non-performing in terms of hard currency. This being so, Bulgaria has significant negative net worth in foreign transactions and this will give rise to a continuing fiscal burden for many years to come.

United Nations embargoes

Immediately before the invasion of Kuwait by Iraq, an agreement was concluded under which the latter contracted to deliver oil to the value of $1.2 billion as payment of debts to Bulgaria. This agreement could then not be fulfilled because of the United Nations prohibition on Iraqi oil exports. But that was not all. The Gulf War came at a time when Bulgarian firms were carrying out major construction projects in Iraq. These projects were halted, no payments were received and large amounts of equipment were destroyed by American bombing, were confiscated or simply had to be left in place. Semi-official estimates (which are very probably over-estimates) put the losses on contracts and from the loss of equipment at $3 billion. Even the Iraqis admit to a debt of $2 billion.[22] More generally, Iraq had been an important trading partner (in the late 1980s that country had accounted for about one-sixth of Bulgaria's exports outside the CMEA) and the enforced cessation of trade involves substantial losses at a time when every export opportunity is needed.

Even more damaging have been the effects of United Nations Resolutions 757, 787, and 820 imposing sanctions on Serbia and Montenegro. The problem here is not only, or even primarily, the loss of markets in Serbia itself, but the isolation inflicted on Bulgaria by the embargo on transit traffic. Bulgaria's geographical position had brought with it major earnings from the transportation of goods between Europe and the Middle East and a central transition strategy involves the reorientation of her own trade in the direction of Central and Western Europe. The only realistic routes lie through Serbia, the alternatives through Romania being totally inadequate. There is no bridge across the Danube between Ruse and the Bulgarian-Serbian border and Romanian roads from the south to the west are incapable of carrying serious traffic. It is this physical isolation which has created the damage.

A study carried out by the ministry of trade in association with the United Nations Development Programme has produced some estimates of the scale of this damage. For the period from the establishment of the sanctions in mid-1992 up to August 1994, total losses are estimated to have been $6.2 billion, trading margins on Bulgarian trade with Europe accounting for $2.2 billion of this and the value of exports lost accounting for $3 billion. The basis of the latter is unclear, however. The effect on the balance of payments depends upon the import content of the lost exports and the effect on GDP depends also upon the domestic opportunity cost of the resources not employed as a result of the loss of markets.

Nonetheless, whichever way one looks at the figures, they add up, not only to a significant depressive effect on domestic activity, but to a high proportion of Bulgaria's external debt. Though the charter of the United Nations makes no provision for direct compensation in cases such as this, some hope exists that it will be taken into account by the UN-associated multilateral lending agencies when considering infrastructural assistance.

198

Conclusion

The collapse of the CMEA trading system made the initial conditions of Bulgaria's transition particularly unfavorable. The terms of trade deteriorated dramatically, the decline in real aggregate demand in partner countries deprived Bulgaria of markets which had accounted for between two-thirds and three-quarters of exports, and the old methods of conducting intra-regional trade were no longer available. In addition to this, the country had large, unserviceable foreign debts and major sources of foreign exchange disappeared as a result of the UN embargoes. Bulgaria was not qualitatively unique in these respects, but no other country experienced these problems to the same degree.

As a result of these factors, the reorientation of trade has become a central objective of transition. Some success has been registered, with increases in the volume of exports to OECD countries, and there are some hopeful signs. First, the debt-rescheduling agreement has relieved Bulgaria of some of the burdens of servicing that debt and, perhaps even more importantly, has opened up the possibility of a renewal of non-official foreign financing. However, the servicing of the remaining debt will continue to pre-empt large amounts of convertible currency for years to come. Second, a reversal in the decline of aggregate demand in former CMEA countries – and especially in the FSU – will offer a revival of trade prospects in traditional markets. Third, the removal of the embargo on Serbia/Montenegro will restore an important source of foreign earnings, especially on transit business, and will remove a serious physical constraint on Bulgaria's trade with central and western Europe.

Nonetheless, despite these good signs, there is a long way to go before the balance of payments ceases to be a serious constraint on real domestic growth. Lack of marketing experience, the need for large investment to effect the technological improvement needed if Bulgarian industry is to compete on free international markets, and the fact that what were major export sectors have little comparative advantage, will all make the task a difficult one. In these circumstances, one cannot avoid noting two domestic policy failures.

First, privatization (which is important not only as an aid to efficient restructuring, but also attracts foreign investors who bring expertise and markets as well as capital) and the restructuring of state enterprises have been disappointingly slow. Second, exchange-rate policy has not been helpful to exporters. Over the first three years after liberalization, the real external value of the lev appreciated significantly – a process which has continued after a brief interruption in early 1994. Although it was correct to attempt to control short-run fluctuations in the exchange rate (there is enough uncertainty facing the real economy without creating yet more through a completely hands-off attitude to the foreign exchange market), the lev has not responded (or has not been allowed to respond) adequately to the high relative level of inflation. A desire to restrain the domestic value of foreign debt obligations has taken precedence over the need to improve competitiveness in trade.

Bulgaria is different from other transition economies, but only in degree. The success stories in the region – and elsewhere in the world – have shown the importance of export-led growth and inward investment. The policy failures in Bulgaria have not been unique, but a country for whom international economic relations are so critical to the transition process might have been expected, in its micro- and macro-economic policies, to have paid more attention to these matters.

Notes

1   This paper draws on Bristow (1996).
2   World Bank (1991), Vol. 1, pp. 152-3.
3   Rosati (1992), p. 65, provides estimates of trade-intensity coefficients which suggest that, in 1989, Bulgaria's exports to the CMEA (excluding the GDR) were five times and those to the USSR 17 times as great as would be the case if the geographical pattern were random. Regardless of the statistical difficulties, these estimates support the qualitative point that the country's trade was massively concentrated.
4   Organisation for Economic Cooperation and Development (1992), pp. 52-5, 99-101.
5   This deterioration in the terms of trade, especially with respect to the FSU, would seem to support a long-standing claim that the CMEA system involved large implicit subsidies from the Soviet Union to other members: that is, the USSR underpriced its exports and purchased overpriced imports. This claim has, however, been challenged – Poznanski (1993).
6   The size of this range is a reflection of the difficulties of aggregating flows denominated in convertible and non-convertible currencies. Official figures suggest the import/GDP ratio to have been only about 20 per cent, whereas other estimates suggest something in excess of 45 per cent.
7   Koves (1992), p. 61.
8   Lazarova and Harsev (1994), p. 16.
9   For a review of the working of this system, see Lazarova and Harsev, op. cit.
10 Hughes and Hare (1992a, 1992b, and 1994).
11 Kostov (1992).
12 The figures in this paragraph are taken from Rollo and Smith (1993), pp. 146, 149-50.
13 Wyzan (1993), p. 128.
14 Bulgarian National Bank, *Annual Report 1992*, p. 51.
15 Wendel and Manchev (1994), p. 20.

16   During 1994, that part of the broad money supply held in leva increased in nominal terms by 51 per cent, whereas that part held in convertible currencies increased by 187 per cent. This process reversed itself during 1995 (thus providing part of the explanation of the stability in the external value of the lev in that year), with leva holdings increasing again by 51 per cent, but foreign currency holdings increasing by only 16 per cent.

17   An alternative index using the rate against the deutschmark shows exactly the same picture, the correlation between the two indices being 0.985.

18   Organisation for Economic Cooperation and Development (1992), p. 96.

19   World Bank (1991), Vol. 1, pp. 157-8.

20   The figures in this paragraph are derived from World Bank (1991), Vol. 1.

21   Known popularly as 'Brady bonds' after a former US Secretary of the Treasury who gave his name to a similar scheme for the foreign debt of developing countries.

22   Iraq's ambassador to Bulgaria, reported in *168 Hours BBN*, 12-18 September 1994.

References

Bristow, J.A. (1996), *The Bulgarian Economy in Transition*, Edward Elgar: Cheltenham, England.

Hughes, G. and Hare, P. (1992a), 'Trade policy and restructuring in Eastern Europe' in Flemming, J. and Rollo, J.M.C. (eds), *Trade, Payments and Adjustment in Central and Eastern Europe*, Royal Institute of International Affairs, London.

Hughes, G and Hare, P. (1992b), 'Industrial restructuring in Eastern Europe', *European Economic Review*, Vol. 36, Nos. 2-3, pp. 670-6.

Hughes G. and Hare, P. (1994), 'The international competitiveness of industries in Bulgaria, Czechoslovakia, Hungary and Poland', *Oxford Economic Papers*, Vol. 46, pp. 200-1.

Kostov, V. (1992), 'The export structure and expansion of participation of the Bulgarian machinery-construction industry in the world market', *Russian and East European Finance and Trade*, Vol. 28, No. 2, pp. 80-92.

Koves, A. (1992), *Central and East European Economies in Transition: the International Dimension*, Westview Press: Boulder and Oxford.

Lazarova, D. and Harsev, E. (1994), 'Clearing between Russia and Bulgaria in 1991-1992', Bulgarian National Bank, *Bank Review*, Vol. 2, pp. 14-21.

Organisation for Economic Cooperation and Development (1992), *Bulgaria: an Economic Assessment*, Paris.

Poznanski, K.Z. (1993), 'Pricing practices in the CMEA trade regime - a reappraisal', *Europe-Asia Studies*, Vol. 45, No. 5, pp. 923-30.

Rollo, J. and Smith, A. (1993), 'The political economy of Eastern Europe's trade with the European Community: why so sensitive?', *Economic Policy*, Vol. 16, pp. 140-81.

Rosati, D.K. (1992), 'The CMEA demise, trade restructuring and trade destruction in Central and Eastern Europe', *Oxford Review of Economic Policy*, Vol. 8, No.1, pp. 58-81.

Schrenk, M. (1992), 'The CMEA system of trade and payments: initial conditions for institutional change' in Hillman, A.L. and Milanovic, B (eds), *The Transition from Socialism in Eastern Europe: Domestic Restructuring and Foreign Trade*, World Bank, Washington, D.C.

Wendel, H. and Manchev, T. (1994), 'The international value of the lev and its effect on domestic prices', Bulgarian National Bank, *Bank Review*, Vol. 1, pp. 16-20.

World Bank (1991), *Bulgaria: Crisis and Transition to a Market Economy*, 2 vols., Washington, D.C.

Wyzan, M.L. (1993), 'Stabilsation policy in post-communist Bulgaria' in Somogyi, L. (ed.), *The Political Economy of the Transition Process in Eastern Europe*, Edward Elgar: Aldershot, England.

Part Five
PRIVATIZATION, RESTRUCTURING OF STATE FIRMS AND SMALL FIRMS

10 Process of privatization in Bulgaria

Hristo Pamouktchiev, Svilen Parvulov,
Stefan Petranov

Introduction

Bulgarian society has accepted privatization as the most significant aspect of the transition towards a market economy. Although the enthusiasm, typical during the first two years of political and economic changes (1991-92), has largely been replaced by more realistic views of existing problems, public support for privatization is still high. It is, however, often based on vague expectations rather than on a precise estimate of economic results connected with the transformation of property.

In this paper we present an analysis of the development of the process of privatization. The process started with restitution of housing property and agricultural land. Although housing privatization is significant as an emotional issue, it was not a very significant move in economic terms since housing has always been private to a large extent. On the other hand, agricultural land was collectivized during the period of central planning and its restitution is a large, painful and difficult process which deserves a separate study.[1]

Here we concentrate on privatization of enterprises either through cash (or market) privatization where assets are privatized against money or debt instruments, or mass privatization where assets are privatized against vouchers distributed to citizens. In the next section we analyze the public attitude towards privatization. We emphasize the fact that, after the initial euphoria, delays in the privatization process created groups in society interested in opposing the process. In the third section we focus on cash privatization. First we describe the basic institutional framework and then highlight some special features of the Bulgarian program where debt instruments can be used by purchasers for payment for newly privatized enterprises. We also provide data on the pace of cash privatization and show that the process has slowed down. In the fourth section we analyze the process of mass privatization. After describing the basic framework, we draw comparisons between the Bulgarian scheme and similar schemes in other East European countries. Then we provide some data which characterizes the enterprises which will be part of the first round of mass privatization. The fifth section concludes the paper.

Public and political attitude

At the present moment, the necessity for privatization of a considerable part of the Bulgarian economy is not being questioned in public debate. On the political level, there is a consensus among the main political powers regarding the necessity for carrying out a large-scale and consistent privatization policy. In practice, however, implementation of appropriate measures for carrying out the process has its difficulties. Privatization has been delayed and in the past several years groups have formed who are interested in halting or at least slowing down the process. These groups have gradually grown stronger and can currently control levers for exercising their influence.

Managerial teams in state-owned enterprises represent one such group. Most of them see privatization as a threat since the new owners will probably assign new managers. For many managers this means more than just losing their positions and salaries. By directing the purchases and sales of the state enterprise to specific firms where they have close connections, some managers have been able to obtain additional income.

Many executives possess high professional skills and loyalty to state-owned property. At the same time, however, a number of cases have become public in which managers of state-owned enterprises have put their own interest before that of the state enterprise. The State is unable to exercise much control over state enterprises. This gives executives in state-owned enterprises relatively wide autonomy. In addition, more recently it has become common to appoint executives of state-owned enterprises for political reasons rather than their professional skills and qualifications. It has become the practice for each newly elected government to change hundreds of state-owned enterprise executives. In this situation, executives can expect that their appointment will last until the election of a new government. Appointment depends on whether or not they supported the ruling party. For the executives themselves the objective becomes maximization of their personal gain during the short period of the current administration. In such an environment, the silent objection of managers to privatization in which they take no part is only natural.

Another group whose interests clash with the process of privatization are middle- and high-ranking government officials who currently supervise the state-owned enterprises in the relevant ministries. When large-scale privatization eventually comes, they will lose their direct power over the decision-making process in the enterprises and over the election, appointment and evaluation of managers. Many of these government officials have been appointed to governing bodies of the enterprises (i.e., Boards of Directors or Supervisory Boards), giving them considerable income and prestige but in practice no real influence on the economic results of the enterprise. Some of them are included in the governing bodies of not just one, but several enterprises. With privatization such officials will suffer considerable losses and this motivates them to give their unvoiced opposition to the process.

These government officials can also influence the privatization process in other ways. They can influence the speed of privatization through specific practical procedures that are undertaken in the administration. Second, as members of the governing bodies of the enterprises, they can have negative influence on prospective privatization initiatives. This influence can be exerted both when the privatization initiative is internal to the enterprise (i.e., by the employees) or when local or foreign strategic investors express interest in the enterprise.

Resistance or opposition to privatization may also arise from large economic organizations which have already developed. They are trying to control particular sectors of the economy. They do not presently have the resources to buy enough enterprises in a sector to control it, but given sufficient time they may be able to obtain enough capital. They are attempting to block the privatization of specific enterprises when they believe that prospective privatization may be detrimental to their interests. Tourism is an example.

Slowing down the privatization process can also be caused by the government, even when it makes frank declarations of its intentions for carrying out the process. Up to the present moment, Bulgarian governments in their realization of the necessity for privatization, remain ideologically associated with particular forms of privatization. The UDF (Union of Democratic Forces) government, driven by purely market-oriented principles, supported only cash privatization and explicitly rejected mass privatization. In their view mass privatization is associated with socialist principles. On the contrary, the current BSP (Bulgarian Socialist Party) government, again driven by ideological principles, already made public announcements that it would primarily support mass privatization. In the present situation, these alternative approaches have different advantages and disadvantages. From the position of economic rationality, the combination and equal treatment of the different approaches is required. The ideological preferences of each successive government to one particular form of privatization inevitably leads to delaying the other forms.

Cash privatization

Privatization in Bulgaria started after a delay of two or three years, when compared with other Central European countries. There are a number of underlying reasons for this delay, but it is also means that the beginning of the process has been carefully prepared. The enabling legislation has been passed and the regulations bearing on cash privatization have now been written.[2] The responsible institutions have been created and a considerable number of state and municipal firms are organizationally prepared for privatization.

Legal and institutional framework

Until the end of 1995 cash privatization was the basic form of privatization in Bulgaria. This differs from other Central and East European countries where mass privatization has been the principle mechanism for privatization. Underlying this decision has been the conviction that Bulgarian enterprises should be owned by persons potentially capable of ensuring their prosperity through investments and modern management. This objective has taken precedence over speed of privatization alone. With this objective in mind legislation was passed which provided equal opportunities for investors, be they Bulgarian or foreign. This was combined with opportunities for employees to acquire shares under preferential conditions (50 per cent discount).[3]

The Bulgarian Privatization Law envisages a many faceted approach to cash privatization whereby different government entities control different aspects of privatization. The law and the extensive complementary regulations issued by the government define the prerogatives of ministries and state and local governments. Small enterprises are privatized under the authority of the relevant ministries. Large enterprises are privatized under the authority of the Agency for Privatization. Very large enterprises need the approval of the Council of Ministers as well. Municipal property is privatized under the authority of local governments. The law also takes into account specific forms of public property in Bulgaria and differentiates across economic sectors supervised by different branch ministries. The institutional scheme for privatization in Bulgaria was intended to be flexible, provide an opportunity to apply different techniques, and restrict bureaucratization of the process.

In practice, many different institutions have been actively involved in the process of privatization. This was suppose to motivate these institutions to assist and enhance the process, as well as improve their expertise. Later it proved that this created tension between institutions and more barriers to the process.

Role of government The main government institution in charge of cash privatization in Bulgaria is the Agency for Privatization. It is a state institution under the direction of the Council of Ministers. Six members of the Supervisory Board are elected by the Parliament and five are appointed by the Council of Ministers for a term of four years. The executive director is appointed by the board. The main functions defined within the law render the Agency virtually independent. It is responsible for general organization and control of privatization of all state enterprises. The Agency is responsible for promulgation of an annual privatization program which includes: the minimal number of state-owned enterprises to be privatized during the respective year, the expected amount of revenue, privatization expenses, a list of industries and/or enterprises which should not be privatized, general lines of privatization of municipal-owned enterprises. It is responsible also for decision-making for state-owned enterprises, provided their fixed assets exceed 70 million levs book value, for licensing of appraisers and for collecting information on the entire process of privatization in the country.

The sector ministries are in charge of privatization of state-owned enterprises whose fixed assets do not exceed 70 million levs book value. In their structure they have departments specialized in organizing and implementing privatization transactions.

In January 1995 a new Ministry of Economy and Development was established. One of its main functions is the general coordination of cash and mass privatization. The Ministry of Finance also assists the process of working out the financial part of the annual privatization program and exercising specific financial operations. The municipal councils are in charge of privatizing enterprises owned by municipalities. All common procedures envisaged by the privatization law for the state-owned enterprises are applied in the privatization of municipal enterprises, as well.

Role of parliament Parliament has a special commission for privatization and property issues. Its role is to assess the annual privatization program elaborated by the Agency for Privatization and submitted by the Council of Ministers. The Parliament debates and approves the program. The commission regularly controls the Agency through hearings on its activities. In addition each member of Parliament can request information from the Agency in accordance with common rules for parliamentary control.

Role of enterprises The law provides for the possibility that the management of enterprises and/or the employees can put forward privatization proposals for their enterprise. Since 1993 most of enterprise privatization programs have been initiated by their managers and employees. One of the principles underlying the Agency's decisions on privatization is to take into account the considerations of managers and employees, although the law does not explicitly state this.

Role of the private sector The law does not envisage that the Agency should necessarily respond to every motion for privatization made by private investors. They could, therefore, initiate privatization indirectly through managers and/or employees or the respective state or local institution in charge of privatization by convincing them of the necessity of privatizing the respective enterprise. For the time being Bulgarian investors are mainly interested in small and medium-sized enterprises.

209

Large enterprises are expected to attract principally big foreign investors.

The law furnishes certain possibilities for 'privatizing privatization'. The institutions in charge of making privatization decisions may authorize other persons to carry out privatization transactions, but this opportunity has not been used actively so far. The evaluation of enterprises to be sold is almost entirely 'privatized' owing to the special requirement that it should be performed by independent appraisers, most of whom are individuals and private consulting firms. The appraisers for each privatization project are chosen on a competitive basis.

The law envisages that privatization should be carried out on the basis of privatization programs which are approved annually, but so far such programs were either not created or approved relatively late. For example the 1995 program was not accepted by the Parliament until May 1995.[4]

The first steps towards privatization in Bulgaria were marked by an opportunistic approach, i.e., privatization started wherever immediate material interest existed. This was also observed in other Central European countries. This approach can be justified because it encourages the process to develop quickly, and privatization criteria and schemes thus crystallize. Nevertheless, the government is trying to focus on a systematic approach based on sector projects. The sector approach allows state organs and potential investors to form a clearer picture of the respective market: its size, level of competition, prospects, substitutes, suppliers, etc. These are factors which are relevant for the organization of privatization and estimation of the prospects for investment.

Debt for equity

The lack of effective demand has always been a serious obstacle for rapid large-scale privatization in Bulgaria. The country is heavily indebted, bearing a burden of domestic and foreign debts that handicap its long-term development prospects. Cognizant of this, authorities looked for a way to reduce debt and help privatization. Debt-equity swaps were introduced as an additional means of payment in privatization. Two main groups of financial instruments were created and allowed to be used in privatization deals:

Domestic debt bonds In 1994 a law was adopted whereby banks were permitted to exchange state-enterprise debt totaling 32 billion levs and $1.8 billion for government securities.[5] The debts in Bulgarian levs were exchanged for low interest bonds with 20-year maturities denominated in levs. The dollar debts were exchanged for bonds with 20-year maturities and denominated in U.S. dollars. Both instruments are tradable and have market prices. The bonds can be used as payment for state property. In order to increase the attractiveness of these instruments a premium of 40 per cent above the face amount is offered when used in privatization. At present the premium is close to that figure as the market price of lev denominated bonds is close to their face value.

Foreign debt bonds In June 1994 Bulgaria reached an agreement with the London Club for restructuring of roughly $9.3 billion in foreign debt. Following the agreement two types of bonds, DISC and FLIRB, covering the debt were accepted as means of payment in privatization under different options.[6] DISCs are accepted at 100 per cent of their face amount. Since the market price is approximately 51 per cent of their face amount, they have a value in the privatization program at almost double their market price. FLIRBs can be used for payment in the privatization process at 50 per cent of their face amount. Since they are trading at approximately 30 per cent of their face value, there is close to a 66 per cent premium if used in the privatization program.

Government has three levers for controlling this program. The premium on domestic bonds will be reduced to 30 per cent after June 1996. Second, bonds can only be used to make part of the total payment; cash must be used to pay the remainder. Initially domestic bonds could be used to make 90 per cent of the payment. This share was reduced to 70 per cent and the use of foreign debt bonds are now limited to 50 per cent of the payment. Third, the market price of domestic bonds has increased reducing the premium they received in the privatization program. Thus the advantage of using bonds in privatization is gradually decreasing as a result of both administrative and market factors.

Economic nationalists oppose the use of debt-equity swaps because they claim that it represents a 'loss of national sovereignty' and 'country's giveaway'. The introduction of these instruments has helped privatization by motivating more investors to look for placement of these new instruments. The structure of payments in privatization in 1995 was 41 per cent cash, 35.8 per cent domestic bonds and 23.2 per cent foreign bonds. This confirms the importance of these instruments in the privatization process.

But there is a serious problem arising from the substitution of debt for cash payment. Bulgarian privatization legislation channels the proceeds of privatization to specific funds. The reduced cash proceeds has decapitalized these funds and reduced their role in restructuring.

Progress of the process

Following the adoption of the Law on Privatization in April 1992 and the creation of the Agency for Privatization in September 1992, several months were needed to prepare for the first privatization transactions. The first, the sale of a servicing shop, was completed by the Ministry of Trade in February 1993. The first big transfer of $20 million was contracted between the Agency for Privatization and the Belgium

'Amillum' company for a modern maize-processing enterprise in north-eastern Bulgaria. In the following months of 1993 and 1994, the number of both enterprises being prepared for privatization and completed privatization transactions increased. This changed when the Bulgarian Socialist Party came to power in February 1995. The new government completed a larger number of privatization transactions, but these were primarily small shops and or small-scale equipment. Often these were separate parts of larger producing units. The total value of privatization transactions decreased in 1995 when the value is calculated in convertible currency (so that it can be adjusted for inflation). The main results of the privatization process in terms of the number and value of transactions are presented in Tables 10.1 and 10.2.

The introduction of new payment instruments, the gradual clarifying of the administrative schemes, and the accumulated experience by the administration were among the conditions which contributed to speeding up the process in 1994. The political environment was definitely unfavorable for privatization in 1993 and 1994. Although the Berov government defined itself as a government of privatization, Parliament failed to pass the 1993 and 1994 privatization programs. Towards the end of 1993 and in the first half of 1994, these contradictions became very clear with regard to both the privatization of tourism and mass privatization. This created an unfavorable environment for the operation of the Agency for Privatization.

The interests of concerned managers of state-owned enterprises and potential investors were promoted through the parliamentary commissions. This provoked debate and eventually increased the pressure on privatization officials. In this period, some of the bigger privatization transactions were subject to severe attacks regarding their economic purpose and legality. As a result, the public began to view privatization as a process for the enrichment of a few who were now acquiring property rights to all the wealth accumulated by society throughout the decades. These feelings intensified during the pre-election campaign in the fall of 1994, and this became a psychological obstacle to the privatization process in the first half of 1995.

Another problem was that important positions in the privatization bodies were occupied by people who lacked experience with the privatization process. They had great expectations regarding the price and other terms of the privatization transactions. As a result, some large transactions were revised on the eve of their conclusion and were not successfully finalized.

On the other hand, a number of favorable conditions for privatization existed in 1995. For the first time, Parliament adopted an annual privatization program, thus legitimizing the ambitious goals set by the government in the field of cash privatization. In addition, a relatively well-functioning scheme was created for the use of debt bonds in privatization as well as opportunities for high discounts. This stimulated the participation of potential investors.

Table 10.1
Number of privatization transactions

	1,993	1,994	1,995
State property	63	162	309
Agency for privatization	6	33	69
Other state bodies	57	129	240
Municipal property	53	384	1,213
Total	116	546	1,522

Source: Agency for Privatization.

Table 10.2
Financial results of state property privatization (in millions)

	1,993.00		1,994.00		1,995.00	
	BGL	USD*	BGL	USD*	BGL	USD*
Revenue	384.80	13.90	10,820.0	199.50	7,464.40	111.10
Liabilities undertaken**	818.90	29.60	2,161.80	39.90	4,937.10	73.50
Future investments contracted	1,464.50	53.00	9,762.20	180.00	10,282.0	153.10

Source: Agency for Privatization.
*   Calculated by converting the value in lev into US dollars on the basis of the official exchange rate of the Bulgarian National Bank.
** Liabilities undertaken are mostly bad debts of enterprises that are taken on by the new owners. These include liabilities to banks, the state budget, and employees.

The number of privatization transactions concluded in 1995 considerably surpassed the results from previous years. To a large extent, however, this was due to a large number of small projects where preferential participation was given to employees or renters. The increased privatization activity also reflected the greater participation of municipalities in the privatization process. A more adequate picture of the situation is given by a comparison of the financial results achieved. These show a considerable decrease in 1995. The same applies to the volume of investments carried out by buyers in the years following the transaction.

The role of foreign investors in the process of privatization has always been considered particularly important, notwithstanding the ever present support for the view that Bulgarian enterprises should remain for Bulgarian investors. Data on foreign investments in privatization are presented in Table 10.3.

Table 10.3
Foreign investments contracted by agency for privatization

	1993	1994	1995
Number of transactions	2	6	4
Revenue (millions USD)	22	123.1	7.8
Liabilities undertaken (millions USD)	-	6.3	13.6
Future investments contracted (millions USD)	30	108.1	49

Source: Agency for Privatization.

According to Foreign Investment Agency data, direct foreign investments in Bulgaria during the period 1991-95 was $530 million. The volume of investments made through the process of privatization was $220 million or about 40 per cent of the total. Both in absolute and in relative terms foreign investments in privatization is low compared to other countries from Central and Eastern Europe or Latin America.

After four years, using primarily a revenue maximizing approach of cash privatization, the amount of privatization is still very limited.[7] Both domestic authorities and international financial institutions (not to mention investors) are dissatisfied. Privatization policy and practice in Bulgaria has been systematically criticized as weak and limited. The failure to successfully carry out privatization programs has been a constant feature during the last four years. Even the 1995 program, backed by an ambitious new government and supported by a majority in Parliament, fulfilled less than 50 per cent its objectives with respect to the key parameter – revenues.

Voucher (mass) privatization

After traveling along a long and winding road, in 1995 the Bulgarian government offered and the Parliament passed a mass privatization program. Different concepts and schemes based on the experience of other Central and East European countries were discussed.[8] Initially a Polish-type mass privatization program dominated by the state was proposed. Then the 'opposite' Czech-type liberal model gained support. Finally, a Bulgarian model, deviating from the others, was adopted.

There are strong indications that no reversal will take place and mass privatization will be implemented as planned. First, the political will of the majority in Parliament can be seen as a guarantee. The credibility of the governmental is higher. Second, and may be more important, is the possible social dissatisfaction if things go backwards. The lack of strong political opposition reduces significantly the probability of blocking mass privatization. Furthermore, 1995 was a relatively successful year for the economy. Lower interest rates on deposits increased the attractiveness of alternative investment opportunities. This combined with positive public expectations makes this the most suitable time for starting a mass privatization program.

The initial time table for mass privatization corresponded with a temporary positive shift in macroeconomic policy. But delays in starting the program threaten a loss of momentum generated by these macroeconomic improvements. At the end of 1995 some negative tendencies are in evidence, challenging the confidence of the public and the attractiveness of privatization. The most important is the growing crisis in the banking system. During 1995 the cumulated loss of Bulgarian banks reached 35 billion levs and the total decapitalization of the banking system was 103 billion levs. A few banks are threatened with bankruptcy. The problem is spreading among both state-owned and private banks, raising doubts about the crucial anticipated role of financial intermediaries in the mass privatization process and their role in corporate governance. The popular dissatisfaction with the destabilization of the financial system can easily be channeled to the privatization funds and the mass privatization program itself.

Legal and institutional framework

Recognition that the existing privatization approach faces severe limitations both on the demand and supply side motivated the acceleration of implementation of a mass privatization scheme. Ideologically it was introduced as a mean of 'restitution of labor', as a counterpoint of the earlier governments' policy of 'restitution of property'. Economically it was introduced to compensate for the chronic lack of effective demand for privatized enterprises.

From the middle of 1991 to the middle of 1993, mass privatization in Bulgaria was a purely academic endeavor, although this was the time when other countries in the region did their most serious preparation work. Mass privatization in other countries under real conditions can now be analyzed, and Bulgaria should benefit from the lessons learned.

The second period of interest in mass privatization began in May 1993, when

215

simultaneously but independently of one another, the Prime Minister and the Deputy Prime Minister put forward alternative proposals for mass privatization. The Prime Minister's proposal was quite different from any proposals implemented elsewhere, but the Deputy Prime Minister's clearly resembled the Polish program, although there were also some elements of the Czech program. After heated debated in the Trilateral Commission and the government, it was decided that, for the sake of unity and uniformity, a synthesized version should be created and brought to Parliament. Once the idea of adopting a separate law for mass privatization was rejected, it became necessary to pass amendments to the already existing Law of Privatization and Reorganization of State-Owned and Municipal Enterprises. This tied mass privatization to all other elements of the law concerning cash privatization and further impeded and slowed the process. Designing the legal framework for mass privatization took more than a year. Over this period there was considerable change in the political sphere, leading to changes in the prevailing ideas of the privatization model. Slowly, the model of mass privatization was altered so that it depended less on the numerous regulations and state control factors which characterize the Polish version. Initially the law regulating mass privatization was very general, consisting of only ten paragraphs. As a result, many important decisions were left to the discretion of the government which was able to influence the process substantially.

In comparative perspective, the Bulgarian model, at least in its present form, is relatively liberal. It restricts the role of the state and the bureaucracy and allows reasonably easy entry of privatization investment funds. It depends to a certain extent on market mechanisms and does not exclude participation of foreign financial institutions.

Mass privatization will be carried out in separate waves (rounds). For each wave the government has to design specific program to be discussed and approved in Parliament. So far, the program for the first wave has been approved. The government declared that it is trying to achieve three main goals:[9]

1. *Abruptly accelerate the privatization process* The achievement of this goal would overcome the difficulties associated with cash privatization: low demand, slow administrative and legal procedures, and conflicts of interest. Achievement of this goal is expected to reduce the alienation towards privatization felt by a considerable part of the population – a problem that is already creating particular public attitudes. At the same time, the government is attempting to create a modern capital market which it views as a basic element in the infrastructure of a market economy.

2. *Involve the people of Bulgaria in the process of property transformation and open up possibilities for participation in the control and management of transformed property* This goal is unlikely to be achieved. What can be expected is an educational process. In the beginning people have a choice whether to participate or not. Over time they will begin to understand that making investments means

taking risks, and incomes are uncertain. It is unrealistic, however, to expect that the program for mass privatization would provide significant possibilities for influencing the management of enterprises, especially given the low concentration of ownership shares and the lack of experience in a corporate environment.

3. *Adjust the specific objectives of the short-run policy measures to the long-run structural policy: recovery of the state budget; improve the management of the state-owned sector; create clear-cut priorities regarding state investments* With successful implementation of the program, the state would rid itself of its present obligations regarding management of and investment in a number of enterprises. This would enable the state to concentrate on a limited number of enterprises. This may lead to improvement in the management investment policies of the remaining state enterprises. At the same time, mass privatization alone is not enough for achieving the desired improvements. The quality of management in state enterprises depends not so much on the number of state-owned enterprises, but rather on the motivation of these managers and the environment in which they operate. Furthermore, the problem of investments in state-owned enterprises may remain, even with fewer enterprises under state control.

The state budget cannot be expected to benefit greatly in the short-run. The program itself does not generate considerable revenues nor does it impose great expenditure obligations. Possible improvements in the state budget will come only after privatization process creates enterprise restructuring leading to improved efficiency and growth.

The program as planned includes the following stages:

a. Proclamation of the program and popular persuasion campaign.

b. Opening of registration bureaus, registration of the population for participation in the process, transformation of limited liability companies on the list for mass privatization into joint-stock companies. This stage will continue for three months.

c. Transfer of investment vouchers of individuals into privatization investment funds,[10] announcement of minimum prices for the shares of the enterprises in the first bidding session. This stage will take at least one month.

d. Centralized bidding for the exchange of investment vouchers with shares from the enterprises on the list. This will be carried out in three bidding session. Each session will take three months.

e. Post-privatization period of six months after the end of the last bidding session.

Under the scheme all adult Bulgarian citizens above 18 years old have the right to participate on an equal basis if they register at local post offices. After registration, a certificate (voucher book) is given to the participant for 25,000 'investment bonds'. The scheme uses the denomination 'investment bonds' instead of levs. The registration certificate and the bonds themselves are not tradable, and their transfer is limited to close relatives. It is expected that it will be difficult to overcome the official restrictions on transferability of the investment bonds. This puts the emphasis on establishing a secondary market in shares of enterprises distributed under the scheme rather than a market for voucher books and investment bonds. The investment bonds can be used only as a means of payment for shares of the enterprises included in the program. The bonds are divisible. Thus an individual investment portfolio can be created by any participant. There is a small registration fee of about $8 with a $1.50 discount for pensioners, soldiers and students. The registration process began on the 8 January 1996 and was scheduled to end on the 8 April 1996. (The deadline was later extended for one month.)

The Law of Privatization and Restructuring of State-Owned and Municipal Enterprise created a Center for Mass Privatization to govern the process of mass privatization. The law guarantees some independence for the center. It is managed as a legal entity and financed from non-budgeted funds. The center oversees the entire set of activities concerned with the development and implementation of the program. This includes the development of proposals for regulation of the program, printing and distribution of vouchers, and the development of a computer network system for the registration of participants and bidding. The scale, complexity, and innovative character of its tasks would present a serious challenge for even the most experienced institution. By contrast, the center was created *ad hoc*, operates on short deadlines in an atmosphere with vaguely defined regulations. It has suffered from serious personnel turnover. The first director was replaced only a few months after his appointment.

There are similar concerns about another key institution, the Securities and Stock Exchanges Commission. This Commission was created to license the activities of the privatization investment funds. According to the law, the government was supposed to establish this Commission by the end of August 1995. Instead, the chairperson and several members of the Commission were appointed in January 1996. Only a couple of weeks before the end of the campaign for the registration of the voucher books, the Commission was organizing itself and seeking the right personnel and premises for its operations. As a result, not a single privatization fund was registered in March 1996, and the promulgation of regulations pertaining to privatization funds were seriously delayed. This has had a negative impact on the advertising campaigns of the privatization funds and lowered the participation rate of the population in the mass privatization program.

Holders of a certificate (voucher book) have two basic options. They can take part directly in the centralized bidding and acquire shares in one or more enterprises.[11] Alternatively they can invest some or all their vouchers in privatization funds. When they invest in a privatization fund they become shareholders in the fund. One investment voucher equals one lev of capital in a privatization fund. With these investment vouchers the privatization funds bid for shares in the newly privatized enterprises.

The activities of the funds are regulated by a specially designed Privatization Funds Law. The main goal of this law is to avoid weaknesses that have arisen in the regulation of other financial institutions.[12] The law puts a number of restrictions on the activities of the funds. These can be grouped under three main concerns:

1. *Securing maximum transparency and availability of information regarding the funds aimed at protecting small investors.* There are specific requirements that funds must observe regarding publicizing information in the form of fliers. These fliers must provide information about the larger shareholders, the professional qualification and experience of executives and the investment and dividend policies of the fund.

2. *Reducing the risk for small investors and stimulating competition among funds.* In order to minimize the risk a number of restrictions have been placed on funds. They are not allowed to invest more than 10 per cent of their capital in shares issued by one company, nor are they permitted to extend credits or to take loans, issue bonds or guarantees, or invest in companies related to members of the fund's governing bodies.[13] Privatization funds are not allowed to invest in other privatization funds without the Commission's approval. There is a limitation on the stake in one company that a privatization fund is allowed to buy. To avoid monopoly control, the law restricts this stake to 34 per cent, which compared to restrictions elsewhere is a relatively large stake and should allow a high degree of corporate control.[14]

3. *Establishing a mechanism for exercising supervisory control over the privatization funds.* The funds are obliged to present annual and semi-annual reports of their activities to the Securities and Stock Exchanges Commission. These reports are required to provide details about securities transactions including buying and selling prices, clients and dates of transactions. The funds are also obliged to present to the Commission quarterly reports for the investment vouchers. Besides the supervision provided by the Commission, many funds are controlled by depositories.

A comparison with the supervision presently in place to oversee other financial institutions is enlightening. Control over the entire banking system is exercised by a department in the central bank that has between 30-40 employees. Due to the lack of a legal regulation, insurance companies have no special regulations and operate within the framework of the commercial code as common joint-stock companies. By contrast, the Securities and Stock Exchanges Commission intends to operate with a staff of about 300 employees.

Most Central and East European countries have already carried out or are in the process of preparing mass privatization programs as a radical means for the fast restructuring of their economies. These programs differ because of specific economic circumstances and differing public attitudes towards privatization.

Russia has already carried out such a program. The Russian model has ended up favoring the large financial institutions and state-enterprise managers. The program started quickly in December 1992, but people did not receive an explanation of how to use the vouchers, and they willingly sold them for a small price. Many vouchers were sold on the secondary market instead of used to invest in privatization transactions. By the end of January 1993, 98 per cent of the total of 150 million vouchers were distributed among the population. This suggested a high level of readiness for participation. The participation itself, however, was much more complicated and limited in scope. For example, sales were often segmented through the application of different payment instruments for one and the same transaction.

Presently there is a strong mass privatization campaign taking place in Slovenia. Each citizen of Slovenia, regardless of age, is eligible to open a 'privatization account' with the national statistics office. The value of the account varies between $800 and $3200 depending on individual's age. The total amount of the operation exceeds nine billion German Marks or 40 per cent of the capital of state-owned enterprises. Participation is fee-free and the expenses are minimal due to the cashless character of the operation. No special papers or documents are issued for either the certificates or the shares in the enterprises. Private investment funds applying to participate in the scheme are licensed on the basis of high capitalization requirements. In addition, the funds must demonstrate that they will be managed by a management company of proven skills and professionalism.

The basic principles of the mass privatization program in Poland are entirely different.[15] By administrative decision, 15 National Investment Funds have been created, each of them governed by a consortium composed of an international investment bank, a consulting company, and a Polish commercial bank. Polish citizens will acquire shares from these funds. The ownership structure of every state-owned enterprise listed in the program is fixed initially with a distribution whereby: one fund gets a 33 per cent stake, all remaining funds receive equal stakes of 1.9 per cent, the employees of the enterprise receive 15 per cent, and the state preserves a block of 25 per cent. The majority stakes of 33 per cent are distributed among the funds on the basis of a specially designed bidding process.[16] The total number of enterprises to be privatized in this way is relatively small, and they account for about 5.4 per cent of Poland's GDP.

From the beginning, the Bulgarian mass privatization was strongly influenced by the Czech scheme and in some aspects it is similar. Based on parallel implementation of two basic streams of participation, direct and indirect, the scheme assumes two basic types of participants. In the transition economy there is a lack of a systematic investment culture and a great number of people will probably be unprepared or unwilling to make strategic investment decisions. For them the scheme offers the indirect participation option, institutionalized through the privatization funds. Others who are willing and ready to risk making an investment themselves can do so by directly buying shares. In this sense the scheme is adaptive.

Political support for mass privatization in Czechoslovakia and later in the Czech Republic is paradoxical. Mass privatization was imposed with strong pressure from the right-oriented political forces of the Prime Minister Vaclav Klaus, not from the left and populist forces. The populist effect of mass privatization was used to balance other unpopular right-wing measures. In Bulgaria, the process is ideologically more straight forward since it is carried out by a new socialist-oriented government.

Mass privatization in Czechoslovakia occurred in two waves. The first, in 1992-93, covered Czechoslovakia as a whole. The second was carried out only in the present Czech Republic.[17] Territorial differences make a comparative analysis of the two waves more difficult, but it is meaningful that the more developed Czech Republic demonstrated greater consistency of action and was quick to start another privatization wave while Slovakia gave up the plan. Nevertheless, experts in both countries share the unanimous opinion that mass privatization is best carried out in one wave, with the maximum volume of enterprise assets involved. The Czech experts admit that they would never have initiated a second wave were it not for the necessity to 'soften' some of the inequities that have emerged from the division of the country. Contrary to this recommendation, the Bulgarian model is designed around several successive waves.

In Czechoslovakia, nearly 80 per cent of the eligible population over 18 years took part in the first wave, although no more than 30 per cent was initially expected. It is generally agreed that the investment privatization funds played a crucial role in encouraging participation through their advertising campaigns at the beginning of privatization. Preliminary estimates on the readiness of population to participate in mass privatization proved unreliable since they had not anticipated the impact on the demand for the privatization funds.

To register, participants in the Czech plan had to pay to $30. In return they received a voucher book of 1,000 points. Unlike Bulgaria, where a voucher book will be equal to 25,000 levs, the Czech scheme is based on points, the price of which is not bound directly to the national currency. For most people in Bulgaria, the price of the voucher book is psychologically connected to the 25,000 levs valuation announced by the government and not with the 500 levs paid for the book. In Czechoslovakia, the advertising was based on a promised return relative to the participation fee of $30, not on the value of the shares acquired against points. Some privatization funds, for example, advertised an amazing tenfold guaranteed increase in the fee invested, from $30 to $300, for instance. In Bulgaria, the market value of shares of privatized enterprises is expected to fall below their nominal value. This makes advertising more difficult and lays the ground work for possible wide-spread discontent due to unsatisfied expectations.[18]

The first wave of mass privatization in Czechoslovakia took 21 months, including one month for promotion, four months for registration of participants, three months for citizens to invest their vouchers in privatization funds, eight months for the five successive rounds of bidding, and four months for summarizing the results. It was only after this technical period that the enterprise shares were actually transferred to their new owners.

The establishment and registration of privatization funds in Czechoslovakia followed a relatively easy procedure. The funds had to meet two conditions: 1) be a joint-stock company and 2) meet a minimum capital of one million Kcs (about $30,000). Their capitalization increased as they acquired additional privatization voucher books from citizens.[19] The funds were obliged to issue shares and thus turn their clients into shareholders of the fund. The registration was assigned to the Ministry of Privatization. No restrictions were imposed on the number of funds that could be registered by one person, legal or physical, nor on the persons who could register a fund. There were 264 investment funds registered by 186 sponsors, including one company which registered 11 funds.

By comparison the Bulgarian legal framework pertaining to investment funds is much more restrictive. The law creates a more complicated procedure of registration with a large number of requirements. It is likely that those who drafted the Bulgarian Law on Privatization Funds paid attention to the Czech experience and are trying to avoid a situation where funds become powerful economic agents which the state might have difficulty controlling. The Bulgarian regulations make a clear attempt to avoid such a phenomenon.

Supply side

A specific feature of the Bulgarian privatization scheme is the bidding procedure. It is regulated in a way which combines acceptable prices, competition on the demand side and perfect price discrimination. Individuals and privatization funds will bid for shares of companies. The process will begin when they bid by announcing a price denominated in investment bonds and the number of shares they are willing to buy of each company. The offers will be ranked and fulfilled according to the bid prices. There will be minimal prices per share for each company announced before the start of each session. If the number of shares demanded is smaller than the number of shares supplied, the differential will be offered at the next session and the minimal price will be lowered. If, after the third session, there are still unsold shares, the remaining shares will be distributed proportionally among those who have already bought shares in the company. Trading in the new shares will be permitted six months after the end of the last session.

While there was no price bidding for the shares in the Czech scheme, Bulgarians must bid by offering a price per share in investment bonds. There will be no canceling of bids if an oversubscription takes place, rather low bids simply will not be fulfilled. Such a scheme is more complicated to execute and difficult for the general public to understand. Analysis is needed not only of the viability of companies but also of the expected effective prices of the targeted shares. These complications should lead to greater participation in the investment funds since they should have better knowledge of the market situation. But common sense is not always present in a society in transition.

The total number of shares to be distributed among the population is 80.461 million with book value of 80.461 billion levs. The number of enterprises included in the scheme is 1,063 state-owned companies out of 3,701 state-owned enterprises from all branches of the economy.[20] In its final version, the Bulgarian scheme demonstrates a desire to broaden the number and volume of shares included. Different companies are offered for privatization with different stakes of their capital. Basically, the companies can be classified in three groups:

Group 1: These are companies where only 25 per cent of the capital is offered for mass privatization.[21] Typically, these are large-scale enterprises with an important place in the national economy. Having the majority stake of 75 per cent, the state clearly wants to dominate the governance of such companies. In this way, the government will have the discretion to look for strategic investors or to keep control over the enterprises.

Group 2: These are companies where 65 per cent of the capital is offered and in a very few cases where stakes of 50 per cent are offered. The enterprises in this group are primarily medium-sized, although some large enterprises are included as well. The state will continue to be a very important shareholder in these companies given the fact that privatization funds are allowed to hold no more than 34 per cent of the shares, while the state will hold 35 per cent. Clearly, the state will exercise control over the strategy of such enterprises even when the private owners have a well-synchronized policy.[22] It is likely that the state will try to gain from the eventual improvement of such enterprises after they are privatized and will probably attempt to sell its stake at a relatively high price later.

Group 3: In this group are companies where 70 to 90 per cent of the capital is offered. These are medium and small enterprises. They will be entirely transferred to private ownership. The remaining stake is being reserved to compensate former owners of buildings or land in these enterprises.

The distribution of the state-owned companies with respect to the relative share of their capital offered for mass privatization is presented in Table 10.4.

223

Table 10.4
Distribution of state-owned companies included in the list for mass privatization

Companies offered with	Number	Book value of capital offered (mil. Lv.)	Relative share of capital offered (book value, %)
<25% stake	199	32,563	40.5
26-65% stake	347	30,218	37.6
>66% stake	517	17,680	21.9
Total	1,063	80,461	100.0

The program includes enterprises from all branches of the economy and in this sense it is well-diversified. Only companies from branches with exclusive legal restrictions on privatization like the extraction industry, ports, and telecommunications are entirely excluded. Probably, a weak point of the selection process was its great centralization and the fact that enterprises were not given a choice. Unlike Czechoslovakia, managers and employees were not asked for their privatization plans, thus losing their cooperation. At the same time, however, this centralization gave the government the opportunity to speed up the process and to follow a more consistent structural and regional privatization policy. In Tables 10.5 and 10.6, the distribution of the enterprises offered for mass privatization with respect to the branches of the economy and to the regions in the country are presented.

Table 10.5
State-owned companies by branches

Branches	Total no. of state-owned companies	No. of companies offered for mass privatization
Industry	1,930	760
Construction	320	79
Agriculture	280	40
Transportation & communications	266	73
Trade & others	692	27
Services	213	84
Total	3,701	1,063

Table 10.6
Regional structure of state-owned companies offered for mass privatization

	Total no. of state-owned companies	Total equity (millions Levs)	No. of companies offered for mass privatization	Equity offered for privatization (millions Levs)	Potential no. of inv. bonds* (millions)
Sofia-city	628	40,134	129	13,333	24,014
Bourgas	316	26,263	104	9,455	16,635
Varna	402	25,800	107	8,911	17,629
Lovech	459	21,605	162	10,746	20,031
Montana	292	12,922	90	5,667	12,427
Plovdiv	468	19,901	138	8,852	23,654
Rousse	351	15,244	107	7,092	14,843
Sofia-region	464	23,131	127	9,880	18,987
Haskovo	321	16,245	99	6,525	16,991
Total	3,701	201,245	1,063	80,461	165,211

*Calculated by multiplying the total number of eligible individual-residents of the region, by 25,000.

Source: Mass Privatization–Where to Invest?, Club 'Economics 2000', authors' calculations.

The financial position of the companies in the list for mass privatization is close to the average for the economy. The 'deadbeats' are deliberately excluded, thus reducing the probability of quick loss of confidence or immediate failure. Still a portfolio weighted by the share of the companies capital, included in the list, is loss-making according to the 1994 data. The distribution of the profitability of companies is presented in Table 10.7.

One of the most important characteristics of mass privatization is connected with the supply of information. Since many individuals are hesitant, good information with respect to enterprises provided in a timely fashion might increase the credibility of the process. Moreover, better information will contribute to better investment decisions and better allocation of investment bonds.

Table 10.7
Number of profitable state-owned companies

	Total no. of state-owned companies	No. of profitable state-owned companies*	No. of companies offered for mass privatization	No. of profitable companies offered for mass privatization*
Sofia-city	628	346	129	77
Bourgas	316	131	104	52
Varna	402	166	107	47
Lovech	459	182	162	69
Montana	292	92	90	25
Plovdiv	468	210	138	72
Rousse	351	137	107	56
Sofia-region	464	152	127	55
Haskovo	321	113	99	46
Total	3,701	1,529	1,063	499

*According to the official financial statements of enterprises in 1994.
Source: authors' calculations.

There are at least three ways in which better information could contribute positively to the process. In each case the situation is far from being satisfactory. First citizens need to understand the importance of the process itself. Why is the mass privatization crucially needed for the country? What are the potential benefits of participation in the program for the common citizen? Do these benefits exceed the registration fee? Why should people pay money for participation? What could people who have never seen corporate shares do with the shares of the privatized companies? These and many other questions have not been explained in the government's campaign. The campaign has dealt only with basic information about who is eligible and where to register.

Secondly, the public is not well informed about the privatization funds. Since funds were not licensed until the very end of the registration period, official advertising was illegal during the period when people were making decisions whether to participate or not. Some funds did a kind of 'semi-official' campaign, but the danger always existed that they could be subject to legal prosecution. Although many financial groups have announced their plans to establish privatization funds, no intensive private advertising campaign took place. This might help explain why participation in the program has been so low. The invasion of funds, if allowed, and official advertising campaigns would increase the number of participants, as it did in Czechoslovakia during the first wave.

Thirdly, more information related to enterprises on the list for mass privatization should have been made available. At the end of the registration period a large number of enterprises had not prepared the information required. The requirement includes information on the economic prospects of the firm, financial indicators, legal analysis on ownership rights, and some additional documents. Table 10.8 presents the state-of-affairs only a month and a half before the registration period. Nearly half the enterprises are still lacking regular documentation, the problems being connected most often with legal analyses. Only three companies have not presented information prospects, while 52 have not presented either information prospects or legal analyses. Many enterprises have the legal status of limited liability companies, and before being offered for mass privatization they must be transformed into joint-stock companies. Additional time will be needed for these administrative procedures. Under the present circumstances people were making decisions for participation without reliable information about the financial and legal situation of many companies.

Table 10.8

Readiness of the mass privatization process in terms of information

	No. of enterprises	No. of enterprises with irregular documents	No. of enterprises which have not presented			
			Information prospects	Legal anal.	Both cases	No. of ltd. liability companies
Ministry of industry	659	363	1	315	42	455
Ministry of regional development	68	27	1	6	0	51
Ministry of agriculture	176	50	0	34	6	175
Ministry of transport	73	7	0	1	4	18
Ministry of trade	27	17	0	10	0	6
Ministry of culture	1	0	0	0	0	0
Committee for tourism	54	8	1	7	0	5
Committee for energy	5	4	0	4	0	4
Total	1,063	476	3	377	52	714

Source: Bulgarian Business, 1996-97.

At the end of the period for registration about 20-25 per cent of the eligible population is expected to buy their voucher books.[23] Judged against the government's expectations, this number is low, but still high if compared to the first month of the Czech mass privatization when privatization funds were not advertising. It is even higher than in Romania where only seven per cent of the eligible population decided to participate in the mass privatization program at the end of the registration period.[24]

Conclusions

Four years of privatization experience after the privatization law was adopted in 1992 the scale of cash privatization is disappointing. Both domestic authorities and international institutions supporting the market-oriented reforms in Bulgaria were dissatisfied. The privatization policy and practice in Bulgaria have been systematically criticized as weak and limited. Annual privatization programs, which by law the government must announce each year, are either not created at all or not fulfilled. The last program, for 1995, backed by an ambitious new government and supported by a majority in the Parliament fulfilled less than 50 per cent of its revenue objective – a key parameter.

The slow pace of cash privatization can be attributed to the time-consuming political debates about what and how to privatize, whether there should be domestic or foreign investors, and whether maximum revenue must be obtained. These delays finally led to the creation of groups in society whose interests opposed the process.

At the same time foreign investors often confronted misunderstanding, slow procedures and political uncertainty. As a result, in 1995 direct foreign investments were small but, more important, even less than 1994.

Recognition that the existing approach to privatization faced systematic failures and severe limitations both on the demand and the supply side created a motivation to accelerate implementation of a mass privatization scheme. The program started but already shows many administrative weaknesses. The program has experienced serious delays and the government still has not prepared some important procedures. This might postpone the program further and conceivably erode the credibility of the program.

Notes

1   See for example Schmitz, A., *et al.*

2   The Law for Transformation and Privatization of State and Municipal-Owned Enterprises was adopted by the Parliament in April 1992. Amendments mak-

ing possible application of a mass privatization scheme passed in June 1994 and December 1995. A bundle of regulation acts was passed by the Council of Ministers, more important ordinances of which are on: auctions, tenders, appraisals, preferential acquisitions of state and municipal-owned shares, information provided to potential investors.

3   Up to 20 per cent of the property rights in the respective enterprise may be bought in this way. As a limitation exists on the maximum value of the discount, which should not exceed a two-year salary, the average value of the preference shares should amount to less than 20 per cent generally, and even less than ten per cent for bigger and technically well-equipped enterprises.

4   The 1995 priority privatization sectors were: tourism, food, agriculture, mechanical engineering, transport, etc. Among the enterprises excluded from the privatization list draft for 1996 were enterprises in the defense industry, mining, power plants and energy transmission facilities, water supply, railway transport and some other with specific functions.

5   The Law on Settlement of Non-performing Credits permitted banks to exchange debt of state-owned enterprises negotiated before 31 December 1990.

6   DISC bonds are discount bonds. These are bonds issued to creditors who have agreed to reduce their claims on the principle. The reduced principle has to be paid in the year 2024 in one payment. The interest is LIBOR +13/16 annually. FLIRBs are Front Loaded Interest Reduction Bonds. These bonds have been issued to creditors who would not agree to reduce the principle obligation but agreed to reduce the interest payments for a certain period. The interest starts at two per cent annually in 1994 and increases gradually until 2002 when it becomes LIBOR +13/16. The bonds must be repaid by July 2012.

7   See Pamouktchiev and Parvulov (1994).

8   See Pamouktchiev and Parvulov (1994).

9   Privatization program through investment vouchers, adopted on 19 December 1995 in Parliament.

10   Investment vouchers, although there are restrictions, can be transferred to close relatives as well as to attorneys.

11   They can also participate through an attorney if they observe specific restrictions.

12   In 1995 many people lost their savings in pyramid schemes. At the end of 1995 and in the beginning of 1996 the first manifestations of a banking crisis began to take shape. The causes were weaknesses in licensing procedures, poor bank supervision, and credit policies.

13   Actually funds can obtain short-term loans with a maturity up to three months after a special approval of the Commission. These loans have to be earmarked for fixed assets related directly to fund's activity.

14   In France, Germany, and Russia this share is ten per cent. In the Czech Republic, Slovakia, and Lithuania it is 20 per cent. In the United States it is

229

significantly lower, five per cent.

15   A similar approach is being used in Romania.

16   The process is similar to the NBA draft system in United States where each fund draws straws to determine the order of first round choices. The order is reversed for the second round, and so on.

17   Slovakia abandoned the idea of carrying out a second wave.

18   It is hard to explain in an advertising campaign that holding shares of 25,000 levs nominal value and selling them for 15,000 levs actually means a profit and not a loss. Since these shares have been acquired for a participation fee of 500 levs, there is a clear profit.

19   This differs from the Bulgarian case. In Bulgaria the privatization funds announce a preliminary capitalization target and a stated number of shares that can be sold in the fund. Once these shares have been sold for vouchers, the fund cannot acquire more vouchers.

20   This is compared to 299.4 million shares from 1,491 companies in the first wave of mass privatization in the former Czechoslovakia.

21   Some cigarette companies are being offered with a 20 per cent stake due to the fact that small stakes in them have already been privatized.

22   According to the commercial code, the most important decisions in joint-stock companies are made by qualified two-thirds majority. In many by-laws of state-owned companies the qualified majority is even higher, i.e., three-fourths.

23   The paper was completed a week before the end of the registration period.

24   As a result, the government prolonged the registration period and started an intensive propaganda campaign including school teachers and church priests. At the end, 30 per cent of the eligible population registered for participation.

References

Pamouktchiev, H. and Parvulov, S. (1994), 'Likely future impacts of Privatization on the Macroeconomic Environment in Bulgaria', draft paper, February.

Schmitz, A., Moulton, K., Buckwell, A., and Davidova, S. (eds) (1984), *Privatization of Agriculture in New Market Economies: Lessons from Bulgaria*, Kluwer Academic Publishers.

11 Nature and role of small firms in Bulgaria

Will Bartlett and Rossitsa Rangelova

Introduction

Throughout the post-war period communist planners in Bulgaria pursued a strategy of rapid industrialization of an agrarian economy based on state ownership of industrial enterprises and a system of central planning. With the exception of some private activities in agriculture and widespread private-owner occupation in the housing sector, there was virtually no private economic activity in the economy. Industrialization was assisted by substantial financial and technological transfers from the former USSR, high domestic investment rates, and growing specialization in machinery exports into the protected market of the CMEA countries. However, the negative side of this progress became more and more evident in the 1980s: environmental degradation, difficulties in maintaining high economic growth, a rapid increase of the external debt in convertible currencies. According to one estimate (Minassian, 1992), industrial output based on a pattern of extensive development eventually stopped growing and began to fall from 1983 onwards.

A key feature of the industrial structure which was developed in Bulgaria under the previous regime was an extreme over-concentration of the economic activities in very large scale enterprises. In the early 1980s the size of enterprises in Bulgaria in comparison with enterprises in other Eastern European countries ranked immediately behind that of the former USSR. This aspect of economic development was reinforced by the complete lack of experience with markets as a basis for trade. In contrast some other countries in the region such as Hungary and the former Yugoslavia, while being heavily dependent on large scale state enterprises had nevertheless begun to introduce some limited experiments in decentralized market mechanisms and therefore had a more favorable set of initial conditions from which to launch the transition process (Bartlett and Hoggett, 1995). The negative consequences from this over-concentration and absence of market incentives to improve the efficiency

231

of production were expressed in decreased economic effectiveness, low returns on investments, high energy consumption per unit of production, inadequate investment in the modernization of fixed capital assets, a low level of innovation and a drop in employees' motivation.

Eventually, as elsewhere in eastern Europe, continuing poor economic performance led to political instability. The fall from power of the communist party leader Zhivkov in 1989 precipitated a process of change in economic, social and political relationships which began the transition to a market economy. This process, however, has been slow and hesitant due until recently to the lack of a clear parliamentary majority committed to economic reform. The first free elections were held in 1990. The absence of a strong independent middle class contributed to the return of the Bulgarian Socialist Party (BSP – the renamed Communist Party) by a narrow majority. Continuing economic difficulties produced further political uncertainty, and in September 1991 new elections were held, which produced a small overall majority for the Union of Democratic Forces (a coalition of 12 non-socialist parties). The UDF maintained a tenuous hold on power for only 11 months. From the end of 1992 the country was ruled by a coalition government. However, government policy with respect to the transition to a market economy lacked direction and the introduction of serious economic reforms in the field of privatization and small business development lagged behind experience in other east European countries such as Poland and the Czech Republic. The coalition government was unable to grapple with a serious economic situation and a sharp decline in living standards, and in 1994 the BSP was returned to power with an absolute majority in Parliament. Nevertheless, under the leadership of 37-year-old Prime Minister Zhan Videnov, the BSP has pressed ahead with market reforms and introduced a degree of stability into Bulgarian politics.

Since the fall of the communist regime Bulgaria has faced a particularly difficult economic situation. In 1990 a series of economic shocks led to the beginning of further economic decline, and Bulgaria defaulted on its $10 billion external debt repayments held mainly with commercial banks. Despite rescheduling, the per capita debt burden remains one of the highest in the region and by 1995 repayments of capital and interest amounted to $1.25 billion on a debt which had increased to $11.5 billion. As a small country Bulgaria's economic development depends to a great extent on foreign trade. Under the communist regime foreign trade had become concentrated on the ex-CMEA and ex-Soviet markets. The break up of this market, the disruption to oil supplies following the Iraq-Kuwait war and the UN embargo on Yugoslavia contributed to a large fall in domestic output in the state sector of the economy. Following the demise of the communist regime and the abandoning of the central-planning system a dramatic reorientation of trade patterns has taken place so that by 1995 about one-half of trade flows were conducted with the OECD market area. However, dependence on Russian oil and gas has meant that about 40 per cent of imports still come from the ex-Soviet area.

A stabilization policy introduced in January 1991 involved price reform, a unified

232

flexible exchange rate, an incomes policy, and tight fiscal and monetary policies (Wyzan, 1993). This policy brought about a significant reduction in domestic demand, and by 1992 the number of loss-making enterprises exceeded the number of profitable enterprises. According to the Agency for Economic Cooperation and Development (1992), there were 2,921 loss-making state enterprises against 2,477 profitable state enterprise, and three-quarters of the latter had a profit rate of less than five per cent. It is estimated that GDP declined by 23 per cent in 1991 and by eight to ten per cent in 1992 (Borensztein, Demekas and Ostry, 1993). The monetary policy was based upon strict credit control and control of the foreign currency transactions of the National Bank. The policy brought about a sharp jump in nominal interest rates from 4.5 per cent to 54 per cent by 1992 (AECD, 1992). High interest rates have remained a serious barrier to investment and in March 1996 were still held at 49 per cent. Despite the high level of inflation (overall inflation reached 62 per cent in 1994) the high cost of credit and tight credit control has been particularly problematic for the small firm sector.

A privatization law was passed in May 1992, but by March 1994 only a tiny proportion of state-owned companies had been sold, including one-sixteenth of large enterprises, 17 out of 870 medium sized enterprises, and 69 out of 5,000 small state enterprises (EBRD, 1994). Around 90 per cent of the fixed assets in Bulgaria remain state-owned, although some of the larger state-owned firms in light industry and services have been subjected to a process of decentralization and restructuring. A new privatization program introduced by the BSP government involves 1,060 of these state-owned firms, representing 56 per cent of the total asset value of the state-owned sector.

The downturn in production in the state sector resulted in a rapid increase in unemployment (Paunov, 1993) as the state sector has carried through large scale dismissals of redundant workers. The level of unemployment began rising immediately after the introduction of the economic reforms at the beginning of 1991 from less than 100,000 to reach a peak of around 600,000 by the middle of 1993 (over 20 per cent of the labor force in the state sector). The prospects for the development of new small scale private sector firms are therefore of crucial importance since this is one of the few areas where employment growth is likely to occur. Since 1993 there have been some signs of recovery. Economic growth resumed in 1994 with a 1.4 per cent increase in real GDP which accelerated to a 2.5 per cent growth in 1995. Underlining the key role of the small firm sector, the most recent indicators show that output from the still small private sector increased by some 50 per cent in 1994 (*Financial Times*, 15 April 1996).

In this chapter we discuss some of the main features of this new small scale private sector. The next section provides an overview of some relevant aspects of the debate on the importance of the small firm sector in transition economies and traces the development of small firm policy in Bulgaria since the early 1980s. The third section presents the findings of some recent research results on the emerging small firm sector based on sample survey methodologies including a recent survey carried out by the authors of this chapter. In the fourth section, the findings from a number of in-depth case studies provide a more qualitative appreciation of the nature of some of the different types of new small firms which have been active in the transition phase. Finally, in the last section some conclusions and an evaluation of the role of small firms in the contemporary Bulgarian economy are developed.

Development of the Small Firm Sector in Bulgaria

In a recent contribution focusing on the role of small firms in transition economies Brezinski and Fritsch (1996) have argued that the growth of the small firm sector can be seen as an indicator of the dynamism of an economic system. Drawing on the work of Marshall (1920) and Schumpeter (1942) they see the importance of the small firm sector being its capacity to regenerate economic activity. As old firms die so the birth of new firms, which are by their nature usually small sized, is an essential component of restructuring and growth. Turbulence in an economy ensures that the old dead wood is replaced by fresh new shoots, to paraphrase Marshall's 'ecological view'. Schumpeter describes the same process as one of 'creative destruction'. In this bottom-up perspective it is argued that small firm entry generates new activity which *replaces* the lost activity from the exit of defunct large state-owned firms, and that the small firms sector represents an alternative economic structure to the dying large scale state enterprises. Policy should therefore be directed to supporting the entry and growth of new firms and facilitating, and if possible speeding up, the demise of the state sector. The drop in state sector output is seen as a necessary step in the transition to a market economy. Moreover, turbulence is expected to be a permanent feature of the new market economy, as many of the new small firms will themselves go bankrupt in the competitive struggle for markets, while other more successful firms will grow to become the new medium and large firms of the future.

In contrast to this approach one may identify an alternative perspective which draws on the work of Penrose (1959). Penrose sees the small firm sector operating *together with* the large firm sector as a coupled dynamic system, in which each depends upon and benefits from the activity of the other, while simultaneously engaging in a competitive struggle for market share. Rather than being seen as an alternative to the large scale state sector, the complementary nature of the small firm sector is emphasized. One key area of complementarity lies in its ability to fill market niches (e.g., in the consumer goods and service sectors) which the large scale sector is unable to supply both due to its lack of flexibility and due to inherent internal barriers to growth in large firms associated with diseconomies of scale. In addition, in the manufacturing sector small firms may sometimes offer support to the restructuring and development of the large firm sector by providing inputs in the

234

form of component supplies and business services. When this occurs the large and small firms together operate as a unified 'supply chain' (Bateman, 1995) which links the fortunes of the large and small firms together. It can be particularly important in providing a domestic employment component when a local supply chain is developed to support foreign direct investment activities which might otherwise rely on imported components. Both these processes reinforce the linkage between the small scale and the large scale sector in the transition to a market economy. In the Bulgarian context the implication is that policy should be directed to support both large and small scale sectors. The appropriate policy is one of balanced growth to ensure interfirm linkages which can underpin the effectiveness of the transition process.

In summary, the Marshall/Schumpeter model emphasizes the importance of turbulence and creative destruction associated with entry and exit of firms from the market. It provides a useful counterpoint to the overemphasis on large firms which dominated Bulgarian industrial policy in the communist system. However, it risks replacing one form of policy bias with another. It tends to neglect the importance of restructuring the large scale state sector and of developing the efficient core of large scale industry built up under the old system. The Penrose model redresses this bias by emphasizing the coupled nature of the large and small firm sectors and provides a more balanced view of industrial policy in transition economies. Nevertheless, the truth probably lies somewhere between these two stylized models, and it is evident that the development of the small firm sector will be an important component of industrial restructuring and regeneration in Bulgaria for some time to come. As Brezinski and Fritsch point out small firm entry may supply a much needed competitive dynamic, foster the emergence of a new middle class to underpin political stability and the transition to democracy, provide a conduit for the transfer of new technologies and help to create new employment opportunities for unemployed workers who have lost their jobs following the decline in demand for labor of the large state sector enterprises. Research into the role of small firms in market economies has identified the key role played by small firms in all these areas (Acs and Audretsch, 1993; Storey, 1994), and their importance is all the greater during economic transition when a market is in the process of being created, virtually from scratch.

In the light of this discussion it is perhaps surprising that industrial policy towards the small firm sector in Bulgaria has been relatively neglected. The genesis of the Bulgarian approach to the small firm sector can be traced back to some innovative policy developments which took place in the final years of communist rule (Jones and Meurs, 1991). In response to the declining efficiency of the industrial sector an experimental policy to enable the creation of new small and medium sized enterprises within the structures of the large state-owned enterprises in the 1980s (Puchev, 1990). Although this policy achieved some success, the extent of the new economic activity generated remained marginal. In 1989 the first steps were taken to liberalize the regime facing private enterprise within what was still essentially a centrally-

235

planned economy. Decree 56, which was adopted in January 1989, was the last piece of legislation of the Zhivkov era. It provided a comprehensive legal framework for the development of private enterprises. It permitted small private firms to hire labor for the first time (but only up to ten permanent workers, while seasonal workers could be employed without limit). By February 1990, 14,011 new private firms had been registered under this law, of which 11,285 were sole proprietorships; 2,556 were partnerships; and 170 were cooperative firms (Jones and Meurs, 1991).

More recently, a new constitution which guarantees private property has been introduced, and a modern commercial code has been adopted. New laws provide a legal and institutional framework for the operation of the private sector, including laws on accounting, ownership and use of farm land, cooperatives, property restitution, competition, foreign investment, and privatization. However, the implementation of this new regulatory framework has been slow, perhaps partly because the change of established patterns of behavior takes time, but also perhaps because of inertia and resistance from established interest groups. At present, the forms of ownership and legal status of private firms in Bulgaria are treated by three main laws, Decree 56 (1989), the Law on Commerce (1991) and the Law on Co-operatives (1991). The Law on Commerce provides a framework for new forms of private enterprise such as limited and unlimited partnerships, private and public limited companies, and unlimited firms under individual ownership. The Law on Co-operatives builds on the long tradition of cooperative enterprise in Bulgaria in the pre-war period (Fotev, 1992), and provides an opportunity for the creation of a new sub-sector of small firms based on a cooperative form of ownership. Another important feature of the Bulgarian path of economic transformation has been the introduction of a Restitution Law which was adopted in February 1992, and provided for the return of property which had been nationalized under the communist regime to the original owners. This law has made an important contribution to the growth of the small firm sector by redistributing property and providing accumulations of capital assets to individual owners.

Over the last three years the emergence of a private sector and the rapid increase in the number of small firms was only partly a consequence of the moves to abolish the monopoly of state ownership. It occurred mainly as a spontaneous reaction of individuals to the process of social and economic democratization. As a result there has been a rapid increase in the number of private firms in Bulgaria since 1991. The latest data published by the National Statistical Institute indicate that by February 1993 nearly 164,000 new private firms had been registered (NSI, 1993) although some estimates indicate that only 70,000 are actively trading (Houbenova-Delissivkova and Puchev, 1996). The overall contribution of the private sector in Bulgaria is disputed, but it probably accounts for only a relatively small proportion of economic activity in contrast to the situation in other transitional economies in eastern Europe such as Poland and Hungary where more than half of economic activity is now accounted for by the private sector. In Bulgaria, despite the rapid development in the number of new small enterprises, the main bulk of employment and output is still accounted for by state-owned companies. Nevertheless the private sector is growing rapidly and it can be expected that it will become a major force in the Bulgarian economy as the transition process gathers speed.

Thus far there has been little in the way of explicit policy support for small business development in Bulgaria. A very limited range of measures to support small firms was introduced through Decree 108 in June 1991. This established a special fund for the support of small firms which was set up in September 1991 with 70 million leva in capital. This fund was designed to provide financial subsidies to small firms through a variety of specialized schemes. The various forms of assistance included a subsidy of up to 50 per cent to cover interest costs of a small business; grants of up to 25,000 leva (or up to 50 per cent of the registration fee) to be paid to incorporated firms; subsidies to cover up to 50 per cent of the costs of communications, energy and water supplies; and grants to support product and process innovations. The small initial capital of the fund was all quickly disbursed to only 17 firms in the food processing industry, although none of it through the scheme to support innovations.

A second phase of funding was channeled through the Bulgarian Chamber of Commerce and Industry in 1992, but at an even lower level of funding. The Chamber's Small Business Encouragement and Promotion Fund had a total value of only ten million leva. To qualify for support firms were required to have fewer than 30 staff, to create new jobs, and to manufacture necessities, so coverage of the scheme was also highly restricted, and it had only a limited impact. In 1992 only three food processing and retailing companies were chosen from 13 competing applicants to receive tied low-interest loans. These firms received soft loans at 18 per cent interest on 12 month loans of 300,000 leva each, which was less than half the effective central bank rate. In addition to central state support, small firms are also eligible to receive support from local and municipal governments. This usually takes the form of joint ventures between local governments and private firms, with limited equity participation in a private firm (equity participation limited to a maximum of 30 per cent). Otherwise, however, local authorities offer little practical help to small firms.

Bulgaria has received substantial financial and policy assistance from the EC PHARE program which has instituted a number of specific policy measures including the creation of enterprise development institutions (agencies, advice center) both in Sofia and in a number of local regional centers. However political uncertainty and the lack of a coherent strategy for the development of small business has meant that outside assistance has been used less efficiently than it might have been.

237

Research findings on small firms in Bulgaria

In the context of the very recent development of the small firms sector in Bulgaria it is not surprising that there have as yet been very few studies of the their development. The policy of promoting small firms within the state sector in the 1980s (under Decree 12 of 1982) has been studied by Puchev (1990, 1991) and Jones and Meurs (1991). Puchev found that by June 1989 there were 650 such small firms established in all sectors of industry with a concentration in food processing, machine building and metal processing, textiles and knitwear, light industry, electrical engineering and electronics and construction materials (Puchev, 1991). Some of these firms were established and owned by local municipalities (34 per cent in 1985), and some 35 per cent (in 1985) were engaged in the production of consumer goods. Jones and Meurs (1991) argue that the program failed in its attempt to stimulate competition in the domestic economy since the new small firms established under this program were confined to niche markets in the consumer goods and high technology sectors.

Nevertheless the experiment did point to some advantages of small scale production. Between 1984 and 1988 mean labor productivity in these small firms was estimated to be between 1.4 and 2.7 times greater than in their large scale counterparts (Puchev, 1990). The productivity differential was partly associated with the incentive effects of decentralized management of these units: management was free to choose both the type and quantity of output. But it was also associated with favorable treatment by the planning authorities: the new small firms received up to 5 per cent of the investment funds allocated by the Plan.

Another study of small and medium sized firms (SMEs) in state, municipal and cooperative ownership (Parvulov, 1992) supported the conclusion that small enterprises had a productivity advantage over larger firms. The study looked at a total of 463 small firms (with up to 50 employees) and 1,813 medium sized firms (with 51 to 200 employees) These represented 44 per cent of the total of 5,158 firms in state, municipal and cooperative ownership in all sectors of the economy in 1989. In small sized firms, the ratio of value added per sales was 20 per cent higher than the national average levels of productivity, while in medium sized firms it was 29.5 per cent higher. The productivity gap was also reflected in improved profits in relation to both sales and assets.

A survey of 105 private firms, 123 small state firms, and 23 small cooperatives by Jones carried out in 1992 revealed some interesting comparative findings between the three types of firms. The main differences observed were that small private firms were more likely to expand employment than either state firms or cooperatives, and that small private firms were more likely to be financed internally from the owners' own savings (Jones, 1996). Although the study was carried out in the very early stages of the transition to a market economy in Bulgaria the fact that these differences should emerge so clearly is an indication of the potential importance of the labor market impact of the small firm sector, and of the problem of lack of external sources of affordable finance (i.e., bank credit) as major factors in explaining the problems facing small firm development in Bulgaria.

The findings of another survey, also carried out in 1992, by the Dutch Research Institute for Small and Medium-sized Businesses, are reported by Houbenova-Delissivkova and Puchev (1996). This study showed that the most serious problems faced by small firms in Bulgaria were the high level of taxation, unfavorable economic conditions, inadequate legislation and policies, poor infrastructure, bureaucracy, lack of credits, and the high level of social security contributions, all of which were reported as serious problems by over half of the firms in the survey. This list of difficulties is not surprising given the general downturn in economic conditions experienced at the time of the survey and the focus of policy on macroeconomic stabilization, restrictive credit policy, and the general incoherence of state support to the nascent small firm private sector.

A further survey was carried out by the authors in 1993 as part of an ESRC project on the development of the small firm sector in southeastern Europe (Bartlett and Rangelova, 1996a, 1996b). It covered a sample of 394 small firms in all sectors of the Bulgarian economy apart from agriculture, employing at least one and no more than 50 workers and excluded consideration of self-employed individuals. The survey was organized as a representative sample survey selected from lists of firms registered with the regional offices of the National Statistical Institute and was carried out by face-to-face interviews with entrepreneurs and managers of the small firms. Overall, one-third of the sample were manufacturing firms, one-fourth were in trade, and one-fifth were in service activities. The relatively high proportion of manufacturing firms was linked to the exclusion of self-employed persons. Nevertheless, most firms were very small micro-firms. Three-fifths (61 per cent) employed fewer than 11 employees, and less than ten per cent of firms employed more than 30 employees. Micro-firms were particularly concentrated in the trade sector, but even in manufacturing almost three-quarters of firms had fewer than 20 employees. Most manufacturing sector firms were engaged in light manufacturing activities such as clothes and dressmaking, and confectionery and soft drinks. An important though small minority (six per cent) were engaged in the production of electronics products which have developed as spin-offs from prior investment in high technology manufacturing under the central planning system in Bulgaria (Bartlett and Rangelova, 1996b). The size distribution of ownership also varied by the form of ownership with very small micro firms more usually being under individual ownership while firms under limited liability tended to be clustered among the larger firms in the sample.

The survey showed that small firms in Bulgaria are mostly family owned, operating mainly under sole proprietorship but with a significant minority of partnerships and limited liability companies. They are largely self-financed from the entrepreneur's own capital, and are independent of outside control. The entrepreneurs have not on

239

the whole entered business as a defensive reaction in the face of unemployment. Most had previously been employed as white collar workers from the state sector who saw and took advantage of favorable business opportunities. On the other hand the survival of the firm was a key consideration. The defense of real incomes, rather than a large improvement, was perhaps all that could be expected under the existing conditions.

The main problems facing small firms in Bulgaria are low levels of demand, high interest rates, high taxes, and bureaucracy. These factors reflect the special conditions of economic transition in Bulgaria. Low demand reflects the collapse of the state sector partly due to external shocks but also reflecting the restrictive fiscal and monetary policies. High interest rates are also a feature of the conventional macroeconomic stabilization policies. Bureaucratic obstacles and high taxes reflect the lingering resistance to small business development. Reflecting this feature of the transition almost no firms report receiving support from the state, and even fewer from local government bodies. There is therefore a need for more focused policies in the area of local employment initiatives and through the further development of a network of business advice centers. In addition there is a need to create and foster stronger social and economic networks. Small firms in Bulgaria are not closely or extensively networked. Although networking links are quite extensive in the area of purchasing, reflecting the legacy of a supply orientated economy, there are only weak links in the area of marketing, and virtually no financial interlinkages between firms. Network capital, reflected through political connections and friendship ties are the least important factors in promoting business success. In addition there is a very tenuous linkage to business associations, to which only a small minority of firms belong. The small firms sector could be encouraged to improve its networking capability especially in the area of marketing, and in the development of business associations.

Another feature of the small firms in Bulgaria which reflects the legacy of the recent socialist past is the evidence of the persistence of an egalitarian ethic. Income differentials between owner-managers and unskilled workers were found to be surprisingly low, with an average ratio of only two to one. The labor relationships within the firm were experienced as very satisfactory, and the skills of the labor force were appreciated as one of the key factors contributing to firms' success.

Most firms operated in a competitive environment, but it is not surprising in view of the underdeveloped state of the market that nearly one-third (30 per cent) of firms reported facing no competition. This is likely to change as the entry of further new firms takes place, which should be encouraged. However, the great majority of firms operated mainly or exclusively for the domestic market, and imported more than they exported. There was a small minority (ten per cent) of firms which were export orientated and exported more than one-fourth of their product. These firms should be candidates for a particular focus of policy attention in the future.

There was little evidence of much in the way of workforce training. Only one-fifth of firms bothered to send their workers on training courses. The entrepreneurs reported that the most useful form of training was in the area of marketing and accountancy. On the other hand, the small firms appeared to be surprisingly innovative, especially in the manufacturing and services sectors. There was evidence of the widespread diffusion of new machinery and techniques, although there was a large tail of firms with older and outdated equipment.

Perhaps the most surprising finding of the survey was the growth orientation of many of the entrepreneurs in the study. Almost three-fifths (59 per cent) of the firms had taken on new employees in the six months prior to interview, and about two-thirds (67 per cent) had plans to expand employment over the following year. To support these plans the entrepreneurs in the survey reported that on average they reinvest over half of their profits for future growth. The entrepreneurs were also surprisingly optimistic. Nearly half expected economic conditions to improve and only one in seven expected them to worsen over the following year. However, this optimism occurred in the very early stages of transition when most firms were newly established and before many entrepreneurs had encountered the painful experience of business failure.

In view of the rapid increase in unemployment in Bulgaria, these fast growth small firms will have an important role to play in the area of job creation. The results from the survey indicated that about two-thirds (67 per cent) of the small firms planned to expand employment. Of those which did not have plans to expand employment most faced external constraints to expansion, and only a small proportion had no job creation potential at all. The subset of firms with an orientation towards employment growth had a number of distinct characteristics. Their owners were more likely to have university education and to employ hired managers to run their firms. They were more likely to report that management skills and good labor relations were the most important factors in their business success. They tended to reinvest a greater proportion of their profits in their business and were more likely to operate advanced numerically controlled machines. They were likely to already employ more than five workers. Firms with these characteristics were more likely to have plans to generate additional employment than other firms. A subset of fast growth firms were also identified. These firms comprised one-tenth of all firms but accounted for nearly one-half (47 per cent) of net job creation over the year prior to the survey. These firms had carved out a niche for themselves in both domestic and foreign markets. They were more likely to be limited liability companies than sole proprietorships, and to adopt procedures of employee consultation over innovation decisions. They faced fewer financial constraints and reinvested a greater proportion of profits than other firms. In addition to the continued promotion of entry of new firms, small firms policy in Bulgaria should be focused on facilitating the further development of these growth orientated firms which have the capacity to generate new jobs.

241

Case studies

Further evidence on the nature and role of different types of small firms in Bulgaria has been gathered through a number of case studies carried out in 1993 as part of the ESRC project reported on in the previous section. In this section we present the findings from three contrasting firms organized as a partnership, a limited liability company, and a struggling municipal company. The case studies reveal the contrasting fortunes of small firms under state and private ownership. The private companies have been successful in taking advantage of new market opportunities and have been innovative and flexible in response to changing market conditions. In contrast, the municipal enterprise has been suffering long-term decline and from an inability to effectively respond to changing market conditions by restructuring the company. The company waits upon assistance from bureaucrats in local and central government offices to offer it a rescue package which never comes. However, the case studies also reveal the extremely recent genesis of the small private firms in Bulgaria and the way in which often state and private capital are intertwined in the establishment of the new small firm sector.

The first firm, 'Rainbow International', is one of the more successful small firms in Bulgaria. The firm was established as a family-based partnership with five employees in June 1990, more than six months before the start of the economic reform. The firm's owner is about 40 years old, an engineer-economist by profession, speaks four foreign languages, and comes from a family of military officers. His professional career began as an editor of a leading economics journal. Several years later he became a specialist in a foreign trade firm and has made good use of the experience and contacts this provided in the branch of ready-made clothing. The original start-up capital of $70,000 was provided as a loan from a Greek investor. Initially, the main goal of the firm was producing and selling a small series of fashionable women's ready-made clothing. This was favorable for two reasons. First, prices were not yet liberalized; and second the firm was not liable to pay different import and export taxes because under the old economic system these costs were covered by the state-owned foreign trade association 'Corecom'. The success of the firm shows that even at that time it was possible for an entrepreneur to create a profitable and effective business with a small amount of initial capital. A key factor in the initial success of the business was the decision to hire skilled designers. Another important factor in the corporate strategy of the firm lay in taking credit only in hard currency so as to take advantage of the fact that foreign currency interest rates in Bulgaria are much lower than rates on domestic currency. But in the owner's view the most important factor in the firm's success lay in the way in which the firm had set up its own production base, both through its own factory and through putting out orders for production to home-workers.

'Rainbow International' is now a well-known firm with its own style which combines high quality with affordable prices. The firm has imposed its own trade mark, has opened a shop in the center of Sofia, and also has a section in the Central Department Store in Sofia. It has a stable distributive network all over the country in over 50 towns. By 1992 the firm had increased employment to 22 workers, and achieved a further increase to 30 employees by 1993. The firm produced 150 different types of clothing and had a production volume of 23,000 units in 1993. However, the low level of consumer goods production in Bulgaria meant that it still faced an excess demand for its products. While the firm had plans to meet this demand by doubling the volume of production, it was constrained from doing so by its inability to raise further credit due to the restrictive monetary policy adopted by the government as part of its macroeconomic stabilization policy.

The firm has been highly innovative in its production methods. Until recently it made dresses mainly from viscose silk imported from Germany. This kind of silk is used by worldwide famous designers such as Pierre Cardin, Vercace, and Armani. 'Rainbow International' was the firm that first introduced this textile on the Bulgarian market. However, the import duty were raised and the supply of raw materials became relatively expensive in relation to consumer purchasing power. In addition supplies became more difficult to obtain because of the conflicts in former Yugoslavia and because of the connected embargo on trade with Serbia. A short study indicated that it would be worth making dresses from Bulgarian textiles, and the firm began to experiment with new materials for its clothing, particularly stretch-velvet. On this basis, in the springtime of 1993 'Rainbow International' established a consortium with the state-owned firm 'Manuela-Haskovo' a large textile company. In the owner's view this kind of combination of state and private firms' activities is a very promising form for the future progress of light industry in Bulgaria.

The second firm 'Namko-Bulgaria' is a public limited company set up as a partnership between a Bulgarian and a Greek owner. Its Bulgarian owner is a 50-year-old engineer, who was previously an army colonel and the director of the most up-to-date and large scale military firm in Bulgaria in the 1980s. People connected the progress of this firm with the personal skills of the owner who holds a PhD in technical sciences submitted in the former Soviet Union. In 1990, due to the start of military industrial conversion into civil production in Bulgaria, several military research institutes and many firms were closed. Many workers and managers were thrown out of work and all military officers over 50 were given compulsory retirement. This provided the cue for the owner to set up a new firm. His first attempt at organizing production activity in the former military repair and engineering works 'Ljulin' was unsuccessful. But eventually he succeeded to organize production of 'Namko Pony-Ford' cars under license. As a new company, the firm is exempt from profits tax for the first five years of operation. The production activity is organized in two Bulgarian towns: Dupnitsa, where a machine-tool plant is sited, and Batak, where an ex-military plant is situated. A group of Bulgarian workers has already been to Greece to specialize in the production of the cars, and by September 1993 the production of the first 50 cars was being carried out in Greece while production began in Bulgaria in mid-1994. The production relies on imported Ford engines. The chassis is produced in Bulgaria resulting in prices about 30 per cent lower than the price of the same class of imported cars. Currently the firm employs just over 80 workers. The legal status of the firm is a public limited company with foreign participation of 50 per cent of the authorized capital. From the Bulgarian side several former military machine repair workers are shareholders. It has received an official permit by the Ministry of Finance to issue its own shares. By a decision of the general meeting of the shareholders (7 April 1993), a subscription was founded for selling 10,000 preference shares at nominal value, 1,000 leva, to raise additional capital to ensure increased production. It was the first Bulgarian public limited company to announce an evaluation of its shares. According to the statute of the firm, during the first five years 80 per cent of the capital distributed for dividends of shareholders are to be reinvested into production. In this way it is expected to increase production and productivity and raise the eventual value of shares to the shareholders.

The third firm, 'Tramcar', is an old established municipal firm set up in Sofia in 1930 as a tram repair workshop. Until the end of the World War II it was known as the best workshop of its type in Bulgaria. In the 1950s several new and modern tram workshops emerged in different districts in Sofia to service the urban transport system. Under the conditions of a centrally-planned economy, the firm was in a very favorable situation. The Sofia City Council regularly provided the firm with funds for capital and current repairs and for the wages fund. In 1987, 400 people were employed, but their numbers gradually began to diminish as working in the obsolete firm became relatively unattractive. From the end of 1989, the firm began to lose business as the economy declined and demand diminished. It began to rely heavily on state subsidies to keep going. In 1990 the firm was reorganized, and many workers and employees in the administration were dismissed. By 1993 only 60 employees remained. The legal status of the firm has not yet been transformed in accordance with the new Law on Commerce, and it is still registered as a municipal firm. During the period from 1989-93 the employees were on strike almost every month for many reasons: against reduction of working places, against the excessive number of administrative and executive personnel, and for more regular payment of wages (because at times workers receive no wages for two or three months).

Due to the weakness of the state budget, partly connected to tax evasion, but also to the shrinkage of the tax base, 'Tramcar' receives very limited wage funds, to say nothing of investment funds. At present it is exceptionally difficult to find funds for repairs, materials, or wages. Lately the firm began to diversify its work into different activities, partly to meet orders coming from new private firms. But the volume of this work is insufficient due to a lack of firms wishing to make orders, and due to the problems of many firms in paying for services delivered to them. Moreover, it is also difficult to obtain bank loans. Nearly all industrial firms are waiting to solve the

244

problem of the so-called bad loans of the banking system which are partly respon-sible for the high interest rates charged by the banks. In 'Tramcar', in 1987 a new workshop for repair activity was started, but it has since been stopped and unfin-ished due to lack of capital. At the time of the interview (September 1993), 'Tramcar' was owed over 500 thousand leva because of the insolvency of other firms. The personnel of the firm 'Tramcar' are desperate, from the unskilled workers to the Directors. Nobody knows what will happen in the near future. A decision should be taken by the Sofia City Council, and in principle by the government. But in the Director's view the prospects are very pessimistic. However, there is an underlying demand for this kind of repair workshop, and so given adequate restructuring the firm could be turned around and remain in business for the foreseeable future.

Conclusions

The research surveyed in this article has begun to put together a picture of the nature and role of small firm development in the specific context of the transition to a market economy in Bulgaria. A number of separate surveys of the small firm sector indicate that the main problems facing small firms remain the high level of taxation, the high level of interest rates and credit rationing associated with the restrictive macroeconomic stabilization policy, and the continuing problems with bureaucratic obstacles to setting up and expanding new business activities. The internal barriers to growth in small firms are much less serious, and most firms report that they have a well trained labor force and good labor relations. Entrepreneurs are on average optimistic about the future development of their firms, are expecting to expand em-ployment in the future and willing to reinvest profits in their firms to ensure this outcome. A small number of firms have proved capable of rapid growth. These tended to be limited liability firms, with good labor relations and high rates of reinvestment. The encouragement and development of such firms should be afforded priority in state policy towards the small firm sector.

The findings from our three case studies broadly supported these conclusions from the more extensive but less in depth survey research. They showed that the private firms were much more dynamic than the state firm which was studied (in this case under municipal ownership). This was due to their greater flexibility in adjusting to changes in market demand and also to their willingness to innovate and try new production methods and new techniques. In two of the case study firms there was some evidence to indicate the importance of foreign investment emanating from Greece in helping to develop the small firm sector in Bulgaria. An interesting fur-ther finding related to the evidence of the importance of private-sector/state-sector partnerships in overcoming financial constraints, and the possible development of new hybrid forms of ownership among some of the more successful small enterprises

245

in Bulgaria. Having said this, the survey evidence indicated that most small firms in Bulgaria remain independent family-owned firms, and even in the manufacturing sector most employ fewer than 20 workers.

Clearly the development of the small firm sector is likely to be a key element of the economic transition in Bulgaria. This is partly due to the slow pace of the privatization of the large state-owned sector, which means that the development of a private ownership market economy in Bulgaria will rely for the most part on a process of 'bottom-up transformation'. It is also partly due to the inherent benefits of the development of a sector of new small private firms, ranging from employment creation, an increased level of innovative activity, an increase in the level of competition in the economy, and the creation of a middle class to underpin the transition to democracy. Although the development of the small scale sector is important in itself, it should not be seen in isolation from other sectors of the economy. The small and large scale sectors are to some extent interdependent, whether through the greater flexibility of the small scale sector in meeting gaps in the market, particularly in the consumer goods and service sectors, or through a more direct interlinkage through the development of supply chain relationships in the manufacturing sector which can directly benefit local employment by replacing imported components for use by large firms whether domestic or foreign. The survey evidence indicates that as yet interlinkages of this type are as yet weakly developed and that more effort is required to develop such interfirm linkages and networks.

Overall, high taxes, high interest rates, bureaucracy, and low levels of demand present the main obstacles to the development of the small firm sector. These factors reflect the conditions of ongoing economic transition in Bulgaria, and progress with the transition should ease their salience for entrepreneurs and enable them to make the best use of the human and technical resources available to develop their businesses. At the same time the pace of transition itself depends to a great extent upon the growth of the small firm sector. In the resolution of this paradox the state will have an important role to play in developing an appropriate policy framework and helping to release some of the constraints on small firm entry and growth which are within its control and which have been identified in the research surveyed in this chapter. If it is able to muster the political will to do so, there is no reason why Bulgaria should not follow other east European economies (e.g., Poland and Hungary) in a fundamental restructuring of her economy involving the rapid 'bottom-up' growth of the private sector which would be likely to bring about a more rapid transition to a market economy than would otherwise be possible.

References

Acs, Zoltan and Audretsch, David B. (eds) (1993), *Small Firms and Entrepreneurship: an East-West Perspective*, Cambridge University Press: Cambridge.

Agency for Economic Cooperation and Development (1992), *1992 Annual Report on the State of the Bulgarian Economy*, Sofia.

Bartlett, Will and Hoggett, Paul (1995), 'Small firms in south east Europe: the importance of initial conditions', in Brezinski, H. and Fritsch, M. (eds), *The Economic Impact of New Firms in post-socialist Countries: Bottom-up Transformation in Eastern Europe*, Edward Elgar: Cheltenham, pp. 151-74.

Bartlett, Will and Rangelova, Rossitsa (1996a), 'Small firms and economic transformation in Bulgaria', *Small Business Economics*, Vol. 8, No. 1, pp.1-15.

— (1996b), 'Small firms and new technologies: the case of Bulgaria', in Oakey, Ray (ed), *High Technology Based Small Firms in the 1990s*, Paul Chapman: London (forthcoming).

Bateman, M. (1995), "Industrial restructuring and local SME development: the case for a 'hands-on' approach", in Malekovic, S. (ed), *Industrial Restructuring and Regional Economic Development*, Economics Faculty: Zagreb.

Borensztein, E., Demekas, D.G., and Ostry, J.D. (1993), 'An empirical analysis of the output declines in three eastern European countries', *IMF Staff Papers*, Vol. 40, No. 1, pp. 1-31.

European Bank for Reconstruction and Development (1994), *Transition Report October 1994*, London.

Futo, Peter and Kallay, Laszlo (1994), *Emancipation and Crisis; the Development of the Small Business Sector in Hungary*, Foundation for Market Economy: Budapest.

Houbenova-Delissivkova, Tatiana and Puchev, Plamen (1996), 'The small private firms in Bulgaria and the impact of the economic reform on their growth and future', in Brezinski, H. and Fritsch, M. (eds), *The Economic Impact of New Firms in post-socialist Countries: Bottom-up Transformation in Eastern Europe*, Edward Elgar: Cheltenham, pp. 116-30.

Izvorski, Ivailo (1993), 'Economic Reform in Bulgaria,' *Communist Economies and Economic Transformation*, Vol. 5, No. 4, pp. 519-32.

Jones, Derek C. (1996), 'The nature and performance of small firms in Bulgaria', in Brezinski, H. and Fritsch, M. (eds), *The Economic Impact of New Firms in post-socialist Countries: Bottom-up Transformation in Eastern Europe*, Edward Elgar: Cheltenham, pp.131-50.

— and Meurs, M. (1991), 'On Entry in Socialist Economies: Evidence from Bulgaria,' *Soviet Studies*, Vol. 43, No. 2, pp. 311-28.

Marshall, Alfred (1920), *Principles of Economics*, 8th edition, Macmillan: London.

247

Minassian, Garabed (1992), 'Bulgarian Industrial Growth and Structure 1970-89', *Soviet Studies*, Vol. 44, No. 4, pp. 699-712.

National Statitistical Institute (1993), *Statistical Reference Book of the Republic of Bulgaria*, Sofia.

Parvulov, Svilen (1992), *Ikonomicheski Harakteristiki na Malkite i Sredni Predriyatiya Predi Reformata*, mimeo, Institute of Economics: Sofia.

Paunov, Marin (1993), 'Labor Market Transformation in Bulgaria,' *Communist Economies and Economic Transformation*, Vol. 5, No. 2, pp. 213-28.

Penrose, Edith (1959), *The Growth of the Firm*, Blackwell: Oxford, England.

Puchev, Plamen (1990), 'A Note on the Government Policy and the New Entrepreneurship in Bulgaria,' *Small Business Economics*, Vol. 2, pp. 73-7.

— (1991), "Development of the 'small business' sector in Bulgaria", conference paper, 36th Annual World Conference, ICSB: Vienna, June.

Schumpeter, Joseph A. (1942), *Capitalism, Socialism and Democracy*, Harper and Row: New York.

Storey, David (1994), *Understanding the Small Business Sector*, Routledge: London.

Wyzan, Michael (1993), 'Stabilization Policy in Post Communist Bulgaria,' in Somoqyi, L. (ed), *The Political Economy of the Transition Process in Eastern Europe*, Edward Elgar: London.

Acknowledgements

This paper arises from a research project on 'Small Firms in South East Europe: New Forms of Ownership and Control' carried out in collaboration with Peter Futo, Paul Hoggett, Janez Prasnikar, and Laszlo Kallay. The project forms part of the East-West Research Programme of the Economic and Social Research Council (ESRC), whose support is gratefully acknowledged. We are grateful to Yuri Aroyo in assisting in the process of data collection for this study. We are also grateful to Anton Angelov, Antonina Stoyanovska, and Anna Vidivona for their advice and assistance at various phases in the research project.

12 Enterprise adjustment during early transition[1]

Derek C. Jones and Stoyko Nikolov

Introduction

The evaluation of firm adjustment and behavior during transition is important as it may shed light on diverse hypotheses including both the microeconomics of behavioral change during transition and also whether changes in macroeconomic policies are accompanied by microeconomic changes (Estrin, Gelb, and Singh, 1995). However, relatively few applied studies to date have examined aspects of enterprise adjustment during transition. In the main, the paucity of such studies reflects the unavailability of sufficient and reliable data with which to examine the topic, often because of the lack of an official (public domain) data gathering apparatus or the unwillingness of managers to cooperate in such research. Typically, the limited work to date has been undertaken for rather small samples of firms that are not necessarily representative of the underlying populations and for firms in a few countries (mainly the Visegrad countries). Analyses also seldom employ statistical testing of hypotheses, but rather tend to be case studies and to employ methods that are predominantly qualitative (e.g., Pinto *et al.*, 1993). Consequently it is difficult to know the extent to which conclusions derived from these studies are generally applicable, especially in countries with very different initial conditions and significantly different transition strategies.

In this paper, by providing one of the first studies of firm adjustment for the interesting case of Bulgaria, we contribute to the debate on these issues. Unlike most previous work, our data are derived from a large sample of firms (n = 490) that is representative of the Bulgarian manufacturing state sector.[2] Moreover, we use both univariate and qualitative techniques to investigate the factors which influence firms' performance during transition. For these reasons, arguably our findings are more reliable than many other studies and also of more general relevance, especially for countries that resemble Bulgaria in important respects. The structure of the paper is as follows.

In the following section we briefly describe the data. Next, after reviewing the relevant literature, we provide a conceptual framework attuned to the Bulgarian case during early transition and outline the empirical strategy. In the main section of the paper we present and discuss the empirical results. In the final section we make comparisons with findings from other studies and draw conclusions.

Data

For this study we use data from what is one of the first probability panel data sets for transitional economies. The data, which were collected in cooperation with the National Statistical Institute, merges two data bases: (1) the Bulgarian Economic Survey (BES), and (2) the Bulgarian Managers Survey (BMS). The enterprises surveyed participated in the Bulgarian Labor Flexibility Survey (the BLFS), a project sponsored by the ILO to assess microeconomic changes in labor practices in Bulgarian industry. The BLFS involved 490 establishments, selected to ensure a nationally and sectorially representative sample. Specifically, the population was defined as all state-owned (in 1989) Bulgarian manufacturing organizations that operated in the so-called productive sector and had more than 80 employees in 1992, the year of the first wave of data collection.

The sampling design for enterprises operated at two levels. First, five groups of the 320 municipal districts in Bulgaria were selected on the basis of geographic and urban variability, reproducing in the aggregate the countrywide industry distributions, and thus minimizing data collection costs. Second, within each of the five regions (Sofia, Pernik, Pleven, Burgas, and Plovdiv), population enumeration lists of enterprises that were state and cooperatively owned in 1988 were compiled by the Central Statistical Bureau. The number of sampled establishments per region was set to reproduce the population proportions of establishments per region. The five regions contained a population of 727 state and cooperatively owned enterprises. Within each region, for each major industry category, establishments were ordered by size and the approximate two-thirds largest were selected up to the desired sample size of 490. Thus the sample contains 69 per cent of the population of establishments which were selected to reproduce population establishments distribution by industry and region. In terms of employment, the sample firms contain about 95 per cent of all employees in state and cooperative manufacturing in the five regions in 1989.

The BMS collected survey data from top managers in the same 490 firms. A wide variety of questions were asked including information about firm characteristics such as ownership and participation in joint ventures, as well as managers' perceptions of employee involvement in decision-making. By comparison the focus of the BES was the collection of detailed financial balance sheet and income statement data. These

250

include measures of profitability, indebtedness, liabilities and size. By merging the two data bases there are 360 firms for which information on key variables used in the statistical analysis for each year from 1989-92 are available.[3]

Hence whereas previous studies are unable to use samples that are representative of the underlying populations,[4] in this study we are able to use data derived from a representative, random sample of Bulgarian enterprises. Moreover, since previous studies contain small samples, any conclusions that are drawn are unlikely to be shown to be statistically significant. In this paper, since we have a much larger data set, we are able to employ some simple parametric tests.

Conceptual framework and empirical methods

One of the few papers to use an explicit conceptual framework concerning enterprise adjustment in transition economies is Estrin *et al.* (1995). After identifying the key initial conditions facing a firm, reform is assumed to produce a series of shocks to the firm which, in turn, are expected to lead to various adjustments. These are cat-egorized as either short- or long-term responses (with the long-term reactions in-cluding restructuring and privatization). The way in which a firm would adjust is hypothesized to depend crucially on the firm's economic situation. To this end a key feature of the empirical method (as in another influential study, Pinto *et al.*, 1993) is to sort firms into three groups. However, whereas Pinto *et al.* focus on enterprise profitability alone, Estrin *et al.* (1995) divide their sample firms by using a broader range of quantitative and qualitative data on the firms' economic situation at the end of the period under study, 1992.[5] To examine their key hypotheses the authors exam-ine the relationship between enterprise viability and indicators of company perfor-mance, such as the total-cost-to-sales ratio, over the period 1988-92.[6]

While both our conceptual framework and empirical method are closely related to the approaches outlined in the previous studies, reflecting both particular aspects of the Bulgarian context as well as the nature of the available data, we make important modifications in both areas. One important point is that the economic environment within which Bulgarian managers and firms have functioned during early transition has been quite unstable and volatile, probably more so than that which has con-fronted managers in the Visegrad countries.[7] Thus changes in key macro indicators have often been larger than expected and often more dramatic then elsewhere (e.g., Blanchard, 1996). During the period 1989-92 the level of industrial production plum-meted by 55 per cent and the rate of inflation was often higher than anticipated reaching a monthly peak of 122.9 per cent in February 1991 (Martin, Vidinova, and Hill, 1996).

Several events contributed to these unfavorable economic outcomes and this dif-ficult context that faced firms including: demand shocks that were more severe than in most transition economies; the dissolution of the country's international trade links with the former communist bloc states (and the accompanying disruption if not disintegration of the inflexible supply and distribution networks of the planned economy); trade liberalization, which damaged firms open to international competition; and macroeconomic stabilization policies. In addition, the political context has been characterized by profound polarization and short-lived, unstable administrations. Also, while legal changes concerning corporate control, both during fading communism (in particular, Decree 56) and early transition (especially concerning the process of corporatization), provided the potential for more managerial control, in an era when privatization was moving extraordinarily slowly, property rights were usually vague and incomplete. This environment potentially enabled diverse interest groups to exert influence and thus provided for the possibility of diverse patterns of corporate governance to emerge (Jones, 1995, Peev, 1995).

These new realities would challenge any managers, let alone those inexperienced in the business of survival in the harsh reality of more open markets. Nevertheless, while we would also expect that all firms would alter their performance and behavior somewhat as a result of the newly established market relations, we would also expect that this confrontation with the new market realities would lead to different adjustment paths. Different responses would reflect not only differences in initial conditions (particularly the financial condition of the firm), but also differences in the environments facing firms (e.g., differences in market structures) and the capacity of managers for change (as well as their different motivation to want to make adjustments). Thus some of the factors which are expected to influence a firm's reaction to macro-level changes include: the initial size of the firm (both the labor force and the capital stock); the form of ownership (especially whether a firm is still completely state-owned); the degree of economic independence (whether a firm is a part of a larger network or not); management characteristics, such as the degree of entrepreneurship and attitude to risk taking in policy decisions; the pattern of corporate governance (especially the extent of employee influence in decision-making); and different environments, as reflected in different sectors and regions.[8]

Several lines of argument exist in the literature concerning why these factors might be expected to influence which Bulgarian firms will adjust best (and thus to be more likely to emerge as efficient, profit-making companies at the end of the four year period of economic turmoil).[9] While it is beyond the scope of this paper to adequately review this literature, in the Bulgarian context, there are important reasons why the arguments may need to be modified. Thus, in general, we expect that, other things equal, larger industrial firms were apt to be least efficient, most often producing inadequate and noncompetitive products, with a high degree of underutilization of labor and most inflexible to change. Hence we anticipate that those firms had major problems adjusting to the conditions of the open market during the four year period. However, at the beginning of transition (during the very short run), because of continuing political forces, the older larger firms were more likely than other newer firms to face softer budget constraints. These larger firms would be better positioned than other firms to be able to exploit the powerful government apparatus of information gathering, product distribution, and resource availability (Ickes, Ryterman, and Tenev, 1995) and thus appear to perform quite well. But as the new policies kicked in and firms began to face harder budget constraints, and the fixed-supply networks collapsed, we would expect that the economic deficiencies of larger firms would begin to surface. For example, large inherited labor forces would make the implementation of retraining programs extremely expensive. Therefore, in the longer run, it is very likely that bigger firms were more likely to become larger debtors, realize larger losses, lay off unnecessary workers, and eventually to become economically nonviable. On the other hand, smaller firms probably performed better during the process of transition. These firms were less likely to be part of nationwide supply networks and thus were apt to be comparatively independent. This financial and operational independence combined with the smaller size of their labor force and capital stock made it a lot easier for their managers to implement changes in response to market signals. Thus, we expect that these firms were much more likely than their larger counterparts, to adjust faster and emerge as the more efficient firms by 1992, by exploring new opportunities in terms of management structure, labor management techniques, and choices of product mix.

We expect that cooperatives or private firms will have performed better than state-owned enterprises due to their superior incentive schemes, closer managerial supervision, and harder budget constraints, all of which promote a higher level of efficiency. It is also reasonable to believe that when firms are dependent on trading partners and suppliers, that would decrease the likelihood that they choose to adjust. In other words, a dependent firm is expected to be inflexible and perform worse than its independent competitors (Ickes et al.,1995). In addition we would expect that firms that were located in sectors and or regions that had been particularly hard hit would be expected, other things equal, to embark on more cautious adjustment strategies.

It is also important to consider the effect of different interest groups and governance structures on enterprise performance during transition. One aspect to which much attention has been paid in the literature is the role of insiders, especially non-managerial employees (e.g., EBRD, 1995). While economic theory is ambiguous as to the expected effects of employee participation in decision-making upon organizational outcomes, including enterprise productivity, the dominant conventional wisdom is that, for diverse reasons, worker participation in control had significant adverse economic effects. However, a more favorable assessment is made by some. For example, Ben-Ner and Jones (1995) argue that for various reasons, certain structures that provide for employee participation in control and in economic returns (through compensation systems such as profit sharing or employee ownership), may lead to enhance individual, group and organizational effectiveness.

In our empirical work we follow Estrin et al. (1995) and create a composite mea-

253

sure to produce three classes of firms based on enterprise performance during the last year in the period of investigation. This composite measure is labeled SEPARATE – it separates the firms into three groups, hereafter 'the good', 'the bad', and 'the ugly'. In constructing SEPARATE we use two criteria, profits and indebtedness in 1992.[10] Firms that fall in the top two quintiles in profits *and* the bottom two quintiles in total liabilities are assigned a score of two ('the good'). The 'good' firms have positive profits in 1992 and relatively low level of indebtedness. Firms that fall in the bottom two quintiles in profits *and* the top two quintiles in total liabilities are assigned a score of zero ('the ugly'). All other firms are given the intermediate score of one ('the bad').

The next step is to select a group of performance indicators and trace them individually over a four year period. Again we emulate the method used by Estrin *et al.* (1995) and construct measures such as: total-cost-to-sales ratio, employment, gross-profit-to-sales ratio, and total liabilities. However, since we have access to a much richer data set than was available in the small sample of Estrin *et al.* (1995), we monitor additional indicators of firm adjustment and performance, such as investment expenditure per worker, the degree of employee participation in decision making, and short-term assets.

In addition, since we have a much larger data set than most other studies, we can test for the first time the statistical significance in the patterns of evolution of the selected indicators. We do this in two different ways. First, we report findings from computing bivariate correlation coefficients between SEPARATE and the indicators listed above. Second, to gain a better understanding of the differences in performance among the three groups, we run simple regressions of each of the four principal indicators against dummies representing two of the three categories for SEPARATE.

Findings

Before examining our findings (reported in Tables 12.1-12.3 and Figures 12.1-12.5) in detail, at the outset we note several important findings. First, for some indicators of adjustment, it is clear that there is evidence of substantial change during 1989-92 for firms in all categories. This is most apparent concerning levels of employment, which fell markedly for firms in all categories (and on average by more than 45 per cent), and rates of investment per worker which also fell precipitously across the board (and on average by more than 65 per cent). Thus it appears that a hardening budget constraint does force firms to respond to a changed environment, even without extensive formal changes in ownership. At the same time, according to some other indicators, change has been less dramatic (for example, patterns of control as suggested by measures of employee influence). Overall this mixed evidence is consistent with the view that the links between enterprise adjustment and policy changes such as privatization are quite complex (EBRD, 1995), though the evidence examined in this paper does not enable us to determine the extent to which strategic restructuring is yet taking place.

A second finding exists when Bulgarian firms are sorted into three groups; we end up with 64 'good', 209 'bad', and 87 'ugly' firms. While to some degree the group sizes reflect the sorting method we have used, we are struck by the fact that the percentage of 'good' firms in Bulgaria is about 18 per cent – considerably below the comparable percentages for firms in the Visegrad countries as discussed by Estrin *et al.* (1995). Third, from the figures, as well as Table 12.1 (in which we report descriptive statistics for these three categories of firms), it is quite apparent that firm-level changes are quite varied. In other words, even before the introduction of widespread privatization of large firms, Bulgarian firms had been responding in different ways to the new environments.

Figures 12.1-12.5 show the evolution of various key indicators for firm category averages during early transition. From Figure 12.1 we see that the total-cost-to-sale ratios increased in all firms from 1989-92. However, the pattern and degree of increase was different for the three groups of firms. For the 'bad' and 'ugly' firms we see that this ratio increased steadily over the four year period from 83 per cent to 129 per cent, and from 91 per cent to 238 per cent respectively. On the other hand, the total-cost-to-sale ratio for the good firms rose sharply in 1990 to 335 per cent before subsiding to 107 per cent in 1992 which is the best level for all three groups at the end of the period.

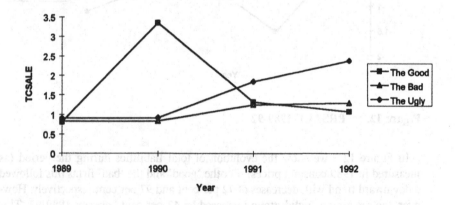

Figure 12.1   TCSALE 1989-92

The profit-to-sale ratios exhibit large differences in starting and final levels for the three groups (Figure 12.2). Initially the 'good' firms have the highest ratio of 58 per cent, compared to 41 per cent and 34 per cent for the 'bad' and the 'ugly'. Then the ratio dips down sharply to -152 per cent for the 'good' firms in 1990. Keeping in mind the steep increase in the total-cost-to-sales ratio for this group during the same year, this result is hardly surprising. By 1992 only the 'good' firms had a positive profit-to-sales ratio of 22 per cent as they clearly demonstrate a more efficient and smooth adjustment. The 'good' firms performed better in this category as they sustained a high level of sales and carefully managed their costs. It is important to notice that the trends of both the total-cost-to-sale ratios, the profit-to-sale ratios support our expectations that the 'good' firms had to overcome severe adversities in the early years of transition, i.e., 1990, before they emerged as 'leaders of the pack'. On the other hand we see that the 'bad' and the 'ugly' firms performed reasonably well during the same stage, arguably still benefiting from continuing government subsidies and other informal contacts.

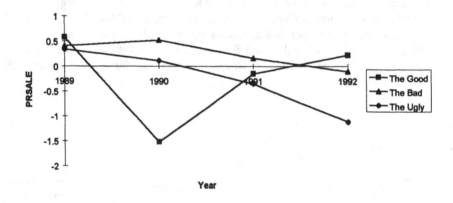

Figure 12.2   PRSALE 1989-92

In Figure 12.3 we show the evolution of total liabilities during the period (as measured in 1989 constant prices). For the 'good' and the 'bad' firms this followed a downward trend with decreases of 72 per cent and 97 per cent respectively. However, the remaining 'ugly' group increased by 42 per cent between 1989-92. This shows that the first two groups managed to effectively impose hard budget constraints while the latter failed to adapt to the decrease in subsidies and fell into arrears. The difference in performance in terms of indebtedness is also consistent

256

with a conservative policy concerning credit in good firms, for which evidence has been found elsewhere (Estrin, Gelb, and Singh, 1995).

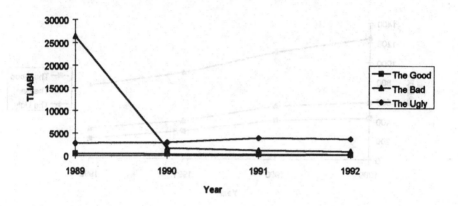

Figure 12.3   TLIABI 1989-92

Employment (Figure 12.4) decreased steadily for all three categories over the entire period. The largest cuts in labor occurred in the 'ugly' firms where the downsizing reached an average of 498 workers per firm. On the contrary the 'good' firms laid off the smallest number of workers, an average of only 220 workers. However, the percentage decrease of labor force for the three groups tells a different story. In the 'ugly' firms it was 40 per cent, in the 'bad' 47 per cent, and in the 'good' 52 per cent. These results suggest that the managers of the 'good' firms curbed the labor costs of their firms by eliminating underutilized labor, which was not the case in the other two categories. We also find support for our surmise that, initially, larger industrial firms were more apt to have labor forces with high ratios of underutilized workers. Hence they were more likely to fall in the 'ugly' group and, as transition continued, be especially likely to contribute heavily to the rising unemployment rates by firing their redundant workers.

Another figure we assemble shows that real investment expenditures per worker fell steadily for the 'ugly' and 'bad' categories over the four year period but increased between 1991-92 for the 'good' firms (Figure 12.5). The percentage drop between 1989-92 for the 'ugly' was once again the largest at 88 per cent, followed by a decrease of 69 per cent for the 'bad', and only 42 per cent for the 'good'. It is important to notice that investment expenditures per worker for the 'good' firms decreased by the lowest percentage, which implies that it is quite important for firms

257

to expend resources on renovating obsolete equipment in order to adjust well in the new environment.

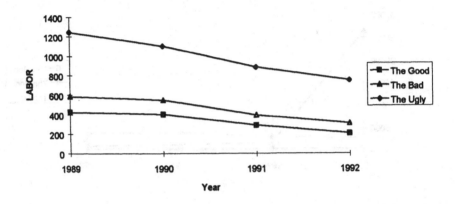

Figure 12.4   LABOR 1989-92

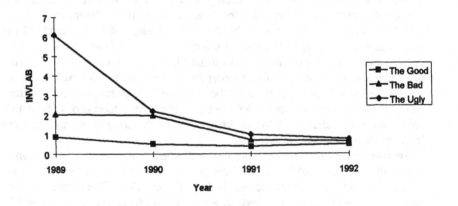

Figure 12.5   INVLAB 1989-92

258

The information reported for 'group A' variables in Table 12.1 is also used in assembling Figures 12.1-12.5. By comparison, the information for variables in 'group B' in Table 12.1 contains additional information (typically these variables are unavailable for all four years). These descriptive statistics suggest several other interesting results. Some indicators suggest a degree of rigidity in institutional evolution (a slow rate of firm adjustment) in Bulgaria, and an unusually slow rate at least when compared with changes in firms in Visegrad transition economies. For example, concerning the dynamics of employee involvement,[11] about 80 per cent of sample firms did not change their type of corporate governance. Beyond that it seems that between 1991-92, firms in the 'good' category moved toward a higher degree of employee involvement in decision making while in the other categories employee influence declined.[12]

Elsewhere, information is also available on other firm attributes which also points towards institutional inertia. For example, very few (less than 1.5 per cent) of sample firms participated in a joint venture (and hence this factor is unlikely to vary across firm type).

However, in other respects Table 12.1 does indicate that there are features which vary across firms and over time. Unsurprisingly, since it is measured in nominal terms, short run assets increased for all three categories from 1991-92. However, we find as predicted that this variable remained lowest for the 'good' firms. In terms of the number of products (NPROD), we see that by 1992 'good' firms had fewer product lines. Arguably they were quicker than were other firms to jettison product lines which had poor prospects in the new environment. We also see that in 1992 fewer 'ugly' firms were independent (INDEP) than were 'good' and 'bad' firms – 'ugly' firms were more apt to be part of larger networks. Finally, the incidence of profit sharing is seen to decrease monotonically from 'good' to 'ugly' firms. This is consistent with the view that profit sharing is positively associated with enterprise performance.

Finally, we note that firms in all categories are present in all industries. This is an important finding, since it implies that it is *not* the case that entire sectors of industry are uncompetitive and obsolete. This is at odds with the claim of some, notably Hughes and Hare (1994), and in turn suggests that it would be unwise to design industrial policy only at the sectorial level.

Table 12.1
Descriptive statistics

Variable	The 'GOOD' Mean	Std. Dev.	The 'BAD' Mean	Std. Dev.	The 'UGLY' Mean	Std. Dev.
Group A						
LABOR89	426.53	520.00	586.41	583.92	1,247.48	1,221.00
LABOR90	401.45	532.61	547.35	596.85	1,101.17	1,037.34
LABOR91	288.48	381.74	394.91	327.28	883.67	700.85
LABOR92	206.22	241.24	309.99	266.03	749.18	599.60
PRSALE89	0.58	1.26	0.41	0.36	0.03	0.41
PRSALE90	-1.52	12.60	0.52	5.95	0.11	0.84
PRSALE91	-0.15	2.08	0.16	1.49	-0.35	2.85
PRSALE92	1.07	1.13	-0.11	0.32	-1.12	3.92
TCSALE89	0.81	0.26	0.83	0.15	0.91	0.33
TCSALE90	3.35	19.44	0.84	0.18	0.92	0.34
TCSALE91	1.32	2.08	1.25	0.87	1.84	2.63
TCSALE92	1.07	0.13	1.29	0.54	2.38	4.04
TLIABI89	475.51	744.00	26,388.45	354,611.50	2,738.44	4,793.79
TLIABI90	367.22	408.58	1,689.53	8,377.73	2,889.20	3,438.88
TLIABI91	309.32	489.16	1,167.69	1,928.91	3,877.49	4,436.21
TLIABI92	133.96	82.27	858.63	1,279.30	3,605.62	3,352.98
INVLAB89	0.87	1.31	2.03	4.77	6.09	19.72
INVLAB90	0.51	0.76	1.97	8.62	2.19	5.40
INVLAB91	0.39	0.68	0.72	1.40	0.99	2.04
INVLAB92	0.50	1.17	0.64	1.07	0.76	2.25
Group B						
INDEP92	0.12	0.32	0.12	0.32	18.00	0.39
INVEXP92	45.42	75.45	177.88	284.82	472.85	1,381.49
NPRODC92	3.13	2.79	4.55	7.10	3.39	3.54
OWNERS92	1.25	0.44	1.18	0.53	1.07	0.40
PROFSHAR	0.70	0.46	0.57	0.50	0.46	0.50
RISK92	0.68	0.47	0.64	0.48	0.84	0.37
RISKCOMP	2.28	0.53	2.18	0.58	2.13	0.56
SALEREPS	4.05	4.36	8.21	15.11	6.47	7.29
SEPARATE	3.00	0.00	2.00	0.00	1.00	0.00
SRASS91	6,005.15	7,235.96	17,600.73	24,796.87	50,233.82	55,041.12
SRASS92	6,537.27	6,306.32	26,863.38	65,068.66	68,160.16	86,764.87
TINCOM92	2,041.73	2,022.67	5,682.60	8,231.66	12,716.88	15,826.36
DMP91	1.96	0.56	1.76	0.56	1.66	0.51
DMP92	2.09	0.62	1.76	0.59	1.64	0.54

Note: all variables are defined in Variable definitions, pp. 270-1.

Table 12.1
Descriptive statistics (cont.)

Variable	The 'GOOD'		The 'BAD'		The 'UGLY'	
	Mean	Std. Dev.	Mean	Std. Dev.	Mean	Std. Dev.
Group C						
IND1	0.06	0.24	0.16	0.37	0.17	0.38
IND2	0.11	0.31	0.14	0.35	0.20	0.40
IND3	0.16	0.37	0.06	0.23	0.09	0.29
IND4	0.34	0.48	0.27	0.44	0.26	0.44
IND5	0.03	0.18	0.11	0.31	0.17	0.38
IND6	0.09	0.29	0.05	0.21	0.03	0.18
IND7	0.02	0.13	0.05	0.22	0.02	0.15
IND8	0.02	0.12	0.04	0.19	0.02	0.15
BOURGAS	0.17	0.38	0.20	0.40	0.17	0.38
PERNIK	0.06	0.25	0.10	0.30	0.11	0.32
PLEVEN	0.14	0.35	0.07	0.26	0.17	0.38
PLOVDIV	0.17	0.38	0.20	0.40	0.14	0.35

Note: all variables are defined in Variable definitions, pp. 270-1.

From the correlation coefficients (Table 12.2), we see that in most years the relationship between SEPARATE and the performance indicator is as hypothesized. Thus typically (and whenever statistically significant) we find that 'good' firms had: lower total-cost-to-sales ratios (all years except 1990); smaller labor forces; higher profit-to-sales ratios (1989 and 1992); lower total liabilities (1990-92); smaller investment expenditures per worker (1989 and 1991); lower levels of short run assets (in 1991-92); and higher levels of employee involvement (DMP91 and DMP92).

Finally we examine results from the regressions. In Table 12.3 we report findings when the omitted category is whether or not a firm is GOOD.[13] From these regressions we are able to see which relationships examined in the figures are statistically significant. Thus from Table 12.3 we see that employment was always statistically significantly higher in the 'ugly' firms as compared to the 'good' firms.[14] Also, the ratio of profits to sales in 'good' firms was significantly better than the 'ugly' firms in 1989 and in 1992. However, in 1990 there was a switch in the coefficient sign for UGLY, illustrated by the sudden 'kinks' in the PRSALE graph in 1990 which was discussed earlier.

Table 12.2
Bivariate correlation coefficients for groups of firms and selected performance indicators, 1989-92

	TCSALE89	TCSALE90	TCSALE91	TCSALE92
SEPARATE	-0.1450	0.0860	-0.1092	-0.2147
	(327)	(341)	(352)	(359)
	P = 0.009	P = 0.113	P = 0.041	P = 0
	LABOR89	LABOR90	LABOR91	LABOR92
SEPARATE	-0.3356	-0.3113	-0.4016	-0.4378
	(332)	(350)	(357)	(360)
	P = 0	P = 0	P = 0	P = 0
	PRSALE89	PRSALE90	PRSALE91	PRSALE92
SEPARATE	0.1179	-0.0638	0.0432	0.2214
	(326)	(340)	(349)	(359)
	P = 0.033	P = 0.241	P = 0.421	P = 0
	TLIABI89	TLIABI90	TLIABI91	TLIABI92
SEPARATE	0.0026	-0.1204	-0.4109	-0.5130
	(334)	(341)	(351)	(360)
	P = 0.963	P = 0.026	P = 0	P = 0
	INVLAB89	INVLAB90	INVLAB91	INVLAB92
SEPARATE	-0.1682	-0.0733	-0.1306	-0.0558
	(226)	(247)	(243)	(151)
	P = 0.011	P = 0.251	P = 0.042	P = 0.496
	DMPOWE91	DMPOWE92	SRASS91	SRASS92
SEPARATE	0.1654	0.2284	-0.4073	-0.2984
	(263)	(276)	(342)	(353)
	P = 0.007	P = 0	P = 0	P = 0

Note: the number of observations for each correlation coefficient is given in parentheses.

262

Table 12.3
Ordinary least squares estimates

Dependent variable	LABOR89	LABOR90	LABOR91	LABOR92
Variable	Coefficient (SE)	Coefficient (SE)	Coefficient (SE)	Coefficient (SE)
BAD	159.88 (117.93)	145.90 (104.13)	106.43 (65.28)	103.76 (53.09)
UGLY	820.94 (134.91)***	699.71 (120.23)***	595.19 (75.28)***	542.96 (61.20)***
(Constant)	426.52 (103.62)***	401.45 (91.19)***	288.47 (57.19)***	206.21 (46.45)***
R-squared	0.13	0.11	0.19	0.23
n	329	347	354	357

Dependent variable	PRSALE89	PRSALE90	PRSALE91	PRSALE92
Variable	Coefficient (SE)	Coefficient (SE)	Coefficient (SE)	Coefficient (SE)
BAD	-0.17 (0.09)*	2.04 (1.03)**	0.31 (0.29)	-0.33 (0.29)
UGLY	-0.239 (0.10)	1.62 (1.18)	-0.197 (0.33)	-1.35 (0.33)***
(Constant)	0.580 (0.08)***	-1.52 (0.90)*	-0.151 (0.25)	0.22 (0.25)
R-squared	0.01	0.01	0.01	0.05
n	323	337	346	356

Note: figures in parentheses are standard errors.
* = significant at 10% level of significance
** = significant at 5% level of significance
*** = significant at 1% level of significance

Table 12.3 (continued)
Ordinary least squares estimates

Dependent variable	TCSALE89	TCSALE90	TCSALE91	TCSALE92
Variable	Coefficient (SE)	Coefficient (SE)	Coefficient (SE)	Coefficient (SE)
BAD	0.013 (0.04)	-2.51 (1.19)**	-0.065 (0.25)	0.220 (0.29)
UGLY	0.095 (0.04)**	-2.42 (1.40)*	0.519 (0.28)*	1.31 (0.34)***
(Constant)	0.814 (0.03)***	3.35 (1.05)***	1.32 (0.21)***	1.07 (0.26)***
R-squared	0.02	0.01	0.02	0.05
n	324	338	349	356

Dependent variable	TLIABI89	TLIABI90	TLIABI91	TLIABI92
Variable	Coefficient (SE)	Coefficient (SE)	Coefficient (SE)	Coefficient (SE)
BAD	25,912.94 (40,339.42)	1,322.31 (984.80)	858.37 (381.19)**	724.67 (273.42)**
UGLY	2,262.93 (46,589.98)	2,521.98 (1,134.79)	3,568.16 (440.35)***	3,471.67 (315.18)***
(Constant)	475.51 (35,345.17)	367.22 (865.39)	309.32 (334.01)	133.96 (239.24)
R-squared	0.01	0.01	0.19	0.31
n	331	338	348	357

Note: figures in parentheses are standard errors.
* = significant at 10% level of significance
** = significant at 5% level of significance
*** = significant at 1% level of significance

In terms of the total-cost-to sales ratio, statistically significant differences exist between the 'good' and the 'ugly' firms over all four years. However, as indicated in Figure 12.1, the coefficient sign for UGLY switches during the period with the 'good' firms emerging as the more cost efficient firms in 1991 and 1992. Finally, from the regressions of TLIABI 89-92, the coefficients for BAD and UGLY show that statis-

264

tically significant differences exist between the 'good' and the 'ugly' firms over all four years and between the 'good' and the 'bad' firms for two years. In all cases the 'bad' and the 'ugly' firms were always larger borrowers than were the 'good' firms, and they became significantly more indebted in the last two years of the period.

Conclusions

In this paper we have examined the adjustment patterns of 360 Bulgarian manufacturing firms during 1989-92. During this period of early transition the overwhelming bulk of older Bulgarian firms continued to be state-owned (indeed, most had not been corporatized). Nevertheless, we find some evidence that firms did begin to restructure. This is most evident concerning levels of employment, which fell on average by more than 45 per cent, and rapidly falling rates of investment per worker. Thus it appears that a hardening budget constraint did force firms to respond to a changed environment, even without extensive formal changes in ownership. At the same time, according to some other indicators, change has been less dramatic (for example, patterns of control as suggested by measures of employee influence). Overall this mixed evidence on adjustment is consistent with the findings from other studies (e.g., EBRD, 1995) that the links between enterprise adjustment and policy initiatives such as privatization are quite complex (EBRD, 1995).

We also find that enterprise adjustments by sample firms have been quite varied. In this respect we confirm findings from other studies of Bulgarian firms, for example, Peev (1995), which typically have used smaller samples of firms. In addition, other evidence that has been derived from data for our sample firms also indicates that responses by economic agents and firms during early transition have been highly variable. While this additional evidence is for other issues (e.g., for patterns of executive compensation, see Jones and Kato, 1995; for patterns of employee participation, see Jones, 1995), these findings taken as a whole point to relationships between restructuring and policy measures which are more complex than some suggested would be the case when transition began.

Many of our findings corroborate those emerging from studies of enterprises in other transition economies. The finding that even without formal changes in ownership, firms did begin to restructure has been observed in Poland (Pinto *et al.*, 1993). Again like Pinto *et al.* (1993) we find that there are 'good' and 'bad' (as well as 'ugly') performing firms in all sectors. In terms of patterns of adjustment, our findings about the patterns of evolution of total-cost-to-sale ratio, profit-to-sale ratio, total liabilities, and labor force over the period 1989-92 are closely comparable to the results obtained by Estrin *et al.* (1995) for enterprises in Poland and Hungary over the same time period. Using a sample of approximately 43 firms, they also

265

found that the total-cost-to-sale ratios rose more sharply for 'bad' firms in both countries. Similarly to our results, they discovered that employment decreased less in the 'good' firms than in the 'bad' ones, again in both Poland and Hungary. Although they witnessed a different behavior for the profit-to-sales ratios in the two countries, the overall trend for this indicator showed a sharper decline for the 'bad' firms. Finally, Estrin *et al.* (1995) found that 'bad' firms eventually emerged as large debtors, which is very close to our findings for the Bulgarian case. Our results, which are based on a larger data set and bear the support of parametric tests, suggest that the preliminary picture of key aspects of enterprise adjustment in Poland and Hungary presented in Estrin *et al.* (1995) is quite possibly a general picture common to many transitional economies.

At the same time, compared to changes that have been found for firms in other transition countries, it seems that there are important differences in the character of the changes taking place in Bulgarian firms. Thus it appears that the falls in employment and in investment per worker in Bulgaria have been much more pronounced that in firms in Poland, Hungary, the Czech Republic, and Russia surveyed in EBRD (1995).[15] At the same time it is clear from case study evidence, including enterprise visits of sample firms, that the pace of change in many other areas, including areas of strategic behavior, has typically been much less dramatic and slower than in several other countries.

In accounting for these differences in adjustment patterns both within and across countries, our analysis for Bulgarian firms suggests that initial conditions play an important role. In particular we find that size is an essential determinant of the process of adjustment during early transition and that large Bulgarian firms performed significantly worse than their smaller counterparts during the period 1989-92. We also find evidence that sectorial and regional location matter much. Our findings on the importance of ownership and employee participation also point to the important roles of property rights and governance structures. However, unlike findings for some other transition countries, our findings on employee participation indicate that under certain conditions this form of insider influence may be a positive force. Finally, the existence of considerable variation in responses across firms which in many respects are substantially similar (e.g., similar policy environment, sector, size, and ownership) points to the crucial role of institutional and organizational change in determining economic outcomes. When economic agents have had scope for discretionary change, it is clear that their receptiveness to change has been quite varied.

However, it is clear that our findings, as are those based on studies of firms in other transition economies, are preliminary. An urgent need exists to extend the analysis to include a broader range of variables – for example, the evidence examined in this paper does not enable us to determine the extent to which strategic restructuring is yet taking place and does not include vital variables such as management compensation. Only after studies based on such richer data sets appear will we be in a position to adequately assess whether there are general patterns of and explanations for enterprise adjustment in transition economies.

Notes

1   Jones acknowledges support from NSF 9010591. The paper has benefited from comments on earlier versions from participants at a seminar at the University of Maryland, especially Christopher Clague and Dennis Mueller, and from Jeffrey Pliskin.

2   Previous studies for Bulgaria are mainly case studies, for example, Peev (1995).

3   There is no reason to assume that these 360 firms are not representative of the initial sample of 490 firms.

4   Compare, for example, with Estrin, Gelb, and Singh (1995), who examine firms in the Visegrad countries and Peev's study of Bulgarian firms. Both studies are essentially a series of case studies.

5   Group A firms are considered economically sound with their future viability not in question. These contrast with category C firms, which are consistently in debt, cannot pay interest on their loans, and also suffer from seemingly insurmountable cash-flow problems. In economies with well-established bankruptcy laws such companies would be liquidated and financially restructured. Average firms which make small profits or minor losses and may occasionally suffer debt of cash flow problems fall between these groups.

6   The authors also examine differences in firms' performance across the three countries from which their sample was drawn and find considerable support for their hypotheses, including an association between variation in enterprise performance across countries and differences in macro policies.

7   Thus most studies of enterprise adjustment are for firms in the Visegrad countries (e.g., see Carlin *et al.*, 1994, and EBRD, 1995 for reviews).

8   This list of factors examined in this study is not exhaustive but rather reflects data availability. In other work we examine the influence of other factors – for example, see Jones and Kato (1995) for an examination of the role of management compensation.

9   For example, see Carlin *et al.* (1994), Estrin and Xavier (1994), and EBRD (1995).

10   In computing this variable we note that there is no obvious theory with which to choose either the particular indicators to be used or the weights associated with the individual components making up the variable. Since no clear definition of the cash flow measure used is provided by Estrin *et al.* (1995), we are unable to replicate the variable they constructed which uses three indicators (profits, cash flow, and indebtedness).

11   To measure the extent of employee influence in corporate governance in our
     sample firms and how this has changed, we asked respondents (top manag-
     ers) in the BMS to assess their perceptions of the influence of employees over
     diverse issues annually during this period. A six point scale was used: '1'
     represents a situation in which management decides alone (without any em-
     ployee input); values of '2', '3', and '4' represent situations in which man-
     agement decides, although there was some small input from employees (e.g.,
     by machinery for consultation or provision of information); '5' represents a
     situation in which there is joint decision making; and '6' indicates that work-
     ers are believed to decide the issue alone (there is no independent role for
     management). For this paper, we collapsed this metric into three categories:
     low (when the score was '1'); moderate (when the score was '2', '3', or '4');
     and high (when the score was '5' or '6'). For more details see Jones and
     Ilayperuma (1994).

12   By mainly using data on individual employee perceptions of employee par-
     ticipation, Jones (1995) examines the evolution of assessments of the extent
     of employee involvement during early transition and how this varies by type
     of firm. Again average levels of employee involvement are found to be quite
     modest and not to change much during early transition.

13   We also repeated the analysis for some of the indicators when the omitted
     category were firms designated as UGLY. Since the pattern of results does not
     change from those reported in Table 12.3, we do not report these findings.

14   In unreported regressions in which the omitted category is UGLY, statistically
     significant differences nearly always exist between the 'good' and the 'ugly'
     firms, and between the 'ugly' and the 'bad' firms.

15   The fall in average real wages has also been far greater. It has continued
     through 1996.

References

Ben-Ner, A. and Jones, D. C. (1995), 'Productivity Effects of Employee owner-
     ship: A Theoretical Framework', *Industrial Relations*, Vol. 34, No. 4, October,
     pp. 532-54.
Blanchard, O. (1996), 'Theoretical Aspects of Transition', *American Economic
     Review*, Vol. 86, No. 2, May, pp. 117-22.
Carlin, W., Van Reenen, J., and Wolfe, T. (1994), 'Enterprise Restructuring in the
     Transition; An Analytical Survey of the Case study Evidence from Central and
     Eastern Europe', E.B.R.D. Working Paper, No. 14.
European Bank for Reconstruction and Development (1995), *Transition Report
     1995*, London.

Estrin, S., Gelb, A., and Singh, I. (1995), 'Shocks and Adjustments by Firms in Transition: A Comparative Study', *Journal of Comparative Economics*, Vol. 21, pp. 131-53.

Estrin, S. and Richet, Xavier (1994), 'Industrial Restructuring and Micro-economic Adjustment in Poland: A Cross Sectional Approach', *Comparative Economic Studies*, Vol. 35, No. 4, pp. 1-21.

Hughes, G. and Hare, P. (1994), 'The International Competitiveness of Industries in Bulgaria, Czechoslovakia, Hungary, and Poland', *Oxford Economic Papers*, Vol. 46, pp. 200-21.

Ickes, B., Ryterman, R., and Tenev, S. (1995), 'On Your Marx, Get Set, Go: The Role of Competition in Enterprise Adjustment', Working Paper Series, No. 11-95-9, Pennsylvania State University, November.

Jones, D.C. (1995), 'Employee Participation in Transitional Economies: Evidence from Bulgaria: 1989-1992', *Economic and Industrial Democracy*, Vol. 16, No. 1, February, pp. 111-35.

—— and Ilayperuma, K. (1994), 'The Determinants of Employee Participation During Fading Communism and Early Transition', Working Paper Series, No. 94/4, Hamilton College: Clinton, New York.

—— and Kato, T. (1996), 'The Determinants of Chief Executive Compensation in Transitional Economies: Evidence from Bulgaria', Working Paper Series, No. 96/2, Hamilton College: Clinton, New York, and forthcoming in *Labor Economics*.

Martin, R., Vidinova, A., and Hill, S. (1996), 'Industrial Relations in Transition Economies: Emergent Industrial Relations Institutions in Bulgaria', *British Journal of Industrial Relations*, Vol. 34, No. 1, March, pp. 3-24.

Peev, Evgeni (1995), 'Separation of Ownership and Control in Transition: The Case of Bulgaria', *Europe-Asia Studies*, Vol. 47, No. 5, pp. 859-75.

Pinto, B., Belka, M., and Krajevski, S. (1993), 'Transforming State Enterprises in Poland: Evidence on Adjustment by Manufacturing Firms', *Brookings Papers on Economic Activity*, Brookings Institution: Washington D.C., pp. 213-61.

Variable definitions

Group A: variables available annually 1989-92 (where suffixes indicate the year)

LABOR = labor force; (e.g., LABOR89 = labor force in 1989).
PRSALE = profit-to-sale ratio (e.g., PRSALE90 = profit-to-sale ratio in 1990).
TCSALE = total-cost-to-sale ratio (e.g., TCSALE91 = total-cost-to-sale ratio in 1991).
TLIABI = total liabilities (e.g., TLIABI92 = total liabilities in 1992) (thousands of leva).
INVLAB = investment expenditures per worker in (e.g., INVLAB89 = investment expenditures per worker in 1989 (thousands of leva).

Group B: variables available for 1991 and/or 1992

INDEP92 = dummy variable; = 1 if firm was dependent in 1992, else = 0.
INVEXP92 = investment expenditure of the firm in 1992 (thousands of leva).
NPRODC92 = number of production lines in 1992.
OWNERS92 = categorical variable; = 1 if state owned, = 2 if coop, = 3 if private, else = 4.
PROFSHAR = dummy variable; = 1 if there existed a profit-sharing scheme in 1992, else = 0.
RISK92 = dummy variable; = 1 if the overall strategic orientation of the firm is opportunistic and risky, = 0 if the overall strategic orientation of the firm is passive.
RISKCOMP = a composite measure of risk; = 0 if the firm is passive, = 1 if the firm is a moderate risk taker, = 2 if the firm is opportunistic.
SALEREPS = number of sale representatives in the firm in 1992.
SEPARATE = a composite measure of economic viability; = 0 if the firm is a persistent loss-maker and heavily indebted, = 1 if the firm is surviving with moderate losses and without excessive borrowing, = 2 if the firm is highly viable and profitable.
SRASS91 = short run assets in 1991 (thousands of leva).
SRASS92 = short run assets in 1992 (thousands of leva).
TINCOM92 = total income in 1992.
BAD = dummy variable; = 1 if the firm is in the 'bad' category, else = 0.
UGLY = dummy variable; = 1 if the firm is in the 'ugly' category, else = 0.
DMP91 = a composite measure of workers decision making power; = 1 if low, = 2 if moderate, = 3 if high.

DMP92 = a composite measure of workers' decision making power; = 1 if low, = 2 if moderate, = 3 if high.

Group C: industry and regional dummies

IND1 = dummy variable; = 1 if the firm is in the food industry, else = 0.
IND2 = dummy variable; = 1 if the firm is in the textiles industry, else = 0.
IND3 = dummy variable; = 1 if the firm is in the wood/paper industry, else = 0.
IND4 = dummy variable; = 1 if the firm is in the engineering industry, else = 0.
IND5 = dummy variable; = 1 if the firm is in the electronics industry, else = 0.
IND6 = dummy variable; = 1 if the firm is in the chemicals industry, else = 0.
IND7 = dummy variable; = 1 if the firm is in the non-metal industry, else = 0.
IND8 = dummy variable; = 1 if the firm is in the mining industry, else = 0.
BOURGAS = regional dummy; = 1 if the firm is in Bourgas, else = 0.
PERNIK = regional dummy; = 1 if the firm is in Pernik, else = 0.
PLEVEN = regional dummy; = 1 if the firm is in Pleven, else = 0.
PLOVDIV = regional dummy; = 1 if the firm is in Plovdiv, else = 0.

Note: All value variables are in thousands of leva. All value variables in group A are in thousands of 1989 leva.

Part Six
AGRICULTURAL REFORM

13 Evolution of agrarian institutions in Bulgaria: markets, cooperatives, and private farming, 1991-94

Mieke Meurs and Darren Spreeuw

Introduction

With the collapse of central planning in East Central Europe, many observers expected that collectivized agricultural producers would quickly return to private farming. These expectations were, in part, inspired by the Chinese experience in which decontrol of the agricultural sector did lead to a large scale return to private farming and was accompanied by rapid increases in income and productivity.

The European experience has been quite different, however. In Romania, where land was decollectivized almost instantaneously through land grabs by the peasantry, 43 per cent of agricultural land had been returned to collective forms of production by 1993 (Brooks and Meurs, 1994). In Hungary in 1993, 53 per cent of land was in cooperative farms (NIS, 1994). In Bulgaria, 54 per cent of rural households surveyed in 1994 planned to place their newly restituted land in production cooperatives (Survey Data, 1994). (All uncited data hereafter refer to Survey Data 1992 and 1994.)

The reluctance of households to begin private farming is often dismissed as irrational, ideologically-motivated behavior on the part of the relatively pro-communist rural population. Theoretical developments in the area of institutionalist economics over the past decade shed a somewhat different light on this hesitation, however. This literature suggests that cooperatives may be chosen over private farming by rational economic agents concerned with finding the most efficient use for their assets.

Recent research has emphasized that where markets are incomplete, weakly developed, or not competitive, agents may turn to alternative institutions to more efficiently allocate resources. Sharecropping is a much-cited example of such a development: where insurance or credit markets are insufficiently developed to effectively reduce the production risk faced by any one individual, land owners and laborers may agree to sharecropping as a means of spreading risk (Stiglitz, 1987). While sharecropping may be inferior to simple exchange of land or labor in a context of more completely developed markets, in the context of weakly developed insurance or credit markets it may improve expected returns on assets.

Production cooperatives may be another example of the use of non-market mechanisms to increase allocational efficiency where markets are weakly developed. Production cooperatives may provide a means of spreading risk in the absence of developed credit and insurance markets. They may provide a means of achieving economies of scale if land or labor markets are weakly developed. Or they may be a means of combating market power of monopolies in agricultural inputs and monopsonies in products. Cooperatives may thus be chosen by producers because they provide net advantages to households over private production, even taking into account the incentive problems often associated with this form of production.

In this paper, we examine the development of rural markets and emerging patterns of private and cooperative production in Bulgarian agriculture. We will argue that although rural markets developed significantly between 1992 and 1994, weak market development has been a significant factor in households' choice of organizational form in agriculture. We find that while communist party influence appears to have played some role in household decisions, the major influence was economic considerations.

In the next section of the paper, we briefly review recent literature on institutional choice, drawing out the implications of this literature for organizational change in East European agricultural institutions. In the third section of the paper, we use original survey data collected by our research team[1] in Bulgaria during the summers of 1992 and 1994 to provide an overview of the reform and to examine patterns of market development and household choice. In the fourth section, a simple econometric model of household choice is developed and tested.

Theoretical background

Rationale for decollectivization

In discussions about rural transformation after 1989, the desirability of private over collective agriculture was frequently asserted, accompanied by an assumption that producers would prefer this form (Aubert, 1988, Brooks, 1991). This position appears grounded in the argument that incentive problems inherent in production cooperatives make cooperatives an inferior form of organizing agricultural production and an inferior allocation of land and labor for the household.

Two types of literature inform this position. The first emphasizes that excessively egalitarian cooperative incentive schemes can cause households to under-allocate labor to cooperative production (Sen, 1966). More recent debates have focused on the difficulty of measuring labor inputs and the resulting problems of free-riding in labor-managed enterprises (see Alchian and Demsetz, 1972). Management incentives may also be inadequate in cooperative farms, due to dispersed ownership and free-riding in monitoring management.[2]

Empirical evidence from centrally-planned economies offers some support for these arguments. Collective farming in Eastern Europe has provided examples of gross misallocation of labor and low levels of labor productivity, and recent studies of the Chinese decollectivization have attributed much of the burst in agricultural productivity between 1978-84 to the move from collective to family farming (Lin, 1992).[3]

The intractability of incentive problems is often overstated, however. As in other organizational forms, labor effort in cooperatives will approach optimal levels to the extent that effort can be efficiently priced and contracts can be enforced at minimal cost, and a number of authors have shown that adequate incentive schemes are feasible in cooperatives (Putterman and Bonin, 1993, Ireland and Law, 1988). Whether these are chosen in a cooperative will depend on the degree to which cooperatives are effectively and democratically governed (so residual claimants can take positive action to adjust pricing and enforcement; see Putterman, 1987), and the degree to which a sense of solidarity exists among cooperative members so that contracts are honored (Ostrom, 1990). To the extent that these conditions are not met, incentive problems in cooperatives are likely to be serious.

Alternative perspectives

Other literature suggests that despite that above-described problems, economically rational producers may choose collective farming, and that this may even offer a more efficient allocation compared to private farming. This analysis focuses on the institutional context in which the households exist. Where markets are well developed, individual households can easily adjust farm size through markets, and cooperative production should offer no particular advantages. Where markets for inputs and agricultural products are weakly developed, however, individual households may be unable to adjust production efficiently.

In this case, production cooperatives can increase the range of input combinations available to producers and increase the market power of farms. In doing so, the cooperatives may increase the efficiency of resource use and returns to households. In East Central Europe, three aspects of weak market development appear likely to undermine the efficiency of private production and thereby influence households' choices of organizational form.

277

In the immediate post-reform period, East Central European households find themselves with combinations of land and labor which they have not chosen (see below for a discussion of how land is being distributed). Land holdings are expected to be small, averaging six ha in Romania and 3.4 ha in Bulgaria (Brooks and Meurs, 1994). Many households will have too little land to form an efficient production unit, while others will have more land than they are interested in working. If land and labor markets are not well-developed, however, households will be unable to adjust the input combinations.

The importance of grain crops across East Central Europe exacerbates this problem. The grain crops (primarily wheat and maize) exhibit economies of scale under the available technology. While economies of scale need not influence the choice of organizational form when a producer can buy or hire additional inputs, poorly developed markets for land, labor, credit or machines create substantial barriers to achieving scale economies.

Thirdly, expected returns to individual households may be influenced by the degree of competitiveness in input and output markets. In a post-central planning context, markets are highly concentrated, putting unorganized individual producers in a weak bargaining position with respect to input suppliers and processing firms. Prices offered to private producers may thus not reflect the best possible exchange.

The choice between individual and collective farming is far from simple. Economically-rational households must weigh possible productivity and income loss due to incentive problems in collective production against possible benefits this form offers due to better input combinations, economies of scale, risk reduction, and improved bargaining positions in inputs and output markets.

Bulgaria background

Prewar background

The prewar legacy of Bulgarian farming is one of extremely small-scale, low technology farming. In 1946, 69 per cent of land holdings were under five ha. In addition, households' land was not consolidated, but rather scattered around the village, with each family holding an average of 17 units (Stoyanova, 1992).

The small and fragmented holdings greatly complicated the implementation of irrigation, machine cultivation, or even crop rotation. In 1944, there were 4,500 tractors in Bulgaria, concentrated on the largest farms. Most villagers continued to use either a traditional wooden plow, or a steel plow drawn by live horsepower. Agricultural production was first for subsistence and only secondarily a commercial venture.

278

Agriculture under collectivization

Substantial changes took place under collective agriculture, of which two are particularly important in understanding households' responses to the current reform: changes in the form of private farming, and changes in agricultural technology. Under collectivization, private ownership of agricultural land was usually limited to yards surrounding private homes, private ownership of agricultural machines was largely prohibited, and distribution of nearly all inputs and most of production were controlled by state institutions. Despite this, widespread private agricultural production persisted in Bulgaria through 1989.

A small amount of land in mountainous areas was never collectivized (about five per cent of arable land); on this land, small-scale, private agricultural production (mainly of livestock) persisted more or less intact. A more widespread form of individual farming occurred on 'personal plots', averaging 0.3 ha in 1986 (Dobreva and Meurs, 1992).[4] This land was used mainly to produce food for household consumption, although households also produced some surplus for sale to the state and, to a lesser extent, for local peasant markets. Commercial private production was usually linked to state organizations and subject to substantial state control (McIntyre, 1988). Most households thus have uninterrupted experience with private production, but the experience is with small-scale production and usually involved little entrepreneurial choice.

Under collectivization, significant changes also occurred in the technology and scale of production in agriculture. Farms grew into gigantic, highly mechanized units, averaging 2,358 ha and 367 workers in 1988. From the 4,500 tractors available in 1944, the number rose to 146,467 by 1985 (CSO, 1988, Vol. 251). Combines increased similarly, resulting in an almost entirely mechanized 'closed cycle' in grain production.

The use of more specialized machinery grew much more slowly, however, and production of certain crops, like tobacco or vegetables, remained very labor intensive. Economies of scale were thus not important in these crops, and household production was often more cost effective than production on collective farms. The suitability of existing technology to small scale production therefore differs greatly by crop.

Land law

The Ownership and Use of Farm Land Act, passed in April 1992, mandates the restitution of land to its previous owners or their heirs. Land is to be returned in its original boundaries, with two exceptions. Land equivalent in size and quality may be given 1) in order to consolidate a household's land holdings, and 2) where the original plot no longer exists. Land received through the restitution may be freely bought and sold, also with two exceptions: a) land may not be purchased by foreign citizens, and b) for two years following the reform, land may not be acquired in excess of 30 ha per family, except through inheritance. Landless persons and those with very small holdings are also eligible to receive land from national and munici-pal land reserves.[5]

Government-appointed Liquidation Commissions are to distribute collective farm property. All those who contributed labor or assets to the farms at or since their formation are eligible to receive a share of property

Current reforms

Rural reform has been taking place against a background of very partial overall economic reform. A privatization law was passed in 1992, but few (30 of over 5,000) state firms have been privatized to date. The demonopolization law, which mandates the breakup of large state firms, often created regional monopolies in the place of national ones.

Those aspects of restructuring which have progressed have generally not created favorable conditions for agriculture. Stabilization policy has perpetuated high nomi-nal interest rates, while inflation (100 per cent during 1994) has encouraged short-term lending and general uncertainty.

Prices of goods with high import content (such as fuel, fertilizer, and machines) have adjusted quickly to world levels, while wholesale prices of food products have not. Food prices have been kept down by falling real wages, as well as price controls and export bans on certain agricultural products. Agricultural producers are again caught in the 'scissors' of rising input costs and stagnant output prices. At least partly as a result of this squeeze, agricultural production fell to 84 per cent of 1989 levels by 1993 (Vienna Institute Database, 1995). All of these factors play a role in the development of rural markets and households' choices of organizational form.

Analysis of household choice

The sample

The Bulgarian Decollectivization Survey was implemented in August of 1992 and again in October of 1994. A stratified sample of 600 rural households in 100 villages was drawn from a much larger, nationally representative sample of households in-terviewed in the national Town and Village Survey in 1986.[6] Unfortunately, the original lists were missing for four of Bulgaria's 28 administrative districts (okrugs),[7] as a result of which our survey is representative for 24 of the 28 okrugs. We believe, however, that we have achieved good coverage of the range of agricultural regions in Bulgaria (by altitude and slope, as well as by crop type) and that our results should represent quite well the dynamics of the country as a whole.

The sample excludes urban dwellers, many of whom received or will receive land in the restitution. Few of these households are likely to return to farming, even as unemployment rises (see Creed, 1995), and these households will find greater difficulty in coordinating private rental arrangements from the city. They are therefore more likely than rural households to place their land in cooperatives. Their exclusion from the sample should understate, if anything, the importance of cooperatives and will help to highlight the local factors which influence the viability of private farming.

In addition to the survey of households, interviewers also gathered data on the general progress of agrarian reform at the village level. This data was collected from village land commissions, mayors' offices, liquidation commissions, and other village officials. In 1994, data was also collected from the newly-formed agricultural production cooperatives found in 67 of the sample villages.

Data on household production from the 1992 survey refer to 1991, since that was the most recent completed production cycle. Other questions in that survey, including all questions asked of village officials about the reform process, refer to 1992. The dates cited in the text reflect this distinction. The 1994 data refer to 1994 production, since the agricultural cycle was largely completed at the time of the survey.

Overview of restitution process

At the village level, the process of collective farm liquidation and land restitution began extremely slowly. By August 1992, the TKZSs in 88 of the 99 responding villages had not yet had their assets liquidated. In 23 of the 99 villages, no land whatsoever had been distributed, while in 51 only small, temporary plots had been distributed. Most land (82 per cent of arable land) was being farmed by the old TKZSs.

The process was uneven, however. Four villages in two okrugs reported that all TKZS assets had been liquidated. In 13 villages, between 50-100 per cent of the land had been distributed. The speed of land distribution reflected some clear regional patterns, with land in the vegetable, livestock and tobacco regions of south and central Bulgaria being distributed much more quickly than in the northern grain regions.

While this situation remained largely unchanged as of the end of 1993 (Ministry of Agriculture, 1993), significant changes began to be seen by the end of 1994. Only six of the 99 villages reported that no land had been distributed, while 55 villages had distributed all land. However, the majority of land was still held only on the basis of temporary-use permits. 63 villages reported that no land had been distributed with legal titles. Without titles, land cannot be sold or used as collateral.

By 1994, regional patterns in land distribution had disappeared. In fact, villages in the non-grain south and central regions had begun to trail villages in grain okrugs in the north and northeast in land distribution.

Despite the initial slow pace of the land reform, both private farming and new agricultural cooperatives had already begun to emerge by 1992. 44 of the 99 villages reported that some villagers were engaged in private agricultural production as their main occupation. Mayors reported that private individuals farmed ten per cent of agricultural land.

In 28 villages, new, registered agricultural cooperatives were also reported. An additional seven villages reported the existence of informal (unregistered) agricultural production associations. 25 of the 35 cooperatives were reportedly functioning.

The formation of agricultural production cooperatives (ZPKs) continued between 1992 and 1994, and by 1994, 67 out of the 99 villages contained at least one registered ZPK. Of the 80 registered ZPKs in our survey, 74 were operating during 1994. 24 villages also reported nonregistered cooperatives. Land worked under the direction of the liquidation committees (the still unliquidated TKZS's) only accounted for 25 per cent of arable land in 1994, while the new cooperatives farmed 47 per cent of village arable land. The percentage of land farmed by private farmers had almost doubled, to 19 per cent.

Clear regional patterns are visible in the emerging forms of agricultural organization. The share of land farmed privately is most significant and has grown fastest in the semi-mountainous regions in western and central Bulgaria. This pattern was already visible in 1992 when, as noted above, these areas decollectivized most quickly. But by 1994, when most of the land had been returned to private owners throughout the country, the emergence of private farming was even more strongly concentrated in the southern and eastern regions.

Emerging producers and their market contexts

Private farming In 1994, sample households expecting land (81 per cent of the sample) expected to own a total of 3.4 ha after restitution. The majority (65 per cent) expected between 5-50 ha. The plots actually farmed in 1994 were smaller, however: an average of one ha, up from 0.5 ha in 1991. Only two per cent farmed over 50 ha.

Private households owned a small, but increasing, number of agricultural machines. In 1994, six per cent of households owned a tractor, up from three per cent in 1991, and 27 per cent owned a plow (up from 12 per cent). Some households could provide minimal traction using draft animals: 17 per cent owned a horse (up from 11 per cent), while about a quarter owned a donkey.

Rural households had few workers available for farming their new land. 42 per cent of households had no member under age 55 in 1994. On average, households had 1.2 workers between the ages of 20-55 and a total of three members. Still, some labor is available for farming. In addition to the pensioners, who make up about half the sample, another 15 per cent of villagers were not employed at the time of the 1994 survey, and near-future employment options in rural areas appear limited.

Nearly all rural residents had some experience with private agriculture (only 16 households in our sample farmed no land in 1991, the year before restitution began) but, as noted above, the experience was generally with very small scale production. The majority of households (67.4 per cent) cultivated under 0.5 ha in 1991, while only two households cultivated one to five ha. In 1994, the majority of households continued to farm only to fulfill household needs or those of extended family members in nearby urban areas in 1994. 57 per cent of those surveyed reportedly did not earn money income from farming, and only four per cent described agriculture as their sole source of monetary income.

Most households thus cultivated a wide variety of crops, including tomatoes, peppers, onions, potatoes, beans, fruit and cabbage, as well as corn or oats for the sheep, fowl and pigs which most sample households kept. In 1994, 34 per cent of households reported having no dominant crop. If a household did report specialization, it was most often vegetables (30 per cent of households), followed by potatoes (nine per cent) and fodder (eight per cent).

This subsistence-style of farming has historical precedents in the Balkans and often enabled rural landholders to live more comfortably than urban dwellers during the last century. Farming is not seen as a commercial endeavor so much as an aspect of household reproduction, like shopping. Villagers expect this pattern to continue, with most villagers (77 per cent) planning to work on private plots next year, mainly for household consumption.

Despite the small size of expected holdings, few households plan to farm all their land independently after restitution is completed. 54 per cent of households planned to put at least part of their land in a cooperative (up from 46 per cent in 1992). Another nine per cent expected to farm it in a smaller partnership with friends (Table 13.1).

While most private producers are small holders producing for household consumption, there are significant regional differences in assets and behavior. In the northeastern okrug of Vidin, for example, households held an average of 6.2 ha in 1994, and no households reported holding below the national average of 2.3 ha. In the mountainous southern okrug of Smolen, on the other hand, households reported an average holding of 0.4 ha and 60 per cent of households reported holding below the national average. Surprisingly, however, land holding sizes in mountainous and plains districts do not show a clear pattern of difference.

Table 13.1
Household choice of organizational form

What to do with land	% Households	
	1992 (n=551)	1994 (n=563)
Cooperative	51	61
Farm it	11	22
Sell it	1	1
Rent it	7	8
Other	20	3
Don't know	10	5

Source: Survey Data.

Households' capitalization also differed greatly by region, with most households in the southeastern okrugs owning no tractors, while in some central regions approximately a quarter of households owned tractors. Clearly, this is linked to the speed and form of liquidation of the TKZS as well as to the initial level of capitalization in the region.

Households reporting a crop specialization were concentrated, with a few exceptions, in the vegetable-growing regions of south-central Bulgaria.[8] Less household specialization was occurring in the grain-growing okrugs of northern and eastern Bulgaria, where high percentages of households planned to place land in cooperatives.

The context in which these private producers farm is one of extremely weakly developed markets. While significant progress can be seen in the evolution of these markets between 1991 and 1994, it is still unusual for households to use markets to adjust their access to land, labor or capital (see Table 13.2).

Land and labor markets are particularly poorly developed, although significant development occurred over the period 1991-94. In 1991 survey, households that received new land received it from the TKZS for temporary use, under the Land Law. No households reported renting land to other households in 1991, and only three per cent rented to agricultural cooperatives.

In 1994, four per cent of households rented out land and the majority of these rented to individual farmers. Another three per cent rented in land, also mainly from private households. Households expected this trend to continue upward, with 6.5 per cent of households planning to rent land out next year. No sales of land were yet legal, but 2.5 per cent of households planned to sell their land in 1995, while another

1.7 per cent of households planned to buy land.

The majority of farm labor was supplied by the household itself. Only one household reported hiring a paid laborer in 1991, while eight per cent enlisted the services of other relatives. By 1994, significant development of labor markets could be seen, with nine per cent of households hiring manual labor for work on their land.

Table 13.2
Development of agricultural input markets

Input	% Households buying or renting	
	1991	1994
Land	3	7
Labor	0	9
Machines	50	45
Credit	0	0

Source: Survey Data.

Reliance on capital markets was also extremely limited. In 1991, only three households reported borrowing for agricultural purposes. In 1994, four households borrowed money for agriculture. Working capital for private agriculture came mainly from non-farm incomes (92 per cent of surveyed households). The system of credit cooperatives which existed before 1946 has not yet reemerged: in 1994 only two villages reported having a credit cooperative.

Given the limited supply of machinery, many households hired machine services for their small scale production, and these markets are becoming increasingly diversified. About half of private producers hired machine services in 1991 and 1994 (50 per cent of households in 1991 and 45 per cent in 1994). In 1991, producers had almost no choice of input supplier: 82 per cent obtained the services from the TKZS. By 1994, only 20 per cent obtained their services from the Liquidation Commission and 15 per cent from a state firm. 33 per cent obtained their services from a private individual.

Only 16 per cent of households rented machines to do the work themselves, but here too the largest supplier was private individuals, with Liquidation Commissions supplying only 28 per cent of households. Despite the increasing diversity of suppliers, the majority of households reported having only one possible supplier for machines and machine services.

Sources of several other inputs were similarly concentrated (Table 13.3). Although many households did not purchase inputs in 1991 (either due to the small scale of their farming or to their close connections with existing TKZSs), most purchased

285

seeds and chemicals from (highly concentrated) state firms, while most fertilizers and fodder came from TKZSs. Veterinarian services were provided evenly by state firms and TKZSs.

Table 13.3
Sources of agricultural inputs for households and cooperatives (C), 1991-94

Source	Seed			Fertilizer		
	1991	1994	(C)	1991	1994	(C)
State firm	49.8	48.6	76.2	32.5	29.9	64.4
Private firm	3.1	7.2	1.6	3.3	14.6	35.6
Cooperative	4.8	5.5	9.5	14.9	22.6	0
TKZS/LC	22.7	17.1	11.1	38.8	10.4	0
Individual	19.6	19.3	1.6	10.5	16.5	0

Source	Chemicals			Fodder		
	1991	1994	(C)	1991	1994	(C)
State firm	64.9	45.6	57.9	15.1	6	100
Private firm	2.1	23.7	42.1	4.2	17.9	0
Cooperative	9.6	10.1	0	8.4	11.6	0
TKZS/LC	9.6	8.2	0	56.9	25.3	0
Individual	13.9	4.7	0	15.4	35.8	0

Source	Machine services		
	1991	1994	(C)
State firm	2.1	15	37
Private firm	5.2	5	--
Cooperative	0.8	9	--
TKZS/LC	82	36	38
Individual	9.9	33	20

Source: Survey Data, 1992, 1994.

By 1994, the dominance of state firms had been reduced. Of the households reporting the purchase of seeds, pesticides, machines and spare parts, about half bought from state firms. Private firms had developed the strongest presence in pesticide

286

markets, where they supplied 24 per cent of households. Private individuals had become important suppliers of certain products, including livestock (supplying 82 per cent of households) and seedlings (67 per cent of households), and new non-agricultural cooperatives supplied nearly a quarter of households with fertilizer.

These markets, too, diversified while remaining highly concentrated. Buyers reported the most choice of sellers in seed markets (39 per cent of households could choose from among at least three sellers). Chemical markets remained more concentrated, with only 13 per cent of households reporting a choice of three sellers. Overall, the majority of private households reported a choice of only one input supplier.

Output markets exhibited a similar pattern (Table 13.4). In 1991, TKZSs did not play a significant role in marketing most goods, and the predominance of state firms appeared to have already eroded in many areas. Vegetables, for example, were most often marketed directly to the population (51 per cent of producer households marketed to consumers in 1991 and 68 per cent did so in 1994), although households apparently had a choice of other marketing channels, including state and cooperative firms. In 1994, 44 per cent of households selling vegetables had choice of more than three buyers, as did 50 per cent of households selling potatoes.

Table 13.4
Marketing channels for agricultural products of households and cooperatives (C), 1991-94

Source	Vegetables			Grain		
	1991	1994	(C)	1991	1994	(C)
State firm	18.2	18	30	0	32	59.7
Private firm	14.5	14	60	20	16	22.6
Cooperative	9.2	0	0	0	5	4.8
TKZS/LC	7.3	0	10	60	0	3.2
Individual	50.9	68	0	20	47	9.7

Source	Milk			Eggs		
	1991	1994	(C)	1991	1994	(C)
State firm	76	46	30	20	9	0
Private firm	0	41	50	4	36	0
Cooperative	16	2	0	52	9	0
TKZS/LC	5.3	0	0	0	0	0
Individual	2.7	12	20	24	46	0

Source: Survey Data, 1992, 1994.

Significant monopsony power still existed for some products in 1991, however, including livestock and grains. 61 per cent of households marketed livestock to state firms, as did 76 per cent of households selling milk. 60 per cent of households marketing grain sold to the TKZS.

By 1994, even these markets appeared to be becoming more competitive. Only 46 per cent of households selling milk sold to state firms, while 41 per cent sold to private firms. With the demise of the TKZS, the new cooperatives did not take over the task of marketing grains. 32 per cent of households sold their wheat to a state firm, while 47 per cent sold to a private individual. Wheat markets appear quite competitive: 69 per cent of households selling wheat reported having a choice of at least three buyers. The market for milk remained highly concentrated, however, with 62 per cent of households reporting only one outlet. Tobacco growers fared the worst, with 100 per cent of sellers reporting only one buyer.

Despite the increasing competition in input and output markets, 23 per cent of private agricultural producers reported that expenses were not covered by production. Another third of producers said that they were just barely breaking even.

Agricultural production cooperatives (ZPKs) At the time of the 1992 survey, the category 'cooperative' included two very different types of organization. A number of the old TKZSs had attempted to protect themselves from dissolution by transforming themselves into 'cooperatives'. These farms were essentially identical to the old TKZS, although there were generally some new membership rights, such as the receipt of rent for land.

In other villages, the Liquidation Commissions were running the TKZS in preparation for their dissolution. While such farms are not included in the above data on *new* cooperatives, the villagers referred to these as 'cooperatives' and are included in villagers responses about their cooperative. These cooperative farms were very large and highly mechanized farms, run in a top-down manner by professional managers. Alongside these transforming TKZS were a multitude of truly new cooperatives – small ventures of villagers using their newly restituted land or land issued for temporary use.

The data suggest that the first category of cooperative included most villagers. 57 per cent of cooperative members surveyed in 1992 describing their cooperative as 'basically the same as the old TKZS' and that it was using land that had not yet been restituted. This situation is clearly linked to the slow start of the reform.

43 per cent of cooperative members reported belonging to more innovative forms of organization, however. These new cooperatives were quite different from the old collective farms (TKZSs), with an average of 356 ha and 87 members.

By 1994, the situation had changed significantly. The old TKZS had disappeared from the majority of villages, and the majority of cooperatives farmed land that had been restituted (without title) to individual households.

288

The transformation of the majority of cooperatives into independent units based on voluntary membership of small landholders did not lead to a proliferation of small units, however. In fact, the average size of new cooperatives grew to 692 ha and 418 members in 1994. In many villages, the majority of land is still farmed by one or two medium-sized, professionally managed units, well-endowed with machinery and other capital acquired by the membership as the old TKZS was liquidated.

The relationship between these cooperatives and their members differs greatly among units. Most cooperatives now pay rent to members – only 11 per cent of surveyed cooperatives did not pay rent in 1994. Most payments are small, and the vast majority were paid in kind and linked to the final output of the cooperative. In-kind rent payments were attractive not only to cooperatives, which could avoid marketing costs, but also to members raising livestock for household consumption. Few member households expected to work in the cooperative: in 1994, only three per cent of households expected a member to work in the cooperative full-time, while eight per cent expected someone to work part-time. This is a significant decline from the 23 per cent of households which expected someone to work in the cooperatives in 1992.

A large proportion of the new cooperatives provided services to members, as well as to non-members. 56 per cent reportedly performed agricultural services, including machine cultivation and the spreading of chemical fertilizers and pesticides. In about half of the cooperatives, members received the services at a lower price than non-members.

The majority of the cooperatives produced grains. In 1994, 92 per cent produced wheat and either corn or barley, and ten per cent of cooperatives complemented this by raising livestock. Only 20 per cent of cooperatives produced fruit or vegetables. In addition to producing agricultural goods and services, a few cooperatives were involved in other commercial activities. About six per cent conducted trade in 1994, and four per cent produced non-agricultural consumer goods.

As with households, some significant regional differences existed within this aggregate picture. Cooperatives in the grain-growing northeast were, on average, larger than those in other areas and owned more machines. As a result, they were more likely to provide services to their members.

Also like households, these new cooperatives function in a context of weakly and unevenly developed markets. Cooperatives were much less dependent on markets for resources, however.

Despite formal liquidation of the TKZS and restitution of land, many new cooperatives are basically restructured forms of the TKZSs. That is, many cooperatives basically inherited large amounts of land, labor and capital from the old TKZSs. Even in villages where two or three new cooperatives exist, they have often simply divided the TKZS's resources. In the restructuring, the cooperatives have worked through traditional methods of negotiation among local interest groups. They have not needed to rely on markets for resource allocation.

While cooperatives have not depended on markets for the acquisition of large contiguous land parcels, they nonetheless appear to have been leaders in the development of a fledgling rental market. Of the member-owned land held by the ZPKs in 1994, cooperatives rented out eight per cent, the majority of this back to members. In this way, cooperatives helped coordinate exchanges between households with excess land of a certain quality with those seeking more of that type of land. 16 of the 79 cooperatives also rented land in. Three rented large amounts (an average of 197 ha) from Liquidation Commissions, while the majority rented small amounts from private persons (an average of 63 ha).

Cooperatives relied on labor markets to a similarly limited extent. Skilled labor was rarely hired by the cooperatives in 1994. The hiring of permanent labor was also minimal – only seven cooperatives hired permanent non-member laborers. 35 cooperatives hired non-member field workers on a temporary basis, however – an average of 204 days per cooperative.

Cooperatives were more likely to participate in credit markets, much more so than private producers: 53 per cent of cooperatives surveyed borrowed within the last two years. Most of the short-term working capital was supplied by banks, both state and private. With the state subsidizing one-third of the interest on agricultural bank loans, 91 per cent of those taking out loans did so through banks. Firms account for the other nine per cent of credit. These were probably agricultural processors, many of which are still state-owned, using their access to credit to provide farmers with working capital in exchange for the right to purchase final production.

As noted above, the majority of cooperatives (67) owned at least some of the machinery used in production. Still, the majority also relied on machine rental and the contracting of machine services. About half turned to state firms, followed by other cooperatives, Liquidation Committees, and 15-20 per cent hired from private firms or persons. Like private households, cooperatives had limited choice of supplier for machinery: about ten per cent of cooperatives reported having a choice of provider for machines or machine services.

In other input markets, cooperatives also faced a limited choice of supplier, similar to that faced by households. State firms supplied the largest number of cooperatives with seeds (48 per cent of cooperatives), fertilizer (38 per cent), herbicides (33 per cent), and spare parts (38 per cent). Private firms had already become important in certain inputs, however, selling to nearly a quarter of cooperatives purchasing chemical fertilizers and herbicides. To date, agricultural supply cooperatives were relatively inactive, selling to only four per cent of ZPKs.

Some competition among suppliers is also apparent. Like households, significant numbers of cooperatives (although less than the majority) reported having a choice of three or more suppliers for seed and chemical inputs (21 and 33 cooperatives, respectively). Markets for spare parts and machines remained more concentrated, however, with few farms reporting a choice of input suppliers.

Market development varied significantly by region. Cooperatives of the northeast, which owned significant numbers of machines, relied much less than cooperatives in other areas on rental markets for machinery and machine services. In the vegetable-growing regions of central Bulgaria, cooperatives relied relatively more on seasonal, non-member labor. The districts closest to Sofia and those in the grain region of the northeast were most likely to have highly competitive input markets, with the majority of purchasers reporting a choice of three or more suppliers for combined purchases of seeds, chemicals, machines and spare parts.

Like households, cooperatives already enjoyed relatively developed markets for many products. Still, they were more likely than households to continue to market through state firms, perhaps due to the large volume of production, which large state firms were better equipped to handle. 60 per cent of cooperatives still marketed grain through state firms, although most cooperatives reported a choice of at least three buyers. 30 per cent of cooperatives marketing vegetables sold to state firms, and few reported a choice of more than three buyers, perhaps because cooperatives were less likely than private farmers to sell directly to the public.

Despite the context of generally underdeveloped and uncompetitive markets, cooperatives appear to be doing quite well. Most (62 per cent) no debts, and only one of the 74 working cooperatives reported losses during its most recent operating year. Six other cooperatives were unable to earn enough to recapitalize their assets, while the remaining 67 cooperatives (90 per cent of working cooperatives) earned positive profits. These farms thus appear to offer an adequate form of resource allocation under the current difficult conditions.

Model of household choice

Since the restitution began in 1991, production cooperatives have been the form of organization preferred by the majority of rural Bulgarian households. In 1992, 46 per cent of sample households planned to incorporate their land in a cooperative. In 1994, the share of households planning to put all or part of their land in a cooperative rose to 54 per cent. The theory outlined in the second section suggests that households incorporating land into a cooperative may be doing so in response to the context of weakly developed markets, which prevent them from adjusting their farm size, inputs or outputs through the market. The cooperative, a previously existing institutional form which has relied only minimally on markets to acquire land or labor, may then be the most efficient available means of using household land.

To test this theory, we developed a simple model of household choice. In 1991, there was little evidence of markets in land, labor or credit, while markets for agricultural inputs and certain products remained highly monopolized. This nearly complete lack of competitive markets made it difficult to test directly for a relationship between marketed development and household choice.

We hypothesized, however, that certain households would be more sensitive to limitations on adjustment than others, and thus more likely to turn to cooperatives as a means of adjusting farm size. Landholding households with few potential agricultural workers or inexperienced in agricultural production would be particularly hurt by the absence of agricultural labor and land markets, while households lacking agricultural machinery would be most hurt by monopolistic markets for machine services. Households in grain regions would be particularly affected, as grain production in Bulgaria is subject to significant economies of scale and purchasing monopolies continued to predominate in this sector, at least in 1991. Households likely to be affected by the lack of land markets included both those with 'too much' and those with 'too little' land.

To perform this indirect test of the impact of weak market development on household choice of cooperative production, we developed a simple logit regression. The probability of a household placing land in a cooperative was expected to increase with the household's need to rely on markets for resource adjustment. That the probability should rise with the household's location in a grain region but decrease with household machine ownership, household experience with agricultural production, and greater numbers of potential agricultural workers.

The variables were measured as follows. Ownership of machinery (MACH) was measured in available units of 18 kinds of agricultural machinery. Agricultural experience (PRIAG91) was measured by the amount of land cultivated by the household prior to decollectivization, and the number of potential agricultural workers (WRKR) was measured by the number of household members between the ages of 20-55 years. To determine whether or not the household lived in a grain region (GRAIN), we used 1987 data on share of the districts' agricultural land planted in grain.[9]

To test the competing theory,[10] that the persistence of cooperative production reflects continued communist influence in rural areas, we included the variable RED in our model of household choice. RED is measured as the per cent of seats won by the Bulgarian Socialist Party in the household's electoral district during the most recent parliamentary election (1991 and 1994).[11]

The equation was estimated for both 1992 and 1994, with the results seen below. The equation explains 77 per cent of the variation in household choice in 1991 and 70 per cent of the variation in 1994. Both GRAIN and WRKR were significant at $p < .10$ in both years. In 1991, AGEXP was also significant, but by 1994 experience with private farming prior to decollectivization no longer played a significant role in household choice. By 1994, MACH had become significant, probably partly due to the increased levels of variation in machine ownership among private households (see Table 13.5). This suggests that in both years those households more likely to need to adjust farm size were, in fact, more likely to incorporate land in a cooperative. Weak market development does seem to have played a role in the persistence of cooperative production

In addition, however, RED played a significant role in household choice in both years. This is not reflected in the 1991 equation, due to the high degree of correlation between the variables RED and GRAIN. When the equation is estimated separately using only RED or only GRAIN, each is shown to be a distinct and significant factor in household choice. While the impact of GRAIN dominates, RED plays a role in both 1991 and 1994.

Table 13.5
Logistic analysis results

	1992 (n=326)			
Variable	Var. mean	Var. SD	Coefficient	Delta P
Constant			-0.3747	
GRAIN	47	16.77	0.0296*	0.007
WRKR	1.35	1.34	-0.1848*	-0.04
MACH	1.97	2.72	-0.0416	
AGEXP	5.12	6.6	-0.0625*	-0.02
RED	49	12.46	0.0181	
Model Chi Square: 40.68*				
	1992 (n=326)			
Variable	Var. mean	Var. SD	Coefficient	Delta P
Constant			0.7148	
GRAIN	46	16.69	0.0414*	0.007
WRKR	1.28	1.34	-0.2218*	-0.002
MACH	2.41	2	-0.1605*	-0.001
AGEXP	5.08	6.77	-0.0115	
RED	57	13.98	0.0209*	0.005
Model Chi Square: 42.97*				

* = significant at p < 0.10.

To examine the relative importance of these factors, we calculated the impact of small change in each an average household (defined as having the mean value for each significant variable). As seen in Table 13.4, the impact of a reasonably small change in any one variable is small. In 1992, the addition of one worker (the smallest possible change, although a large change in relative terms) had the most impact

293

on the household's likelihood of placing land in a cooperative, decreasing it by four per cent. This was followed by the impact of a one dk change in LAND91 (- two per cent). A ten percentage point change in GRAIN increased the likelihood by one per cent. In 1994, the impact of a change in GRAIN was the same, but this had become the most significant variable. A one unit increase in MACH or WRKR generated a change under one per cent. In both years, the impact of a ten percentage point increase in BSP influence increased the household's likelihood of choosing cooperative farming by approximately one per cent.

One possible interpretation of the decline between 1991 and 1994 in the impact of WRKR and in ability of the model to explain variation in the data is the increase in market development during this period. As markets develop differentially across rural Bulgaria, the link between a household's need to adjust resources and the decision to place land in a cooperative becomes less direct. Some households can begin to adjust resources through markets. Indeed, the decline in the percentage of households planning to place land in a cooperative, from 75 per cent of responding, landholding households in 1992 to 65 per cent in 1994 suggests such a trend.

Discussion

The data from the Bulgarian Decollectivization Survey reveal very weak development of credit, land and labor markets in the Bulgarian countryside and a high degree of concentration in many input and output markets. While the comparison between 1991 and 1994 reflects a significant development of markets for both agricultural inputs and outputs, the level and competitiveness of market activity remains extremely limited.

Recent theoretical work suggests that such missing or weakly developed markets provide incentives for the development of non-market institutions for the allocation of resources. This study suggests that the agricultural production cooperatives being formed in Bulgaria can be understood as such an institution. These findings are consistent with other recent work on credit markets in Bulgaria, which found that market imperfections led firms to search for non-market forms of credit allocation (Koford and Miller, 1995).

While our survey data indicate that cooperatives' market opportunities are very similar to those faced by individual producers, the cooperatives have two advantages in dealing with these limitations. They have quickly acquired extensive resources through non-market mechanisms, and they can continue to adjust resources through established bargaining channels.

The statistical evidence suggests that households, which are more likely to need to adjust agricultural land or labor, turn to production cooperatives, perhaps as a substitute for market mechanisms. Under such conditions, the benefits of cooperatives may outweigh any losses due to incentive problems. This is not to imply that such problems do not exist, however, or that the cooperatives produce at optimal levels of efficiency.

Our analysis suggests that as competitive markets develop in agricultural inputs and products, increasing numbers of households use markets to reallocate their land, labor or other assets. The tolerable threshold of cooperative inefficiency will fall, creating pressure for better cooperative management. As of 1994, however, agricultural production cooperatives continued to be the dominant and preferred form of organization in Bulgarian agriculture.

Notes

1   The research team was composed of a group of scholars from the Institute of Sociology of the Bulgarian Academy of Sciences, led by Veska Kouzhouharova and Stanka Dobreva.

2   Although the *de facto* state ownership of collective farms formally concentrates ownership, this just transforms the incentive problem. Since citizens cannot effectively monitor the state, the state in turn is not motivated to monitor managers.

3   Others have argued that other factors were the main driving force behind the productivity growth. See Putterman (1993), for example.

4   These plots were issued by collective farms to members and other villagers for household use during the socialist period. They were usually limited to 0.5 ha.

5   After the victory of the Socialist party in national elections held in December of 1994, amendments to the land law were passed which slightly limited the rights of owners as outlined above. The amendments were then overturned by the Constitutional Court, and as of late 1995 the legal battle continues. Since these changes took place after our 1994 survey, they do not affect the analysis in this paper.

6   By 1994, some of the households in the original sample were not available for the second survey. Of the original 600 households, 445 were surveyed in both 1992 and 1994. The total sample of 569 households surveyed in 1994 is thus comprised of 445 original and 124 replacement households. These replacement households most often occupied the same address as the previously interviewed households.

7   The okrug ceased to be a legal and administrative unit after 1987. We use the unit here because it conforms to the unit of analysis in the 1986 data.

8   Important exceptions were specialization in the tobacco-growing region of Kurdjali and in the semi-mountainous northwestern okrug of Vratsa (vegetables).

9   We used data from 1987 because this was the last year that data were published on the basis of okrugs, the administrative unit on which are lists are based. Data are not published for smaller administrative units in which the households are located, e.g., the obshtina or village.

10   Other dynamics may also be contributing to the persistence of cooperative production. An alternative analysis suggests that cooperatives not may be chosen on the basis of efficiency considerations, but rather in response to a number of other social conditions, including social norms and the relative power of different social actors. An analysis of such factors is the subject of future work.

11   The Bulgarian Socialist Party (BSP) is the renamed and restructured successor of the Bulgarian Communist Party.

References

Alchian, A.A. and Demsetz, H. (1972), 'Production, Information Costs, and Economic Organization', *American Economic Review*, Vol. 62, No. 2, pp. 777-95.

Aubert, Claude (1988), 'The New Economic Policy in the Chinese Countryside', in Brada, Josef and Wadekin, Karl-Eugen (eds), *Socialist Agriculture in Transition*, Westview: Boulder.

Brooks, Karen (1991), 'Decollectivization and the Agricultural Transition in Eastern and Central Europe', Agriculture and Rural Development Department, World Bank, WPS 793.

Brooks, Karen and Meurs, Mieke (1994), 'Romanian Land Reform: 1991-1993', *Comparative Economic Studies*, Summer.

Creed, Gerald (1995), 'The Politics of Agriculture: Identity and Socialist Sentiment in Bulgaria', *Slavic Review*, Vol. 54, No. 4, pp. 843-68.

CSO (State Statistical Office) (various years), *Yearbook of the Peoples' Republic of Bulgaria*, Sofia, Bulgaria.

Dobreva, Stanka and Meurs, Mieke (1992), 'State-Private Sector Relations In Bulgaria Under Collectivization: Implications for Agricultural Development in the Immediate Future', Paper presented at the First Annual Conference on Collectivization and Its Alternatives, July, Budapest, Hungary.

Ireland, Norman and Law, Peter (1988), 'Management Design Under Labor Management', *Journal of Comparative Economics*, No. 12, pp. 1-23.

Koford, Kenneth and Miller, Jeffrey (1995), 'Contracts in Bulgaria', University of Delaware, WP 95-04, June.

Lin, Justin (1992), 'Rural Reforms and Agricultural Growth in China', *American Economic Review*, Vol. 83, No. 1.

McIntyre, Robert (1988), 'The Small Enterprise and Agricultural Initiatives in Bulgaria: Institutional Invention without Reform', *Soviet Studies*, Vol. 40, No. 4, pp. 602-15.

Ministry of Agriculture (1993), 'Progress in the Agrarian Reform to August 8, 1993', Sofia, Bulgaria.

Ostrom, Elinor (1990), *Governing the Commons*, Cambridge University Press: New York.

National Institute of Statistics (1993), personal correspondence, Budapest, Hungary.

Putterman, Louis (1987), 'The Incentive Problem and the Demise of Team Farming in China', *Journal of Development Economics*, Vol. 26, No. 1, pp. 103-27.

—— (1993), *Continuity and Change in China's Rural Development: Collective and Reform Eras in Perspective*, Oxford University Press: New York.

—— and Bonin, John (1993), 'Incentives and Monitoring in Cooperatives with Labor-Proportionate Sharing Schemes', *Journal of Comparative Economics*, Vol. 17, No. 3, September, pp. 663-86.

Sen, A.K. (1966), 'Labor Allocation in a Cooperative Enterprise', *Review of Economic Studies*, Vol. 33, No. 4, pp. 361-71.

Stiglitz, J.E. (1987), 'The New Development Economics', *World Development*, Vol. 14, No. 2, pp. 257-65.

Stoyanova, Rositsa (1992), 'A Periodization of the Bulgarian Collectivization, Part I: Pre-War Background and Early Collectivization (-1960)', Paper prepared for MacArthur Conference on Collectivization and Its Alternatives, Budapest.

Survey Data (1992, 1994), Joint Survey of MacArthur Project on Collectivization and Its Alternatives and the Bulgarian Academy of Sciences, August, Bulgaria.

WIIW Databank (1995), Wirtschafts und Sozialwissenschaftliches Rechenzentrum, Wein, on line.

Part Seven
LABOR MARKETS

14 Bulgarian labor market during early period of transition

Christina Lenkova

Introduction

The transition of the previously centrally planned economies towards market oriented economies has proved to be a painful process characterized by many negative consequences such as the reduction of the standard of living, production decline and a worsening of the income distribution. Among the numerous setbacks caused by the ongoing political and economic reforms, unemployment has appeared as one of the most serious problems for almost all Central and Eastern European countries (CEECs).

The appearance of mass unemployment in Bulgaria happened very quickly and unfortunately reached an unexpectedly high level. Official counting of unemployment in Bulgaria started in July 1990 when the registered unemployed count totaled 31,030 people. By the end of the same year, the figure was 67,079, which constituted 1.5 per cent of the labor force (in December 1990 the labor force was estimated to be 4,161,927). A year later the number of unemployed increased to 419,123 people or 13.7 per cent of the labor force and by March 1993, the officially registered unemployed reached 605,000, representing 16.0 per cent of the labor force. Compared to the other CEECs, Bulgaria had the highest level of unemployment (about 17.0 per cent) followed by Poland (about 16.0 per cent) and Hungary (about 14.0 per cent) by the end of 1993. The data for 1994 showed that unemployment in the Bulgarian labor market continued to stay almost the same. The Labour Force Survey conducted in March and June 1995 showed a decrease in the level of unemployment compared to June 1994 and the beginning of 1995. Within an year the number of unemployed went down by 169,000 people or unemployment decreased by 4.8 per cent (from 20.5 per cent in June 1994 to 15.7 per cent in June 1995). However, even during this period the long-term unemployed continued to constitute a substantial percentage out of all registered unemployed. These were mainly people with a lower level of education, women, and rural population.

301

In Bulgaria, as well as in most of the ex-socialist countries, three phases of a decrease in employment can be pointed out; they refer namely to the early periods of the restructuring of these economies. During all three stages, the Bulgarian labor market exhibited not only a change in the unemployment rate but more importantly – a change in the 'profile' of unemployment, i.e., a change in the duration of the unemployment spells.

By focusing on the importance of unemployment dynamics, this paper tries to shed light on questions related to the length of the unemployment spells. The study covers the period 1991-93 and focuses on two main issues: first, to show the direction of the effect potential explanatory variables (such as personnel characteristics, labor market policies, previous employment history, educational and occupational indicators, place of residence, etc.) have on the conditional probability of completing a spell; and second, to examine the contribution of these factors for the individual's transition from unemployment to the various labor market states (unemployment – employment, unemployment – unemployment, unemployment – out of the labor force).

The basic results of this paper show that a higher educational level (and especially the availability of a university degree) is a reliable guarantee for finding a job. Bulgarian women, individuals with a longer 'unemployment history', and those who have previously worked in the bureaucratic state apparatus and who, in the present analysis fall under the category 'staff' have lower chances for escaping from the unemployment pool. Another two, somehow 'surprising' results are that, compared to those aged 31-40 years, people aged between 41-50 years have a higher exit rate from unemployment, as do those living in rural areas, compared to the urban population. However, these facts should be, treated cautiously since a further analysis of the different transition exits from unemployment gives quite a reasonable explanation of these results.

The paper is organized as follows. First we present an overview of the development of unemployment in Bulgaria since the beginning of transition. The following section explores aspects of the legislation system in the country and stresses the issues which are of considerable influence for the dynamics of the unemployment process. The next section contains a description of the micro-data set used in this study and an explanation of the econometric strategy followed in the empirical analysis. The last section shows the results and presents the conclusions.

Appearance of mass unemployment in Bulgaria

Three stages in the rise of unemployment can be distinguished in the earliest period of economic reforms in CEECs. During the first stage, the increase could be explained by a high level of voluntary separation. This hypothesis seemed to be predominant in Bulgaria for the period 1989-90. At that time, enterprises filled vacancies while keeping over employment. Although the economically active population decreased by 4.7 per cent, this number was small relative to the decrease in industrial production. By the middle of 1990, the number of registered vacancies was two times greater than the number of registered unemployed; but, by the end of the same year, the relationship between vacancies and unemployment was reversed.

During the second phase, the number of vacancies decreased and layoffs went up. This was the situation in the Bulgarian labor market at the beginning of 1991, when the government gave up attempting to maintain full employment in the country (see Table 14.1).

Table 14.1
U/V ratio in the Bulgarian labor market, 1990-93

	Dec. 1990	June 1991	Dec. 1991	June 1992	Dec. 1992	June 1993
Unempl. (in ths.)	65	234	419	476	577	587
Vacancies (in ths.)	28.4	16.5	10	12.5	15.3	8.5
U/V	2.3	14.2	41.9	38.1	80.5	68.7

Source: National Employment Office, Bulgarian Ministry of Labour and Social Welfare.

The third stage could be characterized by mass layoffs from state enterprises. This happened for reasons including cuts in state subsidies, the privatization process, and some restructuring of enterprises. However, it should be noted that mass layoffs started before most of these structural reforms were put in process. In 1991, one-third of the layoffs in the whole economy were due to downsizing or closing enterprises, of which 41.8 per cent had been operating in the industrial branch, 14.4 per cent in the commercial sector, 12.9 per cent in agriculture and 10.6 per cent in the building and construction branch.[1] In 1992, the picture changed and the biggest number of layoffs was found in the agricultural rather than in the industrial sector, due to massive 'dismissals' from the existing co-operative farms.

The statistical information concerning the flows in the Bulgarian labor market is of considerable importance for the present analysis. The aggregate data shows that the incidence of unemployment has varied considerably according to factors such as region, gender, and level of education. However, for various reasons these data should be treated very carefully. Thus it could have taken almost a month until the unem-

303

ployed were registered in the labor office or they may have left the registration system. This lag occurs for two reasons: disrespect for the administrative rules of the system or people leaving for unknown reasons without being re-employed.

Since the subsequent analysis is going to concentrate on data referring to unemployed registered in the labor offices during the last quarters of 1991, 1992, and 1993, Table 14.2 summarizes some key figures which would give a general idea about unemployment in Bulgaria on a macro level for the same periods.

Table 14.2
Newly registered unemployed in the last quarters of 1991-93
(in total)

Time period	Newly registered unemployed (in absolute numbers)
Oct. 1991	60,184
Nov. 1991	50,265
Dec. 1991	45,881
Oct. 1992	68,762
Nov. 1992	64,372
Dec. 1992	60,502
Oct. 1993	44,588
Nov. 1993	50,683
Dec. 1993	42,017

Source: Bulgarian Ministry of Labour and Social Welfare.

Measures for restructuring the Bulgarian labor market

Until the end of the 1980s, the Bulgarian labor market had been one of the most restricted within the CEECs. Legislation determined the exact number of students who were supposed to go to secondary special or secondary general schools, as well as the number of students pursuing different specialities in universities. After graduation the distribution of the labor force was centrally regulated by the State Planning Committee through a network of Labour Departments operating at the district level. Basically, people were allowed to look for a job only in the place of their residence and were rarely allowed to move. Another well-known fact is that during the 'social-ist era' the Bulgarian enterprises were hoarding labor (Jones and Kato, 1994).

The main intention of the new policies at the beginning of the transition was to conduct structural reforms which would put first priority on the restructuring of the state enterprises (most of them were in the industrial sector). However, this 'restruc-turing' process caused a contraction of employment which, within the period of 1991-93 (when the sample was drawn), turned out to be much more than was ex-pected. A possible explanation may be the shock therapy introduced into the Bulgar-ian economy at the beginning of 1991 which caused a sharp decrease in production in state firms, especially in the manufacturing sector: a decrease of more than 22 per cent in July 1991 compared to July 1990 and another 25 per cent decrease by July 1992 compared to July 1991.[2] This sudden decline was far greater than predicted by the policy makers.

This new situation required the setting of new institutional and legislative mea-sures which could deal with the problems arising in the Bulgarian labor market. For the period 1990-92, the official attitude towards labor market policies (active and passive) evolved through three stages.

During the first stage, the policy concentrated on creating a social safety net which would help the unemployed to overcome the 'short' (as it was expected to be) period of job search. When, in 1990, unemployment increased sharply, the government was forced to approve measures for reducing the labor supply. The policy package in-cluded a scheme for early retirement (in Bulgaria the legislation determines 55 years of age to be a retirement age for women and 60 for men). In 1991, the government also approved a penalty tax for enterprises in which people above the retirement age were still kept employed. In that case, the enterprise had to pay 30 per cent of each pensioner's salary to the Fund for Professional Qualification and Re-qualification.

The second stage started with Decree 110 of the Ministerial Council (June 1991) which aimed to stimulate employment. Unfortunately this decree did not fulfill its initial purpose. The only effect was a reduction in the unemployment benefits (UB) intended to activate the job search process, but overlooked the fact that only a small number of vacancies were available and instead put more restrictive conditions on receiving UB. These restrictions led to a decrease in the number of registered unem-ployed and an increase in the number of people without (official) income.

The third stage in labor market policy planning in Bulgaria started at the end of 1992. The newly constructed schemes in that period were aimed at stimulating and helping the private sector with regionally oriented projects, as well as at stimulating the employment of certain groups of the population. Table 14.3 shows expenditures on different applied programs and schemes directed towards dealing with the prob-lem of unemployment in the Bulgarian labor market for the period 1991-92. The numbers clearly show the weak 'popularity' of these measures and programs, and

Table 14.3
Expenditures on and participation in labor market programs in Bulgaria, 1991-92 (in 'real terms')

	Expenditure (in ths. levs)		Participants (no.)		Expenditure per participant (in lv.)	
	1991	1992	1991	1992	1991	1992
Qualif. and re-qualif.	7,101	1,865	20,155	16,618	352	1,122
Measures for youth	104	332	70	125	1,486	2,656
Helping measures for mobility	1	188	2	284	500	662
Subsidized employment						
Social. activ.	no data	343	no data	224	no data	1,530
Direct creation of vacancies	no data	153	30	323	no data	47,461
Subs. credits for the employers	6,246	3,621	550	950	11,356	3,812
Helping unempl. for self-empl.	132	2,382	27	3,955	4,889	602
Measures for the disabled						
Subsid. employment	4	10	-	1	-	10,200
Prof. rehabil.	-	200	-	122	-	1,786
TOTAL	69,748	41,057	20,804	22,592	18,583	69,831
% from GDP	0.58	0.76				

Source: Bulgarian Ministry of Labour and Social Welfare.

consequently the negligible effect they could have had on solving such serious problems as youth unemployment or stimulating self-employment; 70 participants in 1991 and 125 in 1992 respectively were involved in programs dealing with the youth unemployment. Concerning measures for motivating the creation of an own business the expenditures per participant were respectively 4,889 Bulgarian leva (approximately $240) in 1991 and 602 Bulgarian leva (approximately $20) in 1992.

In 1992, 90 per cent of the specialized fund 'Professional Training and Restructuring' was used for UB and for support for the unemployed; 7.4 per cent for covering the expenditures of the labor offices; and only 2.8 per cent was used in all the schemes focused on stimulating employment (see Table 14.4). Table 14.5 presents the spread of the benefits paid out by the Qualification and Unemployment Fund during each year from 1991-94. It shows that the largest part of this fund was used for paying UB (around 90 per cent for each of the years) and the remaining had to be spread to cover the payment of both social benefits and other expenditures (for example, organizing training courses or supporting the participants in such courses).

Table 14.4
Expenditures on the labor market schemes in Bulgaria, 1991-92 (in %)

	1991	1992
Total	*100.00*	*100.00*
A. Income support — in total	92.99	89.77
1. UB and UA	90.43	85.85
2. Family assistance	2.56	3.92
B. Selective measures — in total	0.92	2.80
1. Stimulating self-empl. among the unemployed	0.02	0.15
2. Qualification and re-qualif. of unemployed	0.89	1.25
3. Support for the mobility of the unemployed	0.00	0.01
4. Interest rates on credits given to unemployed	0.00	0.12
5. Wages for recently employed young workers and specialists	0.01	0.03
6. Other selective measures	0.00	1.24
C. Others	6.09	7.43

Source: Bulgarian Ministry of Labour and Social Welfare.

307

Table 14.5
Benefits paid out by fund 'Professional Qualification and Unemployment'

	31 Dec. 1991	31 Dec. 1992	31 Dec. 1993	31 Dec. 1994
Total expenditures made by the fund (in lv.)	720,825	1,214,561	2,356,953	2,967,648
UB paid	684,681	1,025,340	2,053,046	2,660,330
Social benefits	32,189	135,989	209,829	266,630
Other	3,955	53,232	94,078	40,688

Source: Main Macro Economic Indicators, NSI, Sofia, 1995.

Approved in December 1989, Decree 57 of the Ministerial Council was the basic legislative document with which the new labor contract arrangements began. It was changed and extended during the following years, but it remains the main document in the legislative system in the sphere of the labor market.

At the beginning of the transition period, the UB system in Bulgaria was set to be quite generous in accordance with the law. Only employees who were involuntarily dismissed and who had worked at least six months in the year preceding the dismissal were entitled to compensation. UB were paid for nine months on a progressively decreasing scale. Soon after the start of price liberalization, at the beginning of 1991, the indexation of benefits was introduced. This meant that the unemployed were receiving UB which did not differ too much from the average wage. In turn, eventually this required changing the structure of the passive labor market policy in Bulgaria.

A new legislative document (Decree 109) required that the extent of working experience and the age of the unemployed determine eligibility for getting UB (see Table 14.6). The size of the UB was then determined by formula:

min. wage + 20 per cent * (average monthly salary - min. wage).

As a consequence, previous income turned out to have a negligible effect on the size of benefits, thereby equalizing the level of the income based on UB.

Table 14.6
Eligibility for UB

Working experience	Age of the unemployed	Period for getting UB
Up to 5 years	age doesn't matter	6 months
> 5 years	below 40	7 months
> 5 years	40 and up	8 months
> 10 years	45 and up	9 months
> 20 years	51 and up (men)	10 months
> 20 years	51 and up (women)	12 months
> 25 years	56 and up (men)	12 months

Source: 'The Bulgarian Challenge: Reform of the Labour Market and the Social Policy', prepared by the International Labour Organization for CEE, Budapest, 1993.

Since July 1992[3] the amount of the UB was restricted to 60 per cent of the previous wage and it could not 'jump' over the limits between 90 per cent and 140 per cent of the minimum wage set for the country. During that year, the state did not adjust benefits to the price increase. Then in 1993, the Ministerial Council approved a new scheme for indexation. Until June 1993, the minimum wage in the country was indexed to 90 per cent of price increases for April, May, and June 1993. This indexation was also used to determine the size of the UB. After June 1993, the indication was required to be determined quarterly each year.

After 1991, the development of the social safety net was rather restrictive and by the end of 1993 it was considered to be among the less generous systems in the CEEs.[4]

However, the changes in the organization of the Bulgarian safety net didn't contribute significantly to its improvement. This can be confirmed by the fact that in 1992 and 1993 only one-third of all registered unemployed were getting some kind of UB, while in 1992 more than one-third of the budget of the Fund 'Unemployment' remained unused.

The number of people receiving UB over the period of data collection (last quarters of 1991, 1992, and 1993) is fairly constant (see Table 14.7). What was happening is that people whose eligibility for UB was exhausted were replaced by the newly unemployed. Taking into consideration the fact that the number of unemployed in the country was increasing during these years, the ratio of those getting benefits to the number of unemployed was falling.[5]

Table 14.7
Key characteristics of the Bulgarian passive labor market policy

Time period	Registered unempl. (U)	Reported vacancies (V)	U/V	Unempl. eligible for getting UB
Oct.1991	375,922	14,136	266	216,521
Nov.1991	400,812	11,741	341	220,266
Dec.1991	419,123	9,994	419	216,728
Oct. 1992	*	*	*	*
Nov.1992	565,138	7,701	734	218,923
Dec.1992	576,893	7,170	805	226,281
Oct.1993	602,458	8,610	700	203,666
Nov.1993	617,054	6,976	885	214,068
Dec.1993	626,141	7,437	842	227,533

* No data available to the author at the time the research has been undertaken
Source: Bulgarian Ministry of Labour and Social Welfare, and author's calculations.

Concerning the active labor market policy, the conclusion is that during the period examined in this paper, it was just in its 'latent' stage. The number of training courses offered by firms (mainly to the employed) decreased, the labor exchanges started administrating some new schemes for the unemployed and other training programs appeared in the private sector. Nevertheless, at the same time, the extent of training for the employed at the old vocational centers fell sharply.

Econometric strategy and data

We use a duration model to analyze the unemployment spells and the transition probabilities of the unemployed going into another state in the labor market. Duration models started being commonly used in econometrics after Lancaster's famous (1979) paper on unemployment. In the present analysis the basic tool is the hazard function which determines the probability of an individual leaving unemployment conditional on the fact that he/she has stayed unemployed by the time the observation took place (for recent surveys, see Heckman and Singer, 1986, and Kiefer, 1988). In fact we use the Cox *proportional hazard model* and especially its semiparametric

310

specification which doesn't require a parametric specification of the baseline hazard. The intuition is that, in the absence of information about the baseline hazard, only the order of the durations provides information about the unknown coefficients. On the other hand, the partial likelihood specification[6] used in the present analysis is a popular method of analyzing the effect of covariates on the hazard rate and it successfully assesses the influence of predictor variables on the survival times in case of censored observations as is the case with our data set. In the model, the hazard function, which depends on a vector of explanatory variables x with unknown coefficients' vector ß, is factored as:[7]

$$\lambda\ (t, x, \textrm{ß}, \lambda_o) = \omega\ (x, \textrm{ß}).\lambda_o\ (t) \tag{1}$$

where λ_o is a 'baseline' hazard, corresponding to ω (.) = 1.
If we specify the form of ω as:

$$\omega\ (x, \textrm{ß}) = e^{\textrm{ß}x} \tag{2}$$

and using the proportional hazard specification after substituting (2) in (1) we get:

$$\partial \ln \lambda\ (t, x, \textrm{ß}, \lambda_o)/\ \partial x = \textrm{ß} \tag{3}$$

The equation shows that the proportional effect of x on the conditional probability of ending a spell does not depend on duration. This means that the coefficients can be interpreted as the constant proportional effect of x on the conditional probability of completing a spell and their sign will indicate the direction of the effect of the explanatory variables on it.

Typically, the dependent variable of interest in duration analysis is the length of time that elapses from the beginning of some event either until its end or until the measurement is taken (which can precede termination).[8] In our case, this variable will be the individual's unemployment duration, also called the length of the unemployment spell. The availability of information concerning the 'next destination' of the observed unemployed after leaving the registration system provides an opportunity for developing three competing risk models, each one with an exit to a different state. Competing risks models have been developed and used by Diamond and Hausmann (1984), Cox and Oaks (1984), Katz (1986), and Pichelmann and Riedel (1992). Determining separately a hazard function for each of the destination states, and compared to the single risk specification, these models allow us to check whether the effect of the explanatory variables and duration dependance patterns differ considerably for the different types of risks. This is an important remark, since neglecting the different types of exit routes from a certain state (in this case unemployment) may lead to a serious bias in results and conclusions.

311

The exit routes in our models have been constructed in accordance with the information provided about the reasons why an individual quits the registration system: Exit 1 – getting a job; Exit 2 – exhaustion of UB; Exit 3 – other unknown reasons. This last category includes people who quit either because of violating the administrative requirements or because of unknown reasons. The individuals who stay in the category 'no change' are those who are considered to be still unemployed (had not quit the registration system) by the time the sample collection was made (i.e., at the observation time). So this fact leads to these observations being considered as 'censored'. Cox's regression model overcomes the problem with censoring, which appears to be very common when dealing with duration data.

The two types of analyses – single risk and competing risk – have both been applied to the three time waves of data collection (last quarters of 1991, 1992, and 1993) and for all observations pooled together. This approach has been chosen for several reasons. First, looking only at the compressed single risk estimates may be misleading. Not distinguishing the different exit routes may lead to a misinterpretation of the differences in the effects the covariates have on the three specific situations. Also, a comparison among the estimates of the competing risk models will indicate which estimate turns out to be dominant (with respect to sign) for the single risk model. Second, by estimating models for different time periods, we are able to compare the patterns of exiting unemployment over time and thus to look at developments while transition is progressing .

Third, and more importantly – presenting the estimates of the single and competing risk models for the pooled observations makes it possible to point out the prevailing effects among the ones from the preceding time period analyses, i.e., to see which factors have been of most importance for the hazard rate in the single risk model.

The time scale used in the econometric application is *weeks*. Duration has been computed as the difference between the date of deregistration and the date of registration. The fact that the date of separation (the actual date of entering the unemployment pool) is not available for some individuals made the use of the exact 'real' number of weeks representing the unemployment spell impossible. However, a careful examination of the dates of separation available showed that there is a negligible difference between the date of separation and the date of registration at the labor office. Another reason which makes us think that this calculation is a good approximation of the unemployment spell is the specific framework of the legislation system in Bulgaria concerning eligibility to receive UB. Since the time period of eligibility for getting UB is counted from the actual starting date of the layoff, rather than from the starting date of the registration in the labor office, the unemployed have an incentive to register as early as possible.

The data set was prepared according to the OECD standards by the Bulgarian Ministry of Labour and is based on observations from five regional labor offices. The main characteristics of the sample which are used as regressors are classified into three basic groups: (i) personal characteristics; (ii) entitlement to UB; and (iii) previous employment history.

More precisely, the individual data used for the present analysis contain information on: date of birth; registration date; deregistration date; educational level; sector of the last job; previous occupation; place of residence; unemployment status; date of the layoff; reasons for quitting the registration system; starting date of getting UB; ending date of getting UB; size of UB per month (in Bulgarian levs); and participation in a training program.

The sample contains 351 observations for the last quarter of 1991, 640 observations for the last quarter of 1992, and 828 observations for the last quarter of 1993. Information is missing for two districts – Mezdra and Pazardzik for the last quarter of 1991, and Mezdra for the last quarter of 1992. The criteria used when drawing the observations is that the registered unemployed be born on either the seventh, seventeenth, or twenty-seventh of every month.

Since many observations omit information about wages previously received and/or whether the individuals participated in a training program, the decision was made to omit the *replacement ratio* and the *participation into a training program* as explanatory variables in the multivariate empirical work.

Descriptive statistics are presented in Table 14.8. These show that the individuals in the sample are evenly divided with respect to factors such as gender and place of residence. Over the three periods, the sample exhibits a very similar distribution according to the previous occupation of the unemployed – the largest category is 'workers' (ranging between 52-63 per cent during the periods) and 'school-leavers' (around 16 per cent for all three periods). The lowest category is 'top executives' with two per cent. The share of the unemployed without any professional qualification is rather low – around seven to eight per cent.

Characteristics such as age, eligibility for UB, and participation in a training program show rather stable tendencies throughout the periods. For example, the registered unemployed who are eligible for UB and those who are not represent almost equal shares in the sample, while those classified as 'young specialists' (those who had recently graduated from university and are subjected to special regulations concerning the eligibility for UB) constitute a negligible per cent of the whole sample. Since we don't have information about the reasons which forced the individuals to enter the unemployment pool, we may only state the hypothesis that almost half of the registered and not eligible for UB unemployed belonged to one of the following categories: laid off, voluntarily separated from the previous job, housewives, or students who have interrupted their studies (the legislation system in Bulgaria considers all of these categories not eligible for getting UB).

Table 14.8
Data descriptive statistics (in %)

	1991	1992	1993
Gender	100.00	100.00	100.00
male	57.00	52.50	52.00
female	43.00	47.50	48.00
Previous occupation	100.00	100.00	100.00
school-leavers	16.80	15.60	15.80
workers	51.60	61.30	58.80
specialists	10.00	6.10	6.30
executives	6.60	5.00	3.60
top executives	1.70	2.20	1.30
staff and security	5.40	3.10	5.60
no qualifications	8.00	6.90	8.60
Residence place	100.00	100.00	100.00
town	51.00	41.10	31.80
village	49.00	58.90	68.20
Unemployment status	100.00	100.00	100.00
U eligible for UB	54.40	47.30	39.60
U not eligible for UB	43.90	51.60	56.00
young specialists	1.70	1.10	4.30
Reasons for quitting reg. system	100.00	100.00	100.00
(by t observ. time)			
not quitting (censored)	14.50	12.00	79.30
found job	18.00	9.80	3.50
end of UB	25.40	34.50	7.90
other reasons	42.20	43.40	9.20
Education level	100.00	100.00	100.00
university degree	13.10	10.30	6.00
semi-high or secondary special	20.20	15.90	13.40
secondary general	38.50	25.00	32.00
primary & lower	28.20	48.80	47.90
Age structure	100.00	100.00	100.00
up to 29 years	37.00	35.20	37.60
30 to 49 years	51.30	50.20	50.80
50+ years	11.70	14.60	11.60
Participation in TP*	100.00	100.00	100.00
yes	4.60	3.90	2.80
no	95.40	96.10	97.20
Number of observations	351.00	640.00	828.00

* The observations from Lovetch are excluded here.

A relatively large percentage of the sample were young people below 30 years of age (about 37 per cent), which supports the evidence from macro data that youth unemployment in Bulgaria turned out to be a very serious problem. (By December 1991 people below 30 years of age constituted 40.8 per cent of all unemployed; by December 1992 and December 1993 the figures were respectively 44.8 per cent and 43.0 per cent.) As has been mentioned before, for all the observed periods, the participation rate in a training program is very low, less than five per cent.

The characteristics which differ significantly both within the subgroups and across the different periods are 'the reason for quitting' the registration system. The big discrepancy in the percentage of the unemployed who did not quit the registration system for 1991 (14.5 per cent) and 1992 (14.5 per cent), as opposed to 1993 (79.3 per cent), may have its explanation in the fact that by the time the sample had been drawn (in July 1994) the first two groups would have been long-term unemployed (more than two years). The consequence would clearly be the end of receiving UB as well as disbelief in the effective functioning of the social safety net in Bulgaria and mainly its assistance in providing the unemployed with job offers.

Since the duration of unemployment is of particular importance in the investigation process, Tables 14.9a, 14.9b, and 14.9c present the individuals' duration spells for the three separate periods.

Findings

The results from the duration models analysis are given in Tables 14.10-14.13. The first table shows the results from the single and competing risk models for the pooled observations, while the other three tables present the results from the models for each of the three time periods: the fourth quarter of 1991, 1992, and 1993.

The tables present the coefficients' values and their significance level (the non-significant values are given in the tables and used in the analysis as well .

For the pooled data, the result in the single risk model, though rather puzzling, shows that people between 41 and 50 years of age have a higher hazard, i.e., a higher probability to leave the unemployment pool than the base age category (31 - 40 years). However, the estimate values in the competing risks models show that this age group has a higher probability of leaving the unemployment pool because of the exhaustion of UB or 'other reasons', while reasonably the effect the 'job' hazard has is negative, although not very significant. So the two positive, significant hazards prevailed and gave the positive sign of this coefficient in the single risk model.

A possible explanation of this result may be the form of the gender distribution of the people in the discussed and the base age categories, since in Bulgaria older women have better chances to escape from unemployment than the younger ones. The opposite is true for males, who have better chances when they are younger.

315

Table 14.9a
Frequency distribution of unemployment spells, 1991 data (in %)

Weeks	Botevgrad	Mladost	Lovetch	Total
0 to 2	0.00	0.00	0.00	0.00
2 to 4	0.80	0.80	1.85	1.14
4 to 6	4.00	5.00	1.85	3.70
6 to 8	0.80	1.70	0.00	0.85
8 to 10	3.20	1.70	0.90	1.99
10 to 12	0.00	5.90	0.90	2.28
12 to 14	2.40	11.00	0.90	4.84
14 to 16	0.80	4.20	0.00	1.71
16 to 18	2.40	1.70	4.60	2.85
18 to 20	4.80	5.00	0.00	3.42
20 to 22	3.20	5.00	0.00	2.85
22 to 24	0.00	1.70	0.00	0.57
24 to 26	7.30	6.80	0.90	5.13
26 to 28	0.80	5.90	2.70	9.69
28 to 30	0.80	5.90	6.40	3.13
30 to 32	8.00	14.40	0.00	1.99
32 to 34	5.60	3.40	0.00	1.71
34 to 36	5.60	0.00	0.90	1.42
36 to 38	3.20	0.80	0.00	1.14
38+	1.60	1.70	45.40	32.48
still unempl.	33.90	19.50	32.40	15.10
reg. date=dereg. date	11.30	3.40	0.90	0.28

reg. date: date of registration in the labor office.
dereg. date: date of deregistration from the labor office.

Table 14.9b
Frequency distribution of unemployment spells, 1992 data (in %)

Weeks	Botevgrad	Mladost	Lovetch	Pazardzik	Total
0 to 2	1.10	0.00	0.00	0.00	0.20
2 to 4	2.20	1.50	1.80	0.40	1.20
4 to 6	0.00	15.00	0.60	0.00	3.20
6 to 8	1.10	1.50	1.20	0.00	0.70
8 to 10	4.50	3.00	1.20	0.00	1.50
10 to 12	2.20	1.50	0.50	0.00	0.70
12 to 14	1.10	5.30	1.20	0.00	1.60
14 to 16	4.50	5.30	0.00	0.00	1.70
16 to 18	0.00	2.30	2.40	0.40	1.20
18 to 20	0.00	3.00	5.90	0.00	2.20
20 to 22	1.10	1.50	11.20	0.00	3.40
22 to 24	3.40	2.30	6.50	0.40	2.80
24 to 26	6.70	7.50	10.00	0.40	5.30
26 to 28	1.10	1.50	8.80	0.00	2.80
28 to 30	10.10	9.80	11.20	0.80	6.70
30 to 32	4.50	4.50	3.50	0.00	2.50
32 to 34	5.60	3.80	3.50	0.00	2.50
34 to 36	3.40	0.00	3.50	2.40	2.40
36 to 38	1.10	3.00	2.90	4.00	3.10
38+	27.00	18.80	22.40	72.90	41.70
still unempl.	19.10	7.50	2.90	18.20	12.00
reg=dereg		1.50			0.30

reg. date: date of registration in the labor office.
dereg. date: date of deregistration from the labor office.

Table 14.9c
Frequency distribution of unemployment spells, 1993 data (in %)

Weeks	Botevgrad	Mladost	Lovetch	Pazardzik	Mezdra	Total
0 to 2	0.00	0.80	7.40	0.60		1.70
2 to 4	0.00	0.00	8.00	0.80		1.80
4 to 6	3.50	0.80	4.00	0.00		1.30
6 to 8	1.80	0.00	4.00	0.60		1.20
8 to 10	3.50	14.20	2.70	0.60		3.30
10 to 12	3.50	4.20	2.00	1.70		2.20
12 to 14	0.90	1.70	2.70	1.40		1.40
14 to 16	0.90	0.80	2.00	0.80		1.00
16 to 18	3.50	1.70	0.70	0.60		1.00
18 to 20	1.80	1.70	0.00	0.60		0.70
20 to 22	2.70	0.00	0.00	0.20		0.50
22 to 24	0.00	1.70	0.00	0.00		0.20
24 to 26	4.40	0.00	0.70	0.20		0.80
26 to 28	1.80	0.00	0.00	0.00		0.20
28 to 30	0.90	0.00	0.00	0.00		0.10
30 to 32	0.90	0.00	0.00	0.00		0.10
32 to 34	0.90	0.00	0.00	0.00		0.10
34 to 36	1.80	0.00	0.00	0.00		0.20
36 to 38	0.00	0.00	0.00	0.00		0.00
38+	0.00	0.00	0.00	0.00		0.00
still unempl.	67.30	71.20	65.80	91.60		81.60
reg.=dereg.		0.20		0.20		0.20

reg. date: date of registration in the labor office.
dereg. date: date of deregistration from the labor office.

Closest to the pattern exhibited by the results from the pooled data is the model emerged from 1992 duration analysis (results reported in Table 14.12). Its estimates (namely the positive 'other reasons' hazard for younger people) appear as a confirmation of the official statistical evidence for this period in Bulgaria, which shows that the share of unemployed leaving the registration system for unknown reasons or due to non-observance of the administrative requirements (these two categories belong in the 'other reasons' category in our model) increased significantly. By December 1992, 74.5 per cent of the registered unemployed dropped out of the registration system because of non-observance of administrative requirements, and 9.2 per cent quit for unstated reasons, with the younger people prevailing over the older ones.

Not surprisingly, the gender analysis showed that women in Bulgaria have less of a chance to get out of the unemployment pool (for all single and competing risk models). One important thing to notice here is the negative coefficient for 'end of UB' exit throughout the models except for 1993 (and even the insignificant negative coefficient for the 'other reasons' exit). The standard theory of investment in human capital argues that women are more likely to go out of the labor force in order to get involved in activities such as child care, housekeeping, etc. In our case, the argument supporting the empirical evidence which appears somehow counterintuitive is that the low living standard in Bulgaria doesn't allow the household to rely only on the husband's income.

Concerning the effect the passive labor policy may have, the results show that individuals eligible for UB are more likely to stay unemployed than those who are not. There is one exception, the case when UB are ending, which may provide a good incentive for a more intensive job search.

Discussing the 'previous employment history' variables, two basic tendencies appeared to be of interest. The first finding concerns the group's characteristic 'economic branch of last attended job'. In this group those who just graduated from universities have a higher positive 'job' hazard compared to those who previously worked in the industrial branch. This hazard seems to be the dominant one among the other competing risk models and influences the same coefficient for the single model. The suggestion is that young, highly qualified people can find professional realization fairly easily (although not always in the same field for which they have been trained). This tendency is typical not only for the pooled data model but for the time period models as well (except for 1992).

The next finding refers to the group's characteristic 'last previous job occupation'. The pooled data analysis shows that being in the 'staff' category compared to the base one, 'specialists', has a negative impact over all the hazards and especially for the 'job' hazard for all time period models. That result is consistent with the well known fact that in Bulgaria, as in almost all ex-socialist countries, the administrative structure during the communist regime was artificially inflated and there was extensive labor hoarding.

319

Table 14.10
Estimates using pooled data

	Single risk model		Exit 1		Exit 2		Exit 3	
	B	Sig.l.	B	Sig.l.	B	Sig.l.	B	Sig.l.
Age 20	-.0363	.8413	-1.3506	.1920	.1367	.7580	.0336	.8729
Age 2130	-.0258	.7529	-.1847	.3729	-.1895	.2086	.0896	.4357
Age 4150	.2280	.0058	-.2022	.3457	.2808	.0302	.3003	.0178
Age 51	.1188	.3407	-.6371	.1374	.1398	.4065	.3487	.0977
Age 3140-Base								
Gender	-.1621	.0129	-.0639	.7103	-.3159	.0043	-.0474	.6109
Res. place	.1959	.0056	-.2909	.1081	.2235	.0655	.2815	.0054
MC	-.3108	.0000	.7233	.0004	1.6196	.0000	-2.7145	.0000
Y. worker	-1.5890	.0000	-1.7195	.1175	.6180	.2507	-3.5844	.0000
Non-elig.-Base								
Agri	.0220	.8302	-.1818	.4993	.0833	.5754	.0167	.9248
Stud	.6266	.0079	.8285	.0839	-.3308	.4039	.3473	.0000
Serv	.0118	.8873	-.1067	.5972	-.4125	.0037	2.1462	.0066
Tran	-.1393	.5626	-.3815	.5989	.1993	.5905	.3473	.6137
Ind-Base								
Sc.leav.	.3881	.0181	-.1062	.7916	.7638	.0028	.5226	.0801
Staff	-.6431	.0034	-1.0198	.0691	-.7650	.0274	-.3176	.3756
Worker	-.1761	.2018	-.4756	.1563	-.2017	.3307	.0594	.8219
Unqual.	.0382	.8343	-.7545	.1991	-.0332	.9327	.1863	.5281
Top	-.0092	.9550	-.1869	.5776	.1624	.4866	-.0795	.8088
Spec-Base								
Univ.	.5958	.0000	.9961	.0034	.5884	.0135	.6571	.0048
Semi	.5005	.0000	.6059	.0428	.4357	.0237	.6540	.0000
Sec	.4501	.0000	.5370	.0313	.5179	.0008	.4545	.0002
Lower-Base								

Table 14.11
Estimates using 1991 data

	Single risk model		Exit 1		Exit 2		Exit 3	
	B	Sig.l.	B	Sig.l.	B	Sig.l.	B	Sig.l.
Age 20	.4759	.5242	.0720	1.0000	2.1301	.9985	-.1010	.6195
Age 2130	-.0762	.5875	-.2770	.3891	.1748	.5241	.5210	.4922
Age 4150	-.0968	.5645	-.1314	.7003	-.0121	.9676	.1308	.6165
Age 51	0*		0*		0*		0*	
Age 3140-Base								
Gender	-.8468	0	-.3965	.1566	-1.1726	0	-.8091	0
Res.place	.3306	.0153	-.3134	.2986	.2492	.3482	.1376	.0003
MC	-.1942	.1835	.2977	.3376	4.2342	0	-2.3066	0
Y. worker	-1.1986	.0396	-.5944	.6394	1.9181	.2041	-3.4543	.0001
Non-elig-Base								
Agri	-.0130	.9590	.6018	.1892	-.7574	.1675	.0497	.8980
Stud	2.9694	0	1.6357	.0549	3.7380	.0001	5.1458	0
Serv	.0264	.8536	-.1862	.5457	-.1891	.4511	.3838	.1132
Tran	.9162	.1279	-13.1197	.9922	2.1233	.0086	1.2446	.2306
Ind-Base								
Sc. leav.	-.6300	.0387	-.2775	.6688	-.3246	.5439	-1.2128	.0304
Staff	-.0648	.7784	-.1630	.4415	-1.9839	.0612	.0355	.9490
Worker	-.4084	.2325	-.5716	.4387	.2665	.4380	-.3867	.4069
Unqual.	-.0809	.8034	-13.0206	.9723	-10.8025	.9643	-.2271	.6682
Top	-.2052	.5024	.1036	.8498	-.5328	.2920	-.5194	.4337
Spec-Base								
Univ.	.1085	.6692	.8982	.1224	.4568	.3223	-.1390	.7338
Semi	-.1601	.4616	.6183	.1624	.0506	.8790	-.3021	.2915
Sec	.0734	.6758	.5753	.2801	.0989	.8125	.1945	.4480
Lower-Base								

0* - degrees of freedom reduced because of constant or linearly dependent covariates.

Table 14.12
Estimates using 1992 data

	Single risk model		Exit 1		Exit 2		Exit 3	
	B	Sig.l.	B	Sig.l	B	Sig.l	B	Sig.l
Age 20	.0514	.8229	-.6127	.5628	1.2068	.1054	.0968	.7163
Age 2130	.0312	.7901	-.0717	.8252	-.0222	.9199	.1373	.4019
Age 4150	.2690	.0314	-.5234	.1601	-.0020	.9913	.5119	.0076
Age 51	-.0438	.7721	-.3742	.4897	-.2332	.2523	.5019	.0567
Age 3140-Base								
Gender	.1273	.1403	-.0190	.9432	.2311	.1118	.2622	.0384
Res.plac	-.0120	.9008	-.1432	.6090	-.2246	.1734	.0770	.5667
MC	.0654	.5388	1.2267	.0020	4.7972	.0000	-3.1289	.0000
Y. worker	-1.0530	.0782	-10.258	.9732	2.5355	.0192	-3.5999	.0001
Non-elig-Base								
Agri	-.2293	.0949	-1.0939	.0099	-.2832	.1660	-.0881	.6973
Stud	-.2460	.4640	-.4179	.5835	-.4223	.4128	1.6467	.0103
Serv	-.1196	.3099	-.2972	.3441	-.3083	.1271	.0270	.8780
Tran	-.1334	.6606	.5434	.4821	.6433	.2396	.-4339	.3146
Ind-Base								
Sc. leav	1.3432	.0000	.3368	.5815	1.0555	.0025	2.1031	.0001
Worker	-.5202	.1105	-1.2484	.2595	-.6211	.1363	-.3562	.6134
Staff	.1142	.5861	-.3842	.4673	-.4235	.1684	.8281	.0918
Unqual	.5304	.0514	.0467	.9508	.6176	.2869	1.1156	.0364
Top	.0787	.7333	-.3273	.5480	-.4383	.1721	.8741	.1068
Spec-Base								
Univ	.9131	.0000	.5854	.2828	.7197	.0353	1.0984	.0013
Semi	.7782	.0000	.3462	.4234	.4875	.0496	1.0741	.0000
Sec	.5995	.0000	-.1043	.7896	.3037	.1553	.8660	.0000
Lower-Base								

Table 14.13
Estimates using 1993 data

	Single risk model		Exit 1		Exit 2		Exit 3	
	B	Sig.l.	B	Sig.l.	B	Sig.l.	B	Sig.l.
Age 20	-.1135	.7556	-12.764	.9874	-.2269	.7294	.3696	.4515
Age 2130	-.2145	.3478	-.2903	.5973	-.4435	.2638	-.0068	.9841
Age 4150	.2838	.2216	.2347	.6789	.3967	.2718	.1464	.6938
Age 51	.1191	.7364	-.7873	.4723	.2289	.6609	.0689	.9054
Age 3140-Base								
Gender	.1635	.3355	.6012	.1609	.2068	.4704	.0414	.8723
Res. place	.0783	.6555	-.6410	.1389	.3875	.1760	-.0984	.7079
MC	-1.4061	.0000	1.7488	.0082	-2.0643	.0000	-2.6798	.0000
Y. worker	-2.5316	.0003	-13.914	.9887	-1.9073	.1577	-2.8460	.0775
Non-elig-Base								
Agri	.2689	.3240	1.0971	.0911	-.0362	.9247	.2761	.5797
Stud	-.1760	.7724	2.0573	.1889	-3.1194	.0250	12.3339	.9132
Serv	.2550	.2538	.5951	.3223	-1.4918	.1605	.9021	.0116
Tran	-.4898	.4212	-12.998	.9897	-.6644	.3866	-.2941	.7795
Ind-Base								
Sc. leav	1.6534	.0004	-.7063	.6188	13.3955	.7678	-10.853	.9236
Staff	-1.9226	.0688	-14.676	.9873	.7331	.9907	-1.2596	.2584
Worker Unqual	-.3154	.4054	-.9293	.2489	7.9809	.8603	-.0905	.8641
Top	.4524	.3393	-.0648	.9600	9.9753	.8259	-.2587	.6952
Spec-Base	.6107	.1258	-1.5806	.1521	10.3529	.8194	-.4766	.5626
Univ	1.3918	.0011	2.0906	.0559	2.8015	.0068	1.0181	.0969
Semi	1.1302	.0007	.7792	.4489	3.1043	.0003	.8005	.0511
Sec	1.1914	.0000	1.3173	.0908	3.6354	.0000	.1133	.7443
Lower-Base								

Another result is that the school-leavers have a negative, although insignificant 'job' hazard and a positive 'end of UB' and 'other reasons' hazard. The result supports the statistical evidence that by December 1991, although there was a government-sponsored program for providing temporary jobs for the school-leavers, the registered vacancies of that type constituted only one-third of what they used to be in 1990.[9]

The estimated value for the educational levels undoubtedly confirms that the higher the educational level, the greater are the 'single risk' and the 'job' hazards. This appears to support both the investment in human capital theory and the econometric results received from previous empirical studies on transition probabilities in the Bulgarian labor market (Jones and Kato, 1994). The positive 'other reasons' hazard for the people with an education higher than primary can possibly be explained by migration. It may be migration rather than the non-observance of administrative rules for example which made them quit the registration system. The NSI study from 1992 showed that education plays an important role in making a decision to emigrate. In the group of resettlers, 64.0 per cent of the people have a high school or higher educational level.

The other 'surprising' result is the positive hazard for the rural population compared to the urban population in the single risk model. A closer look at the estimates in the competing risk models shows that the rural population has higher 'end of UB' and 'other reasons' hazards. Analysis of rural unemployment in Bulgaria shows that long term unemployment often leads to the so called 'discouraged worker's effect' among the peasants and a part of the rural population deliberately isolated themselves from the economically active population.[10]

Conclusions

Based on the findings of this paper some particular conclusions and labor market policy implications are straightforward.

The results invariably show that labor offices do not seem very helpful in assisting the unemployed in their job search. In very few cases an individual left the registration system because of getting a job. Accounting, however, for the fact that Bulgaria is considered among the countries with a technically well-equipped employment service net, the efforts should be directed towards achieving a better match between the job-seekers and the job opportunities provided by the regional labor offices.

Another conclusion which comes out of the analysis is that during the process of restructuring the Bulgarian economy, female unemployment is going to be of considerable importance. A possible solution in this case would be to provide special social safety measures for women and their dependents.

The other very important issue is labor policy towards rural unemployment. This is a very complicated question which requires further discussion but what should be noted is that a set of instruments appropriate for the Bulgarian conditions and environment must be created which will be effective in encouraging employment among the rural population.

Expanding educational programs to increase assistance (especially to minorities) in getting more schooling definitely will improve workers' chances and opportunities in the labor market.

Finally there is the very important issue not only for the educational purposes but for the training and re-training programs concerning the active labor market policy in Bulgaria which certainly needs more thorough and better planned development. Although the empirical analysis in this paper doesn't deal directly with the active labor market policy, the fact that the number of those who completed training courses in 1991 was 20, 155 (4.8 per cent of all job seekers); in 1992 was 16, 618 (2.8 per cent of all job seekers); and by May 1993 was 9,115 shows that this kind of labor market policy in Bulgaria had not been used very much and, consequently has had little or almost no effect in solving the unemployment problem. The conclusions are that due to limited access to free (public-sponsored) training or retraining programs together with the 'obscure' perspectives of getting a job afterwards, there was little incentive for the unemployed to sign up for such courses.[11]

However, it should be noted that all the findings in this paper are preliminary and that additional work is required. In future research, it is planned to extend the model to include interaction terms (such as sex and age, for example) so that the influence of different factors on transition probabilities may be determined with more precision. Also, access to information about wage level would enable us to include the 'replacement ratio' in future empirical work which, on the other hand, may very well have a significant importance in interpreting the coefficients on some of the variables used in the present analysis. We may think about testing the model for a ten per cent confidence interval because of the relatively small number of observations, as well as to place more emphasis on the role of the size of UB and the influence of the active labor market policy on the dynamics of unemployment in the Bulgarian labor market.

Notes

1   See International Labour Organization for CEECs, 1993.
2   See Jones and Kato, 1994.
3   According to Decree 133 of the Ministerial Council from July 1992.
4   See Burda, 1992.
5   See Jones and Kato, 1994.
6   The proportional hazard partial likelihood specification has been proposed by Prentice and Gloecker, 1978, Han and Hauseman, 1990, Meyer, 1990, Sueyoshi, 1992, Omori, 1994, and Light, 1995.
7   See Kiefer, 1988.
8   See Green, 1992.

9   See International Labour Organization for CEECs, 1993.
10   See Bobeva and Hristoskov, 1995.
11   See International Labour Organization for CEECs, 1992.

References

Beleva, Iskra, Jackman, Richard, and Nenova-Amar, Mariela (1995), 'Bulgaria,
    Unemployment, Restructuring and the Labour Market in Eastern Europe and
    Russia', Economic Development Institute of the World Bank.
Bobeva, Daniela and Hristoskov, Yordan (1995), 'Unemployment in Agricultural
    Areas: An Overview of Central and Eastern Europe', *A Case Study of the
    Bulgarian Region, The Regional Dimension of Unemployment in Transition
    Countries*, pp. 239-60.
Budina, Nina, Dimitrov, Todor, and Worgotter, Andreas (1995), 'Bulgarian
    Country Report', Bank Austria/IHS: Vienna.
Burda, Michael (1992), 'Unemployment, Labour Market Institutions and Struc-
    tural Changes in Eastern Europe', CEPRS Discussion Paper, No. 746.
Greene, William H. (1992), *Econometric Analysis*, Prentice-Hall: Englewood
    Cliffs, N.J.
Ham, John, Svejnar, Jan, and Terell, Katherine (1994), 'The Emergence of
    Unemployment in the Czech and Slovak Republics', unpublished manuscript,
    University of Pittsburgh: Pittsburgh, Penn.
Han, Aaron and Hausmann, Jerry A. (1990), 'Flexible Estimation of Duration and
    Competing Risk Models', *Journal of Applied Econometrics*, No. 5, January, pp.
    1-28.
Heckman, James and Singer, Burton (1984a), 'Econometric Duration Analysis',
    Journal of Econometrics, No. 24, January/February, pp. 63-132.
International Labour Organization for CEECs (1993), 'The Bulgarian Challenge:
    Reform of the Labour Market and Social Policy'.
Jones, Derek C. and Kato, Tako (1994), 'The Nature and the Determinants of
    Labour Market Transitions in Former Socialist Countries: Evidence from
    Bulgaria', mimeo, Hamilton College: Clinton, N.Y.
Kiefer, Nickolas (1988), 'Analysis of Grouped Duration Data', *Contemporary
    Mathematics*, No. 80, pp. 107-37.
——— (1988), 'Econometric Duration Data and Hazard Functions', *Journal of
    Economic Literature*, Vol. 26, pp. 656-79.
Light, Andrey (1995), 'Hazard Model estimates of the Decision to Reenroll in
    School', *Labour Economics – An International Journal*, Vol. 2, No. 4, Decem-
    ber, pp. 381-407.

Meyer, Bruce D. (1990), 'Unemployment Insurance and Unemployment Spells', *Econometrica*, No. 58, July, pp. 757-82.

National Statistical Institute (1994), *Bulgarian Statistical Book*, NSI: Sofia.

—— (1995), 'Employment and Unemployment', *Bulgarian Labour Force Survey*, NSI: Sofia.

—— (1995),'Main Macro-Economic Indicators', NSI: Sofia.

Pichelmann, Karl and Reidel, Monika (1992), 'New Jobs or Recalls', *Empirica*, Vol. 19, No. 2, pp. 259-74.

Steiner, Victor (1995), 'Labour Market Transitions and the Persistence of Unemployment in West Germany', mimeo.

Sueyoshi, Glenn T. (1992), 'Semiparametric Proportional Hazards Estimation of Competing Risk Models with Time-Varying Covariates', *Journal of Econometrics*, No. 51, January/February, pp. 25-58.

15   Fringe benefits in transition: evidence from Bulgaria

Mark Klinedinst and Charles Rock

Introduction

The benefits package from work provided to workers in the former East-Bloc nations rivaled and often surpassed the fringes in other industrialized countries. The transition process begun in many countries in 1989 is bound to have a profound effect on the quantity and quality of many goods and services formerly offered by the workplace. This study will use a rich data set on Bulgarian firms to try to understand the changes taking place in the benefit set during the early period of change to a market economy.

Bulgaria, up until 1989, in some regards can be considered to be a more Soviet-style communist economy than even the Soviet Union. A smaller economy with a more homogenous population combined with a strict central planning apparatus allowed the Bulgarians to implement a fairly complete organization of industrial production according to central design. Hence, Bulgarian industry may be seen as a smaller laboratory to analyze changes brought about in the former Soviet states and other East-Bloc nations.

Workers in Bulgarian firms before the transition were in many cases offered a broad range of benefits from their firms. The most striking difference to a Western observer is the sometimes quite encompassing range of goods and services offered by companies. The firm was designed almost as a big family (or a big brother). Benefits might include a couple of beach and mountain houses for employees and their families to use on vacations, health coverage, drug costs, sick leave, childcare, subsidized housing, supplemental pensions, transportation allowances, training, meals, loan facilities, working clothes, paid vacations, and bonuses. These benefits make up a virtual wish list for many US employees.

In this chapter we will look briefly at the history of benefits in the communist era and then scrutinize the benefits available to industrial employees three years into the transition.

A brief history of benefits before the transition

The benefits available to employees before the efforts to transform the East-Bloc nations were quite extensive. Although relative wage levels in the East and the West were similar, important differences in types of pay and benefits existed (Clark, 1960). The determination of total monetary compensation, although not the focus of this paper, included some items that may be thought of as benefits, e.g., bonuses. Workers in Western nations typically had most of their pay (approximately 60 to 80 per cent) determined largely by how much time was spent at work, East Bloc nations, however, had their pay calculated in large part according to firm performance (Pryor, 1984, McAuley, 1979). Workers in the Soviet Union had up to 90 per cent of their pay through monetary incentives, including both personal and group bonuses. These bonuses could be for overfulfillment of plan norms, punctuality, cutting costs, saving materials, special working conditions, piecework, or on subjective evaluations of job performance.

Firms in Yugoslavia, although following a much more market oriented development that was thought by some to be a potential model for the East-Bloc countries, were similar to Bulgarian firms in the number of employee services provided for by the firm. Calculating the percentage of total income given in the form of bonuses for the Yugoslav firms is not comparable since these firms, until the start of the war, were labor-managed firms. However, the extent and quantity of services were often similar to those found in statist economies (Klinedinst, 1991). Given the Yugoslavian experience there is some reason to expect that the range of benefits may survive in large part in the former East-Bloc, especially if the political leadership is dominated by former communists. Some diminution of benefits can be expected in firms faced with dwindling markets (Nenova, 1993). Assets such as vacation property that are not directly necessary for production are likely in many cases to be liquidated.

Benefits three years into the transition

The data we use comes from surveys conducted in 1992 and 1993 from a randomly selected sample of industrial firms.[1] The breakdown of the distribution of benefits across types of workers is given in Table 15.1. This table shows that, not surprisingly, that managers typically get a fuller range of benefits than other types of workers. Production workers who are full-time have a range of perks that rivals those of

330

Table 15.1
Fringe benefits and summary statistics in Bulgarian industrial firms, 1992

	Yes (%)	No	Occasionally	Not applicable	Do not know
Vacation pay					
Managers	99.6	0.4	0	0	0
Production	99.8	0.2	0	0	0
Temporary	52	40	0	0	0
Civil contract	12	71	3.4	13.6	0
Holiday/ recreation					
Managers	68.4	23	1.7	6.9	0
Production	68.7	22.7	1.7	6.9	0
Temporary	47.6	28.6	4.8	19	0
Civil contract	20.5	60.2	5.5	13.8	0
Sick leave					
Managers	99.1	0.9	0	0	0
Production	99.1	0.9	0	0	0
Temporary	72	20	8	0	0
Civil contract	14.5	68.6	4.3	12.2	0.4
Subsidize housing/ housing allowance					
Managers	5.1	79.1	1.5	13.4	1
Production	5.8	77.9	1.7	13.6	1
Temporary	4.3	69.6	8.7	17.4	0
Civil contract	0.4	78.5	1.2	19.5	0.4
Childcare services					
Managers	13.3	71.7	1.2	12.4	1.4
Production	13.6	71.7	1.4	12.4	1.4
Temporary	4.2	70.8	4.2	20.8	0
Civil contract	2.7	78	1.9	16.6	0.8
Incentive bonuses					
Managers	46.3	42.2	6.7	4.8	0
Production	48.9	39.8	6.7	4.6	0
Temporary	13.6	59.1	13.6	13.6	0
Civil contract	6.7	77.5	4	11.9	0
Profit-sharing bonuses					
Managers	35.3	53.1	3.1	7.6	0.9
Production	34.4	53.7	3.3	7.8	0.7
Temporary	16	60	20	4	0
Civil contract	3.5	78.4	2.7	14.3	1.2

Table 15.1 (continued)
Fringe benefits and summary statistics in Bulgarian industrial firms, 1992

	Yes (%)	No	Occasionally	Not applicable	Do not know
Severance pay					
Managers	45.8	45.6	3	5.6	0
Production	46.5	45.1	2.8	5.6	0
Temporary	8.7	78.3	8.7	4.3	0
Civil contract	1.9	83.5	2.3	12.3	0
Supplementary pension					
Managers	15.4	73.4	0.5	9.3	1.5
Production	16.2	72.5	0.5	9.3	1.5
Temporary	9.1	77.3	4.5	9.1	0
Civil contract	1.2	83.7	0.8	13.6	0.8
Training/education					
Managers	45.9	41.1	7.5	5.3	0.2
Production	45.5	41.1	7.8	5.4	0.2
Temporary	21.7	69.6	8.7	0	0
Civil contract	3.6	79.4	4.4	12.7	0
Transportation allowance					
Managers	44.7	49	3.1	2.9	0.2
Production	45.8	47.7	3.4	2.9	0.2
Temporary	21.7	69.6	8.7	0	0
Civil contract	3.6	79.4	4.4	12.7	0
Meal allowance					
Managers	81.7	16.1	0.7	1.4	0.2
Production	83.6	14.4	0.5	1.4	0.2
Temporary	69.2	26.9	3.8	0	0
Civil contract	23.4	63	3.4	9.8	0.4
Loan facilities					
Managers	37.2	53	3.1	6	0.7
Production	38	52.4	2.9	6	0.7
Temporary	33.3	54.2	8.3	4.2	0
Civil contract	5.4	79.2	1.2	13.5	0.8
Working clothes/ clothing allowance					
Managers	80.5	17.7	1.1	0.4	0.2
Production	94.4	4.2	0.9	0.2	0.2
Temporary	76	20	4	0	0
Civil contract	20.5	63.6	6.1	9.5	0.4

Variable	Mean (%)	Std. Dev.	Min	Max	N
Collective benefits (% of total)	9.9	11.336	0	99	447
Union membership (% in 1991)	75.6	0.231	0.068	1	350

managers, at least in the range of services, but temporary and workers who are under the civil contract fare considerably worse. Workers under the civil contract are supposedly in many cases receiving the benefits through independent sources that they have contracted, hence the firm need not offer severance pay, supplementary pensions to these persons at anywhere near the levels offered to other workers. The managers, according to Table 15.1, receive a slightly greater range of benefits, but this slight difference recorded here probably masks a much greater difference if the monetary equivalents of the benefits is calculated. For example, almost all the production workers and managers are reported to receive vacation pay, but the pay is probably much greater for managers (Klinedinst, 1991b, Crystal, 1989).[2]

Supplementary pensions are offered to only about a seventh of all managers and production workers, a number much less than the reported unionization rate in this sample of approximately 76 per cent. Workers in advanced market economies who are unionized typically also have pensions, hence the low rate for pensions here is probably a hold-over from the communist period. Recent discussions the authors have had with officials of the Confederation of Independent Trade Unions of Bulgaria (CITUB) indicated that indeed the development of pension funds administered by the trade unions was a major goal.

Table 15.2 reports ordinary least squares estimates of different benefits bundles as a function of a number of possible explanatory factors. The dependent variables are collective consumption expenditures as a per cent of employee earnings and indexes that register the total number of benefits available to production workers and managers.[3] Overall these equations, as often happens in cross-sectional studies of this nature (e.g., Estrin, Schaffer, and Singh, 1995), explain very little in the variation of benefits (e.g., the highest adjusted R-squared is 0.07), but there are some important correlations uncovered.

Explanatory variables included here are typical of variables found in income and benefit studies. Unionization would typically add to the breadth and depth of benefits offered by firms and there is fairly strong evidence of that being the case here. Both production workers and managers see an increase in the number of benefits offered, with the effect being weaker, not surprisingly, for managers.

Managers were asked to rank the influence of management versus that of workers on wages, benefits, and employment, ranking that influence from one to six, with one being the case where management alone controls and six being the case where workers alone decide. Managerially controlled firms (MCs) were defined as those firms with a one and in a like manner labor-managed firms (LMFs) were those that registered a six. Firms where both labor and management jointly decide on the above mentioned issues, a five in this scale, are listed here as codetermined firms. All three types of firm management showed no signs of having an effect on the number of benefits offered by the firm.

Table 15.2
OLS estimates of benefits as function of firm characteristics
(absolute values of asymptotic t-ratios in parentheses)

Dependent variable	Collective consumption expenditures as % of employee earnings	Production workers index of fringe benefits	Managerial index of fringe benefits
Intercept	12.77 (4.93)	6.87 (13.26)	6.31 (12.06)
Union membership	-0.36 (0.21)	1.49 (4.13)	1.33 (3.61)
Managerially-controlled firms	-2.13 (1.65)	0.23 (0.84)	0.27 (0.99)
Codetermined firms	-1.62 (0.85)	-0.21 (0.51)	-0.22 (0.53)
Labor-managed firms	-8.70 (1.17)	0.39 (0.31)	0.63 (0.48)
State joint stock	3.34 (1.50)	-0.06 (0.12)	0
Independent cooperatives	2.20 (0.76)	-0.57 (0.96)	-0.46 (0.45)
Private firms	-3.18 (0.44)	-0.48 (0.35)	-0.43 (0.76)
Value added 1992	-1.93E-5 (1.64)	2.47E-6 (0.91)	7.96E-7 (0.78)
Value added 1991	5.28 (0.13)	-1.86 (0.09)	-3.36E-5 (1.71)
Capital stock 1992	-0.001 (1.20)	4.77 (1.38)	2.47E-4 (0.70)
Capital stock 1991	1.45E-4 (0.14)	1.17 (0.04)	-1.00E-4 (0.31)
Region			
Plovdiv	-3.79 (1.88)	-0.10 (0.21)	0.07 (0.15)
Pleven	-2.71 (1.59)	-1.23 (3.49)	-0.96 (2.69)
Pernik	-3.92 (1.49)	-0.46 (0.92)	-0.46 (0.89)
Bourgas	-3.92 (2.04)	-0.14 (0.36)	-0.01 (0.01)

334

Table 15.2 (continued)
OLS estimates of benefits as function of firm characteristics
(absolute values of asymptotic t-ratios in parentheses)

Dependent variable	Collective consumption expenditures as % of employee earnings	Production workers index of fringe benefits	Managerial index of fringe benefits
Industry			
Food	0.50	-0.24	0.26
	(0.19)	(0.41)	(0.46)
Textiles	-2.30	-0.87	-0.52
	(0.85)	(1.56)	(0.92)
Wood/paper	0.70	-0.27	0.06
	(0.23)	(0.44)	(0.10)
Engineering	2.62	-0.61	-0.08
	(1.05)	(1.19)	(0.15)
Electronics	-1.71	-0.58	-0.25
	(0.58)	(0.97)	(0.41)
Chemicals	-0.21	-0.60	0.24
	(0.06)	(0.83)	(0.33)
Non-metal	5.58	-0.84	-0.06
	(1.50)	(1.06)	(0.08)
Mining	-2.73	-0.68	0.22
	(0.69)	(0.81)	(0.27)
Adjust R-squared	0.07	0.06	0.02
N	376	326	331

The level of decentralization and privatization was considered as a possible determinant and hence dummies for state joint-stock firms, cooperatives, and private firms were added to the equations (Rock, 1994). The estimates reported all show insignificant differences from the state firms (the excluded case was state firms), but it is interesting to note that the estimates for private firms were all negative, a possible sign of things to come.

Value added and the capital stock were added as controls. Lagged values were also included to capture longer run effects. The estimates here are typically insignificant. The regional dummies show that most other regions have a lower number of benefits compared to the region surrounding the capital city of Sofia (the excluded case). This was particularly true of the industrial region in the north-central area surrounding Pleven. The industrial distribution of benefits, likewise showed characteristically little significance in the estimates. Two industries, however, textiles and electronics had consistently negative coefficients. Possibly these industries have a higher number of female employees who are receiving fewer benefits as well as smaller wages and more unemployment (see Klinedinst and Rock, 1994, Jones, 1991, Bartol and Bartol, 1974).

Table 15.3 gives the mean values of the production worker and manager index across industries and ownership patterns. Again, production workers almost always are shown to have a greater number of benefits, with mining and the food processing industries offering the most. The separation by ownership shows state joint-stock companies offering the greatest number of benefits with the more independent companies, cooperatives and private firms, offering the least. Perhaps the state joint-stock companies have enough independence to be free of some state strictures on the setting of wages and benefits, but not so much independence in this period as to lose the state's financial clout to offer these higher benefits.

Conclusions

Beginning in 1994 the reformed former statist trade union, Confederation of Independent Trade Unions of Bulgaria (CITUB), was studying the implementation of a pension program to be run by the trade union. An independently run pension program may mitigate the problems of many American workers, e.g., firm-specific plans that take a while for a worker to be vested (hence, a worker could work for a company that was bought several times and end up after 20 years without any pension savings).

The use of profit sharing and bonus pay appears to be declining according to evidence given here and elsewhere. In industrial firms the use of profit sharing dropped 43 per cent between 1989 and 1992, and the use of incentive pay dropped over the same period by 55 per cent (see Jones, Klinedinst, and Rock, 1996). There may be some convergence, or it could be that Bulgarian leaders are missing out on current trends in advanced market economies. A number of studies from both the US and other countries point to the possible productivity effects from these types of compensation schemes (Jones and Kato, 1995, Rosen and Quarrey, 1987). Recent evidence points to the increasing use of variable pay plans in the US. Currently approximately 14 per cent of companies tie pay with performance, six per cent more are installing such systems and another 26 per cent are considering putting them in place in the near future (Wysocki, 1995). The number of workers excluded from the generous benefits of the past is increasing. This increase is indicated in the figures for managers and production workers and also in the increasing use of temporary and workers under the much less generous terms of the 'civil contract'. This increasing use of workers without as many fringes mirrors developments in the US where due to such factors as weakening unions, foreign competition and automation, companies increasingly use temporary workers. In the last decade the number of temporary work-

Table 15.3
Fringe benefits in Bulgarian industrial firms, 1992;
a breakdown by industry and firm ownership

Variable	Production workers index of fringe benefits – Mean (N)	Managerial index of fringe benefits – Mean (N)
Overall	7.22 (358)	6.99 (363)
Industry		
Food	7.51 (53)	7.21 (53)
Textiles	7.00 (50)	6.74 (50)
Wood/paper	7.40 (33)	7.10 (33)
Engineering	7.22 (95)	7.14 (96)
Electronics	7.20 (40)	6.91 (41)
Chemicals	7.36 (20)	7.21 (20)
Non-metal	6.80 (15)	6.85 (14)
Mining	7.85 (13)	7.73 (14)
Miscellaneous	7.06 (38)	6.59 (41)
Ownership		
State	7.23 (289)	7.01 (292)
State joint stock	7.83 (35)	7.50 (36)
Independent cooperative	6.68 (26)	6.41 (26)
Private	6.66 (3)	6.63 (3)

ers has tripled in the US to 2.1 million (Kilborn, 1995). There is some evidence here that not all companies disenfranchise temporary or part-time help. More data is needed to see if this mirrors the movement in the US in increasingly giving partial benefits to workers involved in flextime, job sharing, compressed work schedules, or work at home (Lissy and Morgenstern, 1995).

Benefits for workers in Bulgaria in the next few years will probably not be as numerous as they have been in the past. Our estimates in this chapter are similar to those found in other transition countries (Estrin, Schaffer, and Singh, 1995, Schaffer, 1995). Ironically, the austerity measure suggested by institutions such as the World Bank and the IMF may have actually caused an increase in some benefits. When price liberalization came to Bulgaria, the desire to stop a wage-price spiral led to the creation of a tripartite arrangement at the national level to develop a tax-based incomes policies. Firms that gave wage increases above the suggested guidelines experienced a highly progressive tax structure (Tzanov, 1995). Hence, firms that wanted to keep their good employees would try to compensate for the decline in real wages with an extension of benefits, which were not subject to the high tax. Firms did not get their wage allotment reduced when workers 'voluntarily resigned' during this period, hence even though the range of benefits available to the remaining workers remained approximately the same or in some cases increased, the actual number of workers enjoying these benefits is substantially less.

The inclusion of the assets that the firms own to provide these wide range of benefits, e.g., holiday housing, gardens, etc., would make the Bulgarian firms' investment in benefits quite a bit greater than that found in most advanced market economies (Rein, Tratch, and Woergoetter, 1995). Increased privatization and competition, continuing high unemployment, and the expanded use of temporary workers or workers under the new 'civil contract' point to reduced fringe benefits for workers. Possibly now as the economy becomes more decentralized, accessibility and potentially the quality of services previously provided by firms may be available from other sources, e.g., housing and child care, but will depend on individual's ability to pay. Firms with significant employee ownership may be more responsive to members' preferences for benefits. The labor unions, who still represent the majority of workers in Bulgaria, have started to mobilize their resources to add and strengthen some fringes and they have begun to give employees the benefit of a voice – to participate in firm and national level contract deliberations. The unions may win and expand some benefits, notably pensions, but the full range of fringe benefits available to many workers ten years ago is unlikely to be found in the beginning of the next century. In the meantime, the extensive benefits offered by Bulgarian firms may provide a much needed cushion to workers experiencing the wrenching changes brought about by the transition to a market economy.

Notes

1   The original sample had 500 firms, but to due missing values the number used in some of the following calculations fell below 350.
2   Also we do not include 'under the table' benefits for management, e.g., access to scarce goods without queuing.
3   The calculation of collective consumption expenditures includes items such as holiday houses, firm-sponsored cultural and sporting activities, gardens, etc. It does not include all items reported as benefits in Table 15.1 that may be calculated on an individual basis.

References

Bartol, Kathryn M. and Bartol, Robert A. (1974), 'Women in Managerial and Professional Positions: The United States and the Soviet Union,' *Industrial and Labor Review*, Vol. 28, pp. 524-34.

Clark, Gardner M. (1960), 'Comparative Wage Structure in the Steel Industry of the Soviet Union and Western Countries,' *Proceedings of the Industrial Relations Research Association*, Vol. 13, December, pp. 266-88.

Crystal, G. (1989), 'Seeking the Sense in CEO Pay,' *Fortune*, 5 June, pp. 90-104.

Estrin, Saul, Schaffer, M.E., and Singh, I.J. (1995), 'The Provision of Social Benefits in State-Owned, Privatized and Private Firms in Poland,' Discussion Paper No. 223, Center for Economic Performance, London School of Economics, February.

Jones, Derek C. (1991), 'The Bulgarian Labor Market in Transition,' *International Labor Review*, Vol. 130, No. 2, July, pp. 231-48.

—— and Kato, Takao (1993), 'On the Scope, Nature and Effects of Employee Ownership in Japan,' *Industrial and Labor Relations Review*, January, pp. 252-367.

—— Klinedinst, Mark, and Rock, Charles (1996), 'Structural Adjustment and Efficiency of Firms in Transition: Evidence from a Panel of Data on 247 Bulgarian Firms,' paper presented at the Association for Comparative Economic Systems annual meetings in San Francisco, January.

Kilborn, Peter (1995), 'In New York World, Employers Call All the Shots,' *New York Times*, 3 July, p. 7.

Klinedinst, Mark (1991a), 'Inside the Black Box: Compensation Structures of Efficient Yugoslavian Firms,' *Economic Analysis*, Vol. 25, pp. 363-83.

—— (1991b), 'Are CEOs Paid Their Marginal Product? An Empirical Analysis of Executive Compensation and Corporate Performance,' *Australian Bulletin of*

Labour, June, pp. 118-31.

—— and Rock, Charles (1994), 'Bulgarian Wage Differentials,' International Association for the Economics of Participation meeting in Portoroz, Slovenia, June.

Lissy, William E. and Morgenstern, Marlene L. (1995), 'Currents in Compensation and Benefits,' *Compensation and Benefits Review*, September-October, p. 14.

McAuley, A. (1979), *Economic Welfare in the Soviet Union*, University of Wisconsin Press: Madison.

Nenova, Mariela (1993), 'Wage Controls: The Bulgarian Experience in 1991/ 1992,' Agency for Economic Coordination and Development, Working Paper Series, April.

Pryor, Frederic L. (1984), 'Incentives in Manufacturing – The Carrot and the Stick,' *Monthly Labor Review*, Vol. 107, No. 7, July, pp. 40-3.

Rein, Martin, Tratch, Irina, and Woergoetter, Andreas (1995), 'Social Assets, Privatization and Industrial Restructuring in Ukraine,' *Economics of Transition*, Vol. 3, pp. 260-66.

Rock, Charles (1994), 'Employment and Privatization in Bulgaria's Reform,' International Labour Office, Occasional Paper No. 24, April.

Rosen, C. and Quarrey, M. (1987), 'How Well is Employee Ownership Working?,' *Harvard Business Review*, September, pp. 126-9.

Schaffer, Mark (1995), 'Should We be Concerned About the Provision of Social Benefits by Firms in Transition Economies?,' *Economics of Transition*, Vol. 3, pp. 247-50.

Tzanov, Vassil (1995), 'For a Negotiated Alternative to Tax-Based Incomes Policy in Bulgaria,' in Vaughan-Whitehead, Daniel (ed), *Reforming Wage Policy in Central and Eastern Europe*, International Labour Organization, pp. 87-122.

Wysocki, Bernard (1995), 'Unstable Pay Becomes Ever More Common,' *Wall Street Journal*, 4 December, p. 1.

Appendix: statistical tables

Table A.1
Annual economic indicators
(in billions of leva)

	1989	1990	1991	1992	1993	1994
Nominal GDP	**39.58**	**45.39**	**135.71**	**200.83**	**298.93**	**543.47**
		(15%)	**(199%)**	**(48%)**	**(49%)**	**(82%)**
By sector of origin						
-Industry & construction	23.51	23.15	63.46	90.51	117.13	195.67
		(-2%)	(174%)	(43%)	(29%)	(67%)
-Agriculture	4.33	8.32	20.99	23.53	29.91	61.12
		(92%)	(152%)	(12%)	(27%)	(104%)
-Services	11.74	14.02	63.87	90.48	147.53	251.41
		(19%)	(355%)	(42%)	(63%)	(70%)
-Other sectors, adjustment	-39.58	-45.49	-12.61	-3.68	4.37	35.27
Final domestic demand	**41.10**	**47.39**	**129.92**	**212.58**	**320.92**	**540.08**
		(15%)	**(147%)**	**(64%)**	**(51%)**	**(68%)**
Consumption	28.00	33.59	99.25	172.64	278.49	493.92
		(20%)	(196%)	(74%)	(61%)	(77%)
-Personal	25.18	25.33	75.85	131.93	221.63	401.97
		(1%)	(199%)	(74%)	(68%)	(81%)
-Government	2.82	8.26	23.41	40.71	56.86	91.95
		(193%)	(184%)	(74%)	(40%)	(62%)
Gross investment	13.11	13.80	30.66	39.94	42.43	46.16
		(5%)	(122%)	(30%)	(6%)	(9%)
-Fixed investment	10.33	9.65	24.64	32.58	35.43	53.00
		(-7%)	(155%)	(32%)	(9%)	(50%)
-Change in stocks	2.78	4.15	6.03	7.36	7.00	-6.84
		(49%)	(45%)	(22%)	(-5%)	(-198%)
Foreign trade balance, losses, & statistical discrepancy	**-1.52**	**-2.00**	**5.80**	**-11.75**	**-21.99**	**3.40**

Note: Numbers in parentheses are annual percentage changes.

Table A.2
Annual economic indicators
(index, 1989=100)

	1989	1990.00	1991	1992	1993	1994
Real GDP	**100.00**	**90.90** (-9%)	**80.30** (-11%)	**74.40** (-6%)	**72.60** (-2%)	**73.60** (1%)
By sector of origin						
-Industry & construction	100.00	87.50 (-13%)	71.20 (-16%)	65.40 (-6%)	63.90 (-1%)	65.80 (2%)
-Agriculture	100.00	96.30 (-4%)	103.70 (7%)	88.70 (-15%)	61.80 (27%)	68.50 (7%)
-Services	100.00	95.70 (-4%)	84.90 (-11%)	67.30 (-18%)	65.60 (-2%)	63.50 (-2%)
Final domestic demand	**100.00**	**92.40** (-8%)	**83.00** (-10%)	**82.20** (-1%)	**75.10** (-9%)	**67.80** (-10%)
Consumption	100.00	100.60 (1%)	92.30 (-8%)	89.40 (-3%)	87.00 (-3%)	84.60 (-3%)
-Personal	100.00	98.50 (-2%)	83.00 (-16%)	81.10 (-2%)	81.10 (0%)	81.00 (0%)
-Government	100.00	108.60 (9%)	97.40 (-10%)	91.60 (-6%)	81.10 (-11%)	71.40 (-12%)
Gross investment	100.00	74.90 (-25%)	63.20 (-16%)	66.90 (6%)	49.60 (-26%)	31.90 (-36%)
-Fixed investment	100.00	81.50 (-19%)	65.30 (-20%)	74.20 (14%)	56.00 (-25%)	49.40 (-12%)
-Change in stocks	100.00	50.30 (-50%)	47.40 (-6%)	35.10 (-26%)	23.90 (-32%)	na

Note: Numbers in parentheses are annual percentage changes.

342

Table A.3
Annual economic indicators

	1989	1990	1991	1992	1993	1994
Prices & wages (% change)*						
a. Consumer prices (annual ave.)	6.4%	26.3%	333.5%	82%	73%	96.3%
b. Wages in the state sector (annual ave.)	8.7%	31.7%	165.6%	103%	59%	50.8%
Population & employment						
a. Population** (thousands of persons)	9,000	8,700 (-3.3%)	8,600 (-1.1%)	8,500 (-1.2%)	8,500 (0%)	8,400 (-1.2%)
b. Employment (thousands of persons)	4,366	4,097 (-6.2%)	3,564 (-13%)	3,274 (-8.1%)	3,222 (-1.6%)	3,158 (-2%)
c. Unemployment** (% of labor force)	na	1.5%	11.5%	15.6%	16.4%	12.8%
d. Structure of employment (% of total employment)						
-Industry	37.7%	36.6%	34.5%	32.6%	30.4%	29.6%
-Agriculture & forestry	18.6%	18.5%	19.5%	21.2%	22.1%	22.1%
-Construction	8.3%	8.2%	7.1%	6.2%	6.5%	5.9%
-Services	34.4%	35.7%	37.8%	38.9%	39.8%	41.3%
-Other branches	0.9%	1%	1.1%	1%	1.2%	1.1%
Foreign sector (billions of US dollars)						
a. Current account**	-1.3	-1.2	-0.8	-1.1	-1.5	-0.1
b. Trade balance	-1.2	-0.8	0	-0.2	-0.9	0.2
-Exports of goods (FOB)	3.1	2.6	3.7	4	3.7	4.2
-Imports of goods (FOB)	4.3	3.4	3.8	4.2	4.6	4
c. Foreign direct investment (net)	na	na	0.06	0.04	0.06	0.11
d. Gross external debt**	9.4	9.9	11.9	12.7	13.1	11

Table A.3 (continued)
Annual economic indicators

	1989	1990	1991	1992	1993	1994
Foreign sector (billions of US dollars)						
e. Exports by group of countries (% of total exports)						
-Central and Eastern Europe***	83.5%	80.2%	57.7%	39.2%	36.6%	35.7%
-OECD countries	8.1%	9%	26.3%	42.2%	44.8%	46.7%
-Arab countries	4.2%	6.1%	8.3%	8.6%	4.5%	5.3%
-Others	4.3%	4.7%	7.7%	11.3%	14.1%	12.3%
f. Imports by group of countries (% total imports)						
-Central and Eastern Europe***	72.4%	75.9%	48.5%	36.3%	35.1%	40.3%
-OECD countries	17.2%	14.9%	32.8%	43.8%	43.2%	46.5%
-Arab countries	4.8%	4.3%	4.5%	8.6%	7.2%	1.7%
-Others	5.5%	5%	14.2%	10%	14.5%	11.5%
Government (% of GDP)						
Budget deficit**	1.4%	12.8%	14.7%	15%	15.7%	6.6%

Table A.4
Monthly economic indicators

		Consumer price index		Producer price index****		Exchange rates	
		Jan91=100	Monthly change	Jan91=100	Monthly change	Leva/US$ end of month	Monthly depreciation
1991	Jan.	100.0		100.0		2.9	
	Feb.	222.9	122.9%	218.9	118.9%	20.7	620.0%
	Mar.	335.5	50.5%	248.4	13.5%	15.2	-26.9%
	Apr.	343.9	2.5%	252.7	1.7%	18.5	22.0%
	May	346.6	0.8%	289.1	14.4%	18.2	-1.4%
	Jun.	367.1	5.9%	325.4	12.6%	17.6	-3.8%
	Jul.	397.9	8.4%	335.1	3.0%	18.7	6.5%
	Aug.	427.7	7.5%	376.7	12.4%	17.6	-5.6%
	Sep.	444.0	3.8%	361.9	-3.9%	19.0	7.5%
	Oct.	458.6	3.3%	347.2	-4.1%	20.5	8.3%
	Nov.	481.6	5.0%	365.1	5.2%	18.7	-8.8%
	Dec.	505.2	4.9%	394.4	8.0%	21.8	16.4%
1992	Jan.	529.4	4.8%	402.3	2.0%	23.8	9.2%
	Feb.	560.1	5.8%	412.3	2.5%	24.1	1.4%
	Mar.	582.0	3.9%	420.6	2.0%	23.2	-4.0%
	Apr.	600.6	3.2%	424.8	1.0%	23.0	-0.7%
	May	672.0	11.9%	446.0	5.0%	23.2	0.8%
	Jun.	711.0	5.8%	461.6	3.5%	23.0	-0.8%
	Jul.	730.9	2.8%	483.8	4.8%	22.8	-1.1%
	Aug.	739.7	1.2%	481.4	-0.5%	22.2	-2.4%
	Sep.	764.9	3.4%	487.6	1.3%	22.6	1.9%
	Oct.	812.3	6.2%	490.0	0.5%	23.7	4.9%
	Nov.	866.7	6.7%	492.0	0.4%	24.7	4.0%
	Dec.	906.6	4.6%	502.8	2.2%	24.5	-0.9%
1993	Jan.	969.1	6.9%	512.9	2.0%	25.6	4.5%
	Feb.	1014.7	4.7%	520.6	1.5%	26.6	4.0%
	Mar.	1071.5	5.6%	534.6	2.7%	26.5	-0.3%
	Apr.	1113.3	3.9%	537.3	0.5%	26.4	-0.5%
	May	1172.3	5.3%	551.3	2.6%	26.4	0.1%
	Jun.	1220.3	4.1%	562.9	2.1%	26.7	1.0%
	Jul.	1232.5	1.0%	555.5	-1.3%	27.2	2.0%
	Aug.	1264.6	2.6%	558.3	0.5%	27.4	0.8%
	Sep.	1312.6	3.8%	571.2	2.3%	28.0	2.2%
	Oct.	1367.8	4.2%	578.0	1.2%	29.5	5.3%
	Nov.	1430.7	4.6%	584.4	1.1%	31.2	5.6%
	Dec.	1486.5	3.9%	580.3	-0.7%	32.7	4.9%

Table A.4 (continued)
Monthly economic indicators

		Consumer price index		Producer price index****		Exchange rates	
		Jan91=100	Monthly change	Jan91=100	Monthly change	Leva/US$ end of month	Monthly depreciation
1994	Jan.	1543.0	3.8%	594.8	2.5%	36.3	11.0%
	Feb.	1614.0	4.6%	621.6	4.5%	37.4	2.9%
	Mar.	1735.0	7.5%	678.7	9.2%	64.9	73.8%
	Apr.	2111.5	21.7%	803.6	18.4%	56.9	-12.4%
	May	2278.3	7.9%	872.7	8.6%	55.6	-2.3%
	Jun.	2371.7	4.1%	887.6	1.7%	53.7	-3.5%
	Jul.	2386.0	0.6%	905.3	2.0%	53.3	-0.7%
	Aug.	2510.0	5.2%	949.7	4.9%	57.2	7.3%
	Sep.	2786.1	11.0%	1001.9	5.5%	61.2	7.0%
	Oct.	2978.4	6.9%	1048.2	4.6%	64.9	6.1%
	Nov.	3142.2	5.5%	1073.4	2.4%	65.0	0.2%
	Dec.	3299.3	5.0%	1097.0	2.2%	66.0	1.5%
1995	Jan.	3426.3	3.9%	1134.3	3.4%	66.7	1.0%
	Feb.	3556.5	3.8%	1174.0	3.5%	65.6	-1.5%
	Mar.	3677.3	3.4%	1248.0	6.3%	66.2	0.8%
	Apr.	3714.3	1.0%	1258.0	0.8%	65.2	-1.4%
	May	3784.7	1.9%	1258.0	0.0%	66.0	1.1%
	Jun.	3803.8	0.5%	1264.2	0.5%	66.1	0.2%
	Jul.	3861.0	1.5%	1276.9	1.0%	66.2	0.2%
	Aug.	3880.0	0.5%	1289.7	1.0%	67.9	2.6%
	Sep.	4066.4	4.8%	1356.7	5.2%	68.0	0.1%
	Oct.	4168.0	2.5%	1379.8	1.7%	68.5	0.7%
	Nov.	4279.7	2.7%	1458.1	5.7%	69.8	1.9%
	Dec.	4485.1	4.8%	1523.7	4.5%	70.7	1.3%
1996	Jan.	4588.3	2.3%	1535.9	0.8%	73.8	4.4%
	Feb.	4675.4	1.9%	1571.2	2.3%	76.1	3.1%
	Mar.	4754.9	1.7%	1608.9	2.4%	78.8	3.5%

Table A.5
Monthly economic indicators

		Money (M2)		Average monthly wage, industry****		Unemploym't rate****
		Billion levs	Monthly change	Dollars	Monthly change	% of labor force, end of month
1991	Jan.	49.2		179.8		1.8%
	Feb.	73.7	49.8%	22.1	-87.7%	2.5%
	Mar.	67.2	-8.8%	39.2	77.4%	3.2%
	Apr.	72.4	7.8%	41.0	4.6%	4.3%
	May	73.9	2.1%	44.3	8.0%	5.0%
	Jun.	73.9	0.0%	50.8	14.7%	5.7%
	Jul.	80.6	9.0%	47.3	-6.9%	6.9%
	Aug.	80.9	0.5%	48.5	2.5%	7.8%
	Sep.	85.0	5.0%	63.6	31.1%	8.5%
	Oct.	94.1	10.7%	72.6	14.2%	9.2%
	Nov.	94.2	0.1%	70.2	-3.3%	10.1%
	Dec.	108.4	15.2%	78.2	11.4%	10.7%
1992	Jan.	115.3	6.4%	67.1	-14.2%	11.3%
	Feb.	119.4	3.5%	68.3	1.8%	11.6%
	Mar.	120.2	0.7%	82.2	20.4%	12.0%
	Apr.	120.3	0.0%	84.6	2.9%	12.4%
	May	123.5	2.7%	82.9	-2.0%	12.5%
	Jun.	126.1	2.1%	99.2	19.7%	12.6%
	Jul.	130.9	3.8%	100.0	0.8%	13.4%
	Aug.	138.6	5.9%	100.3	0.3%	13.9%
	Sep.	144.3	4.1%	116.5	16.2%	14.3%
	Oct.	148.5	2.9%	112.0	-3.9%	14.8%
	Nov.	151.6	2.1%	109.8	-2.0%	15.0%
	Dec.	155.0	2.2%	127.2	15.8%	15.2%
1993	Jan.	157.4	1.5%	98.0	-23.0%	15.3%
	Feb.	161.4	2.6%	97.7	-0.3%	15.5%
	Mar.	165.7	2.7%	125.3	28.2%	16.0%
	Apr.	170.6	2.9%	115.0	-8.2%	15.9%
	May	176.2	3.3%	117.5	2.2%	15.7%
	Jun.	184.4	4.6%	136.4	16.1%	15.5%
	Jul.	195.3	5.9%	125.7	-7.8%	16.2%
	Aug.	201.0	2.9%	125.9	0.2%	16.0%
	Sep.	209.6	4.3%	141.5	12.4%	15.7%
	Oct.	213.9	2.1%	128.9	-8.9%	15.8%
	Nov.	220.3	3.0%	123.5	-4.2%	16.1%
	Dec.	229.9	4.4%	131.3	6.3%	16.4%

347

Table A.5 (continued)
Monthly economic indicators

		Money (M2)		Average monthly wage, industry****		Unemploym't rate****
		Billion levs	Monthly change	Dollars	Monthly change	% of labor force, end of month
1994	Jan.	238.2	3.6%	108.0	-17.7%	16.5%
	Feb.	245.1	2.9%	107.9	-0.1%	16.3%
	Mar.	291.8	19.1%	101.4	-6.0%	16.1%
	Apr.	291.9	0.0%	83.9	-17.3%	15.3%
	May	298.2	2.2%	85.0	1.3%	14.3%
	Jun.	309.7	3.9%	98.2	15.5%	13.3%
	Jul.	321.6	3.8%	93.8	-4.5%	13.5%
	Aug.	344.0	7.0%	93.9	0.1%	13.0%
	Sep.	366.7	6.6%	97.9	4.3%	12.7%
	Oct.	383.8	4.6%	87.3	-10.8%	12.2%
	Nov.	386.4	0.7%	92.8	6.3%	12.4%
	Dec.	409.1	5.9%	103.9	12.0%	12.8%
1995	Jan.	413.7	1.1%	93.0	-10.5%	13.1%
	Feb.	425.0	2.7%	95.6	2.8%	12.8%
	Mar.	439.3	3.4%	125.2	31.0%	12.5%
	Apr.	448.7	2.1%	114.8	-8.3%	12.0%
	May	470.1	4.8%	117.0	1.9%	11.2%
	Jun.	497.8	5.9%	134.9	15.3%	10.7%

Table A.6
Monthly economic indicators

		Average monthly wage, public sector****				Nominal interest rates****		
		Dollars	Monthly change	Leva	Monthly change	Base rate	One-month lending rate (% per month)	One-month deposit rate (% per month)
1993	Jan.	88.8		2248		47.00	4.75	3.63
	Feb.	88.4	-0.5%	2322	3.3%	47.00	4.97	3.74
	Mar.	106.6	20.6%	2832	22.0%	51.00	5.11	3.85
	Apr.	105.3	-1.2%	2782	-1.8%	51.00	5.12	3.83
	May	108.9	3.4%	2889	3.8%	51.00	5.13	3.84
	Jun.	121.5	11.6%	3229	11.8%	48.00	4.88	3.39
	Jul.	117.3	-3.5%	3181	-1.5%	48.00	4.91	3.40
	Aug.	117.7	0.3%	3218	1.2%	48.00	4.84	3.37
	Sep.	128.1	8.8%	3531	9.7%	44.00	4.62	3.18
	Oct.	120.6	-5.9%	3433	-2.8%	44.00	4.61	3.19
	Nov.	115.5	-4.2%	3573	4.1%	52.00	5.10	3.51
	Dec.	122.9	6.4%	3930	10.0%	52.00	5.20	3.64
1994	Jan.	100.6	-18.1%	3589	-8.7%	56.00	5.43	3.78
	Feb.	99.5	-1.1%	3668	2.2%	56.00	5.39	3.89
	Mar.	89.2	-10.4%	4211	14.8%	62.00	5.73	3.97
	Apr.	76.5	-14.2%	4221	0.2%	62.00	5.87	4.20
	May	77.7	1.6%	4321	2.4%	62.00	5.94	4.21
	Jun.	87.4	12.5%	4753	10.0%	62.00	5.94	4.33
	Jul.	87.3	-0.1%	4686	-1.4%	62.00	5.88	4.21
	Aug.	86.3	-1.1%	4751	1.4%	62.00	5.85	4.21
	Sep.	86.0	-0.3%	5276	11.1%	72.00	6.42	4.53
	Oct.	80.6	-6.3%	5162	-2.2%	72.00	6.69	4.63
	Nov.	86.2	6.9%	5612	8.7%	72.00	6.74	4.64
	Dec.	95.4	10.7%	6248	11.3%	72.00	6.70	4.64
1995	Jan.	85.5	-10.4%	5715	-8.5%	72.00	6.79	4.65
	Feb.	87.7	2.6%	5822	1.9%	72.00	6.75	4.65
	Mar.	105.6	20.4%	7009	20.4%	72.00	6.77	4.66
	Apr.	101.9	-3.5%	6690	-4.6%	60.00	6.21	4.04
	May	105.1	3.1%	6898	3.1%	54.00	5.37	3.15
	Jun.	118.1	12.4%	7812	13.3%	48.00	5.08	2.93

Source: Bulgarian National Bank, Annual Reports, 1990-94; Bulgarian National Bank, monthly bulletin, March-May 1995.

* Statistical Tables in *The Economics of Transition* (1995), Vol. 3, No. 3, Oxford University Press.

** Statistical Tables in *The Economics of Transition* (1996), Vol. 4, No. 1, Oxford University Press.

*** 1989 and 1990 data include trade with the former GDP.

**** PlanEcon, various reports.

Printed in the United States
by Baker & Taylor Publisher Services